DIPL(

Canad

The warti   United States,
Canada, a   var; in its place
rose up th   th here tells the
story of h   e disintegration
of the alli   nose its place as
a seconda

Smith   ical archives of
the years   stablishment of
NATO. H   de to bring the
United St   t's tendency to
see Russi   i Germany, and
the extent   y as it froze into
the patter   ture emerges of
the relatic   Department of
External   government.

Smith'   nsiderable light
on the ro   d should assist
current ef   nd good sense.

DENIS SM   olitical Science,
University of Western Ontario.

Diplomacy of
FEAR

Canada and the Cold War
1941–1948

Denis Smith

UNIVERSITY OF TORONTO PRESS

Toronto Buffalo London

© University of Toronto Press 1988
Toronto Buffalo London
Printed in Canada

ISBN 0-8020-5770-5 (cloth)
ISBN 0-8020-6684-4 (paper)

Printed on acid-free paper

Canadian Cataloguing in Publication Data

Smith, Denis, 1932–
  Diplomacy of fear

  Bibliography: p.
  Includes index.
  ISBN 0-8020-5770-5 (bound) ISBN 0-8020-6684-4 (pbk.)

  1. Canada – Foreign relations – Soviet Union.
  2. Soviet Union – Foreign relations – Canada.
  3. Canada – Foreign relations – 1918–1945.*
  4. Canada – Foreign relations – 1945–   .
  I. Title.

  FC251.S65S55 1988   327.71047   c87-095168-8
  F1029.5.S65S55 1988

To the memory of two Canadians,

constant, independent, and fearless:

Walter Gordon and Margaret Laurence

Contents

Acknowledgments

This book was written while I held academic appointments at Trent University and the University of Western Ontario; I am grateful to both of these institutions for their congenial ambience and support. For financial assistance in the early stages of my research, I am grateful to the Canada Council; and for later assistance, to the research fund of Trent University and the dean's research fund of the Faculty of Social Science of the University of Western Ontario.

I was led to examine Canada's involvement in the early years of the Cold War, following publication of *Gentle Patriot: A Political Biography of Walter Gordon,* by realization that the subject of Gordon's great public concern – Canada's dependence upon the United States in the 1950s and 1960s – had its political roots in the confusions of the immediate post-war period, not in the 1950s. Other scholars had begun to reflect on the problems of Canadian foreign policy in that era, and to them – especially James Eayrs and Jack Granatstein – I owe thanks for their pathbreaking efforts.

Geoffrey Pearson offered early encouragement and access to the Pearson Papers; the late Brian Heeney provided access to the Heeney Papers; and Fred Gibson of Queen's University assisted with materials from the Dexter Papers. For initial archival assistance I thank Tony Lovink. Donald Page, D'Acre Cole, and the staff of the Historical Division of the Department of External Affairs were helpful facilitators, as were the manuscripts staffs of the Public Archives of Canada, the Public Record Office, the United States National Archives, the Library of Congress, and the Truman Library. Martin Gilbert, John Holmes, Escott Reid, Arnold Smith, and Sir William Stephenson responded helpfully to my enquiries. The manuscript in its initial draft was read by Donald Avery, John Stubbs, and two readers from the Press and the Social Science Federation of Canada, and has benefited greatly from their shrewd comments and criticism.

Linda Brock typed the manuscript with meticulous care, and Beverly Hughes assisted tirelessly in typing the various revisions.

As always, my wife Dawn has offered encouragement and judicious counsel throughout.

The book has been published with the help of a grant from the Social Science Federation of Canada, using funds provided by the Social Sciences and Humanities Research Council of Canada.

Diplomacy of Fear:

Canada and the Cold War

1941–1948

There was, of course, no effective Western response to Soviet policy in these early years; it appeared that Moscow's advance would not stop as she brought under her control hundreds of thousands of square miles of territory in Eastern and Central Europe and more than 90 millions of people. There were Soviet-inspired crises in Berlin. Iran and Turkey were threatened, there was civil war in Greece, and, initially at least, a Soviet-dominated Communist regime in Yugoslavia. Soviet pressure on Norway was particularly disturbing, and political confusion, economic disruption, and a general postwar weariness in France and Italy threatened to bring about in these countries Soviet-supported communist take-overs. There was a general military impotence in the Western European countries and rapid demobilization in the United States, whereas the Soviet divisions seemed war-ready. Thus it is not surprising that there arose a very real fear of new aggressive moves by the Soviet Union westward across Europe to the Atlantic, moves directed by Stalin whose motives and attitudes were to be unveiled for us some years later by his successor, Nikita Khrushchev.

The North Atlantic Alliance was born of this fear ...

Lester B. Pearson,
Mike, vol. 2, p. 39 (1973)

The entire western world was now dominated by the United States, which had just set out on a great ideological crusade for the 'containment' of international Communism. Every nation west of the spiritual divide in central Europe was expected to offer itself, an eager and submissive volunteer, in the fight for freedom under American leadership; and Canada, the Republic's nearest neighbour and closest relative, must obviously be the first to stand up and be counted.

Donald Creighton,
Canada's First Century, pp. 269–70 (1970)

Introduction

When Canada went to war in September 1939 she was a relative novice in international diplomacy, with a record of aloofness from the great disputes of the 1930s that threatened and finally destroyed the twenty years' peace. The Second World War upset the old European and world balance by shattering Britain, France, and Germany and thrusting the United States and the Soviet Union prematurely into the vacuum. Henceforth they occupied the stage as superpowers. Among the countries of the second rank, designated as middle powers by their wartime role and post-war prospects, Canada was unusually prominent. Despite her absence from the Anglo-American strategic councils, her economic and military contribution to the Allied war effort was large, and her diplomats made an impressive showing in the agencies of post-war planning as they pressed for roles appropriate to the country's new economic power.

As the war effort moved towards a victorious conclusion, powerful popular convictions developed in the United States and Canada that the return to normalcy of the mid-1940s would have to differ from that of the 1920s. This time the international settlement would have to involve both the United States and the Soviet Union, as it had not in 1919; all the great powers would have to co-operate to preserve the peace; international aggressors would have to be confronted early rather than appeased while their appetites grew; and world prosperity would have to be maintained through a system of expanding free trade. This liberal internationalist vision dominated opinion among the political leadership as well as the bureaucracy, press, and general public of the two countries.

While the Canadian prime minister, William Lyon Mackenzie King, was a reluctant participant in this vision, he was carried along by its momentum and by the commitment of his allies and advisers. Above all, he desired the return of a peaceful world in which Canada, now freed from its formal dependence on the United Kingdom, could exercise a safe and modest role. If his officials were bolder in their perception of Canada's place in the world than he, they shared his desire for Canadian independence, peace, prosperity, and great power co-operation.

Prime Minister King acted as his own secretary of state for external affairs throughout the Second World War and until September 1946, when Louis St Laurent took the separated portfolio. As secretary of state, King and St Laurent acted on the advice of an under-secretary and a handful of senior officials in the Department of External Afffairs. An increasing volume of diplomatic dispatches and memoranda reached the prime minister's desk as the war came to an end and the problems of the post-war settlement multiplied. The prime minister tended not to share the detail of foreign policy discussion with his cabinet colleagues unless their departments were immediately involved; he did not encourage debate in cabinet or the House of Commons on foreign policy, and in the prim and conservative atmosphere of the King era he was permitted the freedom to make that policy for himself. In doing so he rarely risked advancing beyond the safe limits of popular approval. Public discussion of foreign policy was limited not only by an indifferent and ill-informed parliament, but by an undeveloped academic community and the existence of only a tiny core of journalists with a serious interest in international affairs. Canadians depended heavily for their judgment of world affairs on the American news services and American political columnists syndicated in the Canadian press (as well, during wartime, as the Canadian correspondents following the Allied invasion armies in Europe). Within the Department of External Affairs, in the heady atmosphere stimulated by Canada's large wartime role, there was, by contrast, lively discussion about the shape of the post-war world and Canada's place in it. Canada's young diplomatic service was beginning to feel its oats, and the uncertainties of the early post-war years gave the diplomats a rare opportunity to engage in an extended analysis of possibilities.

Five and a half years of world war had darkened the European world's understanding of its own soul, accustomed it to unprecedented brutality, and simplified the moral distinctions. In this war good and evil were easily identified: the Axis powers were evil incarnate, the Allies were the forces of good. This rationalization salved consciences, reinforced wills, suppressed intellectual doubts and complexities, and no doubt contributed notably to the Allied victory. It also established a habit of careless over-simplification which proved difficult to break in peacetime.

What became evident to Canadian, American, and British diplomats and politicians in the spring of 1945, and to the Anglo-American-Canadian public in the year that followed, was that the peace would not bring a relaxed and secure world, but rather tension and disturbance of a different kind. The source of confusion seemed to be the Soviet Union, which was not behaving as an ally should. Suddenly it was no longer an ally but a dangerous and enigmatic rival, a new enemy. This had to be understood and explained, and policies appropriate to the new reality had to be devised. These policies, it became clear, would involve a rapid descent from post-war idealism to realism in international affairs – or the translation of internationalist idealism into a narrower, regionalist idealism in the West. What was achieved by 1949 was an unstable combination of the two. The translation had the propagandist advantage that it played upon old fears of Bolshevism to produce a new myth of good and evil to replace the wartime myth. Like its predecessor, it was easy to understand: it was a Manichean system of slogans. In the new system of belief, the Soviet Union incarnated evil while the Western, non-Soviet world served God's righteous purposes on earth. The conflict took on the aspect of a crusade. In missionary crusades, as in armies marching to war, there is little room for critical moderation or measured and subtle responses; in both, the preoccupation tends to be the preparation for battle. By 1948, the new myth of the Cold War had been established in the West, and the girding for battle behind American leadership had begun. In its ruthlessness and diplomatic crudity the Soviet Union seemed to offer repeated evidence to reinforce the new Western perception, and for forty years since that time the stalemate between the superpowers has persisted, growing more dangerous in potential as their nuclear arms have mushroomed out of control.

Post-war Canada thus found not security but new anxiety; not quiet independence but new dependence in the conflict of the superpowers. Until the mid-1960s the dominant historical interpretation of that struggle in the United States and Canada was the official version of the political participants and their supporting publics. Post-war co-operation, it was widely believed, had been destroyed by the aggressive and expansionist Soviet Union seeking world domination, against which the United States, Canada, Britain, and Western Europe had reacted slowly and reluctantly to create a new defensive alliance. That alliance had successfully deterred Russian military aggression, or had contained it through a series of proxy wars in which the United States and the Soviet Union did not confront one another directly.

In Britain and Western Europe the orthodox perception of the Cold War was probably more subtle than this: centuries of experience of and reflection upon national conflicts had demonstrated that all nations pursue their selfish interests, that none are pure in motive or deed, and that international relations could best be understood as the endless readjustment of balance in an anarchic universe rather than as a panorama of crusades against evil powers. Europeans, including both politicians and historians, were thus more inclined than North Americans to regard the tensions of the Cold War as natural and predictable, and to apportion praise and blame for events as the evidence suggested rather than by rote.[1] But the United States, as the leading power in the Western alliance, provided both the muscle and the popular catch-phrases of explanation. Because they wanted the American muscle behind them, European leaders frequently accepted or imitated the American language of the Cold War when it was convenient for them to do so.

In the United States the conventional interpretation of the Cold War as a conflict between good and evil predominated until the massive American intervention in Vietnam. But from the mid-sixties the domestic reaction to that disaster prompted reinvestigation of the roots of recent US foreign policy, and a radical redefinition of America's role in the early Cold War. By the 1970s the revisionist critique of American post-war policy was itself massive, largely polemical, and sometimes rudely dismissive of the old orthodoxy.[2] In the crude revisionist image the roles of the United States and the USSR were reversed: the United States had become the expansionist power, the USSR the innocent victim of encirclement, frightened into defence and defiance by American ambition. (There were degrees of variation on the theme.)

Revisionism was an American phenomenon, focused intensely upon American responsibility for the international crisis, and scarcely reflected in European scholarship of the period. Both within the United States and abroad, however, it freshened and broadened historical discussion of the Cold War, especially in its assertion of the economic and domestic political impulses behind American foreign policy. The first critical responses were followed, in the late seventies, by the increasing absorption of revisionist insights into mainstream scholarship, and by a cooling of the temperature of the scholarly debate. By the early 1980s some American historians could speak of a post-revisionist consensus, while others who rejected the notion

of consensus at least concluded that good manners had been restored and
critical history advanced by a new tolerance for complexity and diversity in
Cold War historiography.[3]

One product of post-revisionist interest in the Cold War has been a
growing number of studies of national and regional perspectives on the
early post-war years, demonstrating that American initiatives and reactions
were not produced in isolation, but within a rich context in which the
friends of the United States – above all the United Kingdom – desired and
actively sought a forward and interventionist policy on the part of the
United States.[4] Canadian scholarly participation in explicitly revisionist
and post-revisionist writing about the Cold War has been modest in scale.[5]
Instead, the political and diplomatic participants have maintained their
measured and stately publication of memoirs, while a small number of
political scientists and historians have mined the Canadian archives,
frequently criticizing Canadian actions but only rarely challenging the
larger orthodoxies of American interpretation.[6] In part the absence of
major Canadian participation in the American revisionist debate may
reflect Canada's intellectual position between Europe and the United
States, and the Canadian tendency from the beginning to discount the
extremes of American Cold War rhetoric: lacking the full commitment to
American orthodoxy, we felt less need to combat it. In part, it may reflect
Canada's position on the sidelines in Vietnam; and in part it must reflect,
simply, the small volume of writing about twentieth-century history in
Canada. Where the writer-participants have been influenced by revision-
ism, the effect has been to strengthen their conventional justifications for
Canadian policy rather than to prompt doubts about their wisdom in
retrospect.[7]

Having missed deep immersion in the polemical phase of the revisionist
debate, Canadian historians of the Cold War are in a position to take part in
discussion at the post-revisionist stage, with access to the Western
diplomatic and political archives. (The Soviet side of the record remains
largely unavailable.) This book is a contribution to that discussion. Its
purpose is to examine how the Canadian government saw the political
confusions of the post-war years from its unique perspective between
Britain and the United States, and how it responded to them. What did
Canada think the Soviet Union and the United States were up to? What
kinds of information were available to the Canadian government in making
its judgments on global policy, and how did it make use of that
information? What influences and pressures, from what sources, were

imposed on Canada? What alternatives were open to the Canadian government in its choices of high policy, and to what extent did it consider them?

The country's role in the emerging period of the Cold War, I believe, reveals itself in detail as more complex than the conventional image (which is still, on the whole, the satisfied rationalization of the diplomatic participants). But this role does not fit any simple revisionist pattern of explanation – that, for example, Canada was somehow duped or coerced by the United States into joining the anti-Soviet alliance against its will and better judgment. The Canadian government possessed its own diplomatic sources of information on Soviet foreign policy, shared its documents and judgments widely with the American Department of State and the Foreign Office, and took part forthrightly in the creation of a common appreciation of Soviet intentions and capabilities. In addition, the Canadians possessed a distinct perspective on the United States, initially more sceptical than that of the United Kingdom because Canada was less desperately dependent on American support; yet in the end more complacent before American power – perhaps because Canada lacked Britain's traditions and presumptions as a fading imperial power. Canada entered the Cold War alliance against the Soviet Union not just as a pawn of the United States (at crucial points, indeed, it seemed more subject to British than American influences), but with its own calculations of interest in mind. There were clear limits to Canadian independence in matters of high strategy, however, both objective and self-imposed, both in judgment and in action. This study is, in a sense, an extended reflection on the nature of those limits. Were they realistically and wisely judged? Could other paths have been chosen?

The narrative focuses on the period from 22 June 1941 when the Soviet Union was invaded by Nazi Germany, until 11 March 1948 when Canada agreed to enter negotiations for a Western alliance against the Soviet Union: through the cycle of relations with Russia, from enemy to friend to enemy again. It is concerned almost exclusively with diplomatic and cabinet affairs, with only occasional references to the public background when that intruded itself, because the diplomats and politicians themselves were preoccupied most of the time within their relatively closed universe. That was especially true during wartime, when secrecy was the government's first consideration; it remained true in peacetime because Prime Minister King preferred it that way and the public acquiesced. Although this account is framed within a narrative of public events, it is not so much a history of those events as of the Canadian government's changing perceptions of the USSR and East-West relations: a history of ideas in politics. There is a parallel account to be told of the Canadian public's shifting vision of the Soviet Union in this period; but that is another story, not inconsistent with this one, but less related to the thoughts and acts of the Canadian government than to the movements of popular opinion in the United States and the United Kingdom. This is a tale of diplomats and politicians.

Between America and Russia   1941–1943

Britain's wartime foreign secretary, Anthony Eden, wrote starkly in his memoirs: 'The second world war decided that the United States and Soviet Russia should rule the world; the longer it lasted, the more established the rule. If there had been no dictatorships using war as an instrument of policy in the nineteen-thirties, Europe would have continued to play the leading part for many years.'[1] From early in the war, Eden perceived that Soviet-American relations would be the key to post-war stability, and that those relations would find their major points of encounter in Europe. He was therefore preoccupied, on behalf of the United Kingdom, to anticipate and influence Russian and American approaches to the European settlement.[2] This preoccupation reflected the United Kingdom's long familiarity with the role of a great power, accustomed to dealing with the most central matters of high strategy at first hand. For Canada, the wartime collapse of European power was refracted through the prism of the North Atlantic, and had a different aspect. Russia was a distant presence whose reality only gradually impressed itself on the nation's leaders. For most of the war, Canadian diplomacy worked on the fringes of the Anglo-American alliance, attempting intermittently to gain the influence in wartime planning that Canada's military and economic contributions to the war effort appeared to justify. These attempts met virtually no success, because Churchill and Roosevelt were determined to manage the war in a close partnership that excluded the other allies from the making of high policy.[3]

Initially, the transformation of power that Eden described had a one-sided impact on Canada. American power, American assertiveness, American insensitivity were the preoccupations of Canada's diplomats as they reflected on the world that would emerge from war. From the fall of France in 1940 onwards, a series of departmental papers in External Affairs considered the problem of American power with caution, anxiety and sometimes alarm.[4] The documents, of course, were confidential reflections on diplomatic relationships written by members of the Department of External Affairs and unknown to the Canadian public. They did not echo Canadian public opinion, and the government was careful, throughout the war, to give no hint to that public of its private anxieties about the United States. This loyal unwillingness to use the leverage of public opinion in defence of national interests, while understandable in wartime, had two long-term effects which were of doubtful benefit to Canada. It reinforced a habit in the Department of External Affairs and the Prime Minister's Office of assuming that foreign policy was not a matter for public debate; and it created a gap in perception about the United States between department and public which might later, in peacetime, prove difficult to bridge except by allowing uncritical popular attitudes to override the qualified judgments of the experts.

The first of these departmental documents, by Hugh L. Keenleyside, bore the cumbersome title 'An Outline Synopsis for a Reconsideration of Canadian External Policy with Particular Reference to the United States of America.'[5] It was written in the immediate shadow of the French collapse in June 1940, and foresaw the necessity of a radical change in Canadian external policy to adjust to 'the new world which is being created in the shambles of Europe.' Keenleyside's perceptions had been sharpened by two visits to Washington as the prime minister's personal envoy, for strategic discussions with the American secretary of state, Cordell Hull, and President Roosevelt at the end of May 1940.[6]

Since North America was no longer impregnable, Keenleyside held that 'the Canadian Government and the Canadian people may soon be forced to recognize that the United States will not be prepared indefinitely to protect the Dominion in North America while permitting Canada, without consultation or prior approval, to send expeditionary forces to participate in the execution or attempted execution of British policies in Europe ... Washington cannot long be expected to be willing to accept responsibility for the results of a policy over which the United States has no control.' Whatever the cosmetic appearances, Canada had in fact gone to war in September 1939 'committed to automatic belligerency in defence of a policy which had been formulated by a Government over which Canada had no vestige of control.' The United States was thus required 'to underwrite the foreign policy of *any* British Government in so far, at least, as the effects of that policy threaten war or the incidence of war in North

America.' If American and British policy remained in 'general consonance,' this did not greatly matter; but if British and American policy should diverge, Canada's situation 'would become immediately and wholly impossible.'

This was rhetorical preparation for Keenleyside's two recommendations (which he characterized as 'inevitable' developments): that Canada must in future take full control of her own foreign policy, avoiding any automatic commitments through the British connection; and that she must 'reconsider the whole range of our political, economic and military relationships with the United States.' The first matter he considered relatively easy, involving 'primarily a task of education.' The second was complex and potentially traumatic.

Keenleyside's conviction was that the Roosevelt administration was already preparing to include Canada within its economic and military domains, whether Canada chose to go along or not.

It is no longer any secret that the Government of the United States has been giving detailed and serious consideration to the possibility of reorganizing the whole economic life of the Western Hemisphere. The way in which the Canadian economy can be fitted in to this hemispherical autarchy has been receiving the attention of its United States designers; although up to the present Canadians, in spite of the inevitability of some such development and in spite of its vital importance to Canada, have given it very little thought.[7]

Keenleyside saw an equivalent shift in military necessity. British military power would be reduced by the war; American, Russian, and Japanese (perhaps also German and Italian) would be enhanced. General security would be decreased by the spread of 'poverty, intolerance, fear and the tendency to rely on force.' And Canada's geographic isolation would be reduced by the creation of long-range weapons. All these factors meant that practical measures of North American defence would be essential; and the United States would require Canadian co-operation in that defence. 'If the United States is forced to defend the Americas against encroachments from across either Ocean, Canada will be expected to participate; thus the negotiation of a specific offensive-defensive alliance is likely to become inevitable.'[8]

The short paper made no pretence to be definitive; it suggested merely that there was 'a definite and grave responsibility' on officers of the Department of External Affairs to give urgent thought to such issues. But one concluding sentence rather casually suggested action of an unspecified kind: 'Moreover it may be that by taking the initiative along certain lines now we can hope to achieve a more satisfactory ultimate position vis-à-vis the United States than we can obtain by waiting until events force us to take the best available conditions in a time of crisis.'

The paper undoubtedly reflected the insecurity felt by the Canadian cabinet in the early summer of 1940, when the defeat, even, of the United Kingdom suddenly appeared to be a possibility. In this atmosphere there was no time in External Affairs for the deliberate study of the changing relationship with the United States that Keenleyside had recommended. Less than two months later Prime Minister King, at the call of President Roosevelt, acceded to the Ogdensburg Agreement, creating the Permanent Joint Board on Defence as the common instrument for planning the defence of the northern half of North America.[9] Whether Ogdensburg came closer to taking the best that was offered in a crisis or to taking an initiative aimed at 'a more satisfactory ultimate position vis-à-vis the United States' remains a nice question. Certainly Prime Minister King's concern about Canada's defencelessness and his obsequious relationship to President Roosevelt predetermined the outcome: it was inconceivable, in 1940, that King would reject such a request from Roosevelt. The necessities that bound Canada closer to the United States were personal as well as historical.

In the following months military and economic co-operation between Canada and the United States 'developed apace,' and often as the result of Canadian initiatives. The activities of the Permanent Joint Board on Defence, the Hyde Park Declaration in April 1941, the creation of the Joint Economic Committee in June 1941, and other acts of wartime integration reflected a conscious Canadian purpose. As Cuff and Granatstein write:

The Canadian aim in these critical months of 1940 and 1941 had been to bind the Dominion to the United States. In part this was a plain and simple desire for the protection that could be afforded by the American government. Part, too, was a clear desire to involve the United States more closely with a belligerent, to tie America and the Commonwealth closer together ... In strictly Canadian terms, however, there were both assets and liabilities on the new balance sheet. The gains were in terms of security and the jobs, economic stability, and access to vital components that the new relationship with the United States brought. There was also a new influence in Washington. But Canada was also being linked inextricably into an American-dominated nexus, and its production and resources were increasingly coming to be thought of as joint assets.[10]

The development of linkages continued throughout 1941, while the prime minister reassured himself with the thought that Canada served as the indispensable go-between in Anglo-American relations.[11] (This self-image, which had been flatteringly encouraged by Winston Churchill in the early days of the war, was in fact already being undermined in 1941 by the rapidly growing scale of direct British-American dealings.) The Japanese attack on Pearl Harbor, followed by American entry into the European and Pacific wars in December 1941, demolished the Canadian conceit and immediately confronted the King government with some of the real consequences of neighbourly relations with a great power at war. The new under-secretary of state for External Affairs, Norman A. Robertson, delivered a twelve-page 'rather discursive personal note' to the prime minister on 22 December 1941 dealing with these problems of the American relationship in detail.[12] While the paper took the form of a recommendation on the status and strength of Canadian representation in Washington (Robertson suggested that the Canadian minister should become an ambassador with a substantially enlarged staff), it dealt more broadly with the question of American power and behaviour in the world. The tone was more anxiously practical than that of Keenleyside's document of June 1940.

Robertson noted 'a number of warning developments' in the previous year that the United States was ceasing to regard Canada's interests with special attention and favour.

Canada naturally loomed much larger in the American sphere of things when the President and both political parties in the United States were thinking primarily in terms of continental and hemispheric defence. Now that the world war is joined on both oceans, the United States is, not unnaturally, inclined to take Canadian concurrence and support entirely for granted. In terms of the evolution of United States policy over the last five or six years, the President's cultivation of Canada has probably served its purpose. As an American nation in the British Commonwealth, this country was, in the first years of the war, visible and important evidence of the war's nearness to America. Now that the United States is itself at war with Germany, Italy and Japan, and allied with the British Commonwealth and the U.S.S.R., this phase of Canada's historical role is completed, and Americans are once more viewing Canadian questions in a more modest and more nearly domestic perspective.

The change in Canadian-American relations had been, in Robertson's view, 'rather abrupt and not too tactfully handled.' Underlying the instances which he cited in illustration, the under-secretary perceived a fresh American approach to the use of the country's power in the world.

It has always been sure of its strength and confident that it could control the conditions and degree of its participation in world affairs. For a good many years the President hoped and believed that the United States could save the world by its example, by minding its own business, pursuing a fair and friendly policy toward its neighbours, encouraging and supporting other countries disposed to follow in the same path and frowning on countries who wandered from it.

Now that this era is over, we can see the United States turning everywhere to more direct and forceful methods of exerting its influence.

The American administration, for example, sought before Pearl Harbor to monopolize all direct negotiations with Japan; it was now doing so in relation to Vichy France; and it aimed to speak alone on behalf of all Latin-American countries 'in their major relationships with the rest of the world.' 'In fact, the only major diplomatic relationship which the United States is not yet managing is contact with Russia, and here it is clear that the United Kingdom cannot make further progress in the negotiations with Stalin without bringing in the United States to decide how far they should go to meet his terms.' While American recognition of the country's strength and strategic importance, and willingness to pursue an active foreign policy, were 'very encouraging from the standpoint of the world in general,' the consequent disregard for Canadian interests might have less happy results.

Robertson's conclusions from this analysis were narrowly administrative: the circumstances did not seem to call for any high-flying imagination. There is no suggestion in the paper that Canada could have any influence upon the basic reality of American power. All that Canada might do, while the direction of the war was rapidly being concentrated in Washington, was to ensure that 'we should have the strongest possible representation in Washington and do everything we can to help make it effective.'

This was, in the remaining years of war, the bureaucratic response chosen by the King government to meet the perplexing challenge of American power and presumption. The Canadian Legation was eventually upgraded to an embassy; the establishment was progressively enlarged and staffed with some of the most proficient of the department's promising young foreign service officers; more and more opportunities were taken to develop close contacts within the American administration and when possible to acquire standing in the technical committees of the Anglo-American high command.[13] But in all matters of high military and political strategy (even in the realm of atomic energy where Canada's possession of uranium gave it great potential leverage) the Canadian government accepted the passive role of a loyal subordinate.

The wartime necessities nevertheless grated in External Affairs. Only five days after Norman Robertson's memorandum to the prime minister, H.L. Keenleyside produced another, more acerbic, paper on 'Recent Trends in United States–Canadian Relations.'[14] It covered much of the same detailed ground as Robertson's essay, added some further examples of Canadian frustrations in Washington, and ended with something like a cry of despair.

The fact that Washington is likely to become the centre of all these fundamental and far-reaching activities [of wartime strategic planning and management] gives us a great opportunity, but also involves elements of danger to our position as a separate nation fighting in this war as such. We may find that the Americans are not as conscious of our position and our problems in this regard as the British have become through a long period of education. So far we have not received from Washington – in matters relating to the conduct of the war – that degree of consideration which should be accorded an ally.

Of course, the first essential is to win the war; and no consideration of prestige or constitutional sensitiveness should be allowed to interfere with that end. It is, however, not going to help, but will rather hinder our effort, which is so important to the common cause, if the authorities in Washington feel they can consider us almost as a colonial dependency.

It would hardly be a satisfactory phase of Canada's national development if, having acquired our rightful place as a free and separate nation in the British Commonwealth, we accepted something less than the equivalent of that position in our relationship with Washington.

Within two weeks, in mid-January 1942, one of the most prolific and idealistic (not to say impetuous) members of the Department of External Affairs, Escott Reid, had circulated in the department a further memorandum bearing the provocative title 'The United States and Canada: Domination, Cooperation, Absorption.'[15] Reid carried the discussion beyond the fatalism of Robertson and Keenleyside, focusing on Canadian responsibility for her own plight, and offering a vision of how Canada might escape from the status of a helpless dependent power. He took for granted, to begin with, that there was 'a growing tendency on the part of the government of the United States to order Canada around.' In the long run he judged that this would be unacceptable because 'the people of Canada will eventually get to know it; they will be annoyed; there will be a rising tide of anti-American feeling, and an atmosphere will be created in which an intelligent solution of the problems of Canadian-American relations will be extremely difficult.'

By placing the blame for the Canadian situation squarely on the Canadian government, Reid sought to demonstrate how changes in Canadian policy might alter it: 'No useful purpose is served by being indignant about what the United States is doing. We are being treated as children because we have refused to behave as adults. An adult makes his own decisions; he accepts responsibility for his own decisions. On matters of high policy in the realm of foreign affairs Canada does not make decisions; it has decisions forced on it. We take a positive pleasure in trying not to influence the course of history.' As an immediate example, Reid cited the case of discussions with Japan in the last months before the Japanese attack on Pearl Harbor. 'We refused to take an adult part in those negotiations because to have done so would have made us partly responsible for the outcome of the negotiations.'[16] In general, he supported Robertson's implied complaints about the inadequacy of the Canadian Legation in Washington, pointing out that there were no established patterns of close contact with the Department of State, and virtually no occasions when the Canadian minister was authorized to indicate Canadian policy to the American government. 'From the history of the Canadian Legation as I have known it, except for a period of a few months after Loring Christie had settled down as minister and before he fell ill, the State Department would be justified in concluding that Canada's foreign office was not interested in Europe, Asia, Africa, Australasia or Latin America, that it was interested only in problems arising out of the "line fence" between Canada and the United States.'

The problem stemmed not only from Canadian inactivity in Washington.

It is also one of Ottawa and London. Washington is unlikely to take Ottawa seriously unless London takes Ottawa seriously. Today there is no reason why London should take Ottawa seriously. Ottawa has not asked London for any measure of control over the political, economic, psychological or military strategy of the war. So far as the direction of the war is concerned, Ottawa has been content, at least up to the recent conversations in Washington, to be the capital of a colony. If we don't want to be a colony of the United States we had better stop being a colony of Great Britain.

Reid had two kinds of proposals, one administrative, one strategic, for overcoming Canada's childish restraint in international affairs. There must be 'an entirely new conception of the work of the Department of External Affairs. We must become a planning, thinking, creative body and not be content merely to solve day-to-day problems as they arise or (as we more often do today) pass on to other departments of the government the job of solving the day-to-day problems as they arise.' The legation in Washington must be strengthened to enable it to discuss general issues of foreign policy with the secretary of state and his deputies; and the cabinet posts of prime minister and secretary of state for external affairs should be separated.

Reid's intuition about how Canada might come to act as an adult in the world, accepting responsibilities as it should, was expressed in one paragraph which pointed to the most desirable substance of post-war policy:

The present trend towards the domination of Canada's external policy by the United States is the sort of thing which is to be expected under present conditions. Under a collective system a small state like Canada would have an opportunity to exert a reasonable amount of influence in international politics at the cost of putting various aspects of its sovereignty into an international pool. But under the conditions of international anarchy which exist today the number of big states is likely to decrease and the few that are left are likely to run the small states which come within their respective spheres of influence.

In counterpoint to this vision of a new, collectively managed world system, Reid concluded by proposing a dramatic alternative for Canada. If the country could not 'work out with the United States a modern system of Canadian–United States cooperation, if possible within the framework of a collective system,' then it should throw in its destiny with that of the United States by seeking political absorption.

If we cannot become partners in a democratic world order we should become a part of the master state which will eventually dominate the world. We are, perhaps, the only country that has this choice. The United States might well refuse to let Great

Britain into the American Union but if Canada played her cards at all well she could get favorable terms for entry into the Union ... once public opinion in the United States began to swing in favour of accepting Canada into the Union, the two political parties in Washington would start outbidding each other in the generosity of the terms they offered to Canada in an effort to pick up a good proportion of the new votes to be reaped in Canada.

This stimulating document provoked nineteen pages of comments from six of Escott Reid's departmental colleagues. All of them (as Reid undoubtedly intended) rejected the prospect of absorption into the United States as undesirable and politically unacceptable. All agreed that it was time for Canada to play the adult. All, with varying degrees of warmth or expectation, favoured Canada's entry into a new scheme of collective security as the appropriate means of escaping American domination. But they were noticeably more pessimistic about the prospects for independent Canadian action in the world than Reid had been. Jules Leger expressed his modest hopes for a collective system with the greatest pungency: 'I agree with this and hope it will come true. However, to put it bluntly, the more the Americans participate in winning this war, the more difficult such a collective system will be to establish. Total war also means total victory and total victory has not enough "nuances", in my opinion, to create a good atmosphere for a collective system. If it were not for the U.S.S.R. we would be ripe for a purely Pax Americana and I am not sure if it would be a good thing.'[17]

There was not yet an American peace; there was certainly an American war. In April 1942 H.L. Keenleyside produced another memo for the under-secretary of state for external affairs listing the most recent examples of American high-handedness in wartime arrangements affecting Canada.[18] The paper was starkly titled 'American Imperialism and Canada,' although the text slightly softened this judgment to 'neo-Imperialism.' It noted that Canada fared better, in fact, than most of America's allies because of the existence of various bilateral agencies for co-operation like the Permanent Joint Board on Defence, but said nevertheless that 'there has been a whole series of unsatisfactory episodes, for some of which informal apologies have been received but which have generally gone unrebuked and unexplained. So far no very serious damage has been done but this may not always be true.' The incidents were typified by 'peremptory demands' on Canada by the US government, as well as real invasions of Canadian sovereign territory by the American military. (One case involved the unauthorized installation of '600 men ... anti-aircraft guns, barrage balloons, R.D.F. equipment ... and other military supplies' by the US Army north of the border at Sault Ste Marie in March 1942. Keenleyside recorded that 'informal apologies, or rather explanations were subsequently given. But that was long after the United States units were firmly established on Canadian soil.') Such incidents, small in themselves in the context of a massive war effort, were enough to cause growing anxiety which was soon shared by the prime minister. As early as December 1941 he was reporting in his diary 'a certain aggressiveness on the part of America.'[19]

As the tide slowly turned in favour of the Allies in late 1942 and early 1943, and preliminary planning for the period of post-war reconstruction began, Canada's representatives in Washington expressed renewed anxiety about the American tendency to ignore Canadian interests. In March 1943, Lester Pearson, now the minister-counsellor at the Canadian Legation, directed a memorandum on the subject to the minister, Leighton McCarthy, which McCarthy immediately passed on to the prime minister.[20] Pearson emphasized the dangers for Canada of 'the very intimacy, informality, and friendliness of our relations with the United States':

The American authorities often tend to consider us not as a foreign nation at all, but as one of themselves. This is flattering, but leads occasionally to misunderstandings. Because they take us for granted, they are perplexed when we show an impatience at being ignored and an irritation at being treated as something less than an independent State. They make sudden demands on us, for some concession or co-operation which they consider to be required by the war emergency, and they do not understand why we should not respond, as the Governor of a State would.[21]

Pearson echoed Escott Reid's lament in noting that one source, at least, of Washington's neglect of Canadian sensitivities could be traced to Canada's own diplomatic practices. 'On instructions from Ottawa, we take a firm stand in Washington in opposition to certain United States demands. But as soon as pressure is exerted by the U.S. Government either here or in Ottawa, we give in ... This kind of diplomacy, the strong glove over the velvet hand, has nothing to commend it.'

The document concluded with a general precaution rather than any particular recommendations.

This brings up the question of the attitude likely to be adopted by the U.S. Government towards our aspirations to play an important but independent role in the post-war set-up. There are indications that we may have as much difficulty asserting our position in Washington as we ever had in London during and after the last war. United States understanding of Canada's status and stature in the world in general, and the British Empire in particular, is certainly confused, but I am not sure that this confusion will be cleared up in a way satisfactory to us ...

Suspended, then, somewhat uneasily in the minds of so many Americans between the position of British Colony and American dependency, we are going to have a difficult time in the months ahead in maintaining our own position and in standing on our own feet.[22]

In an effort to sum up the difficulties of the Canadian-American relationship for the possible guidance of those engaged in putting forward the Canadian point of view in the United States, Escott Reid wrote another document for circulation to his senior colleagues in External Affairs and the Prime Minister's Office in April 1943.[23] Two-thirds of the paper consisted of a primer on the disproportionate power of the United States and Canada and a series of sermonly exhortations to avoid a post-war settlement that would place too much authority in the hands of the great powers. Finally, in the last four pages Reid achieved a more precise focus on his perception of Canadian-American frictions in the post-war era. The USSR was by now becoming a significant element in the balance.

The most difficult problem will be the problem of defence cooperation between Canada and the United States. At the present time Canada and the United States are bound not to make a separate peace with the Axis. When peace comes will Canada bind itself not to go to war without the consent of the United States? Will the United States bind itself not to go to war without the consent of Canada? *One cannot rule out the possibility that there may sometime be a war between* the United States and the U.S.S.R. Does the United States expect that, regardless of the causes and occasion of that war, regardless of the allies which the U.S.S.R. may have, Canada will automatically become at least a non-belligerent ally of the United States by granting the United States the right to use the Canadian section of the Alaska Highway for military traffic and the right to fly military aircraft over Canada en route to Alaska and the Far East[?] It is hard to imagine that any self-respecting country would be willing, in the vital matter of peace and war, so completely to give up its right of independent judgment and transfer the making of decisions involving its own destiny into the hands of the government of another country. My country, right or wrong, is a questionable and disreputable doctrine. Somebody else's country right or wrong is an impossible doctrine.[24]

> Canadian participation in international institutions was justified as the means – perhaps the only means – of escaping from subservience to Washington.

It would be easier and more self-respecting for Canada to give up to an international body on which it was represented the decision on when it should go to war than to transfer the right to make that decision from the government in Ottawa to the government in Washington. We have not won from London complete freedom to make our own decisions on every issue – including that of peace and war – in order to become a colony of Washington. It would thus appear probable that effective military cooperation between Canada and the United States is possible only within the framework of an effective world order of which both Canada and the United States are loyal members.[25]

Reid's closing paragraph offered the incomplete beginning of a geopolitical comment on Canada's changing position in the world. At the very moment when Canadians had become accustomed to thinking of themselves as members of an American nation as well as of a British nation, they might now be compelled by advancing technology to undergo 'another mental revolution' in order to see themselves as a northern nation buffering the United States and the USSR. Extensive northern airlifts to Europe and the Soviet Union, hardly conceivable only a decade earlier, were already making that revolution a fact.

The elaboration of this theme occurred a few months later in another memorandum from Escott Reid on 'Canada's position on the main air routes between North America and Northern and Central Europe and Northern Asia,' which was accompanied by 'an air map of the world.'[26] Reid recalled that while Canada was familiar with the role of buffer state between two friendly neighbours – the United States and Britain – 'we have not for many decades had the experience of being a buffer state between two powerful nations whose relations may from time to time become dangerously strained.'

Just as the great naval powers of the nineteenth century 'kept pushing their naval bases farther and farther out from their own shores,' Reid foresaw that without 'some effective system of collective security' the leading powers after the Second World War would seek to extend the line of their air bases ever outwards. For Canada, that might mean heavy American pressure. 'To protect itself from attack across the North Atlantic it may want air bases in Iceland, Greenland, Newfoundland and possibly Labrador. To protect itself against attack from Asia and northern Europe it may want bases not only in Alaska and perhaps the Japanese Kuriles but also across northern Canada.' If the United States desired 'a Maginot line of air defences in the Canadian North,' Canada would be placed in an unenviable position comparable to that of Belgium between France and Germany in the thirties. 'In an effort to maintain some freedom of action on the grave issues of peace and war, we would be most reluctant to have bases built on our territory by one of our great neighbours. To construct and maintain them ourselves would involve us in enormous expense. Moreover to construct bases directed against one of our great neighbours and not the other would line us up in one of the opposing camps – the very thing which we would be trying to avoid.'

Reid could see that by the end of the Pacific war, 'the preachings of Seversky as interpreted by Walt Disney and other popularizers' would already have Americans imagining the outbreak of World War III 'with a dozen simultaneous Pearl Harbors in San Francisco, Seattle, Chicago, Detroit, New York, Philadelphia, Baltimore, Washington, San Diego and Norfolk.'[27] American anxiety was likely to extend even to the granting of commercial air routes in North America to the Soviet Union, since these would offer experience to Soviet pilots that would be valuable in subsequent military operations. Canada would (in the usual metaphor) be caught in the squeeze: restriction of Soviet flights under American pressure would be considered an unfriendly act by Russia; Canada's failure to restrict those flights would be considered an unfriendly act by the United States.

Within ten years, further advances in military technology would mean that Canada would be 'in danger of being involved in a future war either by a direct attack on our own territory or by an attack launched against one of our neighbours over our territory.' All these considerations turned Reid, once again, to the essential importance for Canada of a collective security system rather than 'the alternative system of bilateral and multilateral defensive alliances under which the United States would think of us in terms of the contribution which we could make to the defence of North America.' Reid's fertile mind prompted him to refer in passing to his preference for 'United Nations air bases in Northern Canada' rather than American ones, and to suggest the desirability of 'internationalizing' the major intercontinental air routes and airlines, to remove them from competing national jurisdictions. To carry through all these international projects would require 'a supreme effort of social imagination and social invention based on intellectual integrity and intellectual courage of a high order'; yet Reid worried that the leaders of the major powers would be so exhausted by the war that in peace they would lack the ability 'to imagine, to invent and to construct' the necessary new institutions.

By the late winter of 1944 the phase of preliminary Canadian speculation on the shape of the post-war world was coming to an end. Italy was out of the war; German and Japanese forces were in slow retreat across the world; the Allied invasion of Western Europe was in advanced preparation; and increasingly detailed consideration was being given in London and Washington to some aspects of post-war planning. That consideration had to be followed by the growth of a complementary capacity in Ottawa to plan for the Canadian role in the post-war world. But before this shift to a more detailed and complex phase of planning, Escott Reid prepared one more general analysis of Canadian-American relations for the under-secretary in February 1944.[28]

At the outset Reid noted that the overall record of wartime collaboration between the United States and Canada, despite some irritants, should be regarded as a matter of pride by both nations. However, there was a strong belief in Washington that '"the American way" is by definition the best way'; that the United States was doing humanity a favour by taking part in the war; and that its allies were grasping and short-sighted by comparison. The result of these attitudes was 'a tendency to overlook the rights and feelings of smaller countries and an unwillingness to compromise when United States claims are contested by other nations.' This was by now a familiar refrain in the Department of External Affairs. Reid added to it his analysis of the major reasons for America's increased insensitivity and assertiveness. There were four, he believed: a decline in the influence of the European Division within the State Department (which had been particularly knowledgeable and understanding about Canada) and of the State Department within the administration – both resulting from the proliferation of wartime agencies; the new power of the army and navy, their distaste for the State Department, and their 'easy access to the President as Commander-in-Chief'; the sudden infusion of many blunt and undiplomatic businessmen into the new civil agencies; and the use by the administration, 'almost to the point of political blackmail,' of clamorous public opinion as an excuse for high-handedness.

In illustration of the irritations for Canada, Reid listed six recent matters of dispute involving relations with Latin America, wheat sales, border crossing regulations, defence sales, post-war ownership of US military sites in Canada, and export controls. Again, the complaints were familiar. The paper's conclusion, too, offered no more than a muted repetition of Lester Pearson's admonition of the previous year that Ottawa should choose its disputes with the United States carefully, 'take a strong line only when the issue is important and we have a good case,' and then bargain hard for the Canadian advantage.

The Second World War was a forcing-house for Canadian diplomacy. A government little tested or scarred by international conflicts of power found itself suddenly thrown into the midst of British and American efforts to win a world war, and to hold or enhance their political power in that struggle. An understaffed, inexperienced, and (at least initially) disorganized Canadian foreign service was required to improvise Canadian responses to a distracting range of novel demands, an increasing proportion of which originated in Washington. It seems clear that, by early 1944, the Department of External Affairs' persistent sense of unease about Canada's ability to deal successfully with a muscular great power neighbour (as familiar and attractive as the United States might be) had not prompted and was not matched by any thoroughly considered strategy to contain the American challenge. The only recourse proposed consistently in the department was the vague appeal to 'collective security,' the failed panacea of the twenties and thirties, as a means not only of deterring aggression but also, somehow, of reining in the wilfulness of Canada's dynamic neighbour.

Meanwhile another great power was rising on the northern horizon.

During the months preceding the outbreak of the European war in 1939, Mackenzie King privately recognized that Canada would have to follow Britain's lead into a war against Nazi Germany, and committed his cabinet to that course. The prime minister knew in 1939 that once Britain was at war, the English-speaking majority would insist that Canada too must enter the ranks. (And King stood with that majority.) His political skills were applied successfully to appeasing Quebec and to muffling the fact of Canada's automatic belligerency before the actual event.[29]

King was unhappy, however, that the occasion for war might arise from Britain's new commitments in Eastern Europe undertaken after the German occupation of what remained of Czechoslovakia in March 1939;

he was especially disconcerted by the possibility of an alliance with the Bolsheviks of the Soviet Union. He conveyed his distaste for the Anglo-French-Soviet discussions of spring and summer 1939 to the British high commissioner, and reiterated Canada's device for confronting such unpleasant realities: if Britain were considering an alliance with Russia, he would rather not be consulted in advance.[30] In April, when the high commissioner asked King to make a statement in the House of Commons pledging Canada's support for the United Kingdom against Germany, the prime minister refused angrily to do so, adding that 'certainly our people would not want to fight to help Russia.'[31] The collapse of the Anglo-French negotiations in Moscow, which came with the ominous signing of the German-Soviet non-aggression pact on 23 August, was thus, paradoxically, a distinct relief to Mackenzie King.[32] The treaty may have made war inevitable; but it simplified matters in the prime minister's political conscience. When war descended the Soviet Union could be treated as an enemy. The Canadian Communist party was declared illegal in June 1940 under the Defence of Canada Regulations; and Russian efforts to buy wheat in January 1940 were forestalled by order-in-council.[33]

Two years of commitment to the lonely British cause in wartime made Canada more, not less, dependent on British policy. When the German armies invaded Russia on 22 June 1941, Canadian policy was determined in Whitehall more decisively than in September 1939. This time there was no preparation in cabinet for what was to occur. Churchill had already indicated privately to Stalin that Britain would offer assistance to Russia in the event of a German attack, and had informed President Roosevelt of this resolve.[34] Roosevelt in return had promised, through the American ambassador in London, to support at once 'any announcement that the Prime Minister might make welcoming Russia as an ally.'[35] But in accordance with Mackenzie King's well-established preference, Britain's Commonwealth partner in war was left in ignorance about these preparations. The Canadian prime minister thus learned of Churchill's commitment of the Empire and Commonwealth to the Soviet cause only through Churchill's broadcast on the evening of 22 June, when Britain's historic reversal of policy toward the Soviet Union was proclaimed in a great outpouring of Churchillian rhetoric.[36] ('We have but one aim and one single, irrevocable purpose. We are resolved to destroy Hitler and every vestige of the Nazi regime. From this nothing will turn us – nothing. We will never parley, we will never negotiate with Hitler or any of his gang.

We shall fight him by land, we shall fight him by sea, we shall fight him in the air, until, with God's help, we have rid the earth of his shadow and liberated its peoples from his yoke. Any man or state who fights against Nazidom will have our aid. Any man or state who marches with Hitler is our foe.') Mackenzie King's echo came in a press release the next day, 'though,' as C.P. Stacey comments, 'perhaps with an eye on anti-Communist Quebec, he said nothing of aid to Russia.'[37]

This was indeed a dizzying reversal of policy for Britain and the Commonwealth, and it was not surprising that the Canadian prime minister showed some initial hesitation. (It seems likely, even, that Joseph Stalin was not wholly convinced of British good faith; for several months he sought repeated and tangible reassurance.)[38]

One consequence of the transformation of the Soviet Union into an ally was that the Canadian Communist party, proscribed only a year before, became overnight a fervent advocate of the anti-Nazi cause. The government's security committee was thus faced with the need to review the policy of proscription and internment as it applied to Communists. The Department of External Affairs argued for a reversal of policy, but strong rearguard resistance from the RCMP, the Catholic church in Quebec, and, after his appointment in 1942, the new minister of justice, Louis St Laurent, sustained the ban until 1944.[39]

A departmental paper noted at the end of July 1941 that large public meetings in support of the Soviet Union had been held in Montreal, Toronto, and elsewhere, attended (according to the *Montreal Gazette*) by citizens of 'many races in Europe, including Russians, and also many with a known leaning towards Communistic principles, but there were also representatives of the general rank and file of citizens.'[40] These rallies passed resolutions calling for the establishment of diplomatic relations between Canada and the USSR, the resumption of trade, the signing of a trade agreement, and the release from internment of all 'anti-fascists' and 'labour leaders.' The pattern of orchestrated support for the Soviet war effort soon took institutional form in the Council of Canadian-Soviet Friendship, which allied a wide spectrum of labour, civil libertarian, religious, and public figures in promotion of the Soviet alliance. (Arnold Smith commented in a memorandum from the Canadian Embassy in Moscow in 1945: 'The Soviet Government obviously attaches profound importance to propaganda policy in foreign countries ... The simultaneous creation, in most countries throughout the world, of organisations such as the Canadian-Soviet Friendship Society is an obvious result of a

Communist Party circular directive, though certainly many of the leaders of such societies are unaware of the secret instigation.')[41] The council's activities were complemented, as the Soviet resistance to the German invasion stiffened, by a growing popular admiration for Russian courage and endurance.

In the first weeks after the invasion, the counsellor at the Canadian Legation in Washington, Hume H. Wrong, was engaged (apparently on Soviet initiative) in preliminary discussions with the Russians on the supply of food, shipping, and ship repair facilities; and he soon reported the first, indirect enquiries about the establishment of formal diplomatic relations.[42] The logic of the Churchillian alliance of necessity was working itself out in Ottawa as elsewhere. As the departmental document of 30 July put it:

... in spite of the grounds for mistrust and suspicion, there is little doubt that it is a vital Canadian and Allied interest to keep Russia in the war against Germany. If this can be done, Germany's Eastern Front will become a constant drain on her men and resources, and the Russian front would in time become a stepping-off place for the offence against Germany. If, on the other hand, Russia cannot be kept in the war, the outlook for the Allies is dark indeed. Germany would have solved the problem of the blockade, could move vital war industries still further away from the Royal Air Force, and could hold Europe for years to come.[43]

The circumstances required that Canada 'should give careful thought to possible methods of assisting Russia at the present time. The question of what form this assistance might take i.e. whether economic, military, or political, is worthy of thorough exploration.'[44]

This consideration came, and with it the inevitable extension of military and economic aid and political recognition. But it came in the Canadian way: slowly, cautiously, and safely in the wake of Anglo-American policy. In contrast, the Roosevelt administration – although still technically neutral – demonstrated its support for the Soviet Union quickly and tangibly. In July 1941 Roosevelt sent his personal envoy, Harry Hopkins, to Moscow for talks with Stalin; in August the acting secretary of state assured the Soviet ambassador in a note that the United States would 'give all economic assistance practicable for the purpose of strengthening the Soviet Union in its struggle against armed aggression'; and in the same month American oil supplies were already on their way, the precursors of an eventually vast American effort of supply through Vladivostok,

Murmansk, and Tehran.[45] Britain also began discussions with the Soviet Union on the entire range of the two countries' common interests. In early July they signed a joint declaration making a general pledge of mutual assistance and agreeing that neither would make a separate peace; and by September Britain was delivering the first of four hundred Hurricane fighters, along with other war supplies, for use on the Russian front.[46] Canadian aid was developed slowly under the British umbrella, and justified carefully on military rather than political grounds.[47]

Despite American neutrality, the United States and Britain were now co-ordinating their policies more and more closely. Following Hopkins's visit to Moscow, Churchill and Roosevelt held their first face-to-face meeting from 9 to 12 August at Placentia Bay, Newfoundland, where they agreed upon the Atlantic Charter. This joint declaration, setting out 'certain common principles ... on which they base their hopes for a better future for the world,' henceforth became the basic statement of Allied war aims. In phrases reminiscent of the Fourteen Points, it declared the mutual commitment of Britain and America to the defeat of Nazi Germany and to a new world of peace and international justice. Points two and three, especially, set a Wilsonian standard of expectation almost certain to be disappointed in the post-war conflict of national interest, as it had been in 1919: '... they desire to see no territorial changes that do not accord with the freely expressed wishes of the peoples concerned ... they respect the right of all peoples to choose the form of government under which they will live; and they wish to see sovereign rights and self-government restored to those who have been forcibly deprived of them.'[48]

The Soviet Union, whose own actions in Poland, the Baltic countries, and Finland in 1939 and 1940 had violated these principles, was unhappy that it had not been consulted in drafting the charter, and conveyed its dissatisfaction to the British government. In September 1941 the Soviets formally endorsed the charter at the inter-Allied conference in London; but Ivan Maisky, the Soviet ambassador to the United Kingdom, added the reservation that the charter must be adapted to "the circumstances, needs and historic peculiarities of particular countries,' thus throwing doubt on the commitment as it might apply to Eastern Europe.[49] Stalin made the point explicitly to Anthony Eden when the two met in Moscow in December 1941 and discussion turned to the question of the Soviet-Polish frontier: 'I am genuinely surprised. I thought that the Atlantic Charter was directed against those people who were trying to establish world dominion. It now looks as if the Charter was directed against the u.s.s.r.'[50]

Even while the Soviet Union faced its most critical military challenge from Germany in 1941 and 1942, Soviet diplomacy always pursued political objectives. The first, most desperate Russian purpose (despite Churchill's ringing promises) was to ensure that the countries of the West – chiefly the United Kingdom – would not stand aside while Germany and Russia engaged in deadly struggle, in Eden's phrase, 'as they had watched ours.' 'It was almost as much for this reason as because they needed help, that the next six months were filled with Soviet requests, even demands, for a second front, for enormous quantities of material aid, for British troops to fight in Russia and for a political treaty.'[51]

As Britain gradually reassured Russia that she would not be abandoned, diplomatic discussion turned also to matters of permanent strategic importance: Soviet-Polish relations, the security of Iran, and Soviet-Turkish relations. Under British oversight the Soviet Union reached temporary agreement over the war effort with the London-based Polish government in exile; British and Russian troops acted in concert to occupy Iran in September, thus protecting the trans-Iranian railway link to the Soviet Union; and both nations gave reassurance to Turkey that her interests would not be sacrificed.[52] The Russians pressed insistently for large British contributions of supplies and troops for the Eastern front, and coupled these demands (sometimes harshly) with requests for negotiations over war aims and post-war policy.[53] The British talked, but involved American representatives as closely as they could in these discussions. There were already warnings of potential British-American differences over Russia and the peace settlement – particularly over frontiers. Anthony Eden reported on this subject in his diary of 21 July:

Hopkins and Winant came to see me. They told me that Roosevelt was most eager that we should not commit ourselves to any definite frontiers for any country before the peace treaty. H. said that U.S. would come into the war and did not want to find after the event that we had all kinds of engagements of which they had never been told. Winston was clearly not interested in the peace and H. had therefore been told to speak urgently to me. I explained our position, and that I was as eager to keep my hands free as anybody, but the spectacle of an American President talking at large on European frontiers chilled me with Wilsonian memories.[54]

In December 1941, at the moment of American entry into the war, the British foreign secretary travelled to Moscow to discuss wartime and post-war planning with Joseph Stalin. The Soviet dictator presented Eden with two proposed treaties in draft: 'One was for a military alliance during the war, the other provided for common action to solve post-war questions in Europe and to prevent renewed aggression by Germany. Both these treaties were to be published, but the second one was to have a secret protocol dealing in some detail with European frontiers.'[55] Eden was immediately disabused of any belief that the Soviets might alter their concrete pursuit of national security for the sake of harmony on abstract principles. (Stalin told Eden that he preferred 'practical arithmetic' to algebra.) 'Stalin's suggestions for this protocol showed me that the hope we had held in London, of being able to confine discussion of frontiers to the general terms of the Atlantic Charter, had been vain. Russian ideas were already starkly definite. They changed little during the next three years, for their purpose was to secure the most tangible physical guarantees for Russia's future security.'[56] The Soviet proposal dealt in detail with border and territorial claims upon Finland, Poland, Romania, and the Baltic states – a bold projection of Soviet concern for territorial security, expressed at a moment when the German armies were at the gates of Moscow and these Russian aims were far from immediate achievement. Eden resisted, on the grounds that the United Kingdom could not make an agreement on post-war frontiers before consulting with the United States and the Dominions. Stalin seemed to acknowledge this; and Eden gave the impression that, following such discussion, a treaty might be signed which would bind the Dominions as well as the United Kingdom: 'I went on to explain that I could now sign an agreement, but not a treaty until the Dominions had been consulted and had acceded to it, when the treaty could be signed in London in proper form and ratified.'[57] This was a disingenuous excuse for delay, since Eden knew that it was not necessary or usual for the Dominions to accede to UK treaties. Whatever the treaty's content might prove to be, Eden's presumption (if it was meant literally) could be expected to disturb the calm of Mackenzie King. In 1941 he had given no thought to a Canadian position on the post-war European settlement, and no indication that he might endorse any British treaty commitments on the subject.

Eden returned from Moscow with the strong belief that Europe after the war would confront an unrelenting challenge from the Soviet Union. He reflected on this in a memorandum to the British War Cabinet in January 1942. 'On the assumption that Germany is defeated and German military strength is destroyed and that France remains, for a long time at least, a weak power, there will be no counterweight to Russia in Europe ...

Russia's position on the European continent will be unassailable. Russian prestige will be so great that the establishment of Communist Governments in the majority of European countries will be greatly facilitated, and the Soviet Government will naturally be tempted to work for this.'[58] In anticipation of Soviet pressures, Eden foresaw the need both to cultivate the Anglo-American alliance and to deal co-operatively with the Soviet Union in an effort to dispel her suspicions of the Western powers. 'In practice this means that in order successfully to reconcile American and Russian susceptibilities and to co-ordinate our policy with both of theirs, we shall have to consult the United States Government in all our discussions with the Soviet Government, and try to obtain their approval or at least their acquiescence in all Anglo-Soviet arrangements. Wherever possible we should work for tripartite consultations and tripartite solutions.'[59]

So the British conversations with the Soviet Union over the terms of a formal treaty continued through the winter, in full and intimate consultation with the American administration. While Roosevelt gave his own informal assurances to the Soviet Union that the United States sympathized with the Russian desire for 'complete future security' in Europe, the United Kingdom tried to draw the treaty negotiations to a conclusion by being more precise. The discussions entered an intense stage in London in early April 1942.[60] The British proposal at this point involved a treaty of alliance and confirmation of the Soviet Union's frontiers of 1940, including Russian absorption of Bessarabia and the Baltic countries, but specifically excluding any commitment on the Polish frontier. This opening involved a very substantial concession to Russian territorial claims which it would henceforth be difficult for the United Kingdom to go back upon; the proposal was apparently put forward in the hope that an early settlement of Soviet claims would appease Stalin, reinforce his commitment to the joint war effort, and discourage any larger claims in future.[61]

Britain's promise to consult the Dominions gave her a certain potentially useful leverage in the negotiations. It was never remotely likely that Canada would accede to an Anglo-Soviet treaty negotiated on her behalf by the United Kingdom; but consultation could conversely be used by the United Kingdom to strengthen her case against what she might regard as excessive Soviet claims. Until late in April 1942, the 'consultation' consisted, in Canada's case, of keeping the high commissioner in London informed of the substance of the British treaty proposals, but without soliciting any Canadian response. The request might eventually come, however, and in anticipation of it George Glazebrook of the Department of External Affairs prepared a memorandum for the prime minister which was delivered on 14 April.[62] Glazebrook noted the normal Canadian concerns in assessing a British initiative.

From the Canadian point of view two considerations stand out: maximum efficiency in the conduct of the war, and Anglo-American-Canadian comity. The United Kingdom Government is convinced that, under the circumstances, the first consideration requires a treaty with Russia; but have realized from the first the threat to Anglo-American co-operation involved in following a policy different from that of the United States. In communications between them both the British and American Governments have emphasized the pressure of public opinion. The same factor must be taken into account by the Canadian Government when deciding its policy.

Glazebrook's view was that Canadian reaction to an Anglo-Soviet treaty would depend 'a great deal' on how the treaty was explained to the public. On the one hand, Canadians would be sympathetic to the consolidation of political support for the nation suffering most from the land war against Germany; on the other hand, there might be three sources of Canadian dissent. Canadian anti-Communists (who were probably most influential in Quebec) would oppose any extension of political relations with the Soviet Union; others would object to supporting a British policy different from that of the United States (or, alternatively, an American policy different from that of the United Kingdom); and others would make a challenge of principle.

Opposition to the treaty would also be based on the ground that it destroyed certain small nations and might open the way for further absorption by the Great Powers. The Atlantic Charter has given the impression that such territorial changes would not be made. The Canadian minorities immediately affected – Roumanians, Estonians, Latvians, Lithuanians, and Finns – would suffer disillusionment; while others from small states, such as Poles and Ukrainians, would be apprehensive of the extension of the principle to their homelands. Amongst some of these groups there are divisions, so that some elements would support any move of aid to Russia, but on the whole the effect would probably be bad.

No matter how inconvenient an Anglo-Soviet treaty might be for Canada, Glazebrook made the reluctant point that 'none the less some Canadian policy with regard to it will have to be adopted.' There were three choices: to stand aside (as the United States intended to do); to oppose the treaty on principle; or to support and adhere to it. Glazebrook ruled out the second as impossible, expressed a thinly veiled preference for active support and adherence (on the grounds that it would reduce Anglo-American differences and strengthen the impact of the treaty), but concluded with more extended comment on the option of standing aside which amounted to the discovery of a fourth choice: constructive non-commitment. Canada should stand aside in support. (Glazebrook knew well the tendencies of the King government.) A treaty, he concluded, was unavoidable; 'its value should not be reduced, nor its danger underlined by any action of ours.'

Within a few days the Canadian high commissioner in London, Vincent Massey, wrote to King that the British government sought an entirely informal indication of support for or opposition to the proposed treaty from the four Dominions.[63] Massey noted the delicacy with which the British enquiry was put forward: 'Matter will not come to a formal proposal from here unless United Kingdom Government is assured that all four Dominion Governments would welcome opportunity to enter into such treaty relations with the Soviet Government.'

The Canadian government, for one, would not. At the Cabinet War Committee on 29 April, the prime minister expressed his opposition to participation 'in a treaty with the U.S.S.R. which involved any settlement or guarantee of the pre-war Russian frontiers. The United States were not prepared to do so, though they would not oppose the negotiations, or take exception to the treaties.'[64] Norman Robertson told the Committee that the effect of the British draft would be to establish the 1940 frontiers, with the exception of Poland's, as 'a common principle of Anglo-Russian policy in the reconstruction of Europe.' The navy minister, Colin Gibson, expressed his fear that 'the announcement of these provisions, in essence opposed to the principles of the Atlantic Charter, would create apprehension in democratic countries.' The War Committee thus reached the unambiguous decision that Canada should not adhere to a treaty containing such terms, and on 1 May Massey was instructed in a curt telegram: 'Canadian Government does not wish to enter into treaty relations with the U.S.S.R. along lines of proposed Anglo-Russian Treaties.'[65] Taking the conclusion as a fait accompli (King reported to the War Committee that the United Kingdom believed 'arrangements of this kind were of vital importance' and 'had decided to go ahead, in any event'), the prime minister did not convey to London any direct criticism of the British intention.

There is no indication that Canadian opposition to a frontier agreement in Eastern Europe had any impact in London. But American official distaste paralleled Canadian, and was apparently conveyed more clearly to Eden.[66] Soon afterwards the British foreign secretary presented the Soviets with an alternative draft proposing a twenty year treaty of military alliance and collaboration without any mention of frontiers.[67] The American government at once conveyed its approval for this approach to the Russians; the Dominion high commissioners 'were delighted'; and Molotov, after initial hesitation, agreed to sign.[68] The frontier question was not resolved; only postponed.

Glazebrook now commented in a fresh memorandum that 'the treaty as a whole is a compromise between United Kingdom and Russian policies, but is much closer to the former than seemed possible from reports of the negotiations.'[69] The elimination of a frontier agreement that would have violated the Atlantic Charter and displeased the United States, Glazebrook wrote, 'must be regarded not only as a success for United Kingdom diplomacy but as promising a greater degree of agreement among the United Nations.' There were now no grounds for Canadian opposition to the treaty; in fact, 'the circumstances have now entirely changed, and the Canadian Government can, without embarrassment, express its un-qualified approval.'

The suggestion for Canadian adherence to the treaty had disappeared after the initial cold blast from Ottawa, and was not revived. In a covering note to the prime minister, Norman Robertson observed that there was no provision in the treaty for adherence by third parties, and that, besides, 'I do not think that Canada should, at this stage, assume post-war obligations in other parts of the world which would be different from or go further than those that the United States is prepared to assume.'[70] The outcome exactly suited the cautious preference of the Canadian government: it could conscientiously applaud, but without obligation. This it did, in a telegram to Winston Churchill tabled in the House of Commons by Mackenzie King on 11 June.[71]

Soviet willingness to postpone recognition of its frontier claims, however, had an immediate price, negotiated over the heads of the British and without the knowledge of the Canadians. In direct communication with Stalin in April, Roosevelt had indicated a tacit exchange: if Russia would agree to eliminate references to her borders from the Anglo-Soviet treaty, the United States and Britain would commit themselves to a second front in Europe during 1942.[72] With the Anglo-Soviet treaty in his pocket at the end of May, the Soviet foreign minister, V.M. Molotov, accordingly flew to Washington, returning to London in June with what Eden described as 'an explosive message': a joint Soviet-American communiqué announcing agreement ' "with regard to the urgent tasks of creating a second front in Europe in 1942." '[73] The United Kingdom had not been consulted and could not agree, yet announced its concurrence in order to avoid giving any hint of discord to the enemy. In private Eden and Churchill spoke bluntly to Molotov, and before he departed Churchill gave Molotov 'an *aide-memoire* explaining that it was not yet possible to say whether the plan for a landing on the Continent was feasible that year. We could, therefore, give no promise. Despite this document, the Soviet Government affected to believe, and gave their people to understand, that a second front had been promised. Later in the summer, when the Americans admitted that the operation could not take place, Russian reproaches, particularly against Britain, became violent.'[74] In the months that followed, the pro-Soviet lobby in the West called insistently for a second front, and this propaganda campaign gained intensity from time to time, in parallel with public appeals from Moscow, during the next eighteen months.

Meanwhile discussion of the establishment of diplomatic relations between Canada and the Soviet Union proceeded at a measured pace conditioned by the diffidence of the Canadian government, sensitive above all to the views of the Catholic hierarchy in Quebec.[75] The British foreign secretary, Anthony Eden, was invited to enquire about recognition and the exchange of representatives when he visited Moscow in December 1941; and quickly afterwards the Soviet ambassador to the United Kingdom, Ivan Maisky, presented a draft agreement for Canadian consideration. In early January 1942 the Cabinet War Committee accepted the agreement in principle, and on 5 February 1942 Vincent Massey and Maisky signed the document in London. Another two months were required before External Affairs could convince the prime minister that the exchange should be at the ministerial rather than consular level.[76]

Six months more passed in the selection of a Canadian minister to the USSR. Before that had occurred, the first Soviet minister, Feodor Gousev, arrived in Ottawa on 12 October 1942.[77] Shortly afterwards L. Dana Wilgress, the deputy minister of trade and commerce, one of the few Canadian civil servants with any experience of the Soviet Union, was named as the Canadian representative in the Soviet Union.[78]

Wilgress arrived in the Soviet Union to establish the Canadian mission in March 1943. The mission was initially small and inexperienced, its facilities meagre. The minister was accompanied by a first secretary, R.M. Macdonnell; two third secretaries, Arnold C. Smith and J.A. McCordick; a military attaché, Brigadier H. Lefebvre, and his assistant. Smith alone, apart from Wilgress, had had experience of Eastern Europe, during a year as an editor and teacher in Tallin, Estonia, in 1939 and 1940.[79]

For six months the mission was located in temporary quarters in Kuibyshev, at a time when the Soviet Foreign Ministry was relocating gradually back to Moscow. Wilgress later recalled that 'the foreign diplomats in Kuibyshev had very little to do,' because all important matters were dealt with in Moscow. 'The diplomats in Kuibyshev would spend the morning walking up and down the main street, greeting one another. In the evening they would attend the opera or ballet at the very fine theatre that had become the temporary home of the Bolshoi Theatre. To relieve the boredom they would entertain one another lavishly and never have I partaken of such sumptuous repasts, at a time when Russia was short of foodstuffs and many people were not getting enough to eat.'[80] In spite of the inconveniences, the Canadians set out on their reporting task with vigour. Through the good offices of the British Embassy, the mission began at once to supply Ottawa with a flow of telegrams, dispatches, and letters on a diverse range of military, domestic, and diplomatic subjects. These early communications included reflections on the role the Canadian diplomats sought to play, and the sources of information available to the legation, which are indispensable in interpreting the dispatches sent over the subsequent two years.

At the end of April 1943, Wilgress wrote to Norman Robertson to convey 'a few impressions of the atmosphere in which we work.'[81] The attitude of the Soviet Foreign Ministry, he said, was 'one of non-co-operative accessibility.' Appointments were easily arranged, but the Soviets volunteered little information and no opinions. Most questions had to be submitted in writing, 'and it may be a matter of weeks or months before an answer is supplied.' Informal relations were no better than formal.

It is the general experience of the diplomatic corps that the attitude of extreme caution during office hours is carried even further in matters affecting social and personal relationships. We have not yet had any direct experience in this line and can therefore only repeat what we have heard from other foreigners, but there seems no doubt that it is next to impossible to persuade a Soviet official to accept hospitality. Being seen with foreigners, or have it known that you visit their houses, is regarded as unhealthy by most officials ... I should add that as soon as we get our house in full running order (we still lack China and cooking utensils so we are not yet serving meals) I intend to make every effort to have Russians to the Legation. I am, however, not sanguine enough to imagine that we will have a great measure of success when so many others have failed.

One thing that we are keeping constantly before us is the desirability of making as many Russian acquaintances as possible and the necessity of avoiding the tendency of the diplomatic corps to be a self-contained world unto itself.

Nevertheless, the Canadians were forced to depend for much of their information upon the diplomatic community, which was still small (there were eighteen foreign missions in April 1943). Wilgress offered his initial impressions of those missions, on the basis of his first round of interviews, in a long dispatch on 26 April.[82] He was impressed by the British ambassador, Sir Archibald Clark Kerr, whom he described as 'an able and forceful diplomat ... free of any trace of pomp and ... very proud of his Scottish ancestry. I should judge he is the right sort of man to get along well with Stalin.' The British counsellor in Kuibyshev, H.L. Baggalley, was also 'of the right type. He is a highly cultured, quiet man, with excellent judgment. His views on questions concerning the Soviet Union are marked by moderation coupled with good sense, but he can be critical when this is justified.' Baggalley, unfortunately, was about to be transferred to China.

According to Wilgress, the American ambassador, Admiral Standley, was 'an exceedingly shrewd observer' who 'has a most sympathetic understanding of the problems of this country.' His minister-counsellor, Eugene Dooman, however, was another matter. He had just returned to the United States, which was 'probably a good thing' because 'he had too many prejudices ever to understand this country.'

These initial and superficial judgments on the two embassies were filled out in a letter to Norman Robertson written two weeks later.[83] Wilgress's conclusions were now tartly unfavourable. The Americans, in particular, led 'a peculiar semi-monastic sort of existence keeping very much to themselves and mixing only with the diplomatic corps.' Aside from an obsessive interest in opera and ballet, Wilgress claimed that members of the American mission failed to observe Russian life with any care. 'A new member of the United States Embassy staff arrives in the Soviet Union and is immediately initiated into a sort of monastic brotherhood in which there is instilled into him views of the existing regime handed down from previous incumbents ... These views serve to make him unduly suspicious of the Soviet regime and reluctant to credit good motives to actions of the Soviet Government.' The Canadian minister conceded that 'they run across enough circumstantial evidence in the course of their day-to-day work to confirm what they have been told on arrival,' but insisted that the result was unfortunate. 'I do not wish to convey that the views of the Embassy staff hold [*sic*] about the Soviet Union and the Soviet regime necessarily are incorrect. They are, however, one-sided and tend to make the individual concerned unduly prejudiced. They affect his ability to form good judgements and must seriously interfere with his endeavours to bring about more friendly relations between the United States and the Soviet Union.' Admiral Standley was the exception to the rule among the Americans, 'but then his attitude to the Russian people is very much that of a visitor to the Zoo observing the behaviour of the animals in their cages,' and in any case the job of the minister-counsellor seemed to be to prevent the ambassador 'from deviating too far from the established State Department policy.'[84]

Wilgress speculated that a contributing factor to the American outlook might be 'their method of obtaining information through informers.' While he admitted that he knew little about it, the system of informers did, apparently, sometimes provide the American Embassy with scoops. 'These informers, however, must be men who are risking their lives and cannot be friendly to the Soviet Regime. I would suspect that their information tends mostly to be on subjects which do not show the authorities in the best light.'

Finally Wilgress returned to the puzzling problem of Soviet attitudes.

It must be admitted that the Soviet Government, themselves, are partly to blame for this state of affairs by discouraging all forms of social intercourse between Soviet citizens and members of the diplomatic corps and by the attitude of aloofness which they adopt in the transaction of official business. The people in the Foreign and other Commissariats are undoubtedly guilty of lack of frankness, unwillingness to give information even of a very ordinary character, and sometimes of what in other countries would pass as rudeness. The fault therefore does not lie entirely on one side. Nevertheless the members of the United States Embassy staff do not seem to make the allowance that one would expect if they were really anxious to get on well with the Soviet authorities. I cannot see any remedy for this state of affairs, but I fear that as long as it continues the bringing about of a better understanding between the Soviet Union and other countries will be impeded.

Here the diplomat no doubt exaggerated the significance of diplomatic manners, or mistook symptoms for causes; and he declared himself, with all the charm of the innocent, determined to avoid the faults of his allies.

We are trying and I think succeeding in avoiding falling into such an attitude of mind as that described above by refusing to allow ourselves to be shut off from the current of Soviet life. It is true that we are not likely to be any more successful than the members of the other Missions in making contact with the Russians, but we can keep our eyes and ears open and resist the temptation to look at everything through the darkened spectacles of distrust toward the Soviet regime, which I fear to be the case with most members of the staffs of both the British and United States Embassies.

Among the other foreign missions, Wilgress valued his close relations with the Australian counsellor, Keith Officer, but criticized the Australian tendency 'to relay ... mostly information gathered by the British Embassy.'[85] He regarded as 'the three most interesting missions' those of the Czechs, the Poles, and the Yugoslavs – because 'the countries they represent have most at stake in their relations with the Soviet Union.' The Czechoslovak ambassador, Zdenek Fierlinger, was of particular interest.

Mr. Fierlinger ... is closer to the Russians than any of my colleagues ... He is markedly pro-Soviet in all his views. My Belgian colleague describes him as speaking like 'Pravda'. Actually Mr. Fierlinger is a rather quiet man who rarely talks about matters of high policy. I have had a number of talks with him and have been with him twice to the theatre. He has given me most interesting accounts of various aspects of Soviet economics, revealing an intimate knowledge of the country. He always presents the situation in the most favourable light but not unreasonably so ... Madame Fierlinger, who is with him in Kuibyshev, is a French lady, reputed to have Communist views.

Wilgress described Fierlinger as 'the best informed member of the corps,' and criticized the Americans for keeping their distance from him 'because they were sure he reported to the Soviet authorities everything that was said to him by other members of the diplomatic corps.' While that may have been good reason for caution in speaking to Fierlinger, Wilgress felt that it was 'madness' to ignore him as the Americans did.[86]

Wilgress's other leading pro-Soviet source of information was the Yugoslav minister, Simich, whose embassy was still formally royalist.

Mr. Simich strikes one as a most intelligent man, who takes the trouble to think out for himself the position he takes on various subjects, but obviously his views reflect those of the Soviet Government. He, no doubt, feels that the Soviet Union is likely to be the dominant power in Eastern Europe after the war and, therefore, the proper policy for Yugoslavia is to cultivate close and friendly relations with that power. Undoubtedly Mr. Simich is one of the most interesting and colourful of my colleagues.[87]

In general, Wilgress showed a marked preference for the company and views of those diplomats who were sympathetic towards the Soviet Union – and thus more likely, he judged, to be well supplied with information. He indicated that he had little to learn from the representatives of Turkey, Iran, and Afghanistan, because their fears of Soviet expansionism preoccupied them. The Bulgarian royalist minister was an anti-Communist bore; it was 'fortunate that we have been able to avoid having relations with the Bulgarian Legation.' The Belgian minister was 'a man with a narrow middle-class outlook and full of what the Russians describe as "bourgeois prejudices."' 'He makes no pretence to hide his dislike of the regime and throws scorn on his pro-Soviet colleagues accusing them of having lost their integrity of mind. This is amusing when applied to a man like the Czechoslovak Ambassador, who, while he may be misled, is one of the most honest as well as one of the most intelligent of the foreign representatives here. I do not like to be unkind but I can only classify my Belgian colleague as a rather stupid man.' The Fighting French mission was 'markedly pro-Soviet,' and therefore in close touch with the Russian government; at the same time Wilgress commented that it was excessively and indiscreetly anti-American.

The single clear exception to the Canadian minister's preference for pro-Soviet diplomats was his regard for the Swedes, with whom the Canadians had become 'very friendly.' As neutrals with pro-Western sympathies, they were nevertheless objective in their judgments and 'critical of conditions but without bias.' The Swedish minister was 'entirely without malice and ... very fair in what he reports.' He was 'well-informed [and] a most useful source of information, although it is a good plan to check what he tells with one of the more pro-Soviet diplomats such as the Czechoslovak Ambassador.'

There was nothing devious about the reporting stance of the Canadian mission: it was ingenuous, not to say credulous. The Canadians would make every effort to penetrate the wall of Soviet silence and suspicion, and to interpret events without anti-Soviet prejudice. This meant that Soviet (or pro-Soviet) explanations of their actions and purposes would frequently be reported at face value; although critical interpretations would not be ignored, they would usually be identified as coming from prejudiced sources and therefore discounted. Wilgress was aware, as he frequently noted, of the extreme difficulties of truthful and balanced reporting from the Soviet Union. But in the beginning, for as long as they could conscientiously do so, the Canadian mission would put the best face on the Soviet regime. This disposition to accept Soviet claims in good faith was bound to involve certain conflicts of perception and emotional strain for the Canadians, since it was admittedly at odds with the main currents of opinion in the British and American embassies (on whom Canadian diplomats normally placed great reliance); and it put the Canadian Legation at the risk of innocently serving Soviet propagandist purposes in its reporting to Ottawa. For eighteen months, as contradictions grew, the Canadians maintained this stance.

The prospects for an eventual Allied victory were growing daily more certain in 1943. As the war effort gained momentum, Western diplomats attempted to peer over the horizon and into the post-war world. (A.J.P. Taylor suggests that this was the busy-work of clerks: 'Since the Foreign Office could not win the war it worried about what was to happen afterwards.')[88] By now it was taken for granted in London (if not yet in Washington) that the long-term fate of Europe would depend most directly upon Russian strength and purpose. A British diplomatic dispatch from Kuibyshev tentatively reviewing the subject reached Mackenzie King's desk in January 1943.[89] In it the British Embassy suggested that the Russian government would be forced by the terrible devastation of the war to occupy itself in peacetime primarily with domestic reconstruction, but that it could not let the European settlement go by default.

So far as they are concerned, economic will be subordinated to political considerations. What are these political considerations? In the first place, territorial claims. The Baltic States, a strip of Eastern Poland, Bessarabia; these, at least, the Soviet Union will aim at assimilating to herself in order to secure strategic frontiers in the west. How much further south and west she will be able to go, either in frontiers or in spheres of influence, depends on the conditions existing at the end of the war, on what her other Allies do, and to some extent on what the populations of the Axis-occupied territories do. She may claim a sort of undefined protectorate over the other Slav peoples of Europe, and a somewhat more tangible influence over the destinies of 'Slav-civilised' Bulgaria. Further it would at present be idle to speculate.

The Soviet government discouraged any attempts by the European governments in exile to plan collectively for European reorganization after the war, on the grounds both that they 'were counting their chickens before they were hatched' and that it was 'ridiculous' for them to discuss post-war planning without the presence of the great powers. But despite this disconcerting Soviet attitude, and the paper's sombre reflections on Soviet territorial ambitions, the dispatch concluded by underlining the judgment that Russia, 'after the war, will probably be prepared to take things quietly for a considerable period of time.' The tone was reassuring, though admittedly speculative.

Six months later – and just two months after his arrival in Kuibyshev – the Canadian minister to Russia tried his hand at the same subject, 'the probable attitude of the Soviet Government towards the peace settlement,' with the slightly greater brashness of the new boy.[90] The dispatch reflected his sources. Dana Wilgress emphasized that Soviet Russia, more than any other ally, 'will be anxious for an early peace because the army and people of the Soviet Union will be exhausted from the efforts they will have put forth in driving out of the country the mightiest offensive military machine known to history.' The common interest would dictate the need for close Western co-operation with Russia:

This, however, will be impossible if the Russians have any sense of injustice through not being treated according to their contribution to the defeat of the Axis or through other countries not recognizing their vital interests in Eastern Europe. Seen from this perspective the vested interests of Polish land-owners, Latvian shipowners or Esthonian [sic] politicians seem very insignificant in comparison with the major issues at stake, but the danger is that these vested interests can evoke the natural sympathy for the smaller country and the main issues can become blurred in the haze of endless debate to which such controversies give rise.

American attitudes, Wilgress reported, were the most likely to precipitate post-war conflict over Soviet objectives.

It is because the United States has shown a tendency to support lost causes, because the United States has endeavoured to impose its will without appearing to take proper account of the views of other countries, because the State Department has favoured reactionary rather than progressive elements in certain European countries, because the State Department has not entirely disavowed proposals for a cordon sanitaire in Eastern Europe, aimed ostensibly at Germany but in reality at the Soviet Union, that I believe the Soviet Government is more apprehensive of possible clashes with the United States than they are clashes with other countries in the future peace discussions.

Like the British ambassador, Wilgress believed that 'the dominant desire on the part of the Soviet Government will be to assure the Soviet Union of a long period of peace' to overcome the losses of war and at last to provide material abundance for the Soviet people. But he added that there would be a long-term purpose in this effort of reconstruction, 'in order that the Soviet Union may gather sufficient strength to dispel any threat of future invasion and to continue, when the time is ripe, that onward march of expansion which has characterized the history of the Russian people ever since the Principality of Moscow established its ascendency [*sic*].' Moscow's prerequisites for this renewed phase of imperial expansion were clear to Wilgress: Russia desired 'strategic frontiers' to repel attack and open the paths for further advance; she was determined 'to have no governments in power in Eastern Europe which would be unfriendly to the Soviet Union'; and she hoped as well for 'friendly governments in power in Western Europe in order to assure that no country provides a base for the formation of an anti-Soviet block.' Wilgress judged that the Soviets would not insist on Communist governments in the border states of Central Europe, 'because they are anxious to dispel foreign mistrust of their regime and this can best be accomplished by allaying the bogy of communism.' The Comintern would be used 'very sparingly' as an instrument of Russian policy; instead Russia would appeal increasingly to Pan-Slavist sentiment for the sake of solidarity with her neighbours.

The achievement of these Soviet objectives would require the recognition of two new spheres of interest: a Soviet sphere of paramountcy in Eastern Europe and a British sphere in Western Europe.

They would like to cooperate with and have the other countries of Eastern Europe closely associated with them just as they expect the Scandinavian countries, the Netherlands, Belgium and possibly also France to be united in a close association with the United Kingdom. All this presupposes the exclusion of the United States from active participation in European politics, but it does not necessarily exclude the superimpositon of an organisation such as a League of the United Nations to deal with matters of political and economic cooperation, apart from the internal security of Europe and of other well-defined regions.

Here was a remarkably clear depiction of the post-war international system as seen from Moscow in 1943: a 'regional as distinct from a collective conception of security,' which had attractions for other countries too. 'The United States,' Wilgress wrote, 'even appears to be thinking in these terms, probably feeling that the regional basis will provide a better means of exerting the influence commensurate with the predominance they will have after the war in sea and air power.'

This kind of detailed commentary on Soviet policy and intentions was new to Ottawa. Wilgress demonstrated his capacity to absorb and report both the Soviet government's own account of its objectives and the sympathetic assessment of this account which was available in the Kuibyshev diplomatic community. What was especially intriguing in the dispatch was its description, not just of Soviet determination, but of the traditionalist and realist bases for Soviet foreign policy – with the implied suggestion that the Soviet Union might be satisfied in the short run, her suspicions allayed, by the clear recognition of a Soviet sphere of influence in Eastern Europe. Initially Wilgress seemed to be supporting this view – or at least putting it in a sympathetic light. Was it possible that a realist policy of regional spheres and alliances might contribute as effectively to peace as an effort to substitute for it a universal system of collective security? Wilgress was prepared to grant the Soviet Union her sphere, but his approach to American interests was different. He took for granted that the United States could not be persuaded to renounce an interest in the affairs of Eastern Europe, even though the region might properly be regarded as an area of Soviet interest. Without some overriding and benevolent international scheme which would blunt America's interventionist ambitions, therefore, it was likely that the United States and Russia would clash over the future of the Soviet border states. To avoid this, Wilgress suggested that the United States should be encouraged to associate herself with the leading smaller nations like Canada in promoting a general system of collective security. This, he hoped, might allow America, somehow, to exert her influence constructively rather than abrasively in Europe. The Department of External Affairs' preoccupation with the American presence thus revealed itself, paradoxically, from Kuibyshev too. In a discussion of Russia's international role, Wilgress managed to argue that the primary purpose of a new collective security organization would be to contain the power and ambitions of the United States.

Wilgress's reference to the decline of the Comintern as an instrument of Soviet policy seemed to be more than confirmed two weeks later, with the announcement from Moscow of its dissolution at the end of May 1943. The Canadian minister cabled to Ottawa on 24 May:

Decision of Executive Committee of Communist International to disband organization is interpreted:
(a) As a clever counter-stroke to German propaganda of Bolshevik menace;
(b) As an attempt to allay Communism bogy in Allied countries;
(c) As assisting Soviet Union to assume leading role among progressive countries; and
(d) As a means of strengthening local Communist parties through removal of foreign control.[91]

As he explained in a longer dispatch sent by diplomatic bag the same day, Wilgress gained these impressions at 'an informal gathering' the previous evening among the Swedish minister and secretary, the British commercial secretary, 'Andrechin, who is a Soviet citizen allowed to circulate among the diplomatic corps,' and himself.[92] (Andrechin would have expressed the official line, and was probably a KGB agent.)

The vision of the Soviet Union as the leader among progressive states produced a striking analogy and, for Wilgress, an unsettling train of thought:

They visualize the Soviet Union standing very much in a position analogous to that occupied by the United Kingdom in the last century, when liberal elements throughout Europe looked to London for leadership and this gave the United Kingdom a great moral ascendency [sic].

While I did not, of course, elaborate these views to the others present I could not help thinking that this situation may give rise to a possible conflict of ideas in the post-war world between the Soviet Union and the United States, as the leading representatives of two divergent tendencies. In the case of such a conflict the United Kingdom would play a purely negative role, its foreign policy seeking to keep in with both sides but often having to make a choice between the two. Canada's position would be similar except that we would have no doubt about where our interests lay and we would inevitably have to allign [sic] ourselves with the United States. This prospect is so disheartening and offers such possibilities of conflicts, both internally and externally, that it should be the duty of statesmen everywhere to seek to avoid this development, even by going to the length of appeasing the Soviet Union particularly when her vital interests are at stake.

The Western allies greeted the announcement of the Comintern's dissolution with silence or restraint. Norman Robertson offered Mackenzie King the prudent advice that 'if you feel you have to say something, you might say that it appears to be a sensible move which has been welcomed everywhere except in the Axis countries.'[93] King made no statement to the House of Commons.

Having previously reflected on the inadequacies of the American mission to the USSR (but including the British in his general strictures), Wilgress reported in July 1943, in contrast, on the 'excellent' relations between the British and the Soviets.[94] He attributed this condition to the skilful diplomacy of Winston Churchill and the British ambassador in Moscow, Sir Archibald Clark Kerr, who had successfully broken down Soviet suspicions by their immediate declarations of support in 1941, the provision of material aid, the conclusion of the Anglo-Soviet alliance, and Churchill's care in informing Stalin of every detail of the war effort in the West. In a dispatch that was unusually full of anecdotal detail, Wilgress revealed his own trusted access to the British and American embassies. Churchill's telegrams to Stalin, he reported, were 'nearly all in breezy style,' designed to give Stalin 'the impression of the steadfast loyalty of his chief ally.' Roosevelt's messages, in contrast, were less frequent and more conventional, lacking 'the frank, intimate character of the Churchill-Stalin exchanges.' The British ambassador aided Churchill by his ability to focus on 'the one objective of gaining the confidences of Mr. Stalin and Mr. Molotov.' In Wilgress's wide-eyed view, Clark Kerr offered a lesson in diplomatic style:

He poses as a Scottish squire, fond of the great outdoors and disdainful of the less robust pleasures of mankind. He dislikes diplomatic dinners, hardly ever goes to the theatre and loves to poke fun at his generals, admirals and members of his chancery staff about their enthusiasm for the ballet. He usually regales Mr. Stalin with an account of the latest foibles of these Britishers in their admiration of ballerinas. The remarkable thing is that Mr. Stalin seems to love this banter in spite of the almost sacred regard in which the ballet is held by Russians. Like Mr. Stalin Sir Archibald is a pipe smoker and he always takes along a few pipes which he presents to Mr. Stalin. The latter in return gives him some of his tobacco which the Ambassador smokes when he is with Mr. Stalin but never elsewhere. Sir Archibald's technique is to stay a long time, usually two hours, when he sees either Mr. Stalin or Mr. Molotov. He never allows the conversation to descend to the formal plane. He endeavours to chat informally, brighten up the conversation with touches of humour and intersperse questions on the points he has come to discuss. These tactics are proving admirably successful in gaining the confidence of the two most important Soviet statesmen. Even the most delicate questions are discussed in a frank and friendly manner without tempers ever being ruffled on either side. This is being achieved by an Ambassador who is devoid of any interest in communist ideology.

Soviet relations with the United States, Wilgress believed, were still conducted with 'a certain degree of mistrust,' despite Roosevelt's desire to overcome it. The contrast could be explained, perhaps, by Moscow's careful calculation that Russia and the United Kingdom shared a special interest in close post-war co-operation.

Mr. Maisky, the Soviet Ambassador in London, has been playing an important role in bringing about this realization. He even remarked to a British statesman when the Anglo-Soviet Alliance was concluded how useful this alliance would be to the United Kingdom in lessening their dependence upon the United States. Ever since arriving in this country I have been struck with the fact that the Anglo-Soviet Alliance is regarded by the Soviet Government as the corner-stone of their foreign policy. They are fully conscious of the need for close co-operation between the two countries in the settlement of the problems which will arise in Europe after the war. They are anxious to have the United Kingdom aligned with them rather than with the United States in any differences of view which may arise between the Big Three. Through the talks which have been taking place they have learnt to get along with and trust Britishers. They are not quite sure if they will be able to get along the same way with Americans. They are becoming confident that, if the Soviet Union can be allowed a more or less free hand in Eastern Europe and the United Kingdom in Western Europe, the peace of the Continent can be assured for a long period and it is just such a long period of peace that is the main objective of Soviet foreign policy.

The second front in Western Europe had still not been launched by the summer of 1943, as Allied forces bogged down in their painful advance up the Italian peninsula. The absence of the second front, and evidence of the intimacy of British-American co-operation, led Dana Wilgress to report, at the end of August, a change in the Soviet Union's fragile attitudes. There was now an 'increasing rift in the relations between the Soviet Union and the Western allies.'[95] Following extensive conversations with members of the Moscow diplomatic community (where the Canadian mission had been transferred at mid-month), Wilgress wrote that:

the situation is sufficiently critical to warrant the exercise of the most prudent statesmanship ... on the handling of the present situation depends the chances of future co-operation of the Soviet Union in the tasks of organizing a peaceful and stable world and I doubt if this fundamental truth is fully appreciated in the western capitals. One can understand the impatience with Soviet attempts to dictate Allied strategy by means of press campaigns and with the need of always having to consider the 'touchiness' of a government which itself has consistently followed an arbitrary and chauvinistic foreign policy. We have also to be careful not to fall again into the discredited attitude of appeasement. But in the relations with the Soviet Union a large measure of appeasement can be shown to be justified. Here we have a country wavering between a policy of close co-operation with other countries in maintaining a peaceful and stable world and a policy of isolationism backed up by armed strength. All signs have hitherto pointed to the rulers of the Soviet Union favoring the former policy and they are likely only to adopt the latter policy through mistrust and suspicion of the intentions of other countries. It is surely the duty of statesmanship to attempt to remove all causes for such mistrust and suspicion.

Wilgress could now see signs – admittedly minor – that the Soviet Union was beginning to prepare for the possibility of 'another major conflict.' 'This comes,' he concluded, 'as somewhat of a shock to one who has firmly believed that Stalin's chief aim is to secure a prolonged period of external peace.'

Like the earlier reflective dispatch of 6 May, this one too was widely distributed among the prime minister, senior ministers, and members of the Department of External Affairs. As a distant spectator in the high politics of the alliance, there was little that Canada could do in response to Wilgress's warnings even if she had wished to participate; but the seeds of anxiety and confusion were being planted. On 24 June Mackenzie King had noted, in a personal letter to Wilgress: 'You may be sure that your reports and despatches to the Department from Kuibyshev are studied with very great interest here, and even in the few months that the new Mission has been established, it is quite clear that a great deal of useful work has been done.'[96]

The Enigma

Dana Wilgress's opinion that 'in relations with the Soviet Union a large measure of appeasement can be shown to be justified' was a judgment – or a rationalization – common in Whitehall and Washington in 1943. The British government had already indicated to Moscow that it had no overpowering objection to a post-war territorial settlement which would restore the Soviet Union's expanded 1941 frontiers in Eastern Europe; and Roosevelt, too, had told Stalin that the United States would respect Russia's legitimate need for physical security after the war. Although formal recognition of the 1941 borders was withheld in 1942, the Soviet leaders were given no reason for discouragement about eventually achieving it. The noble words of the Atlantic Charter seemed to conflict with that goal, but the Soviets were not led to expect that Britain or the United States would actually honour the language of the charter when confronted with hard claims of Russian interest in lands far from their frontiers. During 1941 and 1942, instead, London and Washington showed themselves surprisingly eager to court, reassure and supply Moscow. The conflict with Nazi Germany hung grimly in the balance, and the survival of the Soviet Union seemed an essential prerequisite to an eventual Allied victory. By 1943, although – or perhaps because – the balance was tipping against Germany, there was still an urgent desire to keep Russia in the war to the end, fed by intelligence reports of Soviet-German peace feelers in the early months of the year, and by speculation from diplomats in Moscow that the Soviet army might halt its advances at the Russian borders.[1] The Americans, in addition, were increasingly concerned to bring Russia into the Japanese war, where victory could not yet be foreseen.

Beyond these immediate reasons for treating the Soviet Union with consideration and deference, there were also more elaborate justifications emerging for the maintenance of the wartime alliance into peacetime. Franklin Roosevelt's notion of a Grand Design for co-operative great power management of international affairs was both a brilliant wartime propaganda device and a serious (though vague) prescription for policing the world; and plans for a revived and strengthened system of collective security, to supersede the old League of Nations, were also being promoted more and more insistently among the Western allies and their publics.[2] If a peaceful post-war world required international collaboration (which was the lesson drawn by Roosevelt and the Western foreign ministries from the experience of the 1920s and 1930s) both the United States and the Soviet Union would have to be brought into the new international system as satisfied powers. That necessity, for those who accepted it, was bound to encourage a tendency to see the best side of Soviet acts, to overlook or underestimate Soviet objectives which contradicted the goal of co-operation, and to offer incentives to Russia to remain on good terms with her wartime allies.

In the United States, where popular fear and distaste for Soviet Communism had been intense before 1941, the accident of wartime alliance brought a remarkable change in the reputation of the Soviet Union. As John L. Gaddis writes:

Through a curious kind of illogic the Russians' vigorously successful resistance to Hitler purified them ideologically in the eyes of Americans. Surely, the argument ran, any nation which was fighting so valiantly against a common enemy could not espouse so repugnant a doctrine as communism. Reassessing recent events in this light, many informed observers came to believe that Stalin had fundamentally altered the ideological orientation of his own regime; that the Soviet Union was in the process of abandoning communism in fact, if not in name.[3]

Three especially influential American publicists who argued this case for a 'purified' Soviet Union that would co-operate easily with the United States in peacemaking had a major influence in Canada as well. Joseph E. Davies, the American ambassador to the Soviet Union in 1937–38, published his best-selling *Mission to Moscow* at the end of 1941, in which he asserted the peaceful, progressive, and high moral goals of the Soviet regime; and he followed this with a series of promotional tours in the United States and Canada.[4] Wendell Wilkie, the defeated Republican presidential candidate of 1940, travelled the world in 1942 and made a romantic plea for international co-operation in his book *One World,* which was also a wartime best-seller. Henry Luce used all the practised dramatic devices of *Life* magazine, above all in a special issue on Russia in March 1943, to promote the view that the Russians were ' "one hell of a people ... [who] to a remarkable degree ... look like Americans, dress like Americans and think like Americans." '[5] Scholars and churchmen, journalists and politicians, joined the chorus, effectively subduing the dissonant comments of those who remained sceptical or suspicious about the nature and permanent objectives of the heroic ally. Even Roosevelt's Office of War Information promoted the Soviet Union as a 'Western-style social democracy,' the natural partner of the United States in both war and peace.[6]

President Roosevelt's general approach to the problems of the political settlement after an Allied victory was to postpone discussion until the peace conferences, and to concentrate instead upon strictly military goals and vague statements of universal goodwill. As the strategic situation moved in the Allies' favour in 1943 and 1944 this American default had at least two consequences in Europe: it left Russia a relatively free hand to exert its own pressures and seek its own ends in Eastern Europe, where the Russian armies might now, forseeably, supplant the Germans in occupation; and it left to the British the primary initiative in dealing with these Soviet pressures as they arose.

Russian political concerns in Europe, as Dana Wilgress reported in his dispatches during 1943, were concentrated upon the need to settle her western boundaries and to ensure friendly and co-operative regimes in the border states – and beyond if possible. Soviet dealings with the Poles, Czechs, Yugoslavs, and Romanians, however (beyond these basic axioms), showed a flexible ability to adapt to circumstances, rather than any dogmatic certainty about imposing a single pattern of domination.[7] In the case of Yugoslavia, where the Communist party was proving itself, in blood, to be the effective source of resistance to the German forces, Stalin remained aloof, while maintaining correct diplomatic relations with the royal government in exile. Here the Soviet Union only followed Britain's lead after 1943 – and then with reluctance – in throwing her support to the Partisans of Marshal Tito. In the case of Czechoslovakia, Moscow accepted the advances of the exiled government of President Benes, and concluded a treaty of friendship and co-operation in December 1943.[8]

For Britain and the United States, the fate of Poland was the matter of greatest formal preoccupation in Eastern Europe. Its invasion had been the occasion for the British declaration of war; and an American president could not ignore the crucial Polish vote in some states. But this preoccupation was neither chosen nor welcomed. Whatever the public need to maintain appearances, in private the British and American governments recognized their essential powerlessness to affect Poland's fate, and treated the pleadings of Polish non-Communists for support against the Soviet Union as a nuisance to be dealt with cosmetically or ignored. For the Soviet Union, however, Poland was the strategic key to her security against Germany and the object of her most single-minded diplomacy. Throughout the war the British government leaned heavily and hypocritically on the Polish government-in-exile to come to terms with the Soviet Union on the country's borders and the post-war domestic regime; while Roosevelt gave nothing more than empty-handed moral support to the London Poles.[9]

An especially low point in Allied cynicism came in April 1943 when Britain and the United States withheld their approval from the Polish government-in-exile's appeal for an International Red Cross enquiry into the German discovery at Katyn, in the Ukraine, of the mass graves of thousands of Polish military officers apparently murdered by the Russians in 1940. The Soviet Union treated the Polish request with enraged contempt, and used the occasion to break diplomatic relations with the government-in-exile.[10] The effort to patch and restore Polish-Soviet relations became one of the urgent tasks of Anglo-American diplomacy in the remainder of 1943, but always with the purpose of appeasing the Russians rather than the unfortunate Poles.[11]

Canada, too, had a minor role in this ignoble incident. Following the break in diplomatic relations, the London Poles requested that either Britain or the United States should act as diplomatic agent on Poland's behalf in the USSR; both refused. But the United Kingdom approached Canada to undertake this role if asked to do so by the Polish government.[12] On 5 May the War Committee of the Canadian cabinet firmly rejected the proposal, explaining its decision in a dispatch to Wilgress: 'Chief reasons for this decision are that your Mission is too small and too recently established to discharge this most difficult task, that we do not wish to prejudice our relations with the Soviet Government so soon after the exchange of diplomatic missions and that we have as yet no experience of this type of work and no suitable additional personnel.'[13] Two weeks later Wilgress reported laconically to Ottawa that the Australian government (whose mission was equally small and new) had accepted the role that Canada had refused.[14] The ill wind, however, brought Canada a small benefit. With its responsibilities the Australian mission also gained possession of the Polish mission's furniture. Wilgress recalled in his *Memoirs* that the Australians had no need for the furniture themselves, and thus 'agreed to loan it to us for safekeeping.' This windfall permitted the Canadians to decamp from their temporary quarters in the British Embassy to occupy the unfurnished house already assigned to them.[15]

The accumulation of frictions between the Western Allies and the Soviets was a source of anxiety to Churchill and Roosevelt by midsummer 1943. Stalin remained unconvinced about the sincerity of Allied preparation for a second front in Western Europe, and sought reassurance with growing abrasiveness. After Roosevelt and Churchill's first meeting in Quebec City in August, Wilgress reported on Moscow's renewed public campaign for a second front, which was now coupled with a call for a meeting of the three heads of state:

For some weeks there have been almost daily press articles urging that victories of Soviet armies have opened way for a real second front, meaning an attack in western Europe. The latest is an article entitled 'Quebec and the Soviet Union' published in 'War and the Working Class'. It repeats TASS statement of August 13th that Soviet Union was not invited to participate in Quebec Conference. It states military conditions are such that victory over Hitler can be secured this year. That may not mean so much to the United Kingdom and the United States, which are free from invasion, but is vital to Soviet Union with a large part of its territory still occupied by the enemy. Article concludes by stating that a three power conference, including the Soviet Union, with the object of shortening the war, and determined fulfillment of that task, 'would be a glorious step forward in war and towards a lasting peace based on friendly cooperation between the Allies.'[16]

Both Churchill and Roosevelt, as dominant personalities in positions of influence themselves, were inclined to emphasize the effects of personal character and action upon history: and to believe that they could come to terms with 'Uncle Joe' Stalin in face-to-face encounters. When William C. Bullitt (another former American ambassador to Moscow with less generous opinions of the Soviet Union than those of Joseph Davies) told Roosevelt in August 1943 that 'domination of Europe by Stalin's Communist dictatorship would be as great a threat' to free institutions as Nazism, Roosevelt replied to him that Stalin could be handled. 'I just have a hunch that Stalin is not that kind of man. Harry (Hopkins) says he's not and that he doesn't want anything but security for his country, and I think that if I give him everything I possibly can and ask nothing from him in return, *noblesse oblige,* he won't try to annex anything and will work with me for a world of democracy and peace.'[17] What the president meant by 'giving him everything I possibly can' may have been indicated in a conversation a few weeks later, in September, with Francis Cardinal Spellman, who recalled Roosevelt telling him that 'the European people will simply have to endure the Russian domination in the hope that – in ten or twenty years – the European influence would bring the Russians to become less barbarian.'[18] Roosevelt did not expect to be able to convince Stalin to limit Soviet expansion in Europe.[19]

Winston Churchill had a more worldly diplomatic sense than did Roosevelt, but he too believed that the European chess-board could be rearranged to the mutual satisfaction of the great powers, in direct contact with Joseph Stalin. In the autumn of 1943 there commenced, accordingly, a series of strategic conferences among the three allies, directed (on the part of Britain and the United States) at eliminating wartime discord and ensuring the co-ordination of post-war aims through some kind of informal, tacit, and ambiguous concession of a Soviet sphere of influence in Eastern Europe. For Stalin the prospect must have looked promising.

Thus a gradual and 'orderly' growth of Soviet strength from an eastern European base – perhaps with the help of his Communist followers in different countries but not at the cost of a confrontation with his powerful Western allies – emerged as the most desirable goal. The ever more accommodating Western attitude toward a possible division of the continent into spheres of influence abetted Stalin's quest for power and influence. Yet what exactly was worth striving for, in the wide range between his minimum aims and the enticing prospect of Russia's possible hegemony over a prostrate Europe, still remained undecided. The many unanswered questions were to be clarified at the great Allied conferences scheduled in Moscow and Teheran later that year.[20]

For these and the later meetings of the great powers, Canada (like the other secondary members of the alliance) remained on the outside as an observer, dependent even for accurate information on British and American diplomatic sources. Yet it was here, in the wartime conferences of the Big Three, and on the ground in Eastern Europe – rather than at the founding meetings of the United Nations to which Canada would, *faute de mieux,* give her increasing attention – that the initial post-war balance was struck, the Soviet advantage in Eastern Europe was recognized, and the seeds of mutual misperception and misunderstanding were (perhaps inadvertently) planted firm. Dana Wilgress had prepared the Department of External Affairs for the acceptance of an accommodation in Eastern Europe, and there is no indication that the Canadian cabinet or department anticipated such a settlement with any particular anxiety. It was understandable that on this subject, about which the Canadian government knew little, Ottawa would drift in the general direction of British and American policy.

The outcome of the Moscow conference of foreign ministers in October 1943 was in any case difficult to judge for outsiders unaware of the detailed course of negotiations. The official communiqué spoke of 'the atmosphere of mutual confidence and understanding which characterized all the work of the Conference,' and of 'the unanimous recognition by the three Governments that it was essential in their own national interests and in the interest of all peace-loving nations to continue the present close collaboration and cooperation in the conduct of the war into the period following the end of hostilities.'[21] The American secretary of state, Cordell Hull, reported euphorically to the Senate in November that agreement of the four powers (including China) on the 'Declaration ... on General Security' promised an era of unprecedented international harmony: 'As the provisions of the four-nation declaration are carried into effect, there will no longer be need for spheres of influence, for alliances, for balance of power, or any of the special arrangements through which, in the unhappy past, the nations strove to safeguard their security or to promote their interests.'[22]

The conference had indeed proceeded in an atmosphere of mutual accord. The Soviet Union gained the assurance of the Western Allies that the invasion of France would occur in May 1944; Britain's support for the proposed Soviet-Czech treaty; membership on an Allied Advisory Council for Italy; and the suppression of a British draft document which proposed a joint declaration rejecting spheres of influence. The United Kingdom gained the creation of a European Advisory Commission to consult on the technical aspects of policy in the liberated territories; and the United States gained the conference's commitment to proceed with the establishment of a general organization for international security.[23] The Soviet Union showed its willingness to bargain on the terms of general commitments when its immediate advantage was not at stake, while it required in return that Britain and the United States should concede (either explicitly or in silence) her predominant role in the border states of Eastern Europe. Cordell Hull's facile judgment about the passing of any need for spheres of influence curiously contradicted the conference's actual result, which did much to encourage and legitimize Soviet ambitions. Neither the Americans nor the British, however, were willing to admit – as the Soviets did in their enthusiasm for the outcome – what had been conceded.[24] The Canadian minister's first accounts of the conference to Ottawa revealed the same Panglossian optimism shown in public by his British and American colleagues. The conference, he reported, would produce 'extremely useful results' including 'recognition of joint responsibility of the three Powers for all Europe, thereby removing any pretence at spheres of influence.'[25] Not until three months later, after he had received more detailed briefing on the conference, did Wilgress report to Ottawa that this had not, in fact, been the outcome.[26] (The tendency of the great powers to fall back into the unfortunate habits of the balance of power and spheres of influence, he then commented, meant that 'It has been left to the Canadian Prime Minister to sound the clarion call of collective security. While this has rallied around him the small nations and made Canada their leader, it has tended to put the small nations in one camp and the great powers in another. Active support from one or other of the three great powers is badly needed.')

The first Churchill-Roosevelt-Stalin meeting, at Tehran, followed only weeks after the Moscow conference; and here too the United States and Britain showed themselves easy accomplices in the achievement of Soviet aims. The conference was chaotic, and no coherent record of decisions emerged; but the Russians were satisfied that the three allies would co-operate to ensure the permanent weakness of Germany after her defeat, and that the future of Poland and the Baltic countries could eventually be disposed of according to Russian desires.[27] But Roosevelt explained to Stalin that domestic political considerations during a presidential election year would prevent him from acknowledging Soviet political claims in these countries until after the beginning of November 1944. 'It seems likely,' concludes John L. Gaddis, 'that Stalin emerged from this talk convinced that the President's main concern would be to present Russian policy to the American public in the most favorable light, not to secure literal compliance with the principles of the Atlantic Charter.'[28] Roosevelt's domestic worries related both to the Polish-American vote and to his desire to carry the Republican party, including its formerly isolationist wing, in support for American membership in the new international security organization. That, in his view, required maintenance of the increasingly strained myth of Russian altruism, and the concealment of American co-operation (or default) in the creation of a Soviet sphere of influence.[29]

The judgment of Charles E. Bohlen, the State Department's leading Soviet expert, expressed no doubt about the consequences of Soviet aims as they were revealed at Tehran: 'The result would be that the Soviet Union would be the only important military and political force on the continent of Europe. The rest of Europe would be reduced to military and political impotence.'[30] Churchill and Roosevelt, conceding to what they regarded as the force of circumstance, were ready to accept Soviet dominance: hoping only, perhaps, that it would be benign.

Soviet territory up to the 1939 boundaries was virtually cleared of German occupation by January 1944, and the Russian army stood poised for advance into the former Baltic states, Poland and Bessarabia, where Soviet occupation and Soviet claims would soon, again, create grave political problems. The Canadian Department of External Affairs was now giving increasing attention to its efforts to understand the Soviet Union, for which it was dependent above all on the extensive dispatches from the Canadian mission. In February 1944, Dana Wilgress devoted a nine-page report from Moscow to an analysis of changes in the Soviet constitution which purported to increase the roles of the constituent republics in defence and foreign affairs.[31] Wilgress believed that the motives behind these constitutional changes were mixed but generally encouraging: they were meant to comfort sensitivities among the non-Russian nationalities within the Soviet Union and in the Baltic states; to reassure international opinion about Soviet goodwill; and to establish a claim for the representation of some Soviet republics in post-war international organizations.

Wilgress noted that the diplomatic community of Moscow was divided in its interpretation of the constitutional changes according to its political predispositions; but he took his place firmly among the friendly optimists.

The extreme anti-Soviet members of the diplomatic corps see in this new move the fashioning of another weapon of Soviet aggression. They argue that the grant of this bogus autonomy in defence and foreign affairs is designed to make more palatable to foreign opinion the absorption into the Soviet Union after the war of Finland, Poland, Czechoslovakia, Hungary, Roumania, Bulgaria and Yugoslavia. I believe that it is within the range of possibility that some day the Soviet Union may extend to the Adriatic, the Aegean and the Persian gulf, but not in my lifetime. When the war is over the Soviet Union will be exhausted and the prime requirement will be a long period of peace and tranquillity. This will only be possible if fears of Soviet aggression are allayed in Western Europe and in the

United States. There would certainly be no peace and tranquillity if the Soviet Union absorbed any of the above Eastern European countries. The Soviet leaders may impose terms of peace on Finland and Roumania which will involve infringements of the sovereign rights of these countries but this will be the most they dare in the face of western opinion.

These conclusions about the extent of Russian ambitions in Eastern Europe as they had emerged by February 1944 seem, in retrospect, to be reasonable, though naive. The military position was still insecure; and Stalin's dealings with the Allies and the governments-in-exile had not revealed any clear or uniform desire to impose Communist regimes upon Russia's neighbours. Rather, Moscow was actively promoting the Czechoslovak-Soviet treaty as the model for Russia's friendly post-war relations with the states of Eastern Europe; and it was still decidedly ambiguous in its attitude toward the powerful Communist resistance movement in Yugoslavia.[32] It was plausible for Wilgress and other diplomats in Moscow to accept in effect that, in February 1944, Soviet war aims were hardly more definite than those of Great Britain and the United States. What Moscow obviously desired was an early and decisive peace; a permanently weakened Germany; friendly and deferential governments in Eastern Europe; and continuing accord with the other two great powers in the pursuit of these goals. Since Roosevelt and Churchill had apparently indicated their support for these objectives at Tehran – or at least had not repudiated them – it was not surprising for a Western diplomat in Moscow to maintain high hopes, as Wilgress did, for post-war collaboration among the Allies.

But that degree of optimism involved also a considerable ability to ignore, or gloss over, evidences of the Soviet regime's cruel record of centralized tyranny. Wilgress was no more prescient at projecting that record into the future in early 1944 than was Churchill, Roosevelt, or Benes. He could not easily foresee what kind of subordination Stalin might require in Eastern Europe as adequate proof of neighbourly friendship, or the reactions that this subordination might provoke in the West. But as Wilgress did attempt to gaze into the crystal ball, he was swept away, momentarily, by a far-fetched vision of Soviet Communism in its full achievement, the pristine restraint of the Soviet government, and the prospects for perpetual peace:

At the same time it must be admitted that the new move will have a very great influence on future relations between the Soviet Union and neighbouring states. The grant of autonomy to the constituent republics in defence and foreign affairs should increase the power of attraction to the Soviet Union of peoples kindred to those inhabiting the republics. This will not be such a force now, but later on, as the standard of living and material well-being of the border races of the Soviet Union rise, so will there be an increase in magnetic force drawing their kinsmen to the union ... one can imagine that the authors of the new laws believe that they are offering Europe an escape from the evils of nationalism. They foresee the gradual decentralisation of the Soviet state, the grant of more and more autonomy to the constituent republics, the lessening of the need for party discipline and of oppression by the secret police, all of which may make the Soviet Union a more attractive country in which to live than the smaller countries of Europe, plagued by mutual jealousies and by fear of clashes with their neighbours. The dream of a United States of Eurasia centred on Moscow and of a Pax Sovietica is too attractive not to have been entertained by those sitting in the Kremlin who are newly conscious of their immense power, but it is a dream for the far distant future and is not a matter of immediate practical politics. Vyshinsky was sincere when he told a group of British and United States officials during the Moscow Conference that, whereas Tsarist Russia was constantly scheming to annex new territory, the Soviet Union has all the territory it needs and, therefore, there is no reason why it should not be able to get along with the United Kingdom and the United States. Certainly the 1941 frontiers of the Soviet Union embrace all the territory necessary for the further development of Soviet socialism during the immediate future.[33]

The long run might promise bliss, but Wilgress noted (almost as an aside, and out of character with his general optimism) that the maintenance of the Communist party and the security police as centralized bodies would assure that 'in no sense ... can the new move be regarded as endangering the absolute authority of the present ruler of the Soviet Union.'

For the first time, it appears, this report from Moscow stimulated a long memorandum of analysis prepared within the Department of External Affairs by Leo Malania.[34] It placed Russian constitutional changes within the context of Soviet history and constitutional practice, noting that the changes were probably meant to serve certain technical, symbolic, and propagandist purposes, without detracting from Moscow's centralized authority. For Malania, the efforts to appease the major national minorities suggested the Soviet regime's determination to focus on internal development, thus 'raising the moral authority' of the Soviet state. This concentration, he argued, was consistent with the established Soviet policy of discouraging revolutionary Communist activity abroad. 'To Communists abroad this is a clear directive not to act as revolutionary parties seeking to emulate the Russian events of 1917, but to serve either as propagandist societies whose purpose is to extol the achievements of the Soviet Union and in this way to raise its prestige, or as left-wing parties working within the framework of capitalist democracy.'

The Soviet Union's desire for peaceful reconstruction, according to Malania,

will require it to maintain friendly relations with the great powers and to allay the suspicions of the small nations of Europe, so as to prevent the formation of an anti-Soviet bloc among them ...

If, however, the other great powers should again adopt the futile policy of building up a strong European or Asiatic power, or combination of powers, as a counterweight to the USSR, then the latter might well reconsider its present policy. The extent, therefore, to which the potential menace of Soviet expansionism can be kept in check would appear to depend upon the success of the great powers, including the USSR on a basis of complete equality, in organizing a solid framework of international security, within which the small states would be allowed to reconstruct and to develop their economic and cultural life under a system of political democracy. It is safe to assume that the Soviet leaders are sufficiently realistic to be keeping an open mind on this question. But at the present time all indications seem to point to the sincere intention of the Soviet Government to try to [sic] experiment of international collaboration.

The framework of security desired by the Soviet Union, Malania believed, would emerge 'from practices established in the course of war' and would have four elements:

1 A long-term military alliance among the great powers which would underwrite the security of the world;
2 Continuous consultation by the great powers on major questions of world policy;
3 A supplementary network of long-term military alliances among the small powers on the one hand, and their more powerful neighbours on the other, to render one another military assistance in the event of aggression against any one of them;
4 A series of advisory intergovernmental bodies, each dealing with a specific problem and organized upon the basis of functional representation.

In its conclusion, this was a sympathetic and reassuring rendering of the Grand Design, Soviet-style. If Britain and the United States were ready to accept it, as the Moscow and Tehran conferences seemed tentatively to suggest, the possibility of continuing harmony among the great powers looked promising.

Soon afterwards, in early March 1944, Norman Robertson asked Dana Wilgress for a summary dispatch gathering together Wilgress's evidence for his judgments about the post-war foreign policy of the Soviet Union.[35] The Canadian ambassador noted in reply that there was still a substantial belief in the West that 'after the war the Soviet Government will seek to inspire revolutionary communism abroad,' but that this belief accorded neither with recent trends in the Soviet Union nor with his own considered judgment 'in what is of necessity a highly speculative field.'[36] Russian society since the revolution had passed through a series of phases, some of them so striking that 'many people are inclined to form their judgements of this country on phases of the revolutionary process that have long since passed.' It was necessary constantly 'to study ... conditions on the spot and to reach new conclusions unhampered by conceptions based on a previous period.'

Seen in perspective, the dissolution of the Comintern now represented for Wilgress 'the culmination of a tendency that had its origins in the struggle for power between Stalin and Trotsky. It may be said to signify the final eclipse of revolutionary communism and the emergence of the Soviet Union as a national state.' Since the late twenties, in fact, Stalin's regime had concentrated upon the consolidation of central power within the Soviet Union, 'indifferent to the active inspiration of revolutionary communism abroad.'

From now on we may expect the Soviet Union to act as any other national state concerned chiefly with looking after its own interests rather than being concerned with spreading its own ideology by means of a Marxian crusade. This does not mean that the Soviet Union may not attempt to bring about the establishment of communist regimes in other countries if this would further its own interests, but a strong case can be made out for the view that this would be contrary to the interests of the Soviet Union in the post-war period ... the Soviet Union will require a long period of peace and security and this will only be possible if the communist bogy is allayed and other countries are satisfied that the Soviet Government is not interested in interfering in their internal affairs ... Stalin is said to be sincerely desirous of disproving Hitler's contention that the Soviet Union is out to bolshevize Europe.

A country devastated, a civil population terribly wounded and exhausted, would require 'many years of laborious economic reconstruction ... before Stalin can achieve his reputed ambition of giving the people of the Soviet Union a supply of consumers' goods which will raise their standard of living to the level of that of Western Europe.' In this effort of reconstruction, Wilgress reported that the Russians counted on two kinds of assistance from abroad.

The Soviet Government have great hopes of obtaining both machinery and man-power from the Germans in the form of reparations and their demands in this respect may lead to disputes with the other allies. Irrespective of what they obtain from Germany they will be dependent in large measure on the economic cooperation of the United States, which will only be forthcoming if the people of the United States are assured of the peaceful intentions of the Soviet Union. It will be impossible to divert the bulk of the productive capacity of the country to the satisfaction of consumer needs if the lack of external security requires the Soviet Union still to maintain large armaments. The interests of the Soviet Union in peace and security, therefore, are very great and very real.

Wilgress recognized, however, that the Soviet desire for peaceful co-operation with other countries was conditional, not absolute.

It assumes ... that the Soviet Union will not be frustrated in the attainment of what she considers to be her just minimum demands. These include the recognition of the incorporation in the Union of the Baltic States, the fixing of a frontier with Poland which is ethnographically just and strategically satisfactory to the Soviet Union, the securing of adequate reparations from Germany for the damage inflicted by the invaders on Soviet territory, disarmament of Germany and other measures to prevent the recurrence of German aggression until the Soviet Union is strong enough economically to fear no longer the threat of such aggression, and the avoidance by the United Kingdom and the United States of a rapprochement with Germany that appears aimed against the Soviet Union.

If these conditions were met, Wilgress believed that Russia would 'co-operate wholeheartedly' in a general system of collective security, and would act with propriety in her foreign relations. But his conception of Soviet propriety contained some unanalysed contradictions.

The Soviet Government may also be expected to avoid scrupulously interference in the internal affairs of democratic countries and especially the appearance of supporting communist parties in these countries, because to do so would immediately align other countries against the Soviet Union and disturb the system of security she so badly needs for internal reasons. This does not mean that in the immediate period of the restoration of the liberated territories the Soviet Union will be indifferent to the regimes which will be established in these territories. On the contrary she will continue to follow a most forward and progressive policy as she has already shown in regard to France, Italy, Poland and Yugoslavia. That policy will be to make possible the coming to power of regimes likely to have the broadest possible base of popular support and to remove from Europe the last vestiges of fascist-minded regimes. Particularly, the policy will aim at preventing in countries strategically placed like Poland the establishment of regimes motivated by hostility to the Soviet Union, because then such a country would be a base for anti-Soviet intrigues and for the formation of anti-Soviet blocks. This, however, is not the same as endeavouring to establish communist regimes in other countries. I believe that the Soviet Government would be embarrassed if the communists should come to power in any country.

Wilgress added to his explanation of this embarrassment the shrewd perception that for the Soviet Union 'there is hardly room in Europe for two separate communist systems.' Stalin's policy assumed one centre of Communist power, and the absorption by the Soviet Union of 'any Communist regimes established on its fringes.' The Soviet administration did not want competition among independent Communist states; and yet it was not ready to absorb countries that already possessed standards of living higher than that of the Soviet Union. 'It was difficult enough to digest the Baltic States. It would unduly disturb the equilibrium of Great Russian dominion to have to digest Germans or even Czechs, while their standard of living is so superior to that of the Soviet peoples.' The ancient Muscovite dream of expansion had, for the time being, been sublimated in the Soviet desire to improve the conditions of life of the USSR. Once that had been accomplished, Wilgress repeated fancifully, the power of peaceful attraction of the Soviet Union to its neighbours 'may become so strong that they will be able to add to their already huge expanse of territory without provoking the same degree of armed resistance which would now result from any attempts at territorial expansion.'

While Wilgress's account of Soviet aims set the Russian desire for post-war international co-operation very high, the Canadian ambassador also made clear that her minimum demands for territory and influence in

Eastern Europe were large and unyielding. Soviet willingness to co-operate with the United States and the United Kingdom in a general peace settlement would depend upon their acceptance of these minimum demands. By framing his commentary optimistically, Wilgress implied that this acceptance was both possible and legitimate, and that it would appease the Soviet sense of insecurity and satisfy her expansionist ambitions – at least in the short run. For an observer less given to optimism than Dana Wilgress, or for one reading his dispatch in less optimistic times, different conclusions were possible from his evidence. If it was clear that the Soviet Union was no longer interested in stimulating revolutions abroad, it was far from clear that Soviet ambitions in Eastern Europe were compatible with the interests of the countries concerned, or with the potential post-war attitudes of the other great powers. The message was only superficially reassuring.

As usual with Wilgress's major analytical dispatches, this one was distributed not only within the Department of External Affairs and to all Canadian missions abroad, but also to the prime minister and the other members of the Cabinet War Committee: Ralston, St Laurent, Crerar, Power, and Ilsley.[37]

The department pursued its quest for understanding of what the Soviet Union was up to in a series of private conversations, later in the year, between members of the department and Charles E. Bohlen, chief of the Division of Eastern European Affairs in the US State Department. The first two meetings occurred in Washington, in June, between Escott Reid and Bohlen; the third and fourth in Ottawa, in November, among Bohlen and seven members of the Canadian Department – Norman Robertson, Hume Wrong, George Glazebrook, Gerry Riddell, George Ignatieff, Herbert Norman, and Leo Malania.[38]

Bohlen was noticeably less euphoric about Soviet policy than Wilgress was. Reid reported in June that Bohlen appeared, in general, to agree with Wilgress's views as expressed in his recent dispatches from Moscow, but that:

His only major point of difference is that he thinks that it is unwise to attach much importance to the Soviet intention of supporting 'broad-based, representative and progressive governments in Europe'. His interpretation of Soviet policy is that it is essentially negative and flexible. The Soviet want to prevent two things in neighbouring countries – disorder, and the pursuit by governments of anti-Soviet policies. How these two negative objectives can best be attained will depend on the circumstances of the time and the circumstances in the area in question. The local communist parties will be used in each country to prevent the government from following an anti-Soviet line.[39]

Bohlen believed that Russia would be relatively indifferent to the domestic policies of the governments of Eastern Europe provided that they 'follow a pro-Soviet policy in foreign affairs' as Dr Benes had promised for Czechoslovakia. The Soviets might in fact prefer stable right-wing or centre governments to social democratic or popular front ones; as their recent recognition of the monarchy and the military government in Italy suggested, 'they do not attach much importance to constitutional forms and symbols.' The great problem that Bohlen saw in comprehending Russian foreign policy was not its dogmatism but its tactical flexibility – or even its confusion. 'It is often assumed that the Soviets are pursuing a long-run policy, whereas actually they are more inclined to pursue a day to day policy. This increases the difficulty of dealing with them and with leaders who follow their general line. Thus Marshal Tito, who follows their general line, might suddenly switch from attacks on Mikhailovitch to making an agreement with him, or the Soviet might suddenly withdraw their support from Tito.' Dana Wilgress had made a similar point a few months earlier, when reporting on the Soviet Union's unanticipated recognition of the Badoglio government in Italy: 'Their action shows their inexperience and lack of a clear-cut policy in spite of all that the United States press is saying to the contrary. The Soviet Government may know what they want as regards the Baltic States and Poland, but when they go further afield their policy becomes as confused as that of either of the other two great powers. They want desperately to play an equal role but do not know always quite how to go about it.'[40]

Bohlen suggested to Reid that there were two special and related reasons for Russian mis-steps in foreign policy: their ignorance of public opinion abroad, and their insensitivity to the interests of smaller powers: 'the officials in Moscow such as Litvinov and Maisky, who probably understand opinion in the United States and Great Britain, do not carry sufficient weight. Thus the Soviet government might be trying to frame its policies so as not to provoke anti-Soviet feeling abroad and yet by their ignorance of foreign opinion they may unwittingly by their actions provoke suspicions abroad.' The Soviets had not yet learned 'that it is easier to get cooperation of smaller powers if their feelings are spared and if they are not pushed around.' The real prospect was that an anti-Soviet coalition would only be created in Europe if Russian actions precipitated it.

In early November 1944 Bohlen came to Ottawa for discussions with senior members of the department. He emphasized that there were two immediate objectives of Soviet policy: 'to maintain a very close understanding with the other two great powers in the coalition'; and to insist upon friendly governments in the border states. The latter objective, however, might jeopardize the former, because 'friendship' for the Soviets was indistinguishable from subordination, and because the desire for friendly neighbours might be endlessly extended, to the neighbours of neighbours as well. Bohlen argued that Britain and the United States should make absolutely clear to the Russians that pursuit of an ambitious policy in Eastern Europe 'may arouse public suspicion to such an extent that co-operation among the three Great Powers, to which they attach so much importance, would become impossible.' Americans 'felt very strongly' about the future of Poland, and that subject should therefore provide the occasion for a determined stand by Britain and America. But Bohlen also reflected on the dilemma that would face them in protesting against Soviet policy:

In taking a stand against undue extension of Soviet influence, the Anglo-Saxon powers should be careful to avoid giving the impression of a 'united front' against the Soviet Union, as this would defeat its own purpose by arousing Soviet suspicions, and encouraging them to proceed unilaterally. The way to get around this difficulty was for the United Kingdom and the United States to make independent approaches, wording their representations differently. When controversial issues were under discussion between the three powers, satisfactory agreements would never be reached if the United States and United Kingdom always acted together; they must constantly be careful to treat the Soviet Government in all respects as an equal, and give no cause for suspicion that they were acting in concert in bringing pressure to bear on Moscow.

Poland should be where the Western Allies draw the line against Russian dictation; and Czechoslovakia would be the test case for 'the possibility of a friendly neighbouring state of the u.s.s.r. retaining real internal independence.' 'Benes had done everything possible to show his good intentions. Mr. Bohlen wondered whether in view of this the Soviets would tolerate any private criticism of the u.s.s.r. in Czechoslovakia.'

This general assessment of Russian policy and the prospects for post-war collaboration was even gloomier than Bohlen's earlier judgment had been. While he believed that a display of firmness toward the Soviet Union was now necessary, he added pessimistically that such a warning might be taken by Stalin as proof of Russia's isolation and justification for further assertions of will.

Presumably Bohlen made the same call for firmness in Washington and London; but his call was not heeded. After the opening of the second front in June 1944, the renewed Soviet advance into Eastern Europe rapidly altered the strategic balance, giving the Russians both fresh confidence and the power of their military presence in Poland, the Baltic states, and within a few months in Romania, Bulgaria, Czechoslovakia, Hungary, Austria, and Germany. In July Stalin recognized the puppet Polish Committee of National Liberation; and for six weeks after mid-August the Soviet army waited passively across the Vistula while the Polish Home Army in Warsaw rose against the German occupation and was crushed. In the face of these indications of Stalin's ruthlessness, Roosevelt and Churchill engaged in nothing more threatening than hand-wringing.[41]

George Kennan, a colleague of Charles Bohlen and the other most experienced State Department specialist on Russian affairs, returned to Moscow in that summer of 1944, after an absence of seven years, as minister counsellor in the American Embassy. Kennan, like Bohlen, was a realist about the Soviet Union. In his bleakly penetrating view, there was no prospect of Anglo-American co-operation in peacemaking with a Stalinist regime that was determined to impose its will on the whole of Central and Eastern Europe. The evidence of Soviet intentions had revealed itself to him throughout the year, as military victories made Moscow less and less dependent on the Western Allies and more indifferent to their moralizing appeals for a liberal world order. Kennan's vision was complex and unsentimental. It coincided neither with Franklin Roosevelt's lingering conviction that he could deal as a friendly equal with Joseph Stalin, nor with the State Department's emerging zeal for a new international organization to secure the peace through collective action. But Kennan did not expect to persuade his government to share his convictions. 'Russia remains today, more than ever, an enigma for the Western World. Simple American minds imagine that this is because "we don't know the truth about it." They are wrong. It is not our lack of knowledge which causes us to be puzzled by Russia. It is that we are incapable of understanding the truth about Russia when we see it.'[42] When Kennan submitted his pessimistic reflections on Soviet policy to the ambassador, Averell Harriman, in September 1944, Harriman returned the paper to him without comment.[43] 'The apprehension of what is valid in the Russian world is unsettling and displeasing to the American mind,'

Kennan wrote; and for another eighteen months he remained isolated with his convictions 'on a chilly and inhospitable mountaintop where few have been before, where few can follow, and where few will consent to believe that he has been.'[44] Bohlen shared his isolation.

While anxieties accumulated (in varying degrees) among the diplomatic observers of Soviet conduct in Britain and the United States, these anxieties were effectively blocked by the heads of state in 1944 in their preoccupation with winning the war and maintaining the Grand Alliance into peacetime. The worries and perplexities of the experts were conveyed neither to the Anglo-American (and Canadian) publics nor to the Soviet Union itself – except, presumably, through their secret intelligence sources within the three governments. For Stalin, on the contrary, the overt signals from the West were still unmistakably favourable. One of the clearest indications of his ability to act without hindrance in Eastern Europe was his agreement with Churchill on 'degrees of interest' in the Balkans, negotiated in October 1944 in Moscow without the active participation, but with the knowledge, of the United States.[45] While Winston Churchill may have been moved to impress upon the Soviet Union that the United Kingdom intended to restore its influential role in Central Europe before the Soviets had fully occupied the vacuum, his readiness to deal, and his easy concession of Russian dominance in Romania, Bulgaria, and Hungary in return for British dominance in Greece, was remarkable evidence of British willingness to play the game of power on Russian terms – and to play it without finesse.[46] The Canadian Embassy in Moscow was regularly briefed by the British Embassy on the Stalin-Churchill discussions, and was aware of the general nature – if not, apparently, of the particulars – of the 'percentages agreement.'[47]

On 9 November 1944 Dana Wilgress sent a further major review of Soviet policy to Ottawa, this one decidedly less confident about Russian purposes than his previous dispatches had been.[48] Wilgress still believed, in spite of 'some recent manifestations of Soviet policy' in relation to Poland, Turkey, Iran, Romania, and Bulgaria, that Russia desired above all to maintain harmony with Britain and the United States. The qualification, however, was emphatic: 'the main objective will be the avoidance of international unrest if this can be accomplished without jeopardizing their vital interests.' Wilgress added that even this qualified judgment was now disputed by many observers, who held that the Soviet Union was 'motivated by aggressive intentions and ... aiming to incorporate within the Soviet Union many of the territories on her western, southern and eastern borders.' As evidence to the contrary, Wilgress remarked on the 'magnanimity' of Russia in its armistice negotiations with Romania, Bulgaria, and Finland; its active participation in planning for new international institutions; and the propriety of its attitudes toward Czechoslovakia, Yugoslavia, Greece, Afghanistan, and China. 'The one rock on which future co-operation between the Soviet Union and the other two great powers is most likely to founder,' he concluded, 'is the treatment to be meted out to Germany,' where the Soviets would require a hard peace. The impression Wilgress conveyed in this dispatch was one of deepening uncertainty, typified by his puzzling remark that 'functional non-co-operation' by the Soviet Union in European ventures would not be a sign of her unwillingness to co-operate in maintaining the peace, but rather a reflection of her suspicions and fears for her security. In his efforts to explain the motives behind Soviet policies, Wilgress was inclined to underemphasize or ignore the external effects of those policies, both real and psychological. But it was upon the basis of those effects that other nations acted.

Following Prime Minister Churchill's inconclusive discussions with Stalin over Poland in October 1944, Soviet determination to impose the Lublin Committee of National Liberation upon the country became ever more obvious.[49] In January 1945, with the entire Polish territory cleared of the German army and under Soviet occupation, the committee transformed itself into a provisional government which was immediately recognized by the Soviet Union over the futile protests of the United Kingdom and the United States.[50] 'Further correspondence,' wrote Churchill, 'did not seem to me to be likely to do much good. Only a personal meeting gave hope.'[51] This next meeting of the three leaders had been under discussion for months. Now, under the shadows of the Polish dispute, the undecided fate of Germany, and disagreement on voting procedures in the United Nations, Churchill, Roosevelt, and Stalin arranged to meet at the Soviet Black Sea port of Yalta in February 1945. Despite these shadows, Churchill's fatigue, and Roosevelt's declining health, however, the two Western leaders 'did not come to avert a crisis; elated by the impending triumph over Nazism, they were self-confident and optimistic about the future.'[52]

Seven days of meetings at Yalta produced ambiguous results for each of the participants, who nevertheless put the best face on the outcome. None of them was willing to risk the appearance of a rupture in the alliance in the concluding days of the war: none thought there had been a rupture. But agreement on German reparations was postponed; the understanding on

Poland was vague enough for the Soviets to believe they could proceed as they wished while the Western Allies thought they had gained an understanding on free elections; and the ringing 'Declaration on Liberated Europe' which reaffirmed 'the right of all peoples to choose the form of government under which they will live,' was obviously regarded by the Russians as a piece of hollow rhetoric to be ignored wherever they wished.[53] Later, during the Cold War, Yalta gained a popular reputation in the United States as the place where Britain and America had surrendered their European interests to the Soviet Union. But the outcome was less dramatic and clear-cut than that. On some subjects, such as reparations, the Soviets were stymied. On others, such as Poland, the prospect was uncertain but entirely dependent on Russian good faith. On the Pacific war, the United States regarded the Soviet commitment to entry as wholly beneficial (although by that time it was probably unnecessary for Japan's defeat). The conference gained its significance only in retrospect, when it came to stand as a symbol of Western weakness and Soviet duplicity. But the weakness had been more evident in the meetings at Tehran and Moscow; and Soviet duplicity was only the common coin of diplomacy, given inflated attention because of the Western Allies' readiness to take general commitments at face value. If Yalta could be described as any kind of triumph, it was no more than the last triumph of Western illusion about the USSR. As Vojtech Mastny writes: 'Measured by achievements, Yalta was, despite its later notoriety, the least important of the Allied chiefs' wartime gatherings ... Yalta was certainly not a glorious occasion for Western statesmanship, but neither was it in any tangible way "Stalin's greatest victory." If it stands out as a landmark, this is because of the precipitous breakdown that soon followed, a shock to all its participants.'[54]

 **Disenchantment**

For many Western diplomats, the moral simplicities and expectations of war gave way rapidly in the spring of 1945 to the realization that there would be no new world after the peace. This disillusionment was in part a natural product of the coming surrender, the result of facing – in exhaustion – the new and arduous problems of relief, reconstruction, political rehabilitation, and demobilization. But it was sharpened by what was seen as a self-interested hardening of Russian policy after Yalta, which would render the chances of post-war co-operation with the Soviet Union remote. Whether profound or tactical, sudden or cumulative, that transformation was not what the British and American governments had prepared themselves and their publics for in the aftermath of war. Their policies of postponement and appeasement, to the extent that they had any long-term rationale, had been based on the belief that the Soviets would be reasonably altruistic partners in the creation of a just world (as that was conceived in liberal internationalist imagery), or at least that they would behave tolerably in what was discreetly conceded to be their sphere of prominence in Eastern Europe. For four years Allied governments had promoted such complacent beliefs, as reinforcement for the fighting spirit. There were now large investments of habit, interest, and faith in the accuracy of such claims; and when the balance of the evidence no longer easily justified them, the difficulties of readjustment proved to be immense, in both human and political terms. For the next three years that readjustment occurred, until a new, simplified faith and a new, simplified policy took root – as misleading and imprudent in their ways as those of wartime had been.

Altered perceptions of the Soviet Union led logically to a reassessment of Allied policy and tactics towards it. Both changes came first among the diplomats who were closest to events: the members of the Western embassies in Moscow. The signs of change can be traced over months, in 1944 and 1945, through shifts of tone and emphasis in their dispatches, as the views of the 'realists' like George Kennan gradually gained ground and those of the liberal optimists lost it. Winston Churchill and Franklin Roosevelt, too, came to the point of disenchantment in March 1945. But as the leading advocates of the Grand Alliance, still seeking to maintain it, they conveyed their anxieties to Joseph Stalin in decidedly uncertain language.

The breakdown of trust in 1945 was the product, in the Western mind, of Soviet bad faith. At the end of February the Romanian government was overthrown and replaced by a Communist-dominated cabinet through the direct intervention of the Red Army and the Soviet deputy foreign minister Andrei Vishinsky. In Moscow, the Soviets made clear that the ambiguous Yalta agreements on Poland would not result, as the British and Americans led themselves to believe, in reconciliation between the Lublin government and the non-Communists. Late in March the Soviets transported the sixteen Polish Home Army delegates with whom they had been negotiating to Moscow, placing them under secret arrest as traitors; and shortly afterwards they proposed that the Lublin government should represent Poland at the founding conference of the United Nations in San Francisco. When Britain and the United States rejected this suggestion, Stalin told them that Molotov would be unable to come to San Francisco.

Allied discussions on a joint occupation policy in Gemany faltered in the face of Soviet delays and obscurities; and in March the Russians revived their plans for a swift military drive to occupy Berlin. At the same time the Russians probed beyond their sphere by publicly denouncing the British-sponsored Greek government, and announcing that they intended to end their non-aggression pact with Turkey.[1] Vojtech Mastny concludes that an element of panic lay behind this hardening of Russian attitudes: 'Though unmistakably more aggressive, the pattern of Soviet policy since Yalta had been erratic and inconsistent rather than premeditated and methodical. Stalin must have anxiously recalled the consequences of his last great miscalculation, concerning Hitler's intentions in 1941.'[2]

Beneath the surface of almost daily tactical wavering, what had apparently become clear with the advance of the Soviet armies was the Russian realization of what could and would be done in the lands under Soviet occupation. 'This war is not as in the past,' Stalin told the Yugoslav Military Mission in April 1945; 'whoever occupies a territory also imposes on it his own social system. Everyone imposes his own system as far as his army can reach. It cannot be otherwise.'[3]

The tensions over Poland and Romania, in particular, prompted Churchill and Roosevelt to make joint complaints to Stalin at the beginning of April. Since these took the form of anxious pleading for co-operation, however, they cannot have impressed Stalin by their firmness. The only hint of a threat in Churchill's message of 1 April 1945 was that he might have to admit the failure of the Yalta agreements to the House of Commons:

If our efforts to reach an agreement about Poland are to be doomed to failure I shall be bound to confess the fact to Parliament when they return from the Easter recess. No one has pleaded the cause of Russia with more fervour and conviction than I have tried to do ... It is as a sincere friend of Russia that I make my personal appeal to you and to your colleagues to come to a good understanding about Poland with the Western democracies, and not to smite down the hands of comradeship in the future guidance of the world which we now extend.[4]

Roosevelt's hint of the consequences of failure was also far distant from the political world of Joseph Stalin:

I wish to convey to you how important it is for the development of our programme of international collaboration that this Polish question be settled fairly and speedily. If this is not done all of the difficulties and dangers to Allied unity which we had so much in mind in reaching our decision at the Crimea will face us in an even more acute form. You are, I am sure, aware that genuine popular support in the United States is required to carry out any Government policy, foreign or domestic. The American people make up their own mind, and no Government action can change it.[5]

Stalin delivered a slightly mollifying reply on 7 April; but at the same time what Churchill calls 'a far more bitter and important interchange' over armistice negotiations with the German forces reached its climax. When German agents in Switzerland approached the Americans to discuss the possible surrender of German units in Italy at almost the same moment in early March as the American army crossed the Rhine at Remagen and began an unexpectedly rapid advance into central Germany, the Soviets saw revived the spectre of a separate peace and an Anglo-American-German alliance directed against them.[6] The Soviet Union asked to participate in the secret meetings, and when the request was obliquely deferred, Molotov protested that the talks must be broken off.[7] On 3 April Stalin cabled Roosevelt to accuse the United States and Britain of having reached agreement with the Germans 'to open the front and permit the Anglo-American troops to advance to the east,' in return for which 'the Anglo-Americans have promised ... to ease for the Germans the peace terms.'[8] Roosevelt's reply, sent two days later, bluntly rejected Stalin's accusations and ended in an outburst of anger:

Finally I would say this: it would be one of the great tragedies of history if at the very moment of the victory now within our grasp such distrust, such lack of faith, should prejudice the entire undertaking after the colossal losses of life, material, and treasure involved.

Frankly, I cannot avoid a feeling of bitter resentment toward your informers, whoever they are, for such vile misrepresentations of my actions or those of my trusted subordinates.[9]

Stalin responded blandly that he had not challenged the integrity and trustworthiness of either Roosevelt or Churchill; suggested in the next breath that the behaviour of the Germans in continuing a 'crazy struggle' with the Soviet army while yielding in the West was 'more than curious and unintelligible'; and insisted that 'my informants ... are extremely honest and modest people who discharge their duties conscientiously and have no intention of offending anyone.'[10] Churchill commented to Roosevelt that 'this is about the best we are going to get out of them, and certainly is as near as they can get to an apology'; and Roosevelt closed the incident by appealing to Stalin on 12 April 1945 that 'There must not, in any event, be mutual mistrust, and minor misunderstandings of this character should not arise in future.'[11] That afternoon, at Warm Springs, Georgia, President Roosevelt died; and at the White House later in the day, Harry S. Truman was sworn in as president.

While the two Western heads of state fenced inconclusively with the belligerent Soviet leader, Western diplomats in Moscow rallied their arguments for a fundamental change of course. For Canada, the key documents were contained in a long dispatch from Moscow on 16 April 1945 containing four memoranda on Soviet policies and diplomatic techniques, and recommendations for a Western response.[12] The memoranda were the work of Arnold C. Smith, and in the absence of the ambassador (who was on his way to the San Francisco conference), the covering dispatch was signed by the new Canadian chargé d'affaires, Leon Mayrand.[13] Both the interpretations of Russian policy and the tactical judgments about how to deal with the Soviet Union contained in this dispatch are in startling contrast to the general approach of previous messages from the Canadian mission in Moscow. Clearly a watershed had been reached.

Mayrand reported that Smith's papers were meant to explain a number of sombre conclusions suggested by recent events:

(i) That the Soviet government at present seems intent on creating relatively exclusive zones of influence for itself in Europe and probably elsewhere.
(ii) That the Soviet government seems at present unwilling to cooperate seriously in international economic planning, or to contemplate meshing the economies of countries in 'their' zones of Europe with those of the rest of the continent and the world. It is intended, however, that they be closely integrated with the economy of the Soviet Union.
(iii) That there has recently been a marked deterioration or stiffening in Soviet diplomatic techniques during the first three months of 1945, and an attitude of increasing unwillingness on the part of the u.s.s.r. to cooperate closely and frankly with their major Allies, especially in matters affecting the 'Soviet' sphere in Europe.
(iv) That it is therefore time for a firm diplomatic line to be taken by the Western powers in their dealings with the Soviet Union, and that it is also desirable to consider building up those areas in Europe and elsewhere where Western influence is or can be dominant.
(v) That continued Western firmness may induce the Soviet Goverment to modify, at least temporarily, its present clearly isolationist trends.
(vi) That cooperation between the Western powers and the Soviet Union is in any case not ruled out. But it will have to be on rather other terms than those generally contemplated during recent years.

Mayrand reported that the arguments of the Smith memoranda paralleled the changing views of the British and Americans.

The United Kingdom and United States Ambassadors in Moscow have been reluctantly forced to the conclusion that it is now essential for the Western powers to adopt a much stiffer attitude in diplomatic relations and policy regarding the Soviet Union than has been followed at any time during recent years. I understand that Mr. Churchill is now of this opinion, and that Mr. Roosevelt came reluctantly to a similar tentative decision shortly before his death. Events have forced us to general agreement with this view.

Since Soviet policy aimed at the consolidation of 'a powerful bloc of its own, a bloc of Western civilization would seem necessary by default. The chief danger to avoid is thus not a Western bloc, but two distinct and exclusive "British" and "American" blocs which would compete between themselves.' It was essential that the Western Allies should attempt to contain Soviet influence, by concentrating

without further delay on the building up of areas in western and southern Europe which during the emergency period are our main responsibility and the populations of which can in the post-war period be our reliable friends. In this connection an early and adequate supply of relief necessities, and an improvement in the food situation, would seem essential, if serious disorders are to be minimized and if Communist influence is to be kept within reasonable limits in these countries. The real dangers of Communist influence lie of course not in their social and political philosophy but in the fact that they seem so often to be in effect instruments of the external policy of a foreign Great Power, the U.S.S.R.

This effort of containment should also be extended, through aid, capital investment, and propaganda, to the poor countries of the Middle East, China, and Africa, in order 'to bring these "backward" populations into contented and therefore reliable partnership with Western democratic civilization. This policy alone can make democratic civilization permanently and overwhelmingly strong. Since the Soviet Government seems always careful to maintain a relatively free hand in foreign policy, and has demonstrated its ability both to make quick reverses in policy (e.g. 1939) and to bully when it feels its own position sufficiently strong, such a nurturing of potential friends and allies is the best long-run political guarantee of continued Soviet cooperation and thus of our security.'

Mayrand reviewed the proposal for a change in Western diplomatic approaches to the Russians which was developed at length in the Smith memoranda. 'A long-run policy of increasing the strength of Western civilization, coupled with a flexible diplomatic technique which would use firmness against firmness, yield advantage usually only against advantage, and that would always be ready to encourage cooperation but would offer no temptation through softness for the undue seeking of expansionist advantage, would seem a necessary educational technique.'

While Mayrand judged that 'the honeymoon period of collaboration between the Western powers and the Soviet Union' was over, and that 'the dream' of easy post-war co-operation had been vain, 'there is nevertheless no reason whatever for alarm.' The Soviet Union was not aggressive; it would continue to seek harmony 'in such specified and carefully delimited fields ... as contain clear material benefit to themselves, or alternatively which involve relatively limited commitments and appreciable gains in prestige or propaganda opportunities ... Excellent possibilities of sincere and mutually beneficial co-operation nevertheless remain, if the problems are approached without illusion and without weakness.'

Arnold Smith reported that in spite of all the evidence of Soviet determination to establish Russia's own, exclusive economic zone in Eastern Europe (evidence which he noted in detail) the American and British governments were still pleading helplessly to the Russians for programs of general European relief and economic reorganization.[14] Now, both the British and American ambassadors in Moscow had come to George Kennan's view that 'such further pleas would be not only useless but dangerous,' that the Soviets 'probably only regard as a sign of weakness the apparent inability of the United Kingdom and the United States to organize "our area" without Soviet participation.' They had therefore appealed to their governments, as a matter of urgency, to concentrate their relief in Western and Southern Europe and to inform the Soviets of this decision.

The Ambassadors hope that this strong and realistic policy may force the Russians to cooperate with western civilization on the basis of a post-war Europe less sharply divided into two spheres. They feel however that nothing less than this pressure could create such a swing back in the basic aims of present Soviet policy, and are not too optimistic that ... the Soviets can be persuaded to cooperate except possibly on a temporary and tactical basis ...

I should add that I know the profound personal reluctance with which Mr. Harriman and Sir Archibald Clark Kerr have been forced to adopt these conclusions.

In a fascinating memorandum on 'Certain Aspects of Soviet Diplomatic Techniques,' Smith reviewed some 'unexpected and unpleasant' features of Russian diplomacy, citing examples of 'extremely sharp practice,' 'hypocrisy and even outright lying' in dealings with Britain and the United States.[15] He noted that observers in Moscow had previously distinguished Soviet manners from the substance of policy, and forgiven their manners:

It has long been customary to regard these techniques and irritations with almost limitless tolerance – as mere bad manners; as a proud unwillingness to admit inefficiencies due to inexperience, shortages of trained staff, and pressure of work; as a hangover from long and not unjustified suspicion of 'capitalist' nations, suspicions which patience and understanding on our part could eventually remove, etc., etc. Insofar as the *technique* of negotiations is concerned ... the United States and United Kingdom methods hitherto used can be described almost without exception as patiently 'turning the other cheek.'

But the charitable analysis and the soft response were now inadequate. They had 'been given more than a fair trial, with results that seem not merely negative but progressively harmful.'

On the plane of high policy, too, the 'soft' technique of diplomacy seems to have proved inadequate. Here of course no moral credit can be claimed for softness, but the lesson would appear to be the same. If firm post-war agreements and commitments on serious issues had been reached in 1942 or 1943, at a time when militarily the Soviet Union, like all of us, was appreciably weaker than today, and when Lend-Lease and Mutual Aid supplies were of decisive importance, then it may well be that solutions more satisfactory to us than any now possible could have been attained. In fairness to the Soviet Government it should be emphasized that they made repeated early efforts (in 1942 and 1943) to get us to 'talk turkey' regarding post-war settlements, and that we consistently refused.

Because the Anglo-Americans had been unduly suspicious of progressive and left-wing elements in German-occupied Europe, they had followed for too long a self-defeating policy of support for disintegrating 'conservative or socially reactionary groups.' 'It took the United Kingdom and the United States Governments a long time to recognize the inevitability of a "leftward" trend in Europe, and the consequent desirability of harnessing the dynamic forces of this evolution to our purposes of national resistance and to the eventual creation of satisfactory post-war regimes whose relations with ourselves shall be dependently close and friendly.' European progressives, as a result, were suspicious of the British and Americans; and progressives within the United States and United Kingdom in their 'only partially-informed' criticisms, had added to the confusions of Western policy. This progressive pressure had been partly responsible 'for a widespread misinterpretation of Soviet policy as essentially democratic ... and .... for various gratuitous concessions to Soviet expansionism for which, though many of them were on the whole necessary and desirable in themselves, we could have obtained a useful *quid pro quo*.'

The heart of Smith's documents was devoted to this matter of diplomatic tactics. The arguments for 'toughness' in bargaining with the Soviet Union were complex and powerful, in his view; and they had finally been accepted by Churchill and Roosevelt, as they should be by President Truman.

It is hoped that this 'tough' bargaining technique can prove to be an educational process. Soviet negotiators, bred exclusively in totalitarian conditions, are accustomed to take their orders from above, to pursue them as inflexibly as possible, and to avoid compromise except on a *quid pro quo* basis. This is the reverse of the attitude of easy give-and-take which democratic experience breeds.

Mr. George Kennan, the United States Minister in Moscow, has a theory that by the very nature of Soviet (and Communist Party) social structure and traditions their negotiators must inevitably try to obtain all they can in any given negotiations, and yield as little as possible. The United Kingdom Minister, Mr. Frank Roberts, has told me that he shares this view. A further characteristic is that even without definite expansionist objectives there is, as it were, an automatic tendency to fill any political vacuums that may exist, unless constantly and consciously restrained ...

The corollaries are that the western democracies should i) carefully avoid political vacuums in areas in which they are interested; ii) should, as Mr. Kennan puts it, maintain constantly a moderate and flexible pressure; and iii) should adopt realistic 'horse-trading' or bargaining methods as the technique of negotiations with the Soviet Union.

... A sensitive and flexible western policy of firmness against firmness, immediate benefit only against benefit – which would always welcome cooperation but give Soviet leaders no grounds for believing that western statesmen and diplomats are 'suckers' – is probably the only way of inducing, on a permanently reliable basis, such cooperation from the Soviet Union.

It was also, he suggested, the best means of assuring stability and consistency in public attitudes to the Soviet Union, which democratic foreign policy eventually relied upon.

Incidentally, the 'firm' technique is also perhaps more likely to enable democratic countries to pursue a consistently cooperative attitude with the Soviet Union on their own part. A contrary policy of hiding from the public disagreeable facts and accepting one-sided arrangements is likely, over a period of time, to yield to an ingrowing sense of frustration and an eventual over-marked sense of revulsion which could be dangerous. Over the long run, therefore, a firm policy is likely to involve more unity, and more consistency, in and among the democracies themselves.

Because a policy of firmness and bargaining for advantage would have to be maintained over a long period, Smith emphasized that the Western powers would have to 'take care constantly to have a safe preponderance of weight and of bargaining counters in democratic hands.' He therefore devoted a separate memorandum to this subject of the material basis for a strong policy, titled 'Our Own Cards.'[16] Western occupation of the main industrial zones of Germany would give Britain, the United States, and France the decisive voice in making reparations policy; they should be careful only to exchange an agreement on reparations (which the Russians 'banked mightily' upon) for Soviet fulfilment of its obligations in Eastern Europe. Post-war financial credits to the Soviet Union should not be committed for the long term, but only on a year-to-year basis according to current political calculation (a case that Averell Harriman was making concurrently to the American administration). The preponderance of Western long-term capital investment should instead be directed to the world outside the Soviet sphere. The friendship and loyalty of Western Europe, especially, should be assiduously cultivated through relief and capital aid, support for progressive regimes, and close cultural relations. (That effort should include a policy of removing the Franco regime in Spain, in order both to make amends for the democratic 'betrayal' of republican Spain and to deprive the Soviet Union of one fertile ground for subversion in Europe.)

The Soviet Union was adept in its use of propaganda, Smith continued, not only to promote the admirable features of Soviet policy, but to disguise 'the ruthless totalitarian control of every aspect of life and thought,' to cover the pursuit of its external interests, and to attract new recruits to Communist parties abroad. To put this propaganda into balance, there should be, in the West, 'a judicious revelation of the fuller facts – including especially many of the facts until now shrouded in diplomatic secrecy, and a suitable emphasis on the real meaning of democratic concepts.'

These reassessments of Western policy, as Smith acknowledged, closely paralleled the views of George Kennan, who had come to the conclusion late in 1944 that 'not only our policy toward Russia, but our plans and commitments generally for the shaping of the postwar world, were based on a dangerous misreading of the personality, the intentions, and the political situation of the Soviet leadership.'[17] Like Kennan, Smith argued that it was necessary to recognize that Europe was already divided into spheres of influence; to abandon any facile attempt to integrate these spheres; and to act towards the Soviet Union with steadiness and firmness, refusing to surrender further advantages or to believe that friendly collaboration would continue after the end of the war. Smith's exposition of April 1945 was in fact a fully developed anticipation of Kennan's case for containment of the Soviet Union, which was elaborated in his 'long telegram' to the State Department of February 1946.[18]

But such unequivocal and discouraging realism was not easily accommodated in Washington or Ottawa in the spring of 1945. President Truman's lack of experience in foreign affairs, for one thing, meant that he would take time to find a coherent voice. In the meantime the momentum of wartime co-operation and planning for the peace would be maintained, with all the force of American popular idealism behind it. President Truman was fully briefed on the recent strains in the alliance; in private he used typically gritty language in speaking of the Russians; but his actions continued to demonstrate to Moscow that the United States desired friendship with the Soviet Union and would concede a great deal to maintain it.[19] American policy was uncertain and inconsistent, as it would remain, to a large degree, for the next two years.

In the aftermath of Franklin Roosevelt's death, Averell Harriman persuaded Stalin that Molotov should attend the founding conference of the United Nations, and arranged that he should visit Washington to meet President Truman on his way to San Francisco. Harriman then returned at once to Washington to brief Truman on his newly pessimistic view of Russian policies and objectives, and on his (and his staff's) case for a tough line. Harriman could now count on substantial support for this position among Truman's cabinet and advisers, chiefly from the secretary of the navy, James Forrestal. Only the secretary of war, Henry Stimson, and the army chief of staff, George C. Marshall (who still sought Russian participation in the Japanese war), seriously opposed Harriman's recommendation. Truman took the predominant advice, and declared himself determined to talk tough to Molotov. The blunt and undiplomatic interview took place on 23 April 1945. It could have left Molotov in no doubt that Truman disapproved of Soviet action in Poland and Eastern Europe, and perhaps suggested that there had been a change of American policy with the accession of a new president.[20] But seen in context it was something less:

Truman's tough rhetoric of April, 1945 was just that – rhetoric – and did not signify an end to American efforts to reach an accommodation with the Soviet Union.

... to view the new President's confrontation with Molotov as the opening move in a well-planned, long-range strategy for dealing with the Soviet Union is to presume a degree of foresight and consistency which simply was not present during the early days of the Truman Administration.[21]

Within a few weeks Truman had dispatched Roosevelt's special assistant, Harry Hopkins, to Moscow with Harriman to seek a fresh accommodation with Stalin; while Joseph Davies, the friend of the Soviet Union, was sent to London in an effort to contain Winston Churchill's growing antagonism to Moscow.[22] The result of Hopkins's mission to Moscow was a further provisional agreement on the Polish government which made only face-saving concessions to Britain and the United States; a renewed Soviet promise to enter the Pacific war; a compromise agreement on voting procedure in the United Nations Security Council satisfactory to all three great powers; and Stalin's approval for a further meeting of the Big Three in Berlin in July.[23] The Soviet leader once again displayed his aptitude for making timely concessions on secondary matters, without damage to Soviet interests of first priority.

Beyond the transformation in personal style from courtly to brusque, the change in the American presidency had thus led, for the moment, to no substantial change in American policy toward the Soviet Union. It remained the administration's overwhelming desire to co-operate with the Soviet Union over Germany, the creation of the United Nations, and Soviet participation in the Japanese war; and that meant that the United States would do nothing of consequence to interfere with Soviet rule in Eastern Europe, or even bargain firmly for advantage as the embassies of Britain, the United States, and Canada had recommended from Moscow. In June, when Churchill proposed to Truman that American and British occupation forces in central Germany should not retreat to their agreed 'lines of occupation' until satisfactory agreement on many subjects had been reached with Russia, the President refused to delay the withdrawal because this might risk Soviet displeasure. Churchill expressed his 'profound misgivings' at the consequent entry of the Russian army 'into the heart of Western Europe and the descent of an iron curtain between us and everything to the eastward.'[24] Both Britain and the United States complied in the early post-war months with Soviet demands for the forceful return to the Soviet Union (and thus to death or imprisonment) of thousands of anti-Communist refugees from areas of Western occupation.[25] There were scores of further examples, at all levels of occupation administration, of British and American failure to press their bargaining strength in dealing with the Soviet Union. In these months it was evident that Britain, under Prime Minister Churchill's direction, was more inclined than the United States to hold the diplomatic line. But it was also suddenly clear that, with the end of the war in Europe, power had shifted decisively to American hands, and that Allied policy towards the Soviet Union would henceforth be made in Washington.[26]

To the extent that Canada made a choice, in the spring of 1945, between British firmness and American flaccidity, Canada chose the American line. It did so in the full and discomforting knowledge that the embassy in Moscow urged otherwise. At the United Nations conference in San Francisco, where the energies of the Department of External Affairs were concentrated from mid-April to the end of June, the general Canadian policy was to do everything possible to ensure that both the United States and the USSR would accept the charter and enter the new international organization.[27] The delegation was initially headed by Prime Minister King, who directed that Canada should not take a forthright role in the conference.[28] But King's mind was focused on the Canadian general election which he had called for 10 June, rather than on San Francisco; and that left effective direction of the Canadian delegation in the hands of Norman Robertson and his substantial External contingent.[29] By 15 May the politicians had departed. The Canadian delegation was anxious about the accumulating evidence of Soviet intransigence summarized in the Mayrand-Smith communiqués from Moscow and omnipresent in the newspaper headlines; but if anything the effect of their anxiety was to soften rather than stiffen the delegation's approach to the Soviet Union – the very opposite of Arnold Smith's advice. On key clauses of the charter such as the great power veto in the Security Council, the consequence of Canada's desire to bring the Soviet Union into the organization was to subject the Canadian delegation inexorably to Russian pressure. As Escott Reid wrote on 6 June 1945: 'Norman (Robertson) and I are pretty much on the same side. My view is that once we are convinced that the Soviet Union is not bluffing when they say such a provision is in (or not in) we have to give in to them. Otherwise we precipitate the formation of two rival alliances.'[30]

There was a division of opinion in the delegation over this question of tactics: Hume Wrong and at least one other diplomat were 'ready to contemplate the immediate formation of two alliance systems';[31] but under Robertson's direction the Canadians made the choice for conciliation rather than confrontation. With only minor exceptions, this was also the American choice at San Francisco. Escott Reid was impressed with the technical skill of the Soviet achievement, and wrote about the veto rule on 8 June:

While the conference may still have some hot arguments it is no longer possible that it will break down. The Russians have played their cards beautifully. Whether they planned it that way from the beginning, I don't know. They took an extreme position and then after precipitating a crisis retreated to something only a little less extreme. Now we are supposed to be (and in fact are) so grateful to them that we can do little but swallow under protest the old voting formula which is so repugnant.[32]

The Canadian diplomats left San Francisco in a state of despondency about the prospects for world peace. Dana Wilgress told Escott Reid in April that he 'feels he has misled the government by his prophecies about the moderate line which the USSR was likely to adopt after the war.'[33] Reid reflected that 'something big has to be done soon to stop the steadily increasing speed with which we are setting about to construct two rival heavily armed camps in the world.'[34] And Norman Robertson asked the delegation not to discuss the United Nations charter's weaknesses openly 'since the sole result would be to destroy the public's faith in the new organization.'[35] This advice, too, contradicted that of Arnold Smith from Moscow that public illusions about international co-operation should be dispelled by realistic discussion, in order to avoid later and greater disenchantment in the public mood.

During the San Francisco conference, John E. Read of External Affairs dispatched to Norman Robertson a memorandum on 'Recent Trends in Soviet Foreign Policy' written by Leo Malania.[36] Read wrote that the paper had not been revised or circulated for comment and 'could not, of course, be complete or definitive; but you will find it interesting and suggestive.' In notable contrast to the Smith memoranda, Malania's analysis offered an even-handed explanation for recent Soviet actions in Eastern Europe which, while not denying the 'drastic and ruthless' nature of Soviet interference in domestic affairs, sought to show that it varied according to national circumstances and was reasonable and tolerable.

While in Roumania, for example, the Soviets were roughly ejecting General Radescu, their own appointee, Finland under President Mannheim, long considered by the Soviet press as a symbol of Fascism, was preparing for democratic elections which took place a month later without any evidence of interference by Soviet occupation authorities. In Yugoslavia, while it is true that the Soviets gave considerable moral support to the partisan movement in its formative years, they were in no position to interfere directly until that movement had demonstrated that it enjoyed sufficient popular support to be described as indigenous.

The general conclusion might be attempted that direct Soviet interference in the internal affairs of its neighbours has been in direct proportion [he seems to mean inverse proportion] to the readiness of their governments to contribute' to the security of the Soviet Union by adopting a foreign policy which assured friendly collaboration with the U.S.S.R. and an internal policy which would provide the necessary basis for the continuance of such collaboration. The contrasts in Soviet policy provided by Poland and Czechoslovakia, Finland and Roumania appear to be striking illustrations of this broad generalization.

The Soviets, Malania argued, regarded the Anglo-Soviet treaty of 1942 as a key to the long-term provision of security in Europe; and they believed that it implied 'that each party would respect those European interests of its Ally which were vital to the security of the other partner. The Churchill-Stalin conversations in October 1944, resulted in an agreement with regard to Eastern Europe which appears to conform to this Soviet interpretation of the Anglo-Soviet Alliance.' (This was undoubtedly true.) 'The chief difficulty' in implementing the Yalta agreement over the reconstitution of the Polish government, Malania suggested, rested not in bad faith but rather in conflicting interpretations of the agreement which had recently, perhaps, been resolved.

Malania laid out the case in detail for a sympathetic understanding of the Soviet Union's admittedly arbitrary and unilateral acts in support of the Lublin government. In effect, he suggested that the government 'is attempting to perform a difficult task in difficult circumstances and not without a measure of success'; and that, in order to minimize the extent of direct interference in Poland, it was necessary for the Soviets to give full support and trust to a united domestic regime. While the disappearance of the Polish underground leaders remained disturbingly unexplained, and while the London Poles spoke of 'arrests, shootings and deportations,' the truth about these reports could not yet be discovered.

'Another factor which must be taken into account,' according to the paper, was Soviet apprehension that the United Kingdom and the United States were ganging up against it, 'that the coalition of three is turning into a coalition of two and one'; and that this might result in a Western effort to soften the peace terms against Germany.

It would probably be a mistake to attribute the Soviet apprehension over the close and intimate collaboration of the two Anglo-Saxon powers to mere childish petulance and wounded pride. The Soviets cannot but recall the pre-war isolationist trend in United States policy and the replacement of this trend by a kind of moral perfectionism especially where problems of Eastern Europe are concerned. The marked deference of the United Kingdom to the susceptibility of American public opinion must no doubt make the Soviet leaders wonder whether the United Kingdom can be counted upon to display the necessary firmness and resolution when the problem of the post-war treatment of Germany becomes a matter of practical policy. For this in Soviet eyes is the acid test by which the policy of foreign states is judged ... If this estimate of the Soviet position is correct, the problem of consolidating a security belt on the frontiers of the U.S.S.R. must appear as a first priority of Soviet policy, as an urgent task to be pushed ruthlessly, regardless of the feelings of friend or foe.

In the case of Romania, the paper made the startling suggestion that Britain had withheld intelligence information from Russia revealing a German network to sabotage Soviet military communications; that the existence of the network justified the Soviet-directed coup; that the Soviets 'either knew or suspected British Intelligence of being in possession of this information'; and that the Russians might therefore 'be tempted to place a rather sinister interpretation on both the United Kingdom's failure to disclose it to the Russians and on the diplomatic protests over Soviet action in forcing the resignation of Radescu.' This set of claims (which was dependent for its confirmation upon access to both British and Russian secret intelligence) was immediately balanced by a list of 'other instances of Soviet unco-operativeness.'

The paper, in conclusion, emphasized that while the Soviets were cold-blooded in pursuit of their strategic interests in the border states and Germany, they followed a policy of non-interference 'in the spheres of special interest to the Soviet Union's allies,' and desired to co-operate in creating the United Nations provided that they could safeguard their position in Eastern Europe. While Soviet policy had become 'non-aggressive, more self-reliant,' it was still too early to judge the prospects for continuing co-operation with the USSR in peacetime.

The paper did not go beyond this analysis, as Arnold Smith's did, to examine the appropriate Western tactics in dealing with the Soviet Union. But the argument suggests that this was a counter to the Moscow memoranda, and implies that the Western allies should accept the legitimacy of Russian policy in Eastern Europe and seek to maintain co-operation in other realms. The contrast with the current line from the Moscow embassy must have been noted by those who studied the document; but there is no indication in the files of reactions to it.[37]

On 18 May 1945 the Canadian Embassy in Moscow delivered an addendum to its long dispatch of 16 April noting that further events 'have persuaded us that we erred if anything on the side of understatement.'[38] The Polish government, in clear violation of the Yalta agreements, was assuming responsibility from the Russians for the administration of German territories in the north and west whose disposition was to be left to the peace conference; and the Yugoslavs, with apparent Russian support, had occupied former Italian areas in Istria, Trieste, and Venezia-Guilia which military agreements had also left for allocation to the peace settlement. Both cases had been the objects of protest by the British and American governments. For the Russians, the Trieste case in particular could be seen 'probably as a probe, to test out the strength of western reactions and therefore to provide pointers useful in guiding Soviet policies elsewhere.'[39]

From Washington, in June, T.A. Stone of the Canadian Embassy reported that he had exchanged various papers on Russia with Jock Balfour of the British Embassy (who had been recently transferred from Moscow). Balfour was especially interested in the Smith memoranda, which he described as 'excellent jobs of work ... in line with his own views.'[40] 'Balfour has a great admiration for Smith's ability. He told me that at first he was a little concerned that Smith was too starry-eyed about the great Russian experiment to observe it entirely objectively. He thinks that these memoranda now bear out the conclusion which he himself had reached before leaving Moscow, that Smith had found his feet and that he was standing on them firmly.'

Following the King government's comfortable victory in the general election of 10 June, John Read sent the Mayrand-Smith papers to Prime Minister King for a second time on 20 June, noting that: 'It is possible that you may not have had time to read the despatch and memoranda as they are very long. It may be helpful to bring to your attention the summary and comments which have been prepared by Mr. Malania.'[41] Malania's comments constituted, in fact, a new and spirited challenge to the line of argument put forward by Arnold Smith. If Smith's object in arguing for the creation of a Western bloc was, as he said, to induce the Soviet Union to integrate its economy and policies with those of the West, Malania responded that Smith should consider the likely Soviet reaction.

This policy would in effect confront the Soviet Union, a Socialist state, by a bloc of 'western', i.e. capitalist powers ... Smith does not discuss the probable reaction of Soviet leaders to this policy of pressure and encirclement, but it is difficult to see how it would fail to arouse those very suspicions, which the western powers have been attempting to allay, and which have resulted in the Soviet Union taking unilateral action to forestall the sort of encirclement which is here envisaged.

Malania wrote that in his discussion of Soviet diplomatic techniques, Smith 'lists a series of incidents all showing that the Soviets can employ, though perhaps not too smoothly, such time-honoured diplomatic devices as ambiguity, procrastination, evasion, and even prevarication, and goes on to advance the thesis that the United Kingdom and the United States have hitherto pursued the policy of "turning the other cheek" to Soviet rudeness.' But this softness applied 'only on the procedural level'; on the level of high policy, the Western Allies had failed to come to terms with the Soviet Union on virtually all the significant problems of European frontiers and governments, as the Soviet Union had wished. That failure was the source of Soviet mistrust.

This attitude aroused the strong suspicion that the United Kingdom expected the Soviet Union to be so weakened by the war, that the latter would willy-nilly have to accept the verdict of the other powers on matters of first importance to Soviet security. It was this suspicion which underlay the second front agitation, as well as the Soviet decision to proceed, in the absence of agreements with the United Kingdom, to make as many unilateral decisions as possible in order to have a strong bargaining position at the final settlement. The efforts of the United Kingdom to associate the United States with its policy in Eastern Europe and Iran merely strengthened Soviet suspicions. Instead of lessening these suspicions, the end of the war with its attendant confusion in Germany has intensified them.

Moscow had as much reason to suspect London and Washington as they had to suspect her.

Malania deprecated Smith's proposal for a 'tough' line towards the Soviet Union by suggesting that neither Europeans nor Americans would be prepared to support their governments in such a risky policy. 'The recent statements by Mr. Grew and by a group of the State Department's heads of divisions, as well as President Truman's actions in seeking to improve relations with the U.S.S.R., indicate that it is futile to seek a solution of European problems by organizing pressure blocs.' Not 'toughness,' but only 'persistent effort to face troublesome problems and to solve them before they have become explosive issues' was called for; and in all situations 'the limits of our effective intervention should be clearly recognized.'

Like previous papers by Leo Malania, this was an articulate presentation of the case from the Soviet perspective. Malania's claim was that the Soviet Union was justified in taking all the material steps it could to enhance its strategic advantage and bargaining strength, while Britain and the United States were not justified in doing the same where they could do so. To the imperfect extent that it was expressed in the memorandum, Malania's case for this imbalance seemed to be that the Soviet sense of insecurity was justifiably greater than that of other states, and could only be overcome by conceding to the Soviet Union's essential claims. This had been the view of President Roosevelt in 1943 and of Dana Wilgress in 1944; but now that the security zone of the Soviet Union had been established by force of arms, it was perhaps an anachronism to continue discussing Western diplomatic approaches in such terms. Malania did not confront Smith's central argument, which concerned Soviet acts rather than feelings: that a persistent display of Western determination to hold all its material advantage in bargaining with the Soviet Union, and to trade concessions only in return for concessions, would moderate the claims of a power that Smith (like Malania) considered to be fundamentally cautious in its foreign policy. Malania conveyed the strong impression in this paper that he was attempting to discredit Smith's reliability as a judge of Soviet foreign policy. That tendentious edge is also reflected in further glosses on Moscow dispatches prepared in July and August 1945 by Malania for circulation within the department.[42]

The conflict of views was in a sense academic. Since the Canadian government's general position was to fall in with American policy, there was apparently no pressing need for (and some risk in) Canada alone coming to a decision about tactics in dealing with the Soviet Union. The debate within the Department of External Affairs therefore remained inconclusive. Prime Minister King may have shared the anxiety of his External advisers about the prospects for peace in the early summer of 1945, but he did not reveal it, even to his diary. The Canadian delegation had made a quiet impression of technical competence at San Francisco, especially upon the Americans; the war was at an end in Europe and almost at an end in Asia; the Big Three were engaged in their last wartime meeting at Potsdam in July; and at home Mackenzie King had his new parliamentary majority. Summer 1945 was, for the first time in seven years, one in which Ottawa could relax into oblivion.

The United States and the Soviet Union emerged from the Second World War as dominant powers. The military and economic foundations for this dominance had been established in four years of conflict; the realization of it came after the German capitulation in May 1945. The impact of victory, and the occasion for reflection that it provided, stimulated both Americans and Russians to exuberant expressions of pride and the sense of power. Two British diplomatic dispatches, from Moscow and Washington (both passed on to the Canadians), described the remarkable parallels in Soviet and American self-assessment in victory.[43] Sir Alexander Clark Kerr wrote from Moscow of 'military exuberance,' 'confidence ... without measure,' a Soviet Union 'teeming with vitality and bent upon making her influence felt, even far from her frontier ... indifferent to arguments about the unwisdom of stirring up fresh troubles in a troubled world.' Russia was 'rejoicing in all the emotions and impulsions of very early manhood that spring from a new sense of boundless strength and from the giddiness of success. It is immense fun to her to tell herself that she has become great and that there is little or nothing to stop her making her greatness felt. Why resist therefore the temptation to put a finger into every pie? Why be patient of correction?'

From Washington, Jock Balfour wrote similarly of the United States, 'endowed with colossal productive and fighting capacity,' 'the amphibious Leviathan of modern times,' inspired with 'the liveliest satisfaction and patriotic pride,' perceiving its interests for the first time in global perspective. Each state saw the other as the only significant competitor; each recognized certain ill-defined boundaries between their two spheres of interest where power gave them the right of intervention and definition; neither regarded the interests of third powers as significant except as those interests affected their own. Outside the Russian orbit, the United States felt no uncertainty about the use of its power. 'Here a blend of idealism, hard business instinct, and motives of security is propelling the United States to a greater extent than ever before into international fields far beyond the limits traced by the time-honoured Monroe Doctrine and notions of hemispheric defence.'

From the wartime conception of the Grand Design, involving the 'coequal collaboration' of the United States, the Soviet Union, and Britain, both powers now saw 'a world that rotates into two orbits of power.' For the United States, 'Great Britain, whilst occupying a highly important position as the bastion of Western European security and as the focal point of a far-flung oceanic system, will nevertheless be expected to take her place as a junior partner in an orbit of power predominantly under American aegis.' For the Soviet Union, dealings with the United Kingdom were shifting from the great power relationship of the Anglo-Soviet treaty to a phase in which the British connection would be manipulated, when possible, to encourage friction and misunderstanding between the two English-speaking nations.

For the short term, however, peace in Europe and the signing of the United Nations charter at the end of June brought a relaxation of tension on both sides – sought, apparently, to allow some soothing of frayed nerves. Administrative arrangements for the occupation regimes in Germany and Austria were established; and the Potsdam conference passed in relative concord with the creation of a three-power Council of Foreign Ministers to continue discussion of the peace settlement. Potsdam, too, marked the Soviets' face-to-face introduction to new Western leadership: Harry Truman and his secretary of state, James F. Byrnes (who had replaced Edward Stettinius after San Francisco); Prime Minister Clement Attlee and his secretary of state for foreign affairs, Ernest C. Bevin (who replaced Churchill and Eden following the British general election midway through the conference).

Two events – one public, one private, both profoundly discomforting – brought Canada temporarily to the centre of high politics during the summer and autumn of 1945. On 6 August United States dropped the atomic bomb on the Japanese city of Hiroshima, and three days later a second bomb on Nagasaki. As a confidential partner with the United Kingdom and the United States in the 'Tube Alloys' project, Canada had supplied the uranium fuel for the bomb, sat on the Combined Policy

Committee which co-ordinated the development, and provided sites, in the Montreal and Petawawa laboratories of the National Research Council, for the work of the British scientific teams engaged in atomic research.[44] Mackenzie King had four initial reactions, three political and one personal, to Hiroshima. He wrote in his diary for 6 August that the bomb was a 'great achievement in secrecy – a tremendous secret to have kept over four years. It shows what control by a government of publicity can effect.' He reflected callously on the target of the attack: 'It is fortunate that the use of the bomb should have been upon the Japanese rather than upon the white races of Europe.' He speculated on the possible reaction of the Russians: 'I am a little concerned about how Russia may feel, not having been told anything of this invention or of what the British & the U.S. were doing in the way of exploring & perfecting the process.' (Truman had in fact told Stalin of the weapon at Potsdam ten days earlier, and Stalin had received the news with outward calm.) And finally, King made one of his more distasteful allusions to providential coincidence, noting 'the number of great events today,' which had included his own re-election to the House of Commons in the Glengarry by-election – as well as the extinction of eighty thousand residents of Hiroshima.[45]

More considered reactions to the bomb were supplied to the prime minister by the associate under-secretary of state for external affairs, Hume Wrong, in a memo on 18 August 1945.[46] He thought that a declaration of government policy on atomic weapons would be necessary, since 'the successful development of the bomb is of such far-reaching importance that it may profoundly affect international affairs even to the point of altering the whole balance of international forces overnight.' Both Churchill and Truman had 'taken the view that the secret should be kept by those who now hold it at least for the time being. There will doubtless be strong pressure, especially from the Soviet Union, for detailed information. (I understand that the Soviet Government has already requested us to provide them with 50 tons of uranium.)' Some kind of control of the weapon would be necessary, but the United Nations Security Council, with the great power veto, would be unlikely to provide it. The political problems were bound to proliferate.

It seems too soon to estimate with any certainty the effects of the bomb on our own defence planning with relation to the size and disposition of our post-war forces. There is even a possibility that the discovery will heighten tension between the great powers rather than reduce it. Furthermore, jealous eyes may be turned towards the sources of the essential ingredient and we may feel compelled to take special measures to protect these sources within Canada. We may also find that our part in the development will lead for the first time to a serious effort to plant foreign agents in Canada with the object of securing information on secret processes.

(Leon Mayrand had offered a similar, prophetic comment in his dispatch of 3 August from Moscow, noting that one of the roles of western Communist parties 'is presumably espionage.' According to the US Embassy, the American Communist party 'appears to be making a determined effort to organize technical espionage in the United States Navy.')[47] These warnings made no particular impact – for a few weeks.

The second event, King wrote, fell 'like a bomb on top of everything else' on 6 September, the opening day of the new Canadian parliamentary session. It was a time bomb. Just half an hour after the event, Norman Robertson and Hume Wrong met the prime minister urgently to tell him 'that a most terrible thing had happened': a man and his wife, apparently from the Russian Embassy, had come to the office of the minister of justice offering to turn over documents he was carrying which 'would be seen to disclose that Russia had her spies and secret service people in Canada and in the U.S. and were practising a species of espionage ... he said that he had enough evidence there to prove that instead of being friends, the Russians were really enemies.[48] Robertson and Wrong sought the prime minister's advice about how to deal with the affair: King preferred to leave it altogether alone.

I said ... that I thought we should be extremely careful in becoming a party to any course of action which would link the government of Canada up with this matter in a manner which might cause Russia to feel that we had performed an unfriendly act. That to seek to gather information in any underhand way would make clear that we did not trust the Embassy ...

Robertson seemed to feel that the information might be so important both to the States and to ourselves and to Britain that it would be in their best interests for us to seize it no matter how it was obtained. He did not say this but asked my opinion. I was strongly against any step of the kind as certain to create an issue between Russia and Canada, this leading to severance of diplomatic relations and as Robertson pointed out, might have consequences on the meeting of the Council of Foreign Ministers which might lead even to the breaking up of that organization.[49]

While King temporized, the desperate man was left to wander the streets, and eventually to return to his home, fearing kidnapping by the Soviets and threatening suicide. The prime minister suggested that a plain clothes police watch might be mounted on the apartment: 'If suicide took place let the city police take charge and this man to follow in and secure what there was in the way of documents, but on no account for us to take the initiative ... Both St. Laurent and I felt that no matter what happened we should not let it be assumed that the Government of Canada had itself sought to spy on the Embassy or to take advantage of a situation of the kind to find out something against a trusted ally.'[50]

By morning, following a break-in at the apartment by four members of the Soviet Embassy staff and the involvement of the Royal Canadian Mounted Police, Igor Gouzenko, a cipher clerk in Soviet military intelligence, was in secret custody under RCMP protection offering his evidence of Russian espionage to the police. The previous evening Robertson had sought the advice of William Stephenson, the Canadian head of British Security Co-ordination in New York, who urged that Gouzenko should be taken into protective custody; now, more by inadvertence than planning, that had occurred.[51] Over the next two days Robertson reported to King the alarming news that Gouzenko had turned over abundant evidence of Soviet spy networks in Canada and the United States, reaching into External Affairs, the British High Commission, the State Department, and the atomic research laboratories of the National Research Council. He had also said that at the Russian Embassy 'there was the freest talk among themselves about the next war.'[52]

King and Robertson were alarmed – panic-stricken might be more precise – that if the Soviets discovered this information was in Canadian hands the entire framework of Western co-operation with the Soviet Union might be pulled down. Robertson told King once again 'that what we had discovered might affect the whole meeting of the Council of Foreign Ministers; that if publicity were given to this it might necessarily lead to a break in diplomatic relations between Canada and Russia and might also lead to that in regard to other nations as well, the U.S. and the U.K. All this might occasion a complete break-up of the relations that we have been counting upon to make the peace. There was no saying to what terrible lengths this whole thing might go.'[53]

Robertson's initial suggestion that he should visit the Soviet ambassador to confront him with what had occurred was quickly dropped. Instead the British high commissioner, Malcolm MacDonald, was informed and advised to convey the information to the foreign secretary, and through him to the American secretary of state, James F. Byrnes. British Security Co-ordination provided a safe communications network to London via New York (since Gouzenko's evidence suggested that the links through External Affairs and the British High Commission were both compromised), and William Stephenson returned quickly to Ottawa with officers of the FBI and the British secret intelligence service (MI6) to assist in Gouzenko's interrogation. They in turn made their reports to Washington and London.[54] But beyond taking information from Gouzenko, confidentially briefing the two Allies, directly engaging their counter-intelligence agencies, and placing those implicated under RCMP surveillance, the whole effort of King and Robertson was directed at smothering the affair in silence: 'Robertson and I both agreed that great caution must be used from now on in the matter of avoiding any kind of publicity, hoping that matters can be straightened out without the public ever becoming aware of what had taken place.'[55] To co-ordinate planning and diffuse responsibility, King asked Robertson to chair a consultative committee made up of Robertson, Wrong, two RCMP counter-intelligence officers, and the British high commissioner and his deputy; this committee met daily for the next few weeks to reflect on Gouzenko's revelations as the documents were translated one by one.[56]

There was one awkward and dangerous possibility, however, which seemed to require additional precautions. One of Gouzenko's reported agents, the British physicist Dr Alan Nunn May, was about to return to England after three years at the NRC's atomic research laboratory in Montreal. He was 'almost second in the knowledge pertaining to the atomic bomb, and ... knows practically all that has been done in Canada and the United States ... if he got away to Moscow he would be able to inform the authorities there of everything within his knowledge.'

The question was what should be done with him. Robertson strongly advised the passing of a special Order in Council very secretly which would re-enact certain clauses of the Defence of Canada Regulations, so far as May was personally concerned, which would enable us to have him watched by the police and if necessary arrest him; also to see that he did not get away with papers, etc. To this I agreed and signed the recommendation to Council which was to get the signatures of four Ministers: Ilsley, Howe, Abbott and myself – only enough to be told the others to justify their signing. Nothing to be said to the rest of the Cabinet. The order to be kept in the vault of the Clerk of the Council. I immediately signed the recommendation which was subsequently signed by other Ministers.[57]

Since May could be legally detained in Canada, but not in the United Kingdom for offences committed in another country, King's advisory committee agreed that May and the other suspects would have to be arrested before the date of May's departure for London. That plan was aborted when the Gouzenko documents revealed the instructions for May's covert meetings with a Soviet controller in London in October. The British security service (MI5) suggested that the rendezvous should be allowed to take place so that the new controller could be identified and watched, as a possible means of making 'a vital break into a Russian spy ring in Britain'; so all action was delayed, and May was allowed to return to England where he was kept under close watch by MI5 and identified in secret communications by the code-name 'Primrose.'[58]

At an early point in the affair, the Soviets learned from their British agents that Gouzenko and his documents were in Canadian custody. Peter Dwyer reported to the director-general of MI6, Sir Peter Menzies, who asked his director of Soviet counter-intelligence, H.A.R. Philby, to fly to Ottawa to question Gouzenko further. Philby was preoccupied with protecting his own cover as a Soviet agent, which was coincidentally threatened by another potential Russian defection in Turkey. After consulting his KGB controller, Philby suggested instead that Roger Hollis, the director of Communist counter-intelligence for MI6's companion agency, MI5, should be sent to Ottawa. Hollis came, and participated in the continuing joint discussions on the disposition of the spy case. At this time, in September 1945, he apparently did not see Gouzenko.[59]

Hollis later became director-general of MI5, and his direct role in the Gouzenko investigations appears in retrospect to have been one of the most significant elements in the entire enquiry. One of Gouzenko's key assertions was that he had seen evidence, as a cipher clerk in Soviet military intelligence headquarters in Moscow in 1942, that there was a GRU agent, code-named 'Elli,' at a high level in MI5. Even more than the evidence about Alan Nunn May and the source in the British High Commission, this suggestion had ominous implications for both Britain and the Soviet Union. Confirmation of the claim, and discovery of the Soviet penetration agent, would have shut off a central source of Russian intelligence, and might have led to the early exposure of other GRU espionage operations in the United Kingdom. However, the lead was not followed, and Gouzenko's references to the MI5 agent 'Elli' were suppressed in all public discussion of the case for thirty-five years after 1946. Subsequent investigation points to the possibility that Roger Hollis

was 'Elli,' who, like Philby at the same time, was in that event able to take
the lead in smothering the evidence against himself. When Hollis finally
interviewed Gouzenko briefly in 1946, Gouzenko was left with the
impression that the British had no interest in pursuing his claim – an
impression that seemed correct.[60]

The whole affair had acquired a cover: it was now being referred to as the
'Corby' case, in honour of the Corby's whisky carton in which Norman
Robertson was hiding the files. As the revelations worked away at
Mackenzie King's preoccupied mind over the next two weeks, he
repeatedly connected the existence of Soviet spy networks with a vast
Russian plan to conquer the world in a new and terrible war: a conclusion
based on Gouzenko's assertion and a flimsy construction of suppositions.
In the small circle with whom King shared his secret, he talked of this
danger and considered how the spy case should be treated on that
assumption. The ultra-cautious Canadian did not wish to be remembered
for bringing on the apocalypse. By 23 September, in a meeting of his
advisory committee at the British High Commission, King had come to the
view that a private and joint approach to the Soviets at the highest level was
the choice of prudence.

The first question discussed was the alternative method re security; one was to
allow everything to be hushed up and not proceeded further; another was to take
action at once and let the British and U.S. governments know the situation with a
view to taking what steps might be best to prevent further developments. The third
was adopting a course which would make the whole thing public, immediate
arrests made and getting additional information at trials, etc. My own view was
that the second course was the appropriate one, and I found that that was the view
that appeared to be generally held. It was discussed in relation to the larger
question of what was wisest from the diplomatic and political points of view. We
all agreed that it would not do to let the matter pass as though it were something
which should not be disclosed to the Russians, nor would it do to have publicity
given to the whole business at this time. That the best course would be to have the
British and United States Governments and ourselves work together on the highest
level, and let the Russians know what we know with a view to discovering from
them whether they intended to really try to be friends and work for a peaceful world
or whether a course should be taken toward them which would lead to having all
nations against them.[61]

Since the unwelcome burden had been thrust upon him, King now reassured himself that a higher purpose must be involved. On 11 September he recorded in his diary: 'I cannot believe that this information has come to me as a matter of chance. I can only pray for God's guidance that I may be able to be an instrument in the control of powers beyond to help save a desperate situation, to maintain peace now that it has at least been nominally established.'[62] On 24 September he wrote: 'It is strange how this business should have come right into my room in the East Block on the morning of the Opening of the 20th Parliament. I can see that from now until the end of my days, it will be with this problem more than with any other that, in all probability, I shall be mostly concerned.'[63] On 26 September he added: 'I had a feeling when the whole matter came upon us at the start that perhaps this was the big mission that I may have after all to perform. To use the judgment that may be necessary to help to avoid a break which might lead to another war very shortly, and to find some better means of coping with the situation. That is where we stand tonight.'[64]

So King and Robertson, both weary from the unrelieved strain of years of war, decided to travel together to Washington and London to seek the advice of Canada's Allies in the Soviet espionage affair. What made the trip urgent was that the British were now impatient to arrest Nunn May at once, and assumed that the Canadian and American governments, too, would begin criminal actions at the same time. King still feared anything precipitate.

The message indicated that H.M.G. was prepared to meet whatever situation might arise out of these arrests. Robertson had talked this over with me and I agreed with him this was not the course to pursue. We must move very slowly and cautiously. We were not ready in Canada to take proceedings and our leading advisers up to the present say it would be very difficult to get a conviction on material we have considering its source, etc. We agreed the course to be taken should be on the top level. That Attlee, Truman and myself should agree on the course to be taken.[65]

Two messages went off to London calling for delay; and on Saturday, 29 September, King and Robertson flew to Washington with the first purpose of engaging the Americans in a common front against the British desire for immediate action.

When Norman Robertson and the Canadian ambassador, Lester Pearson, met the acting secretary of state, Dean Acheson, that evening they were relieved to learn that he shared the Canadian conviction and would convey the American request for delay to the United Kingdom the next day. 'Dean thinks,' Pearson wrote to Hume Wrong, 'that you people are handling this matter with coolness and intelligence and compared you favourably in this regard with London.'[66]

On Sunday morning, 30 September, Prime Minister King met President Truman and Acheson for two hours in the Oval Office of the White House, reading extracts to them from the police reports gathered from Gouzenko which Robertson had provided in a green folder. King was pleased that Truman came spontaneously to his own cautious conclusion:

While proceeding with the discussion and speaking of our view of being careful not to disclose anything until the situation had been worked out, the President of his own volition said he felt every care must be taken to get full information before anything at all was disclosed ... The President also volunteered the statement that he thought the matter should be discussed between Attlee, himself and myself. That we should all be agreed on the course that was to be taken. Two or three times he repeated his view that nothing should be done without agreement between the three and above all nothing should be done which might result in premature action in any direction.[67]

Truman was proving to be a man after King's own heart. By now, the prime minister had refined the outlines of a scheme which might allow him to fulfil his providential mission, and he proceeded to explain it to the president. He claimed that he had played a crucial mediating role for Theodore Roosevelt over Japanese immigration to the United States in 1908, and said: 'I thought there was a possibility if the Russians were confronted in a similar way with known facts that it might be a means of meeting the situation.'[68] (This seemed to imply that King should be the spokesman for the three leaders in confronting Stalin.) King's plan involved a master-stroke of stupendous naivety:

I thought we should relate the information we have to the question of the veto on the Security Council of the U.N. organization. If at all possible, we should get the Russians to realize there must be confidence all in all or not at all and that their insistence on agreement on the part of the Great Powers to any action or use of force, was creating suspicion in itself. That they should be willing to do in the matter of the action to be taken, what the other four Great Powers were prepared to do. One must know the kind of a world we wanted to live in and be assured they were prepared to help to co-operate in furthering a similar kind of world.[69]

King does not record Truman's response to this extraordinary suggestion. It must have provoked some surprise in Truman and Acheson, since it suggested that King did not know that Britain and the United States were also determined advocates of the veto power, and that Stalin – once confronted face-to-face – would admit and atone for the foolish mistakes he had made in achieving the veto and engaging the Soviet Union in espionage. Truman's kindest response would have been silence; what King reported was that the president 'said something about Attlee coming out to have a talk with him.'[70]

Immediately afterwards King went to the British Embassy to inform the ambassador, Lord Halifax, of his meeting with Truman and to renew the call for caution. Halifax told King that he agreed. The prime minister, now in full flight, repeated his proposal for a deal with the Soviets – with, he thought, a somewhat more positive response.

I spoke to him about my view as to using this evidence to help secure a removal of the right of the Russians to veto any course of action which implied use of force against one of the Great Five. Said it seemed to me that they could have to do something which would let us see that they merited our confidence. This espionage system had shaken that completely especially when it was carried on during the years that we were fighting together as allies and seemed to be intensified now up to the end of the present year. Halifax seemed interested in this point of view. He agreed the secret of the atomic bomb would probably become known to the Russians. I pointed out it would have to be shared. I said I thought it would have to be shared ultimately and all of it might as well be made part of one piece. Halifax expressed a real interest in what I had suggested. Evidently he had not been thinking on those lines.[71]

The package of mutual concessions King proposed to carry to Moscow was gaining weight: it now contained the secret of the atomic bomb as well. The third man in the room for this interview was the counsellor of the embassy, Donald Maclean, whose 1951 defection revealed him as a long-time Soviet agent.[72] Moscow's information on the joint response to Gouzenko – particularly the facts of Canadian and American hesitation to act, and King's desire to dispose of the affair in a heart-to-heart chat with Stalin – was thus further filled out from another source. Here was renewed evidence for the Soviet leader of Western confusion and lack of resolution, and added reassurance that even so potentially damaging a lapse could be played out to Russian advantage.

Set against the prime minister's messianic scheme were Mackenzie King's fears of war, which Dean Acheson helped to confirm as the two drove from the White House to the Canadian Embassy. In pressing for immediate arrests, Acheson felt, the British were acting out of impatience with the Russians 'and were prepared to take any chance.'

That was all very well so far as Britain was concerned but that we were in the Western Hemisphere and we had to consider our position. He felt that the United States and Canada would be more immediately affected by consequences of any action which severed relations with Russia, than even the U.K. He thought the position we had taken was the only sound one. He spoke about the possibility of war and certainly if war came of it coming on this continent with Canada as the battleground. I agreed that would be inevitable; this continent would be the one in which war would take place.[73]

Acheson went on to say that this danger made desirable the standardization of military equipment between Canada and the United States – a remark which was anything but casual.[74] (It is just possible that Acheson's mention of war was a dramatic means of raising the subject of military equipment, rather than a disinterested comment about the international situation.) According to King's report, Acheson 'did not say he believed war itself was inevitable.' Given the prime minister's state of mind, however, that probably reinforced King's sense of the potential significance of his mission of salvation. That evening King and Robertson, 'thoroughly exhausted, and looking forward to a leisurely voyage,' travelled to New York for embarkation the next day on the *Queen Mary*.

During King's sea voyage the British government again indicated to Ottawa its desire to arrest Nunn May. On 6 October 1945, as a result, Louis St Laurent, as acting prime minister, arranged for the adoption of a second secret order-in-council giving the Canadian government power to detain and interrogate suspected foreign agents without the normal guarantees of civil liberty under the common law.[75] The measure was apparently intended to prevent publicity and to give the authorities unusual means of gathering evidence sufficient to allow the laying of charges. When King and Robertson reached Southampton on 7 October, they were met by Roger Hollis of MI5, who conveyed a dual message: the Foreign Office requested approval for Alan Nunn May's arrest that night, when he was due (according to Gouzenko's evidence) to rendezvous with a Soviet contact outside the British Museum; but a telegram from Washington renewed

President Truman's pressure for delay to allow for further investigation. King reiterated his own desire, which was identical with Truman's, for joint action and no precipitate arrest unless it were absolutely necessary for reasons of security. When May failed to appear as scheduled that night (or on two subsequent occasions), the joint pressure for delay prevailed once more.[76]

During four weeks in London, King's sense of alarm over the spy affair was gradually calmed, and his purposes redirected, by the subtle diplomatic ministrations of the British – who may not always have spoken with a single voice.[77] In a series of meetings at Chequers and Downing Street, Prime Minister Attlee raised King's sights from Gouzenko to the larger strategic question of controlling atomic weapons (which was Attlee's current preoccupation), and engaged King's vanity in his proposal for an early meeting in Washington among Truman, Attlee, and King on this and other questions. The subject of the atomic bomb would not only provide an appropriate cover for further conversations on Soviet espionage, but might also give the spy case the proportion that came more naturally to Attlee than to King. While King worried that the British had not thought through the implications of treating the spy affair as a relatively minor and discrete matter, he recorded Attlee's comments on 11 October that: 'this could not be a matter of surprise to the Russians. As a matter of fact, they would come back with the reply that Britain herself had her spies. Was getting all the information she could about Russia. Russia also would say she had not kept her promise as an ally in not letting Russia know that she was developing the atomic bomb and had found the secret.'[78]

When the Canadian prime minister propounded his theory to Ernest Bevin that the recent meeting in London of the Council of Foreign Ministers had perhaps collapsed because the Russians had learned in the course of it of Western possession of Gouzenko's evidence, Bevin dismissed the thought firmly and completely. He was sure that there were larger influences at work.[79]

In the meantime a new anxiety – peculiarly political and bizarre – gripped Mackenzie King in his contemplation of relations with the Soviet Union. He related his worries confidentially to Bevin:

I then said that once the statement were publicly made, the motive would be misinterpreted and it would be said that I was trying to further annexation views but it was this. That I was certain that unless we secured in some satisfactory way the relations with Russia – in a manner which would remove fear, our own people in British Columbia and on the Prairies, Alta., Saskatchewan, etc., would all become very strong for looking to the U.S. for the protection that we needed. That this would inevitably lead to annexation movement which it might be hard to control.[80]

All the more need to confront the Russians privately with the evidence, in pursuit of a general understanding.

On 21 October Attlee again raised the question of May's immediate arrest, noting that

their intelligence officials were feeling that they ought to disassociate him from the work that he is doing in connection with atomic energy and that if there was a much longer delay, the whole business would be getting cold and blame might attach for not having taken some immediate action. They proposed as what they would like to do, to examine him privately under some military protectionist measure – I have forgotten the name of it, not with a view to publicity being given but simply to bring out information which would be helpful in discussing the matter later with the Russians.[81]

King favoured this course, but in ignorance or forgetfulness of the Canadian order-in-council, doubted that Canada 'had the same authority at law for examining individuals on the score of suspicion.'[82] He would nevertheless inform President Truman that both the United Kingdom and Canada hoped to question suspects secretly 'to verify ... the information we already have so that this might be available before the conference at Washington.'[83]

Norman Robertson, however, was even more cautious than Mackenzie King; he warned against any action, and counselled that King should now inform the Canadian cabinet about the affair. King took these suggestions with ill grace, reflecting that Robertson was too inclined 'to get things into the hands of the permanent officials,' and that 'I would have to take the decisions myself ... I do not propose to yield my own judgment to any man living.'[84] He directed Robertson to prepare telegrams for Truman and St Laurent concerning the intention to question suspects at once. Robertson nevertheless managed to convince King the next day, with the support of British intelligence (that is, on the probable advice of Roger Hollis), that if eighteen persons were questioned in Ottawa there was bound to be publicity, and that the wise course therefore was to delay any action until after meeting Truman. The discussion had come full circle. 'This has been our view from the start but Attlee had represented on Sunday night that MI5 ... were anxious to apprehend criminals at once and had asked if we could not proceed at once.'[85] King felt at ease again with the renewed agreement on inaction: 'I am sure the course of caution, secrecy, etc., is the right one. Direct approach to the Russians is the right thing.'[86]

By late October the extended interlude in London (which included most of a week in sittings for a portrait by Frank Salisbury) had become the kind of relaxing change that King had hoped for. The strangest event of the visit took place on 31 October, when King accepted an invitation from the Russian ambassador, Feodor Gousev, to lunch at the Soviet Embassy. King knew Gousev, as the first Russian minister in Ottawa in 1942–43; he was also identified by British Security as the director of KGB operations in the United Kingdom, and would thus have been briefed about Gouzenko's defection and carefully instructed for the occasion.[87] Whether King knew that is unclear; but he had received his own intelligence briefing and assumed that Gousev was aware of the defection. The conversation, as the prime minister recounted it in his diary, involved an elaborate dance of mutual deflection. Gousev both flattered and frightened King by suggesting that Canada 'had a good deal to do with the making of the atomic bomb; also Canada knew the secret.' King conceded that Canadian scientists had worked with the British and Americans on atomic research, but insisted with some fervour that Canada neither knew the secret nor was a partner in manufacturing the bomb. After this exchange King noticed 'a certain restraint in conversation.' 'I felt sure he knew about Primrose and he must have known that I did, too. From what he said, I could see that the Russians may come back on any disclosure we make, presenting the view that the bomb was really conceived in Canada and worked out there by scientists of Britain and the U.S. That this was done at Montreal. This will be the excuse they will make for having found it necessary to have espionage.'[88] But before his departure, King and Gousev exchanged warm words of personal and national friendship. Soothed by the course of this bibulous lunch ('I was careful not to do more than taste some of the wines that were served'), King's sense of alarm over the possibly catastrophic consequences of the spy affair seemed by now to have disappeared. If the Russians were treating it calmly, so, perhaps, could he.

Further conversations with the king and queen, Viscount Addison, Edward Stettinius, Field Marshal Montgomery, and Winston Churchill all fed King's ruminations on the nature of the Soviet challenge. Addison offered the opinion, in explanation of their behaviour, that 'we must remember that they are orientals' – a convenient image then coming into favour, which James Forrestal had used a month earlier in a meeting of the American cabinet.[89] Churchill emphasized his conviction that the Soviets, whom he described as 'hard realists,' '"realist lizards," all belonging to the crocodile family,' had to be confronted with absolute firmness.[90] When King revealed his information about the spy networks, Churchill showed no surprise. While urging careful preparation of a response, he argued that it should in the end be public: 'that the world ought to know where there was espionage and that the Russians would not mind that; they had been exposed time and again.'[91] Churchill had already passed the point of expecting friendly reconciliation with the Soviet Union; he believed that what mattered now was an Anglo-American alliance 'as one people against the rest of the world,' to which Mackenzie King's frustrated sense of mission might turn again in familiarity: 'He stressed this again when I was leaving, stating to me that my mission was to get that alliance between the U.K. and the U.S. He asked me if I had spoken to the Government here on those lines. I told him it was precisely the line I was emphasizing to everyone. He said you have the key position and you can do more than any other man toward bringing this about.'[92] Churchill also told King of his invitation to lecture in Missouri the following spring on world affairs – an invitation he was inclined to take up.

Less alarmed by espionage and superficially more worldly after a month's immersion in London, Mackenzie King prepared to sail for New York at the beginning of November in proud anticipation of his forthcoming meeting in Washington with Attlee and Truman. King's reflections on the president's Navy Day speech of 27 October, however, suggest that while the prime minister's anxiety had fallen, his intellectual muddle had, if anything, increased. Truman (he recorded with approval)

makes clear that the U.S. will not give up keeping up its power in the world. I like the emphasis which the President puts on Christian behaviour in the world ... All things ... are moving to the preparation of the world for a meeting in Washington of the President, Attlee and myself which will be taken by the world as most significant. I will go back from England ready to enter on a larger sphere of work than ever – a sphere of work which will identify me with this new age of atomic energy and world peace. It is the thing that I am sure is a part of the purpose of my life. All that I get from my own inner feeling through psychic sources, etc., stresses this very clearly.[93]

When the three heads of government and their advisers met in Washington from 10 to 15 November 1945, their preoccupation was the use and control of atomic energy. Various drafts of a statement prepared by the three delegations were examined, revised, and integrated, and on 15 November Truman, Attlee, and King signed and released a joint declaration on the international control of atomic energy.[94] The declaration asserted their concern that 'the new discoveries shall be used for the benefit of mankind, instead of as a means of destruction'; promised to share information on the industrial application of atomic power 'as soon as effective enforceable safeguards against its use for destructive purposes can be devised'; and proposed the creation of a United Nations commission to prepare recommendations on the elimination of atomic weapons, international inspection and control, and exchanges of atomic technology for peaceful purposes. As Lester Pearson recorded, the declaration meant that 'the world organization was being given a very severe test at the outset of its existence';[95] and that the Western powers had decided to use the issue of atomic energy as one prominent means of probing the co-operative intentions of the Soviet Union. The realists among Western diplomats had already forsaken the possibility of co-operation according to any optimistic liberal design; but the political leaders (and many of their advisers, especially in the United States) were not yet ready to do so. The declaration marked the beginning of an intensive effort, lasting fifteen months and doomed to failure, in which the Western powers tangled with the Soviets over mutually incompatible conceptions of their interests as reflected in their strategies of atomic development.

At some time during the discussions in London and Washington, a 'draft agreement on procedure for dealing with the "Corby" case' was prepared, consolidating the understandings that had apparently been reached during Mackenzie King's weeks of worried consultation.[96] It is not clear whether this agreement was actually consummated in Washington. But the document's proposals for dealing with Gouzenko's evidence are consistent with all that had gone before. There were, it said, four 'controlling considerations' in the case:

(a) The practices of the Soviet Embassy in Ottawa, which undoubtedly are followed also in the United States and United Kingdom, are not to be tolerated.
(b) While the case should be handled firmly, it should be dealt with, nevertheless, so as to disturb as little as possible the continuance of normal diplomatic relations with the U.S.S.R.

(c) The case provides an opportunity for exposing the uses to which the Soviet Government puts local Communist elements, and one objective should be to make it as difficult as possible for them to continue (or, in Canada, to reconstruct) their network based largely on these elements.

(d) It should, however, be so handled as to give the least possible substance to charges that our action has been taken for ideological reasons.

The nature of 'appropriate police action' to be taken in Canada, with 'supporting action' in the United States and United Kingdom, was defined: 'In the first place, it should consist of the interrogation of agents, accompanied when legal power exists and this course is considered desirable, by temporary detention. In all cases in which enough evidence is discovered, prosecution should be instituted. In Canada, the police interrogation may be followed by an investigation by a judge, acting as a Royal Commissioner and authorized to sit in camera.' An annex described 'the position in the United Kingdom,' where there was no power, as in Canada, to detain persons for secret interrogation without charge. Nunn May would 'therefore have to be questioned without being detained.' The annex warned that, since 'the greater part' of the existing evidence was Gouzenko's, without documentary or first-hand proof, 'the authorities are not very sanguine of obtaining a confession from Primrose on which it will be possible to bring a charge against him.'

Canadian diplomatic action was to begin at the commencement of police action, and was to be limited to requesting the departure from Canada of those diplomats 'directly implicated in espionage,' with a short explanation of the reasons. The recall of the Russian ambassador was not to be requested. Publicity in the case 'should be guided and controlled as far as possible,' initially in a public statement by Prime Minister King. The Canadian prime minister's proposal for confronting Stalin in a session of all-or-nothing bargaining was reflected only in pale and uncertain shadows: 'It is for consideration whether action against agents should be accompanied by the despatch of a message to Marshal Stalin from Mr. Mackenzie King.'

The draft concluded by setting a date for co-ordinated action 'in the course of the week beginning November 25th.' For some reason this did not occur: it seems, instead, that King and Robertson reverted to a stance of complete passivity. King told his cabinet in February 1946 that 'we had waited to give the U.S. an opportunity to follow up the revelations that they had received'; but he also said that 'I had hoped, and had said so to the

President and Bevin, that we might find a way of communicating the facts to the Russian government itself without disclosing them in court, giving the government a chance to clear up the situation itself.'[97] Following his lunch with Ambassador Gousev in London, King seemed satisfied that the Soviets knew from their own sources that Gouzenko had defected with his evidence; since they were prepared to maintain a cordial façade, the issue could perhaps be allowed to fade away. For King the quietist that would be the safest way.

In a memo to the president of 22 December 1945, Dean Acheson indicated that the initiative now lay with Canada: 'I had a talk with the Canadian Ambassador and told him that we no longer requested delay in any action which the Canadian Government might think desirable or necessary. The Ambassador communicated this to Ottawa and informed me that his Government was not contemplating any immediate action but would inform us prior to any which might be taken.'[98]

These were months of continuing confusion in official Western attitudes to the Soviet Union. The spy case was caught up in this atmosphere of indecision, a Soviet provocation which, like others, the three nations could not easily decide how to confront. For Mackenzie King the case was the primary symbol of Soviet treachery; for Truman and Attlee it was one among many signs (and not the most important) of Soviet untrustworthiness and obscurity. The West wavered between conciliation and challenge; and without a firm lead from Washington, King was not the man to act boldly and alone. Now, however, the information was shared by three governments and beyond the prime minister's exclusive control. The time bomb ticked for another two months.

 **The Curtain Descends**

While Mackenzie King fussed over the spy affair, the diplomacy of war's end became intense and complex. The Department of External Affairs' Soviet analysts in Moscow and Ottawa, still ignorant of the Gouzenko revelations (only Robertson, Wrong, and Pearson were informed at the outset), continued their efforts to describe and understand Russian purposes. The disappointments of spring and summer brought a new tone of sobriety to Wilgress's and Malania's commentaries, which were now devoid of any exuberant idealism. But both persisted in explaining events from the Soviet perspective; and both held out modest hope for a *modus vivendi* if the West could appreciate the workings of the Kremlin's mind. There was an implicit contrast, in particular, between the Wilgress dispatches of the autumn and the Mayrand-Smith dispatches of the previous spring.

Dana Wilgress returned to the USSR in mid-September after an absence of five months, and on 25 September he attempted his first reassessment of the view from Moscow.[1] He commented: 'I have come back to a situation entirely different to that which prevailed when I left.' The war had ended, and three conferences had occured at San Francisco, Potsdam, and London 'which had provided the testing ground for the ability of the Soviet Union to cooperate with the outside world.' These events were 'complicated' and 'world-shaking'; and until he was once again familiar with Moscow, he asked Ottawa's indulgence for not writing with assurance. It would take some time before he could find his bearings again 'in what is now for me the uncharted sea of Soviet diplomacy.'

Wilgress suggested that Washington and London were equally at sea.

The conclusion I am groping towards but do not yet feel sufficiently confident to state categorically is that the Anglo-Saxon powers are still a long way from finding the proper method of dealing with the Soviet Government. The United States Government have shown a refreshing readiness to assume more of the measure of responsibility that is commensurate with their great power. Unfortunately the advent of the Truman administration to power has coincided with the ascendency [*sic*] of those advisers who have been preaching 'toughness' towards the Soviet Union. I am not sure if toughness for the sake of being tough may not at times take the place of that policy of being 'firm but fair' which I would like to see applied to dealings with the Soviet Government. The United States Government have also taken as their starting point for the new policy the Yalta Declaration on Liberated Europe which brings them very definitely into clash with the Soviet Union in that part of Europe where Soviet power is paramount and where the Soviet Government consider their interests to be most vital.

This was precisely the area which the British-Soviet percentages agreement had led the Russians to believe had been left to their disposition; but now Britain appeared to have abandoned that understanding in its support for the Yalta Declaration.

The British, in the Soviet view, had begun to tip the balance of their relations away from Russia to the United States (as Wilgress believed inevitable and correct); but that raised the suspicion that 'their chief ally is not living up to what the Soviet Government expected of it under the alliance.' 'This may explain partly why to-day the United Kingdom is more the object of resentment than the United States, although the basic reason for this is that in so many parts of Europe and the Middle East there is a direct conflict between United Kingdom and Soviet interests.'

Thus there had been a general deterioration in Soviet-Anglo-American relations and an increase in mutual mistrust. On the Soviet side this took the form of charges of Western obstruction in the Balkans, fear of renewed capitalist 'intrigues,' and the revival by the Soviet Union of a 'war of nerves' over Turkey and Iran. 'It is this irresponsible readiness to play with fire,' Wilgress said of the Soviets, 'that makes me uneasy about the ability to avoid conflagrations.'

It seemed clear to Wilgress that at the Conference of Foreign Ministers the Soviet foreign minister, Molotov,

with more than usual daring and with less than his usual sense of responsibility has been playing a game of colossal bluff. On the defensive in the Balkans he has carried the attack to what is to the British an equally vital sphere of interest – the

Mediterranean. The hypocrisy of the trustee arrangements worked out at San Francisco has given him an admirable instrument for this purpose. By claiming for the Soviet Union a voice in the administration of Italian colonies he can play power politics without alienating left-wing opinion throughout the world.[2]

In the Far East Soviet policy was quiescent, because the lines of influence were clear: the Soviets were 'doing nothing to provoke the United States in an area where American power has become predominant and where American public opinion would be quick to react to any Soviet moves that savoured of aggression towards either China or Korea.' In Western Europe the Soviet Union was on the defensive; it was pressing only in Iran, Turkey, and the Mediterranean, probably for tactical reasons.

By carrying the offensive to the special sphere of influence of the British Mr. Molotov may hope to get his way in the special sphere of Soviet influence in south-eastern Europe. By placing the British in the position of claiming the Mediterranean as a British sea Mr. Molotov is on firm ground in claiming that the Black Sea is Soviet. The atomic bomb is also surely a factor. By making extravagant claims Mr. Molotov may hope to strengthen the hands of those idealists who advocate giving the secrets of the atomic bomb to the Soviet Union as a grand gesture of appeasement. In any event he probably feels that it is incumbent upon him to show that the Soviet Union has not been deterred from playing the role of a power equal to the United States through possession by that country of such a formidable weapon.

The rhetorical Soviet challenge to Turkey was probably a preliminary to hard bargaining over the straits; the threats against Iran appeared more like 'frank aggression,' intended to establish Soviet control of Iranian oil reserves. 'The master minds in the Kremlin may have concluded that the soft under-belly of the Atlantic Community now in embryo is this region of the Persian Gulf ... the Soviet leaders may have decided to entrench themselves in Iran before the Americans realize their new responsibilities as policers of the seas and the importance of Iranian oil to the execution of those responsibilities.'

The key to current instability, in Wilgress's judgment, was the fluidity of the situation: the Western oscillation between idealism and realism, and the uncertainty about where the boundaries between spheres of influence were to be set.

... the world is now in a state of flux and what is decided upon in the coming weeks will set the pattern for many years to come. The Soviet leaders are out to take as much advantage as they can of this fluid situation. Once things settle down they will work within the framework of existing instruments according to the balance of forces prevailing at the time. Everything would have been easier if we could have removed that atmosphere of mistrust and suspicion that so long has permeated relations between the Soviet Union and the Western world. As things are now I fear we may lose the substance of genuine Soviet cooperation for the shadow of elections in the politically immature countries of Eastern Europe.

(For that was now one of the chief objects of Anglo-American diplomacy at the Council of Foreign Ministers.)

Simultaneously in Ottawa, Leo Malania prepared a paper on 'Present Trends of Soviet Foreign Policy' following a meeting on the subject in Norman Robertson's office, and gave Robertson a copy to take with him to Washington and London.[3] In a note accompanying the copy sent to the Prime Minister's Office, Malania explained his approach:

In assessing any difficulties that may arise between persons or governments it seems to me that an essential prerequisite to intelligent discussion should be an earnest attempt to see the situation with the other fellow's eyes on the assumption that the other fellow is neither a knave nor a fool. If such a point of view does not yield any plausible explanation for conduct which may appear to be strange, then – but not till then – would one be really justified in examining the situation to find out whether it's foolishness or knavery that is causing the difficulties. Hence the memo attempts to look at the world from Soviet eyes, more or less.

With the end of war, Malania suggested, the Russians believed that 'the purpose of the western democracies is to restrict Soviet influence in world affairs to the borders of the Soviet Union.'

The fact that the Soviets were able to obtain what they wished in Poland only after vigorous unilateral actions ... must have confirmed the Soviet belief that in negotiations with them, the Western Allies were responsive only to the strongest pressure. The current Anglo-American concern to establish democracy in the Balkan States, which hardly had any experience of democratic forms, while tolerating totalitarian regimes in Portugal, Spain and Turkey must appear to Moscow as an attempt to limit the influence of the Soviet Union rather than as the pursuit of purely idealistic aims.

From December 1941 until October 1944, Malania argued, the Soviets
had sought, in co-operation with Great Britain, to define mutual spheres of
influence in Europe. In October 1944 they seemed to succeed in doing so.
The current Russian diplomatic offensive, however, stemmed from the
point, in February 1945, when Britain injected itself into Romanian affairs
in response to Soviet acts. Moscow was also disturbed by 'the attempt to
bring the United States into questions which the Russians would appear to
feel are a matter primarily for the United Kingdom and the Soviet Union.'
In their study of American attitudes, the Soviets had judged 'that the United
States is not prepared to go nearly as far as the United Kingdom would like
in support of the latter's policy.' There were many indications to Moscow
'that the United States is far from unanimous in its backing of the United
Kingdom's foreign policy.' Chief among these, for Malania, were Walter
Lippmann's recent suggestion that the United States should act as a
mediator between Britain and Russia rather than taking the British side too
closely; and the results of a *Fortune* magazine poll of leading executives
(published that month) indicating that there was overwhelming support for
long-term trade and credit arrangements with the Soviet Union. Malania
reported that State Department officials were unhappy about the possible
deterioration of relations with Russia over its Romanian and Bulgarian
policies, and left a lingering hint that the Soviets might be aware of these
confidential attitudes. (His source was the British Embassy in Washington;
as subsequent defections indicated, this intelligence had almost certainly
been available to the Russians.)

Given a Russian assessment that US policy was soft and UK policy hard,
Malania concluded:

One might hazard the guess that under these circumstances the Soviet tactic in the
Council of Foreign Ministers has been to delay decisions on Eastern European
issues, by raising issues of greater concern to the United States, such as the
principle of trusteeships. For it is clear that if the Soviet Union were to agree to
Anglo-American demands in Eastern Europe at this stage, they might lose the
bargaining advantage which they now possess when discussions turn to questions
of vital concern to the United States, such as problems of United States security in
the Pacific.

(Malania was mistaken in his judgment that the Soviets were responding to
a soft American attitude at the London conference, where James Byrnes
had in fact shown his belligerence.)

There was no possibility, according to Malania, of immediate war with the Soviet Union: neither side wished to fight. The urgent problems of physical survival confronting Western Europe meant that the West needed agreements on supply and reconstruction more than the Soviet Union needed them – because Russia was already proceeding unilaterally with economic reform in Eastern Europe. The Soviets were in the stronger bargaining position, and were determined to assert it.

To conclude, it would seem that the current Soviet attitude is based upon a realization that the Soviet Union has 'arrived' as a world power of first magnitude and upon the fear that an attempt would be made to deprive it of this position. The Soviets probably feel that mere diplomatic recognition and condescending admission to a 'select club' of Great Powers is not enough to secure their present position. If the United States can have exclusive bases, the Soviets intend to have them also. If the United Kingdom has colonies, the Soviets intend to have full equality in this respect also. If both of these powers have areas where their influence is predominant, the Soviet Union feels justified in claiming a position of equality with them.

Malania was more confident than Wilgress was that a new accommodation would eventually be reached between Russia and the West; and he implied that this would involve, essentially, Anglo-American recognition of the new fact of Soviet power. 'The adjustment of any group of powers to a completely changed political situation is never easy and can only be reached through a series of crises, which define the new inter-relationships. But the current trends of public opinion in the democracies and the facts of the situation point to an ultimate readjustment through the process of bargaining and concessions to the power which is dominant in those areas where the other powers have no means of effective intervention.'

This was the last commentary on the Soviet Union prepared for the department by Leo Malania, whose career was altered by an indirect link to the Gouzenko affair. For several months Emma Woikin, an External Affairs cipher clerk with a background of misfortune, had lived with the Malanias. On 28 September 1945 (the date of this paper) Woikin was transferred from the Cipher Division of External Affairs on evidence received from Gouzenko that she had passed information to the Soviets; and soon after that Hume Wrong informed Malania in confidence of the evidence against her. Although there was no indication of Malania's own involvement, he was embarrassed and recognized that his future in the department had been compromised. In November he was posted as secretary of the Canadian delegation to the Preparatory Commission of the United Nations in London, and secretary-general of the delegation to the first General Assembly. Following his return to Ottawa in the late winter of 1946, a position was offered to Malania, through Hume Wrong's intermediacy, in the office of the UN Secretary-General, which he accepted gratefully. Malania was never regarded as a security risk, and remained in close and influential liaison with the Canadian mission to the United Nations through the late 1940s and 1950s. He eventually became an Episcopalian priest with a New York City parish.[4]

By early October Dana Wilgress judged from 'the little bits of evidence we have of Soviet motives' that Molotov's disruption of the first Council of Foreign Ministers meeting had been a response to the American attack on Soviet influence in Romania and Bulgaria.[5] James Byrnes's use of the Yalta Declaration on Liberated Europe as the basis for his challenge appeared to the Russians as a partial and hypocritical act, given that British manipulation of Greek politics was not also an object of American condemnation. Now some fresh approach to a compromise on Western recognition of the Romanian and Bulgarian regimes and the peace treaties would be necessary to restore relations with the Soviet Union. The Russians did not appear unduly concerned by the failure of the London conference, regarding it as only one incident in a continuing negotiation; the effect had been far greater in the West, where goodwill towards the Soviet Union had been largely dissipated. 'It is so typical of Soviet psychology,' Wilgress wrote, 'that they have been willing to risk all (these) results ... in order to prevent being pushed around in the Balkans.' The policy of Britain and the United States in dealing with Russia would have to be more finely tuned: Wilgress searched for the elusive golden mean.

I have long instinctively felt that this isolating of herself by the Soviet Union would be the result if those who preached toughness towards the Soviet Union had their way and so I fear it has come to pass. But the other extreme of appeasement without clearly recognised limits would be still more dangerous, particularly at the present juncture. Now is certainly not the time to woo the Soviet Union back to the respectable comity of nations by unloosening the purse strings of the United States money bags or by magnanimously disclosing the secret of the atomic bomb. On the contrary Mr. Molotov should be made to realise that he cannot obstruct with impunity the efforts to achieve compromise on difficult international questions.

But we on our side have also much to learn from the recent happenings in London. It is not so much a question of teaching the Soviet Union that there is a limit beyond which the United States will not go. Rather it is a question of the United States learning the difficult art of adjusting its policy to the new fact that accommodation must be found in the family of nations for a newcomer with different manners and different modes of thought.[6]

Meanwhile the Canadian ambassador in Washington reported that the State Department's first response to the collapse of the London conference was to take the Soviet Union's technical protests over Chinese and French inclusion in discussion of the Balkan peace treaties at face value.[7] Pearson quoted George Kennan's view from Moscow that the failure in London was 'a profound shock to the Soviet public and, indeed, to most Soviet officials' which had led to 'some pretty serious stock-taking ... in Moscow.' In mid-November the British Embassy in Moscow reported, in a dispatch passed on to the Canadian government, the deepening suspicions of the Soviet Union over the global ambitions of the Anglo-Americans – not only in Eastern Europe, but in Asia and Western Europe as well.[8] 'The feeling is growing here,' wrote Frank Roberts, 'that we are meddling in the affairs of South-Eastern Europe, where we have no major interests, refusing to recognise vital Soviet interests and working for the creation of a coalition which would inevitably become hostile to the Soviet Union.' Roberts, even more than Wilgress, believed that there were no 'sinister motives behind Soviet policy,' and that Russian suspicion of the British and Americans was 'genuine enough.' Soviet objectives were limited and would remain so; above all, 'there is no reason to doubt M. Stalin's sincerity when he stated recently that the Soviet Union needed fifty years of peace to restore the ravages of war and to bring her economy up to the level of the Western world.' The great problem was not to counter an aggressive foe, but somehow to break the descending spiral of mutual mistrust. For Roberts as for Wilgress, the diagnosis was clearer than the treatment, which tended to be defined in appeals for restraint rather than in specific antidotes.

In a dispatch of 14 November 1945, Dana Wilgress explicitly challenged the policy of 'toughness' towards the Soviet Union advocated by George F. Kennan.[9] 'I have very great respect for the ability of Mr. Kennan,' said Wilgress, 'and for his deep knowledge of the Soviet Union, but he suffers from having been here in the pre-war days when foreign representatives became indoctrinated with anti-Soviet ideas as a result of the purges and subtle German propaganda.' The Russians were well satisfied with the military and diplomatic gains of the war and early post-war period, disappointed only in their failure to dominate the Dardanelles; but they recognized that this could not be achieved without a war they were unprepared to fight. The essential source of their belligerent tone, he repeated, was 'the ascendency [*sic*] of the tough school in the United States,' and the related possession of the atomic bomb by America.

What is more necessary than anything else ... is an attempt by the United States to allay Soviet suspicion and mistrust by abandoning the philosophy of the tough school and resorting once more to the Roosevelt touch – even though the master hand is no longer present. In this allaying of Soviet mistrust and suspicion the handling of the atomic bomb secret must play the leading part. I am not one of those in favour of disclosing the actual process of manufacturing the bomb to the Soviet Union unless the proper safeguards are given in return, which I doubt if the Soviet Government are in a position to give. I am all in favour, however, of the secret being brought some way into the United Nations Organisation in order to bolster up that body and inspire new trust in international cooperation for peace and security.

'Bringing the secret some way into the United Nations Organisation' was the deceptively vague formula chosen the same week (as a test of Soviet goodwill) by Truman, Attlee, and King, who thus demonstrated that Western policy was not, as Wilgress believed, a consistent expression of the tough school.[10] But if it was not, then his explanation of Soviet conduct as a response to Anglo-American attitudes was also inadequate.

Secretary of State Byrnes, too, had been reassessing the results of his unyielding and forthright approach at the London conference, and in the face of divided counsels at home, adopted a more conciliatory attitude to the Soviet Union. Against strong British objections he proposed that the next meeting of the Council of Foreign Ministers should be held in Moscow in December, and gained British acquiescence only by threatening to meet in Britain's absence.[11] He decided to take to Moscow the three-power proposals for international control of atomic energy, in order to seek Soviet concurrence before submitting the scheme to the first United Nations General Assembly in January 1946.[12] And he decided also to soften his line on Soviet policy in Romania and Bulgaria in order to hasten negotiation on the peace treaties.[13]

The decision to discuss atomic energy in Moscow raised the question, to

Mackenzie King's dismay, of whether Canada should participate in the Council of Foreign Ministers' meeting. On 7 December Bevin cabled Lord Halifax in Washington:

Seeing that the Canadian Government has been intimately associated with all the work on atomic energy it is particularly important to warn them in advance not only of the meeting but of the fact that His Majesty's Government and the United States Government propose to exchange views with the Soviet Government on the subject of the control of atomic energy. Seeing that it is desirable on all grounds to continue this close association, I think that Mr. Mackenzie King should be given the opportunity of associating a Canadian representative with the discussions in Moscow on the subject of the control of atomic energy. Mr. Mackenzie King's representative might be the Canadian Ambassador in Moscow, Mr. Wilgress ... Please ascertain immediately whether Mr. Byrnes agrees that we should put this suggestion to Mr. Mackenzie King.[14]

On the same day this telegram was conveyed through the British high commissioner in Ottawa to Prime Minister King.[15] The Canadian government's reply was swift and unequivocal. As the high commissioner cabled that evening:

1 Robertson has just been in touch with me with message from the Prime Minister who wished to convey it to you at once.
2 Mackenzie King feels it will avoid embarrassment for everybody concerned if proposal that Canada be associated with Moscow talks be dropped.
3 If this is agreed it would be awkward for the Canadian Government that specific reference to the Canadian Government on atomic energy should be included in the communique. He therefore much hoped that this reference can be omitted. He of course fully understands that the talks on the subject will and must take place in Moscow.[16]

The prime minister was determined to keep his head down in Moscow; this was no time for a new Canadian excursion into high diplomacy. In any case, the American secretary of state's reply to the request (also delivered the same evening) rejected the proposal on the ground that the complications of excluding France and China would be compounded by Canada's presence.[17] In London the thin file was opened and closed in a single day.

The disposition to seek compromise in Moscow by now extended to London as well as Washington. Dana Wilgress (who had gone to Britain for the meetings of the United Nations Preparatory Commission) reported a long conversation with Ernest Bevin on 11 December, in which Bevin 'shared to a remarkable degree the views I had expressed.'[18] There seemed to be an Anglo-American-Canadian consensus in explaining the reasons for Moscow's belligerence of the early autumn. 'He said that the difficulties which led to the breakdown of the Council of Foreign Ministers at the beginning of October last could be attributed in large measure to the attack which Mr. Byrnes made on the Soviet-sponsored Governments in Roumania and Bulgaria.'

In the next approach to the Soviets, Bevin seemed prepared to fall back to a policy of mutual non-interference.

Mr. Bevin believes that a deal can be made with Mr. Molotov on a definition of spheres of influence. This course is forced upon the United Kingdom Government by reason of the arrangement made by Mr. Churchill whereby the Soviet Union agreed to keep their hands off Greece in return for a free hand being given to the Soviet Union in Rumania.

Mr. Bevin's approach to the problem, and the one he intends to pursue in Moscow, is to ask Mr. Molotov exactly what he wants, and then to propose a series of what he calls 'Monroes'. This would mean that the United Kingdom would be chiefly responsible for the Mediterranean, the United States for the Pacific, and the Soviet Union for South Eastern Europe. Each Power would be responsible for maintaining international order within its own sphere, but it would be a necessary condition that each Power agreed not to interfere in the internal affairs of the countries in its sphere, and to allow freedom of access to the other Powers and to other countries in establishing trade relations with the countries in the sphere of influence of each Power.

I told Mr. Bevin that this approach was the realistic one, but that in order to provide a broader development of a more idealist approach it would be essential to tie up the arrangement in some manner with the United Nations ... With this he readily agreed.[19]

Bevin's desire for a comprehensive agreement on spheres of interest was not satisfied in Moscow; but James Byrnes came out of the meeting convinced that he had successfully traded off concessions with the Soviet Union. Stalin promised some widening of membership in the Romanian and Bulgarian governments, sufficient in Byrnes's eyes to permit diplomatic recognition and the conclusion of peace treaties (although George Kennan described the concessions accurately as 'fig leaves of

democratic procedure to hide the nakedness of Stalinist dictatorship');
Byrnes offered in return a token and advisory Soviet role in the American
administration of Japan; a general conference was agreed upon to ratify the
peace treaties with Nazi Germany's wartime allies; the Soviets accepted
the American proposal for a United Nations Atomic Energy Commission;
and Stalin reaffirmed his acceptance of the Chiang Kai-shek government in
China. Bevin and Byrnes failed only to gain Russian agreement on the date
of Soviet withdrawal from the northern Iranian province of Azerbaijan. By
toning down his democratic rhetoric and engaging in specific bargaining
for mutual advantage, Byrnes seemed to have produced the accommoda-
tions that had eluded him in London.[20] Dana Wilgress commented
approvingly that 'the results of the December conference in Moscow have
been sufficient to indicate the failure of the approach advocated by the
tough school.'[21]

Byrnes's and Wilgress's emphasis upon traditional diplomatic tactics
and superficial accommodation, however, failed to take account of a tidal
shift in American attitudes to the Soviet Union. To his surprise, Byrnes
returned to Washington to face widespread charges – both within and
outside the administration – that he had engaged weakly in appeasement in
Moscow.[22] Truman rebuked Byrnes for acting beyond his authority to
produce only the illusion of success; and the president made clear to the
secretary of state that American policy towards the Soviet Union would no
longer be conciliatory. 'Unless Russia is faced with an iron fist and strong
language,' Truman wrote, 'another war is in the making. Only one
language do they understand – "how many divisions have you?"'[23]

Truman had now been decisively influenced by the evidence of Soviet
barbarism in Eastern Europe in the wake of its military occupation. He was
also determined to cover his political position against growing press and
Republican criticism, and Byrnes – once he appreciated that bipartisan
support for American foreign policy was in danger of collapse – was ready
to join the president in reverting to the tough line.[24]

From the end of the war in Europe, the problem of how to deal with the
Soviet Union had never, for the United States, been a matter simply of
diplomatic technique. Soviet intransigence had shocked American idealism. If Russia was no longer a trusted ally, American understanding
required some satisfactory historic or philosophic justification for a
permanent break in the wartime alliance, and some relatively simple
guide-lines for a new policy. These new foundations – or rationalizations –

for policy were provided for the American administration in February and March 1946, although the public signals from Washington to Moscow remained confused for at least another year. As the bases for American policy towards the Soviet Union solidified, the uncertainties of Canadian (and British) official attitudes, too, were resolved in general acceptance of the American world-view. The extent to which this parallelism was the result of deference to American power and prestige, or of genuinely independent analysis, is impossible to measure with precision.[25] But there can be little doubt that official Canadian uncertainty about Russia would not have been resolved without the American lead.

On 9 February 1946 Joseph Stalin delivered a major speech which was examined carefully in Washington.[26] The leading advocate in the Truman cabinet of a tough line towards the Soviet Union, James Forrestal, took it as one of two touchstones for his approach. Stalin emphasized the continuing Soviet conflict with the capitalist world as background for the next five-year plan of heavy industrial and military production, 'to guarantee our country against any eventuality.' Forrestal quoted Justice William O. Douglas's description of the speech as 'The Declaration of World War III,' and the editor of the Forrestal diary commented that 'this speech and the program it laid down came close to convincing him that there was no way, as Lippmann had hoped, in which democracy and Communism could live together. It is clear that from this time on he felt increasingly that policy could not be founded on the assumption that a peaceful solution of the Russian problem would be possible.'[27] This was a Manichean shift, allowing no space in great power diplomacy between friendly co-operation and aggressive preparation for war. It depended on a certain reading of Marxist-Stalinist thought more than it did on a careful judgment of the historical evidence. Stalin had not threatened or predicted war between the Soviet Union and the capitalist countries in his speech, but rather had foreseen conflict leading to war *among* the countries of the West, resulting from uneven economic development and rivalry.[28] Forrestal ignored such subtleties, and considered the Soviet emphasis on heavy armament to be particularly ominous, given the accelerating pace of American demobilization – which, as secretary of the navy, he vigorously but unsuccessfully resisted.

Forrestal found his other, utterly convincing, touchstone in a dispatch from the American chargé d'affaires in Moscow, George Kennan, of 22 February 1946.[29] The secretary of the navy entered this eight-thousand-word dispatch (which became known as the 'long telegram') in his diary, and circulated it with missionary fervour in the administration and among the armed services.[30] Kennan recalled drily that 'the effect produced in Washington by this elaborate pedagogical effort was nothing less than sensational.'

If none of my previous literary efforts had seemed to evoke even the faintest tinkle from the bell at which they were aimed, this one, to my astonishment, struck it squarely and set it vibrating with a resonance that was not to die down for many months. It was one of those moments when official Washington, whose states of receptivity or the opposite are determined by subjective emotional currents as intricately imbedded in the subconscious as those of the most complicated of Sigmund Freud's erstwhile patients, was ready to receive a given message.[31]

Kennan's long telegram argued that the Soviet regime saw the world as divided into two conflicting realms, socialist and capitalist, between which there could be 'no permanent peaceful coexistence.' Kennan denied the historical accuracy of this judgment, and therefore concluded that 'the Soviet party line is not based on any objective analysis of the situation beyond Russia's borders; that it has, indeed, little to do with conditions outside of Russia; that it arises mainly from basic inner-Russian necessities.' The original source of Moscow's 'neurotic view of world affairs' was an 'instinctive Russian sense of insecurity.' Over centuries, Russian rulers had 'learned to seek security only in patient but deadly struggle for total destruction of rival power, never in compacts and compromises with it.' The Bolsheviks, whose sense of insecurity was still more extreme, had provided the perfect cloak of Marxist dogma for traditional Russian attitudes.

In this dogma, with its basic altruism of purpose, they found justification for their instinctive fear of [the] outside world, for the dictatorship without which they did not know how to rule, for cruelties they did not dare not to inflict, for sacrifices they felt bound to demand. In the name of Marxism they sacrificed every single ethical value in their methods and tactics. Today they cannot dispense with it. It is the fig leaf of their moral and intellectual respectability.

The Soviet government lived in an 'atmosphere of oriental secretiveness and conspiracy' which probably prevented anyone within it – and certainly Stalin – from receiving accurate reports of the external world. With that background of misconception, the regime conducted a foreign policy (both official and subterranean) aimed at increasing the power and prestige of the Soviet state, advancing Soviet power abroad, and weakening the influence of the advanced nations of the West. Communist parties abroad, whatever their public stance, were 'in reality working closely together as an underground operating directorate of world communism, a concealed Comintern, tightly coordinated and directed by Moscow.' The Soviets acted from the belief that with the United States 'there can be no permanent *modus vivendi,* that it is desirable and necessary that the internal harmony of our society be disrupted, our traditional way of life be destroyed, the international authority of our state be broken, if Soviet power is to be secure.'

This was an alarming message. Kennan was not gently tinkling a bell, but ringing the tocsin. Twenty years later, he regarded the dispatch with 'horrified amusement.' 'Much of it,' he wrote in his *Memoirs,* 'reads exactly like one of those primers put out by alarmed congressional committees or by the Daughters of the American Revolution, designed to arouse the citizenry to the dangers of the Communist conspiracy.'[32] Kennan attempted to balance the stark warning with an optimistic assessment of how the Soviet Union might be successfully confronted. The Soviets, he judged, had no fixed plans for expansion and took no unnecessary risks. They were 'highly sensitive to [the] logic of force,' and withdrew 'when strong resistance is encountered at any point.' The regime was not firmly based on the allegiance of the Russian people, and could face severe domestic strains. If the United States met the reality of the Soviet Union without illusions, and developed the strengths of its own society in self-confidence, it could expect to 'solve' the problem of Russian power – 'and that without recourse to any general military conflict.'

In the atmosphere of unease which now pervaded Washington, it was the image of a hostile and ambitious Soviet regime, unaffected by diplomatic gestures of compromise, which was influential. Kennan's implicit message that reason, forbearance, and persuasion would not work in dealing with the Soviet Union, that only a steady display of firmness backed by 'sufficient force' – whether diplomatic or military was not made clear – took root. Finely tuned diplomatic efforts to appease Russian insecurity, and the complicated analyses on which such efforts might be based, were suddenly discredited.

While George Kennan was writing and dispatching his decisive telegram to the State Department, another major statement on Soviet policy was being prepared for the American public. On 12 February Lester Pearson wrote to Mackenzie King and Norman Robertson to report that he had spent an hour with Winston Churchill at the British Embassy.[33] Churchill was in Washington (before a holiday in Florida) to consult with President Truman about his forthcoming speech, planned for 5 March, at Westminster College in Fulton, Missouri. Pearson wrote that Churchill was critical of Anglo-American uncertainty towards the Soviet Union.

He does not think that the Russians are dangerously aggressive in the sense that the Nazis were, but he is convinced that they will exploit the present situation, with its waverings and uncertainties on the part of London and Washington, to the very limit in order to achieve certain objectives. He is convinced, as most observers are convinced, that the Russians know exactly what they want, whereas neither London nor Washington does. Therefore, in his view, the first requirement of British and American policy toward Russia is agreement on their own policies. They should then let the Soviets know exactly where these policies are in opposition to U.S.S.R. objectives. All cards should be put frankly and openly on the table. According to Mr. Churchill, Mr. Stalin understands this kind of approach and does not bear resentment when it results in opposition to his own policies. The great sin, according to Mr. Churchill, is weakness and uncertainty.[34]

Pearson conveyed Churchill's hope that King might visit him in Florida before the Fulton speech; and on 28 February Churchill telephoned King to renew the invitation.[35] King was unable to make the trip; but on 1 March, Churchill called King again to say that he intended to emphasize the need for closer Anglo-American co-operation in defence, 'along lines of our Permanent Joint Board on Defence.'[36] This, in Churchill's view, would be 'a steadying force in the world'; King 'thought that was excellent.'[37] He sent off to Churchill at once copies of his own speech of 1940 on the Ogdensburg Agreement ('On reading it through, I was amazed to discover how very apposite it was and how very helpful it would be to him. It really would be an anticipation in large part of what he had to say.') On 3 March, after Lester Pearson had read the full text of Churchill's speech at his bedside in Washington, Churchill called King again, who repeated Pearson's view that the speech was excellent, 'as fine a speech as Churchill had ever made.'[38] Pearson meanwhile wrote to King that the text had been read as well by Truman's personal aide Admiral Leahy (who expressed his 'hearty agreement'), and by James Byrnes. He did not think President Truman had read it, 'but, of course, as he is travelling with Mr. Churchill and introducing him at Westminster College, it will be difficult for him to dissociate himself entirely from what Mr. Churchill says.'[39] In his choice of occasion and his consultations on the text of the address, Churchill carefully sought to be once again, as he had been in wartime, the voice of the Anglo-American alliance – now centred in Washington rather than London. For the Truman administration, the speech was the opportune occasion for an expression of its new firmness of purpose towards the Soviet Union – safely expressed by a prominent visitor.[40]

At Fulton, Missouri, on 5 March, Churchill called for 'the fraternal association of the English-speaking peoples,' in peace as in war, to preserve the common values of freedom and democracy.[41] 'Fraternal association,' he said, 'requires not only the growing friendship and mutual understanding between our two vast but kindred systems of society, but the continuance of the intimate relationships between our military advisers ... the continuance of the present facilities for mutual security by the joint use of all naval and air bases in the possession of either country all over the world': a world-wide extension, he suggested, of the Canadian-American permanent defence agreement to include the whole British Commonwealth and Empire.

Unless the two English-speaking families worked together, Churchill foresaw disaster. 'The dark ages may return, the Stone Age may return on the gleaming wings of science, and what might now shower ... immeasurable material blessings upon mankind, may even bring about its total destruction. Beware, I say; time is plenty short. Do not let us take the course of allowing events to drift along until it is too late.' This great new fraternal association, 'with all the extra strength and security which both our countries can derive from it,' should be displayed to the world, so that 'it plays its part in steadying and stabilizing the foundations of peace.'

The new challenge to peace and security, Churchill continued, came from one source. He deplored the spread of Soviet-dominated 'police governments' in Eastern Europe where, 'from Stettin in the Baltic to Trieste in the Adriatic, an iron curtain has descended across the Continent'; he deplored Soviet attempts to create a pro-Communist Germany; Soviet pressures upon Turkey and Iran; and domestic Communist agitation throughout the world but especially in Italy and France, 'in complete unity and absolute obedience to directions they receive from the Communist centre.'

Churchill's estimate of Soviet objectives was sombre: 'I do not believe that Soviet Russia desires war. What they desire is the fruits of war and the indefinite expansion of their power and doctrines.' His own (and by extension,

Britain's and America's) objectives were stated in equally absolutist terms: 'what we have to consider here today while time remains is the permanent prevention of war and the establishment of conditions of freedom and democracy as rapidly as possible in all countries.' These contrasting objectives were obviously incompatible; what was needed, therefore, was a settlement. If that prospect seemed slight in the light of what Churchill had said before, he could suggest a means of achieving it. 'From what I have seen of our Russian friends and allies during the war, I am convinced that there is nothing they admire so much as strength, and there is nothing for which they have less respect than for weakness, especially military weakness.'

Churchill had come full circle to his initial suggestion for an Anglo-American military alliance – but with its goal now clearly established. That goal could not be, as in the thirties, a balance of power 'on narrow margins, offering temptations to a trial of strength': it had to be an overwhelming preponderance of power in Anglo-American hands, which would force the Soviet Union to a 'good understanding through many peaceful years.' The speech was thus more than an appeal for realism about the Soviet Union. It offered, beyond that, its own missionary vision of righteousness triumphant and the end of politics. This was not, perhaps, quite the lesson in diplomatic sophistication needed by the American public in 1946.

But the speech, in all its parts, caught the admiration and envy of that inhibited missionary Mackenzie King. Soon after hearing the address on radio, King reached Churchill and Truman by telephone in Missouri, and spoke to Churchill in tortured superlatives. 'I told him what I thought about his speech, being, all circumstances considered, the most courageous made by any man at any time, having regard to what it signifies at the moment and for the future.'[42] Churchill (ever the politician) asked King if he would be willing to express those sentiments to Prime Minister Attlee. King agreed and sent off a cable the same evening:

To me, it was the most courageous utterance I have ever heard by any public man and one that has been made none too soon ... I personally feel that there is only one way to meet a threatening danger and that is to fight it in the open. Churchill has sounded a note of warning to the free nations of the world which cannot be heeded too fully. With all that he said of effectively facilitating and strengthening utmost cooperation between the United States and the British Commonwealth, I am in complete agreement. I believe that Canadian opinion will be strongly behind Churchill in what he said in his address today.[43]

To his diary, King confessed more personal feelings of inadequacy provoked by the iron curtain speech.

I confess it gave me very much the feeling that I had not made the use of my life that I should have made ... I should today be speaking out to the countries of the world as Churchill himself was speaking and should have been able had I applied my time and talents to really equipping myself for public life, – to speak, if not with the same eloquence and words at least with a like power of influence on world problems. Perhaps the mistake was not marrying early in life and having a home where my whole thoughts could have been centred in a great public mission. But if I had had the problems of a home I might not have been able to give the public life and work the time I have ....

With Smuts and Churchill I am pretty much today in the position of one of the few remaining men who stand out in their separate countries as the older statesmen. I should be more worthy of being so classed. I never feel that I am doing justice to the position I hold. Addresses like Churchill's on the questions of the day, which give expression to thoughts, feelings and convictions I so strongly feel and entertain, but to which I give such little expression in public always cause me to feel a bit disappointed and sad. I might have done much better. Churchill's address today was all built around the Ogdensburg agreement, which was essentially and wholly something worked out by myself.[44]

King's enthusiastic response to the Fulton speech was less than universally shared in the United States and Britain. While the press analysis section of the Canadian Embassy in Washington reported that the speech had had an 'explosive impact,' congressional reaction was depicted by the Associated Press as 'generally unfavourable.'[45] L.B. Pearson wrote that reaction was 'about what I expected; mixed, but with the preponderance of opinion critical.'[46] Opposition had been tempered by Churchill's high popularity in the United States, and by the fact that the normally anti-British elements in the country were also anti-Soviet. The major American complaint centred on Churchill's proposal for an Anglo-American alliance, which aroused 'the traditional and deeply rooted fear of being linked with "Imperialism," ' and suggested to the supporters of the United Nations that it would be bypassed and weakened. The conservative press generally admired Churchill's forthright condemnation of the Soviet Union, but showed 'marked coolness' to his proposal for an English-speaking alliance; the liberal press was either unsympathetic or 'hesitant but troubled ... doubting whether Churchill had adequately probed the present problem or contributed anything to its solution.'[47] Since President Truman was assumed to have approved the speech, the criticism of Churchill fell also on the President. The United States public was not yet ready for the harsh regimen proposed by Winston Churchill.

In Britain, too, Labour party opposition to Churchill's views made any public expression of support by the Attlee government impolitic, although privately the British prime minister expressed his approval.[48] Having made his dramatic impact to his own satisfaction, Churchill somewhat tempered the message at a press luncheon in Washington on 11 March by insisting that he had not advocated 'an English-speaking military alliance,' but only an informal 'fraternal association' – 'a distinction without as much difference as Mr. Churchill implied,' in Lester Pearson's judgment.[49]

Mackenzie King's preoccupation during February 1946, which contributed to his palpable sense of relief at Churchill's suggestion for an Anglo-American alliance in which Canada would be cradled and protected, was once again the Russian spy affair. Canada's continuing inaction, which had now lasted for five months, was the source of increasing frustration in the US and UK administrations. Three curiously coincidental events at the beginning of February had the effect of embarrassing the King government over its indecision in the affair. On 1 February President Truman's chief of staff and intelligence adviser, Admiral William D. Leahy, met alone with the prime minister in Ottawa and urged him to commence action against the Canadians implicated in the spy network revealed by Igor Gouzenko.[50]

On 2 February the new Soviet military attaché in Ottawa, Grigori Popov, was arrested on Jarvis Street in Toronto, in possession of a pistol and a medical receipt in the name of one of the spy network.[51] (Popov had replaced Nickolai Zabotin as both military attaché and chief of GRU [Military] intelligence operations in Canada when Zabotin was suddenly recalled to his death after Gouzenko's disappearance the previous autumn.[52]) The evidence, conveyed to Prime Minister King the next day, indicated that Soviet intelligence was once again active in Canada, in brazen defiance of the government's irresolution. Finally, on the evening of 3 February, in a radio broadcast, the Washington journalist Drew Pearson revealed the Gouzenko case in outline, compelling the King government to take action.[53] While King thought that 'may be all for the best,' he suspected that the revelation must have been inspired: 'I have a feeling that there is a desire at Washington that this information should get out; that Canada should start the enquiry and that we should have the responsibility for beginning it and that the way should be paved for it being continued into the US. This may be all wrong, but I have the intuition very strongly. It is the way in which a certain kind of politics is played by a certain type of man.'[54] According to his own testimony, the 'certain type of man' was William Stephenson of British Security Co-ordination, who had not only supplied Drew Pearson with information on the Corby case, but had also arranged the trap for the Soviet military attaché in co-operation with the RCMP security service.[55] Stephenson suggests further that these actions were the 'joint inspiration' of Winston Churchill and himself.[56] (No confirmation of this can be found in the Churchill papers.) Stephenson's motives, he later suggested, were to expose Russian espionage to the public and to demonstrate to the British, Canadian, and American governments the urgency of continuing their co-ordinated intelligence operations in peacetime – concerns that he undoubtedly shared with Churchill. (Both British Security Co-ordination and the American secret intelligence service, the OSS, were being dissolved.)

On 5 February, for the first time, King told the Canadian cabinet of the information in the government's possession, and informed it of an order-in-council appointing two Supreme Court justices, Robert Taschereau and R.L. Kellock, as royal commissioners to conduct a secret enquiry commencing at once.[57] By this time not only the Soviet military attaché, but also his two principal aides, had been recalled to Moscow (the ambassador too was absent), and King was convinced that the Soviets were 'pretty well aware that we have knowledge of some of the things which have been going on which could not stand the light of day.'[58] Nevertheless he told the cabinet of his extreme anxiety over the possible consequences of the steps he was now taking:

They might help to set aflame a controversy of extensive and bitter proportions, throughout this country and the U.S., and also to further suspicion and unrest in other countries. That Canada would be a marked country, so far as Russia was concerned in the future. We were the most vulnerable of any country in our proximity to the U.S.S.R. That I had hoped ... that we might find a way of communicating the facts to the Russian government itself without disclosing them in court, giving the government a chance to clean up the situation itself. I pointed out, however, that on the other hand there was a need to clean up our own service, and that now that Drew Pearson's statement was out, there would be questioning and we would not be able to conceal the situation effectively.[59]

King denied to the cabinet that the timing of action was the result of the Pearson broadcast, insisting that it was being taken because both Britain and the United States were now prepared for and urging it.[60]

King braced himself for domestic as well as international repercussions, noting in his diary for 13 February that when arrests were made, 'I can see where a great cry will be raised, having had a Commission sit in secret, and men and women arrested and detained under an order in council passed really under War Measures powers. I will be held up to the world as the very opposite of a democrat. It is part of the inevitable.'[61] On 15 February there was a rush of activity: fourteen arrests in the early morning; a briefing of the opposition leader John Bracken; an interview with the Soviet chargé d'affaires and second secretary; and the release of a press statement at 5 p.m.[62]

One of the Russians who appeared in the prime minister's office in response to the summons was Vitali Pavlov, the chief of KGB intelligence operations in the Soviet Embassy and the leader of the break-in at the Gouzenko apartment the previous September.[63] King cautiously reviewed Gouzenko's defection and the evidence of Soviet espionage he had conveyed. Robertson then read an official Canadian apology over the arrest of the Soviet military attaché which King privately felt 'went a little far in expressing an apology.'[64] As they rose to go, the prime minister told the two Soviet diplomats 'how sorry Robertson and I were that it was necessary to speak of these matters at all; that we were close friends, and that nothing should destroy that relationship. I wanted to repeat again what I said about the care we had taken not to deal with other than members of our own public service. Disclosed nothing further than what was essential to indicate the seriousness of the offence which justified the action we had found it necessary to take against them.'[65] This muted protest must have reinforced the Soviet conviction that the Canadian government remained both naive and fearful in its attitude to the Soviet Union.

The brief press release stated that 'information of undoubted authenticity' about the disclosure of secrets to unauthorized persons (including the staff of a foreign mission) had led the Canadian government to create a commission of enquiry, and to arrange for the detention for interrogation of a number of persons, including some present or former civil servants. The government intended to lay charges in cases in which the evidence warranted.[66] The Soviet Union was not named.

As the case made its front-page impact in Canada, the United States, and Britain, Mackenzie King sought solace once more in the belief that he was acting as a divine instrument 'in the play of world forces and unseen forces beyond.'[67] He told the cabinet secretary, Arnold Heeney, that the revelations marked a new and ominous phase in 'the effort toward world conquest by other powers.' 'Now the conflict is whether the U.S. or Russia shall control the world. What has now been disclosed must inevitably lead either to world war No. 3, in which Russia will seek to destroy the States, and of course Canada, and of which Canada will become the battlefield, or whether by these disclosures the Russian people themselves may come to have their eyes opened and decide they will not be made victims of the new military power that has gained control there.'[68] King's consolation in his role as God's instrument was that he would thus be responsible, not for war, but for the self-liberation of the Russian people from their jailers. That would bring about 'a real brotherhood among the common people of the earth.' 'To help toward that end is unquestionably my mission and the thing for which I was born. It is my grandfather's life effort only on the arena of the world instead of the small arena to which in his day his efforts were necessarily confined.'[69]

In King's confused imagination, the threat of Soviet retaliation against Canada caused him continuing worry. He conceded on 21 February that 'my name is now anathema throughout the whole Russian Empire,' and expected that a break in diplomatic relations with Russia was unavoidable.[70] While he gave himself credit for the spy exposures, he sought also to spread responsibility to the United States and United Kingdom (as he had from the beginning) in order to divert Soviet animus and to ensure Canada's protection by the great powers. When Secretary of State Byrnes publicly expressed doubt that Soviet espionage had extended to the United States, King was 'amazed' (in his knowledge that Gouzenko had named several senior American public servants as agents) and reflected that the denial revealed something unfortunate about the Democratic party. The administration would suffer for it 'when, inevitably, what they do know now, comes to be disclosed. I am coming to feel that the Democratic party have allowed themselves to be too greatly controlled by the Jews and Jewish influence and that Russia has sympathizers in high and influential places to a much greater number than has been believed. Indeed, I used to feel that even with Franklin Roosevelt, he was perhaps trusting Russia far too much, sympathizing of course with the mass of the people.'[71]

Since there was a direct link between Canada and Britain in the person of Alan Nunn May in the Gouzenko case, King was able to rely upon a more effective sharing of responsibility with the United Kingdom than with the

United States. He was relieved to hear on 21 February that Nunn May had made a full confession. 'I said to Robertson I thought it would be best to arrange for his trial in England. Let them see that everything is not put off on Canadians. When he is arrested, and his trial comes, bring home Britain's responsibility and this is certain to lead very far in the U.S.'[72] When the first charges were about to be laid in Canada in early March, King insisted on a flurry of anxious telegrams to Britain to ensure the simultaneous arrest of May: 'it was important that the public should see that British civil servants and scientists were involved and that the whole burden was not on the shoulders of the Canadian Government in relation to its own civil servants. Moreover, the statement would make clear too that the Russian espionage was not restricted to Canada or Britain but extended also to them and the U.S. It was all-important that this larger aspect of the situation should be made clear at once.'[73]

The official Soviet response to the Canadian action confounded King's fears, and confirmed the expectations of those who looked on espionage with a certain relaxed cynicism. On 21 February 1946, in Moscow, the Soviet government took the unusual step of admitting that espionage had occurred, although denying that the information received had any significance.[74] Because of the inadmissible acts of his staff, Moscow said, the Soviet military attaché in Ottawa had immediately been recalled. (The statement did not mention the attaché by name; by now both Zabotin and his successor Popov had gone, along with Ambassador Zarubin.) The official statement went on to deplore the current 'unbridled anti-Soviet campaign' inspired by the Canadian government's actions; but this rhetoric did not conceal the admission and apology. The Soviet Union clearly wished to play down, rather than make an issue of, the Canadian affair. There would be no diplomatic rupture; no third world war; no popular revolt against Soviet rule in the USSR: only somewhat bruised business-as-usual. Mackenzie King sought to repair the diplomatic damage by insisting piously in his statement to the House of Commons on 18 March 1946 that he remained a good friend of the Soviet Union and that he was sure Joseph Stalin 'would not countenance action of this kind on the part of officials of his country.'[75]

The effects of the Gouzenko case could be seen, instead, in its influence upon popular attitudes to the Soviet Union in Canada, the United States, and the United Kingdom; and in the damage done to the rule of law by the Canadian government's procedure in the affair. The Canadian prime minister's alarmist explanation of Soviet espionage in the language of general conspiracy theory – as part of a sinister Russian plot to conquer the world by force – was just one expression of a view now increasingly accepted in the three English-speaking countries. King put the view in its most extreme, simplified, and distasteful form; but more or less diluted, more or less complex, it was also the message of Winston Churchill and George Kennan in the spring of 1946 to an audience that was receptive to such explanations. The confusions and uncertainty with which Soviet policy had been greeted since the end of the war were profoundly unsettling after the easy certainties of total war, and could not be sustained. However unpleasant it might be, politicians and public in the United States and Canada seemed to require a new secular faith, and greeted its emergence with relief. Its elements had been in the air since 1917, and could therefore be grasped with a sense of familiarity. From this point on – although policy still remained far from clear – the anti-Communist faith dominated the North American public consciousness, providing a touchstone of 'loyalty,' narrowing the range of speculation and enquiry about Russian intentions, and progressively limiting the margins for diplomatic maneouvre in relations with the USSR.

Although Mackenzie King fretted in his diary during February and March 1946 (and occasionally also to the minister of justice, the cabinet, and counsel for the royal commission) about the Star Chamber methods being employed to extract confessions from the alleged Soviet agents, the hard fact was that the King government deliberately adopted these methods and did not alter them in the months that it had to consider its course before action was forced on it in February 1946. The justification for the suspension of civil liberties in the case was *raison d'état*; and, for that, the nature of the challenge had to be regarded as severe. Despite their uneasiness, King and Robertson always insisted that the methods were justified by the threat. While some members of parliament (especially C.G. Power, A.L. Smith, and John Diefenbaker), civil liberties organizations, lawyers, and friends of the Soviet Union harassed the government for its arbitrary acts, it was evident – to King's political satisfaction – that parliament and public were overwhelmingly prepared to support the government and forgive its indifference to due process.[76] The government's extraordinary action, and its public acceptance, reinforced the sense that a continuing emergency might justify further invasions of the rights of citizens in defence of national security.

A more mundane (and humane) alternative would have been to expel the Soviet diplomats for spying and to use normal police methods in gathering evidence against citizens, even if that reduced the chances of charges and convictions. But in the atmosphere of growing fear, once the spy network was revealed, Mackenzie King seemed desperately to need the evidence of confessions and convictions (however obtained) to prove to the Soviet Union and the Canadian public that the revelations were justified – and thus, perhaps, to prevent potential Russian retaliation. The Soviets, who were after all the instigators of espionage, presumably did not need the proof of their activities that King seemed to think they did. And the belated response to Gouzenko failed even as a counter-espionage operation. With apparently minimal damage to their networks, the Soviets renewed and intensified their spying activities in the three countries – as later prosecutions and defections were to reveal.

During March 1946 the royal commission issued three interim reports, preparing the ground for a series of arrests and charges under the criminal code and the Official Secrets Act. Mackenzie King, who was increasingly sensitive to criticism of the government's detention of suspects without charge or access to counsel (and unable any longer to satisfy himself that the course was justified by the threat of Soviet retribution), now pressed his minister of justice for cancellation of the emergency order-in-council. Finally, on 1 April, the prime minister told the House of Commons with 'immense relief' that the order had been revoked.[77] By this time he was also able to write with some objectivity that the case 'has raised an issue in the minds of the people even more important than that of the espionage and will probably result in several of the persons being freed altogether when they come before the Court, or given trifling sentences. It will be an interesting study in the power of public opinion and preservation of freedom.'[78]

In July, before publication of the final report of the Kellock-Taschereau Commission, the Canadian government informed the Soviet Embassy that seventeen members of its staff had been identified as active espionage agents by the commission. Six of these remained at the time on the embassy staff, and were declared *personae non gratae*.[79] Vitali Pavlov was at the top of the list. The Russian government withdrew these diplomats from Canada under conventional protest a few days later.[80]

The royal commission found that twenty-one persons had been engaged in disclosing secret information to the Soviet Embassy, or were aware of its disclosure. The commission found evidence sufficient for charges to be laid against nineteen of these persons (and in several cases, in effect, passed judgment before trial in its reports). Two of those implicated disappeared before they could be detained; eighteen were eventually

136 Diplomacy of Fear

charged with conspiracy or offences under the Canadian Official Secrets Act; and Alan Nunn May was tried in the United Kingdom. Among the Canadians, eight were convicted and had their convictions sustained, two were discharged on the ground of insufficient evidence, and eight were acquitted.[81] Dr Raymond Boyer of McGill University and the National Research Council was sentenced to two years on conviction for conveying information on proximity fuses to the Russians; Fred Rose, the Labour Progressive member of parliament for Montreal-Cartier, was sentenced to six years for conspiracy; and Sam Carr, the organizing secretary of the Labour Progressive party, was apprehended in 1949 and sentenced to six years of imprisonment for conspiracy.[82]

By midsummer 1946, while the trials continued, public interest in the affair had subsided in Canada. The commission's final *Report* in July, however, which contained detailed accounts of the activities and methods of Soviet military intelligence, was widely circulated and carefully studied among officials in London and Washington as well as Ottawa. For London at least, the lessons were doubly exemplary: while the high commissioner in Ottawa wrote that the *Report* was 'a masterly uncovering of the spy organisation ... a brilliant study ... thorough, clear and forceful,' he added: 'On the other hand, one cannot avoid the impression that the attempt to give dramatic effect has led at times to unjustifiably extravagant language; the search for brilliance has not necessarily always led to an impartial judicial conclusion. Indeed, on close examination it appears remarkable at times that the document should have been issued over the signatures of two judges of the Supreme Court.'[83]

On 3 August *Pravda* commented that the 'trifling affair' could have been settled through normal diplomatic channels, but that the Canadian government had instead allowed itself to become a tool of international warmongers who were seeking, unsuccessfully, to undermine Canadian-Soviet friendship. *Pravda* found its convenient scapegoat in Igor Gouzenko, 'a traitor to his Soviet Motherland,' whose 'vulgar slander, stupid invention, unpardonable lies ... bubbling, slanderous fabrications and generally unpardonable ravings' were the deceptive source of the 'whole shameful comedy.'[84]

Under this onslaught the hardening of Canadian official attitudes developed apace. While returning by ship in February from the first session of the UN General Assembly in London, Escott Reid wrote a personal paper for Norman Robertson on current problems of foreign policy.[85] In his view, there were three possible means of confronting the schism between the Soviet and Western worlds, which should be pursued simultaneously: the creation of a more stable geographic balance between the two realms; the removal of divisive internal conflicts in the Western world; and a long-term effort to end the Soviet-Western conflict. The first would require the resigned acceptance of 'an extension of Soviet influence over border territories especially in the Middle East'; but this should occur as slowly as possible, both to minimize the cost in 'human suffering and moral values' in these areas and to allow the strengthening of economic and political defences in 'the next line of border territories.' The removal of conflict within the Western world would be 'a long and slow process' of economic and social reform; during that effort Western governments would have to engage in propaganda campaigns to 'try to disillusion the Western proletariat about the good faith of the Soviet agents who are trying to capitalize on their discontents.' Most important, the schism between Russia and the West would have to be mended; and that would require a clear understanding of its nature. Reid put the conflict in the absolutist language of religious faith: which made the West's goal the conversion of heretics.

The essence of Western Christian faith is that the individual is eternal and the state and the community are temporal. The individual is an end in himself. The state and the community are mere means by which the individual may be helped to attain the good life. Opposed to this faith is the totalitarian heresy that whatever serves the interests of the state or the community is right ...

In order that the schism may be ended without in the process destroying the values of civilization the Western world must convert the Soviet world from its heresy. In order to prevent war we must launch a war for men's minds. We cannot win that war unless we practise it, unless we preach it with fervour.

Reid focused his attention on the opportunities for Western propaganda and good works in the United Nations. There, the West must 'preach its own gospel and attack the heresies of the Soviet world'; bring the colonial world rapidly to independence; 'formulate a declaration of the rights and duties of states and a declaration of the rights of man' (these would become 'the creeds of the Western world – its articles of religion'); and promote the rapid growth of employment, income, and equality throughout the world. This positive use of the United Nations for progressive Western ends should lead in the end, he believed, to world government. In the process considerations of 'national prestige, particular national advantage,' should be ignored. Escott Reid was donning his armour and raising his banners for the crusade.[86]

Churchill too put the conflict in moral and ideological (if not religious) terms; but Reid considered his purpose to be different. While Churchill sought to rally worldly faith as an element in the conflict of power, Reid suggested that his crusade would be an alternative to it. Churchill foresaw the need for Anglo-American military predominance to force the Soviets into political agreement; Reid aimed more radically at conversion to replace the conflict for power. He had perhaps forgotten, or hestitated yet to admit, that crusades can lead to holy wars.[87] Both, in the winter of 1946, foresaw the need for eventual Russian capitulation.

Hume Wrong, the leader of the Canadian delegation to the United Nations General Assembly, produced a general commentary on the London meetings of the assembly and Security Council on 27 February 1946 which contrasted sharply with Reid's rhetoric.[88] While Wrong recorded that the basic institutions of the United Nations had been created 'without serious friction and in a constructive manner,' he noted that the Soviet delegation had dominated proceedings in a series of propaganda battles against Britain, France, Holland, and Belgium. Wrong expected that the Soviets would continue to exploit the United Nations for its propaganda value, especially 'in an effort to depict themselves as the defenders of dependent peoples, small countries, and organized labour'; and that they would effectively frustrate the work of the Security Council. He therefore concluded, in disagreement with Escott Reid, that 'the talk of turning the United Nations into an agency of international government, by the delegation to it of a portion of the sovereignty of the members, is in present conditions wholly unrealistic.'[89] The forum provided by the United Nations had encouraged the creation of rival blocs, and the value of the organization, in those conditions, was doubtful: 'Without a great alteration ... in the attitude towards each other of the great powers – and it should be emphasized that this alteration is required not only on the part of the Soviet Government – the first meetings of Security Council and the Assembly leave open the question whether the establishment of the United Nations has in fact furthered its primary purpose – the maintenance of international peace and security.'

The British and Canadian embassies in Moscow both produced their counterparts to Kennan's 'long telegram' in the spring of 1946. In two telegrams on 17 March, Frank Roberts reviewed the historic sense of insecurity of the Russian state since the sixteenth century, and the long record of conflict and reconciliation between British and Russian interests in the Baltic, the Middle East, southern Europe, and Asia.[90] Until 1945, however, 'Britain and Russia were never left face to face'; they lived in a diplomatic universe involving a series of other powerful European states. 'Now all that has changed ... The only other world Power is the United States, and there is clearly no reason why Britain and Russia should be brought to combine against her as a menace to their interests or to the peace of the world. Therefore Britain and Russia are now in immediate contact as never before, with no other Power to unite them in self-defence or act as a buffer between them. And between them there is now a greater ideological gulf than even in the 19th century.'

Roberts outlined the Soviet Communist view of capitalist encirclement and internal capitalist contradictions in terms very close to those of George Kennan and, like Kennan, emphasized the dogmatic misconceptions and misinformation that clouded Soviet understanding of the Western democracies. Beyond this, Soviet diplomatic techniques did not involve any belief in the finality and good faith of agreements.

The Soviet Union ... approaches a partner, whom she regards as potentially hostile, endeavours to exact the maximum advantage for the Soviet Union, if possible without any return, and, having obtained what she wants, reopens this issue or raises another at the earliest possible moment in order to achieve the next item on her programme ... All nations are, of course, guided by self-interest; but most other great nations approach the problems of common interest ... with a greater or lesser desire to make their contribution and not only to exact the maximum advantage for themselves.

While other nations shared a certain sense of world community, the Soviet Union had further isolated herself since the end of the war. 'In short, the Soviet Union is ideologically and economically a closed community, controlled by a small handful of men, themselves cut off from the outside world, whose system of government is based upon an all-pervasive police system and the most widespread propaganda machinery.' They despised Western ideas of liberty, tolerance, and justice, and had faith that they represented 'a chosen system destined to spread throughout the world.'

To balance these worrying judgments, Roberts offered some re-assurances. The Russian people and intelligentsia were not hostile to the outside world; and in addition they possessed 'a fundamental streak of laziness, indiscipline and inefficiency.' The revolution had now stabilized, and world revolution was no longer part of the Soviet program. The Russian regime differed from the Nazi in its tactical realism and flexibility; it was pursuing a long-term Russian national policy of gradual aggrandizement rather than any short-term goal of conquest.

British policy, according to Roberts, should be framed on the assumption that Russia sought to expand its borders; that security was her first consideration; that British and Soviet interests in any particular conflict could be reconciled, 'granted the right mixture of strength and patience and the avoidance of sabre-rattling or the raising of prestige issues'; and that no new, overriding common threat would be likely to draw the Soviet Union and Britain together again as it had in 1812, 1914, and 1941.

In the second dispatch, Roberts commented that the Russian experience of the wartime alliance had been that 'all the concessions, approaches and even gestures came from one side, and the Kremlin must have found the course of Anglo-Soviet relations a very pleasant and convenient arrangement under which they received big gains ... They probably hoped and expected that this would continue after the war, and the present crisis in our relations is largely due to a realisation on both sides that the time for one-sided appeasement and concessions is past.'

'It is easier,' Roberts admitted, 'to draw the conclusion that none of the methods adopted over the past thirty years should be repeated than to put forward any very positive or inspiring substitute for them.' The first essential, he believed, was to plan Britain's political strategy as carefully as its military strategy had been planned in wartime – after intensive study and in readiness to face the facts, however unpleasant they might be. Simultaneously, the public should be educated by government and the press out of its illusions, either blindly pro- or anti-Soviet – 'which are equally dangerous counsellors.' Britain should contribute to the economic, social, and political progress of the whole non-Communist world, to inoculate it against Soviet influence. In dealing with the Soviet Union, she should not expect easy benefits; should bargain only for mutual advantage; should apply firmness, 'perfect politeness and ... a formal correctness' to all negotiations; and should show endless patience (to match that of the Russians) in every deadlock. Above all, Britain must earn respect: 'we must be strong, and look strong. But this strength should never be paraded unnecessarily and it should always take account of Soviet susceptibilities and prestige.' The Russians had reacted strongly against Churchill's Fulton speech; but what they objected to, Roberts reported, was not his reference to Soviet respect for strength, or even a closer Anglo-American alliance. They simply considered so frank a public statement of the case to be provocative.

This was all a calm counsel of realism – something, as Roberts concluded, that the United Kingdom knew how to live with. 'I realise that the above may not seem a very inspiring policy and will indeed be a sad disappointment to those who had set their hopes of post-war Anglo-Soviet relations very high. But British relations with Russia were for three centuries maintained not unsuccessfully on such a basis of distant realism between Governments. If we do not aim too high, we shall at least avoid constant irritations and disappointments.'

Dana Wilgress returned to Moscow from the United Nations General Assembly on 6 March, and commented in a dispatch two weeks later that 'the Soviet Union apparently has decided to go its own way.'[91] It had chosen Iran as 'the main object of Soviet aggression at the moment' because it could attack British interests there in the hope of dividing Britain and America. 'If they can get away with it in Iran they can then proceed to treat with Afghanistan, another area remote from the United States and unlikely to concern seriously the people of that country. Only after Anglo-American lack of common policy and inability to act decisively has been demonstrated in the case of these remote areas, are the Soviet Government likely to test possible reactions to territorial encroachments on more delicate regions, such as Turkey and the Middle East generally.'[92]

Wilgress continued to believe that Soviet policy was opportunist rather than carefully designed according to a plan:

... apart from the overall programme of doing everything possible to strengthen the position of the Soviet Union, I believe that the day-to-day manifestations of Soviet policy are nothing more than revelations of the intuitions of Generalissimo Stalin and of his beliefs of the extent to which he can go in pushing Soviet interests without incurring undue risks ... Stalin must often have chuckled to himself over the ease with which he secured the tremendous concessions to his point of view at the Teheran, Yalta and Potsdam Conferences. In fact the price paid to keep him fighting to the last Russian must have convinced him that an equally high price will be paid to keep his remaining Russians at peace. He must contrast the debate over whether or not to divulge the secret of the atomic bomb with the manner in which he would have exploited this advantage if the position had been reversed. He can only interpret as a sign of weakness the feverish efforts of the United States Government to satisfy the demands of the American people for the return home of their sons and husbands. In the centre of this picture he sees ... the imminent breakup of the British Empire. The pickings seem too easy for him not at least to have a try at helping himself.

Wilgress described the appropriate response to this 'irresponsible opportunism' as 'Not that policy of toughness which in the minds of its advocates means treating the Soviet Union as an inferior or as a pariah, but a policy of firmness based on a coalescing of American and British policies on a high moral plane.' It was not quite obvious how 'toughness' and 'firmness' could be distinguished.

When Norman Robertson wrote to Dana Wilgress in March 1946 to suggest that there was a slight chance that Mackenzie King might wish to visit Moscow during the summer, Wilgress was direct in his response.

I cannot now advise the Prime Minister to come here, at least not until after some months have elapsed since he was publicly abused in the Soviet press for disclosing the information leakages in Canada. This is referred to now by the Russians as 'the King affair'.

The Soviet Government and the Soviet public would regard a visit by the Prime Minister to Moscow so soon after the events of the last two months as a sign of weakness and a step of appeasement comparable in kind if not in degree to Chamberlain's visit to Goetesberg [sic] in 1938. They would interpret it as an indication that after their all-out attack on Great Britain Canada, the country occupying the key position between the United Kingdom and the United States, is thoroughly scared and will pay almost any price to appease them. Instead of making them more reasonable I fear it would encourage them to a continuation of their disruptive tactics.[93]

Mackenzie King was, certainly, 'thoroughly scared' by the Soviet Union in the spring of 1946, and his instinct was to appease. But Wilgress was expressing the new line of both Britain and the United States in rejecting any symbolic acts of appeasement, and whatever King's private preferences, he would not act in defiance of Canada's partners. The will-o'-the-wisp of a visit to Moscow evaporated.[94]

Dana Wilgress's own 'long telegram' was a ten-page dispatch of 24 April 1946, in which he sought to answer a series of questions about Soviet objectives in the world.[95]

(a) Are the Soviet leaders prepared to risk another war in the near future?

(b) Is Soviet foreign policy at the present time primarily concerned with the security of the Soviet Union?

(c) Have the Soviet leaders any aggressive aspirations which they wish to see fulfilled in the near future?

(d) Are the Soviet Government sincere in expressing the desire of making the United Nations Organization a success?

(e) Do the Soviet leaders really wish a stable world?

(f) Is the spread of Communism now one of the chief objectives of Soviet policy?

(g) What does Mr. Molotov mean when he complains about lack of equality among the members of the Anglo-Soviet-American coalition?

(h) What are the principal objectives of the present Soviet foreign policy?

Wilgress's judgment about the Soviet desire for war had never wavered: Russia was in no state to wage a major war, and it was inconceivable that she would deliberately seek one. The next three five-year plans would have to be completed before she could face a long war against a powerful antagonist like the United States. Security was the essential justification for all the sacrifices demanded from the Russian people, and the claim that the Soviet Union was encircled by unfriendly capitalist states – though curious in a huge, continental nation – was effective at home.

Wilgress noted, however, that the claim to security or self-defence was always made as a preface by aggressive powers. He referred to his previous dispatches (stemming back to 1943) describing 'the remarkable expansion of the power of Moscow during the past five hundred years,' an expansion which now had the impetus of a doctrine of inevitability and 'the halo of a crusade' to give it dynamism. He was no longer prepared to regard himself as an 'apologist of the Soviet Union,' and could not explain away Soviet expansionism as simply the search for security. However, like Kennan and Roberts, Wilgress was convinced that the Soviet leaders were not reckless, but cool and cautious. They would seek advantage where they could find it. The state of post-war flux, and the uncertainty of the Anglo-Americans in meeting it, had encouraged that instinct. The example Wilgress cited was the experience of autumn 1945:

They have found that all they have to do is to stand firm in the war of nerves and sooner or later the other side come round to them. This was well illustrated by United States policy after the breakdown of the meeting of the Council of Foreign Ministers in September, 1945. A few weeks later the State Department instructed their Ambassador in Moscow to go to the Caucasus to see Stalin, who kept him waiting ten days before signifying his readiness to receive him. Then in December all of the Soviet demands rejected in September were agreed to by the other two powers.

The Soviet attitude to the United Nations, Wilgress believed, was positive (but inconsistent with Western idealism). For Russia the United Nations was a source of international prestige, a vehicle for propaganda, and a means by which she could involve herself legitimately in the resolution of minor conflicts.

Did the Soviet leaders desire a stable world? For Wilgress the answer was simple: they wanted stability in their own sphere and instability beyond it – in Germany, Europe, and the decaying world of colonial territories, where their own interests might gain by unrest, civil war, or economic distress. While there was a comfortable Soviet faith that the triumph of Communism in the world was inevitable, the faith was passive: the Soviet Union appeared to be actively interested in the spread of Communism abroad only in those countries where it might serve Russian national interests.

The Soviet foreign minister's reiterated complaint about lack of equality among the great powers obviously represented a grievance of some kind. Wilgress put it down, as he had previously, to the new boy's sense that the Anglo-Americans did things in their own spheres of influence which they would not countenance from the Soviet Union in its sphere – a claim from Moscow which had considerable strength.

If this is so it indicates the extreme difficulty of reconciling the divergent approach to world problems of the two points of view. Mr. Molotov says in effect that each of the three partners of the coalition has the right, for reasons of security, to its own sphere, in which the others should not intervene, but that outside of these three spheres there should be equality between the three partners. In the case of the United Kingdom the Soviet Union is prepared only to recognise a sphere necessary for the security of the British Isles alone and not for the Empire as a whole. This is derived perhaps from the entire absence of sea power as a factor in Soviet thinking. The Anglo-Saxon powers, on the other hand, while willing to concede to the Soviet Union a zone of security, are not prepared to countenance too much Soviet interference in the world outside of the Soviet sphere. Instinctively they regard this as predestined for the hegemony of the Anglo-Saxon race. In essence it boils down to the difficulty of adjusting the balance between land power on the one hand and sea and air power on the other.

What were the Soviets' principal objectives? That was difficult to answer, because they mixed so much bluffing with their earnestness. They believed they could continue to count upon 'the lack of cohesion between the Anglo-Saxon powers and ... the vagaries of United States foreign policy': Britain and America would always retreat in a war of nerves. Concessions thus prompted further demands, in an endless process allowing no stable understandings. Since there were no fixed Soviet objectives, there was only one appropriate response to Soviet claims: 'resort must be had to that policy of firmness now being pursued by the other two partners of the coalition. The pursuit of this policy is a frank recognition that the attempt to prevent the world being divided into two camps has failed. It is a new attempt to find an equilibrium between the two camps on the basis of relative power.'

Wilgress, like Frank Roberts, was settling in for the long haul. After the period of confusion and uncertainty which he had shared with the political leaders of the United States and Britain, he had now accepted with resigned satisfaction that the new firmness of Harry Truman and James Byrnes was the appropriate response to Soviet power. His approach, like that of the British diplomats in Moscow, remained calm, empirical, and discriminating. He saw no need for panic, religious crusades, or urgent preparation for war. The message was appreciated in Ottawa, where dispatch no. 185 was widely distributed to ministers, the chiefs of staff, government departments, and all missions abroad.[96] But fine distinctions of tone were not easily recognized now in Western dispatches from Moscow, and Wilgress, the former challenger of George Kennan's 'toughness,' was henceforth identified with him. Thomas A. Stone (of the Canadian Embassy in Washington), in a 'Note on a Comparison of some of Mr. Wilgress's recent despatches with some of Mr. Kennan's telegrams to the State Department from Moscow,' commented on the 'striking similarity' of the two in concluding that no policy of appeasement could succeed with the Soviet Union.[97]

The analysis of Russian psychology, the reports of the position of the party, and the estimates of Russian intentions in these two sets of papers are so very similar that it is almost possible to say that when one has read one set it is unnecessary to read the other. If it were possible, therefore, to add more weight to Mr. Wilgress's excellent and interesting reports, this is done by placing them beside the reports of another Russian expert.

In all three English-speaking capitals the determination to hold the line against the Soviet Union had been accepted; but the moral and emotional foundations for this determination remained unstable. As Mackenzie King, Arnold Smith, and Escott Reid had demonstrated, there were other responses – more volatile than Wilgress's – to the Soviet enigma in Ottawa; and they too formed part of the atmosphere.

Preparing for War?

On both sides of the European divide, after the confrontations and challenges of February and March 1946, the months of summer and fall were a time for consolidation. The Truman administration at last seemed confident in its attitude of firmness, as it pursued its policies on Germany, the peace treaties, and atomic energy with a view to its own interests rather than to accommodation at any price with the Soviet Union. On American initiative the Council of Foreign Ministers met again in Paris on 25 April to draft peace treaties for Italy, Finland, Hungary, Bulgaria, and Romania.[1] After weeks of patient negotiation in which the Soviet Union made more significant concessions than did the British and Americans, the draft treaties were brought before a peace conference of twenty-one states in Paris at the end of July.[2] A Canadian delegation headed by Prime Minister King and Brooke Claxton attended the conference, playing a minor role in what was in any case a window-dressing exercise to confirm the treaties already agreed to by the five great powers. Canadian officials found the ten-week conference excruciating, while Mackenzie King sought more interesting diversion in visits to Dieppe, the Normandy battlefields, Berlin, and Nuremberg.[3] While Herbert Evatt of Australia goaded the Russians, the Canadians kept their silence and brooded. 'Suspicion between the Western nations and the Soviet Union,' wrote J.W. Pickersgill and D.F. Forster, 'was only highlighted and accentuated by the tediousness and wrangling which featured the Paris conference and, henceforth, great power tension and conflict became the major factors conditioning the development of Canadian foreign policy.'[4] But the treaties emerged from the conference in October, were refined by the Council of Foreign Ministers in New York in November, and signed in Paris in February 1947.

The occupying powers had delayed dealing conclusively with the

German settlement in 1945, but by 1946 the political vacuum required filling. At the opening of the Foreign Ministers' Conference in April, James Byrnes offered the Soviet Union a four-power guarantee of German disarmament for twenty-five years 'as a test of Soviet objectives in Germany.'[5] Senator Vandenberg, an American delegate at the meeting and the original author of the proposal, wrote that 'If and when Molotov finally refuses this offer, he will confess that he wants expansion and not "security" ... Then moral conscience all around the globe can face and assess the realities – and prepare for the consequences.'[6] The Russians (and the French) had been resisting the creation of unified economic institutions for the whole of Germany, and in May the American military governor, General Clay, suspended reparations shipments from the American occupation zone to Russia pending agreement on a single economic policy. In July Molotov rejected the proposed treaty of guarantee on the ground that reparations payments had to be completed first; and henceforth both Russians and Americans acted on the assumption that Germany would remain divided into zones that would be progressively integrated into their own political and economic spheres. In Stuttgart, in September, James Byrnes outlined American policy favouring unification of the three western zones as the alternative to a united Germany under Soviet control.[7] By this time, it appeared, Soviet and American tests of each other's objectives in Europe were self-confirming. Neither power was willing to concede territory or influence, and the defensive choices of one appeared threatening and expansionist to the other.

On home ground in North America, Canadian ministers and officials had been considering the nature of post-war defence arrangements with the United States for over two years, since the creation of an Advisory Committee and a Working Committee on Post-Hostilities Problems in 1943.[8] In their wide-ranging discussions, the committees attempted to place Canadian defence planning within the larger political and strategic framework of relations among the great powers – in particular, those of the United States and the Soviet Union. As Norman Robertson pointed out to Dana Wilgress in a letter on 5 August 1944:

We have been giving an increasing amount of thought to the question ... of Canada's position between the United States and the Soviet Union. We have not wanted to over-emphasize the danger of a clash between the U.S. and the Soviet Union. Our fears have been based not so much on the prospect of an actual war over our territory between the U.S.S.R. and the U.S. We did fear, however, that the U.S. military policy might be based to such an extent on preparation for a possible war with the Soviet Union, that pressure would be placed upon us to co-operate in defensive measures which the Russians would not consider to be friendly or neutral.[9]

The only means of maintaining Canadian independence between her large neighbours, in the event of discord, would be to provide appropriate defences on her own, sufficient to prevent 'one power from making use of our territory for attacking another. If we do not maintain adequate defences, we cannot blame the U.S. for wanting to interfere in order to protect itself.' Robertson's opinion reflected an earlier judgment of General Maurice Pope, the head of the Canadian military mission in Washington, that the Canadian-American wartime joint defence plan, 'ABC-22,' should be renewed in peacetime to calm the anxieties of the United States:

... should ... the United States go to war with Russia they would look to us to make common cause with them, and, as I judge their public opinion, they would brook no delay.

So, therefore, my view is that the defence relationship between the United States and Canada in the Post-War Period should just be that intimate technical relationship that we enjoy at present. We should renew ABC-22, and take good care that in our defense establishments we should provide adequate forces, not so much as to defend ourselves against possible raids from the enemy (though this would be necessary), but more to ensure that there was no apprehension as to our security in the American public mind. As I used to hold ten years ago when I was in operations, what we have to fear is more a lack of confidence in United States as to our security, rather than enemy action.[10]

The problem of satisfying both great powers that their security was not endangered in Canada was something, as Mackenzie King told his cabinet, that 'may have to be worked out with very special care.'[11]

In May 1944 the Canadian army staff submitted its draft paper on 'Post-War Defence Arrangements with the United States' to the Working Committee on Post-Hostilities Problems.[12] The committee, in applying King's 'very special care,' focused its attention on 'the possibility of tension between the U.S.A. and the U.S.S.R., in which Canada, being sandwiched between the two, would inevitably be involved.' The first instinct of the committee was one of extreme caution: it questioned both the granting of air bases to the United States in peacetime, and the very existence of the Permanent Joint Board on Defence because these 'might give rise to mistrust on the part of third powers' about Canada's neutral and defensive objectives. The revised paper, as it came from the Working Committee a month later, took the obvious but not very helpful line that it would be best for Canada if friction between the United States and the Soviet Union could be avoided.[13]

The committee regarded the next ten years as a reasonable maximum in estimating the dangers of another war. Germany and Japan, defeated and disarmed, would offer no threat. 'Even if tension were to become acute between the U.S.S.R. and the U.S.,' the report added (reflecting the view of Dana Wilgress), 'the problems of recovery and development in the U.S.S.R. are so great that the possibility of warfare between these two Great Powers during the next decade is extremely remote.' The challenge which Canada would face, as the committee suggested in its preliminary conclusions, was therefore to discourage rumours of war rather than war itself. This could be done by maintaining the consultative machinery of the Permanent Joint Board on Defence; planning with the United States for 'the facilities required for the deployment of North American forces in the northern half of the continent' should that become necessary; permitting no American defence installations on Canadian territory in peacetime (perhaps with special exceptions under international agreement); and assuring that Canadian-American defence arrangements fitted within 'the general organization of world security.' General Pope commented on these proposals that, since the prospect of an American-Soviet war fought across the wastes of Siberia and Alaska was 'somewhat far-fetched,' there would be no forseeable occasion for the deployment of American forces in Canada. 'My feeling therefore is that we should not bring such ideas to the attention of our American friends, but on the contrary we should await their doing so (and I am not sure that they will) but from the very outset make it clear to them that actual Canadian defence will be undertaken by Canada.'[14] In two memoranda on 29 June 1944 Escott Reid made a still broader protest that the PJBD should not be invited to discuss any bilateral defence arrangements between Canada and the United States, since this would cause friction between Canada and the USSR.[15] These comments, or similar ones in the advisory committee and the Cabinet War Committee, had a significant effect on the revised document as finally approved by the War Committee on 19 July 1944.[16] The assessment of the likelihood of war as 'extremely remote' remained, now reinforced by the assurance that 'on present prospects Canadian planning for the ten years after the war need not take account of the possibility of attack on North America or of the outbreak of war between the U.S. and the U.S.S.R. The proposal that planning for the emergency deployment of American forces in Canada should take place in the PJBD was removed; and all references to the possibility of hostile American assessments of the Soviet Union and consequent US military pressure on Canada were eliminated. What remained was the general Canadian commitment 'to consult and cooperate on defence matters' through the Permanent Joint Board on Defence; the balancing commitment to refuse permanent American bases in Canada; and a plea for Soviet-American friendship.

When the Canadian military staff in Washington was asked to seek informal reactions to this statement of Canadian policy, General Pope reported strong American reservations – and revealed how easily the subject could become entangled in congressional lobbying.[17] One US member of the PJBD 'whose judgment merits respect' commented that 'the Canadian assumption had been drawn up somewhat conservatively.' The deputy chief of staff of one of the American armed services responded more emphatically.

His reaction was immediate and categorical. He thought it extremely unlikely that the U.S. Joint C.O.S. would be disposed officially to state their agreement with the tentative assumption. The United States services both were hoping and planning to make compulsory military service a feature of the post-war period. They certainly proposed to retain a powerful navy. As for their land and air forces they proposed to remain in a position which would enable them rapidly and at any time to mobilize an army and air force of four and one-half million men. To achieve this policy they would be dependent on Congress. This being so it would be most unwise on their part officially to subscribe themselves to the proposition that the possibility of a major war during the first decade of the post-war period was extremely remote. For if word of this ever reached the ears of congress the hopes they now cherished and planned to achieve would be dashed against the rocks. We were left in no doubt whatever under this head.

Pope suggested, in consequence, that the Canadian document should not be presented officially to the American chiefs of staff.

These informal American objections to the Canadian view that war with Russia was unlikely were sufficient, it appears, to prompt a major rewriting of the document. Following a further round of discussion in the autumn, a new paper was presented to the Cabinet War Committee on 8 January 1945, and finally approved on 28 February.[18] It was more discursive, more sensitive to American military sentiments, more subtle, more ambiguous than the original – and certainly intended for Canadian eyes only. The paper began by warning that the only serious threat to good Canadian-American relations was likely to arise from differing attitudes towards 'events in other parts of the world,' particularly Soviet-American dealings. 'The possibility, however, of the United States being moved to exert undue pressure on Canada, particularly as respects matters of defence, should not be overlooked.' The experience of war, and the new significance of air power, had revealed this possibility starkly. If Canada had been unwilling to co-operate in the wartime joint defence plan, 'the United States was willing and even anxious to proceed alone.' While the United States had now agreed that Canada would purchase all American defence facilities constructed in Canadian territory, American defence planning in future would nevertheless also encompass Canada, and would be carried out either with Canadian co-operation or if necessary in spite of its absence.

The report asserted the positive value to Canada of the Permanent Joint Board on Defence as a means of co-ordination and a medium for informal discussion of such 'potentially controversial questions of defence before government policy in either country has become fixed.' Canada would 'accept full responsibility for such measures of local Canadian defence as the moderate nature of the risk to which we are exposed may indicate to be necessary'; it would leave open for discussion the precise form of these measures; and it would remain alert to the possibility of American pressure based on a more extreme assessment of the military challenge from Moscow. While the advisory committee and Cabinet War Committee had not, by February 1945, altered their judgment that war between the United States and Russia was unlikely, they had begun to face the prospect that American anxieties might force Canada into a military role on the continent which it would prefer not to accept, and which the Soviet Union might consider provocative.

During 1945 the American military members of the Permanent Joint Board on Defence engaged in persistent prodding of Canada over the maintenance of defence communications in the Canadian northwest (between Alaska and the continental United States) and the desirability of standardizing Canadian and American military equipment.[19] The Canadian members of the Board made a considered reply to these advances in

September 1945, noting that they could only be assessed on the basis of a joint appreciation of the threat to be resisted; yet the Canadian military had received no information from the American armed forces about the nature of that threat. The way ahead seemed obvious to the Canadians.

We should both seek to agree as to the international picture of the coming post-war period in so far as this has a bearing on the question of North American defence. This having been done, it should only be necessary for us to revise Defence Scheme No. 2 (ABC-22) which has governed the employment of our forces disposed for home defence during the course of this war, so as to bring it into line with our new joint appreciation of our defence position. This having been done and the new plan having gained the approval of our respective Governments, it can be held in readiness (subject of course to periodic revision) to be put into effect by Governmental agreement in the event of an emergency arising.[20]

In November 1945 the American military members of the Permanent Joint Board, speaking on behalf of the US secretaries of war and navy, made the same proposal for a joint revision of ABC-22.[21] The recommendation was conveyed to the Canadian Cabinet Defence Committee, which in turn recommended to the cabinet on 4 December 'That the United States proposal for continued collaboration in defence planning be accepted and that the Chiefs of Staff Committee, with the addition of appropriate civilian officials, be given the responsibility for coordinating Canadian participation in the preparation of joint plans.'[22] The exercise was important for Canada, the memorandum asserted, because the United States might intend Canada to accept heavy responsibilities for defence; and because joint planning would enable Canada to 'learn as much as possible about the plans being formulated in the United States,' which were bound to affect Canada's own military planning. The cabinet accepted the proposal on 19 December 1945.[23]

With this authority, a planning operation of substantial and rapidly growing scale was undertaken by the Canadian and American military staffs in 1946.[24] Almost immediately Canadian officials in Washington and Ottawa expressed concern that the PJBD, acting on the initiative of the American members, was engaged in 'inappropriate and premature' planning for a full-scale security treaty, without reference either to the United Nations charter or to Canada's position in the Commonwealth.[25] Following these private cries of alarm, the board subsequently proceeded more cautiously to make two technical recommendations for military co-operation between the forces of the two countries, while a special Canadian-American joint committee on military co-operation undertook to prepare the 'joint appreciation' of the strategic threat which the Canadians were seeking, along with a revised basic security plan.[26]

As guidance for the Canadian members of the joint committee, George Glazebrook and Gerry Riddell prepared a 'Memorandum on Soviet Motives in Relation to North America' in February 1946.[27] The paper noted the continuity of Russian policy in seeking security on the country's borders, and asked 'the central question ... whether the expansion of the Soviet Union can be regarded as being limited to the achievement of these objectives.' The 'case for limited expansion' was supported by the evidence that the Soviet Union still permitted the existence of an autonomous government in Finland, and had not conclusively revealed its intentions in Poland, Romania, and Bulgaria. It had not yet incorporated within its boundaries European territories 'as extensive as those which were under the direct jurisdiction of the Czarist regime,' and seemed to have no further annexationist claims except in Turkey. However, 'the case against limited expansion' was that Russian claims of influence beyond her borders were capable of indefinite extension. 'The same kind of argument could be applied to strategic claims and lead, for example, to demands in the Mediterranean going beyond the expressed interest in the Italian possessions on the southern shore. Similarly it might be felt that the Soviet expansion will progressively extend through Siberia to the north-west areas of Canada and the United States.' This piece of hyperbole was neither offered with conviction nor sustained. The paper went on to reassert the view that 'the Soviet Union pursues, largely to the same extent, the same ends as those of the Czarist regime,' and concluded decisively: 'it may be suggested that the foreign policy of the Soviet Union, while pursued by different methods and sponsored by a government which is foreign in its political institutions and social structure, is nevertheless the normal expression of the interests of that country. There have been no indications of undue Soviet interest in North America and politically, therefore, it may be judged that there is an absence of evidence to show the development of any aggressive designs on the part of the Soviet Union against this continent.' Glazebrook made the prudent suggestion that this assessment should be shown only to Canadian officials, lest it should appear to the Americans to be 'an expression of government policy.'

The joint 'Appreciation of the Requirements for Canadian-u.s. Security' which emerged from a four-day meeting at the Pentagon on 23 May 1946 reflected instead the American military view of the Soviet military threat – although without ever identifying the Soviet Union by name.[28] The draft document submitted to the meeting by the American members, the Canadians believed, had already received the approval of the US joint chiefs of staff; in Arnold Heeney's phrase, it was 'amended somewhat' in discussion with the Canadians.[29] The paper contained no intelligence information not available to an informed layman. Only two brief paragraphs discussed the international political situation – and these in the most sweeping and elliptical language. While it was 'impossible to estimate firmly the likelihood of a major war or when it might occur,' the appreciation nevertheless asserted that 'the possibility exists that a major world power might precipitate war or might extend its policies to a point which Canada and the United States, in their own vital security interest, could no longer tolerate. This possibility is emphasized by the present delicate international situation which is characterized by the divergent tendencies in several critical areas each of which contains the seeds of possible global conflict which could germinate with unusual rapidity.' If war broke out in Europe, the continent might be overrun; but in that case the 'hostile powers' (henceforth referred to as the 'enemy') would know that the military potential of the United States, Canada, and the other unconquered Commonwealth countries would be decisive; and they 'might therefore become targets for attack.'

The paper acknowledged that no potential enemy possessed a strategic air force, naval surface forces, or the atomic bomb, sufficient to make possible an immediate attack on North America; it was thus probable 'that any war-minded nation would make every effort to overcome these weaknesses prior to the commencement of hostilities.'

Although enemy capabilities for offensive action against the U.S. and Canada are limited in the immediate future, they will progressively increase as ostensible weaknesses are overcome – attaining culminating proportions when any potentially hostile power has available a weapon of the destructive effectiveness of the atomic bomb. Prior to overcoming these weaknesses, it is reasonable to assume that any war-minded nation would attempt maximum gain by all methods short of a major war.

On the other hand, the completion of a vigorous program of economic and industrial development plus possession of the atomic bomb would change the picture. With such a weapon, any war-minded power would feel confident of the ability to inflict significant damage to Canadian and U.S. war-making ability and the will of our people to fight. It is the consensus of informed scientific thought that it will probably require three to five years for any potential enemy to develop and produce the atomic bomb.

From the speculative assertion that there was a possibility of global war, the paper slid to the position that within three to five years the Soviet Union (though unnamed) 'would feel confident' in attacking the United States and Canada, and would be fully capable of doing so. There was no assessment of whether Russia was in fact planning or developing its ability to do so. The paper then asserted the potential for significant damage to North America by an enemy in the interim, through limited northern invasion, submarine warfare, sabotage and subversion, harassing long-range air attacks, and biological warfare. These claims, too, were unsupported by any evidence of Soviet intentions or real preparations.

By now the paper had become an exercise in military fantasy, soaring free of political reality. The primary targets of the enemy in a major attack on North America would be, first, the 'nerve centers of executive, military and industrial control' – 'Washington, Ottawa, Montreal, New York and Chicago, for example'; major industries, transportation, and communication on the Atlantic seaboard; 'the atomic bomb factories, and the uranium mines at Port Radium'; and the major centres of population, where 'the shock effect ... of a devastating attack' might prompt that choice. The avenue of approach for an attack would have to be by air over the polar ice-cap, since a major assault by sea was inconceivable; the most likely route would be from the northeast, over the stepping-stones offered by 'Spitzbergen, Iceland, Greenland, and the northern Canadian islands.'

North American defences would accordingly have to be developed with 'the firm necessity of keeping our measures for security ahead of (the enemy's) capabilities.' This would require an integrated continental air defence system, including air warning, weather forecasting, and communications networks; interceptor air bases covering 'all avenues of approach at the maximum practicable distance from vital strategic areas'; sufficient interceptor aircraft deployed at these bases; effective air and surface surveillance; naval and antisubmarine forces to control all sea approaches; garrison and mobile forces sufficient 'to deny the enemy lodgment in the northern part of the Western Hemisphere'; and an adequate emergency command structure. Since the capabilities of a potential enemy could reach 'menacing proportions' by 1950, some elements of the defence system were already urgent: the essentials of the air defence system; air photography and mapping; and military training exercises in extreme arctic conditions.

If the Canadian government entirely failed to gain solid information about the reality of the Soviet challenge from this American-inspired joint appreciation, the revelation of US military ambitions for North America was revealing. The US joint chiefs of staff or their delegates were proposing a fully developed system of integrated air, sea, and ground defences, substantially to be located on Canadian soil. The authors took for granted, as justification for this elaborate scheme, the likelihood of a major Soviet attack on the continent, over Canadian territory, after 1950. What was more, the Canadian members of the joint planning committee had endorsed the American appreciation, and had conveyed it at once to the Canadian chiefs of staff and the Department of External Affairs before submission to the Cabinet Defence Committee. A certain momentum had been created in favour of Canadian approval of the document.

The associate under-secretary of state, Hume Wrong, was quickly alerted to the weaknesses of analysis in the paper and its potentially vast implications. On 11 June 1946 he circulated a memo expressing his reservations to senior colleagues in the department and to the cabinet secretary, Arnold Heeney.[30] 'My feeling,' wrote Wrong, 'is that the appreciation while sound in its general analysis is defective in its estimate of the possible time factors involved and also overemphasizes some of the potential dangers. It seems to me to assume a greater capacity in the USSR for waging an offensive war than seems likely to exist now or even within the next decade.' Wrong drew attention to the key Wilgress and Roberts dispatches from Moscow (of 24 April and 17 March respectively), noting especially the paragraphs that emphasized Soviet caution, traditionalism, and incapacity to fight a major war. He expressed extreme scepticism about the chances of 'a long-drawn out struggle with the military occupation of the North-American continent as its major objective,' and dismissed the dangers of wartime sabotage on the evidence of the Second World War. 'The consensus of informed scientific thought' that the Soviet Union could produce an atomic bomb in three to five years was unknown to him. This judgment, he believed – like others – was an exaggeration.

In general, I think that there is next to no danger of any great power deliberately choosing to provoke a major war for at least a decade and probably a good deal longer than that. In the present state of international relations, however, there is a constant friction with the U.S.S.R. and one must admit the possibility that this may lead to local clashes which might grow into a general war against the will of the great powers involved. On the short-term we should be ready to do our part to minimize by adequate defensive measures the effect on North America of a conflict so arising. We need not, however, begin in 1946 to approve plans and incur expenditures based on the conception of a malevolent Russia building up her strength so as to be able to engage successfully in a deliberately chosen contest with the United States.

Wrong and Heeney attended three meetings of the Chiefs of Staff Committee in June to consider the joint appreciation, and simultaneously organized their own, political responses to the paper. On 12 June Heeney wrote to Prime Minister King to brief him on the document on his return from the Commonwealth prime ministers' conference in London.[31] The cabinet secretary reported that 'the conclusions of the draft appreciation are grave.'

There is no doubt that, from several points of view, these developments will constitute one of the most difficult and serious problems with which the government will have to deal, within the next few years. The initiative has been wholly that of the United States but our own military advisers will certainly, on purely defence grounds, reach similar conclusions. They may feel, however, that, on all the evidence, we have more time than u.s. authorities have estimated. It is, I think, likely that the importance which the u.s. government attach to acceptance and implementing of joint plans will be emphasized by an approach on the highest level.

In these circumstances, the government will probably have to accept the u.s. thesis in general terms, though we may be able to moderate the pace at which plans are to be implemented and to some extent the nature of the projects which are to be undertaken.

Within the next fortnight, Charles Ritchie, George Glazebrook, and Hume Wrong each wrote critical assessments of the joint appreciation. Ritchie pointed out its numerous analytical flaws, and dismissed the capability or intention of the Soviet Union to fight a major war in the near future – although he believed that it would be making long-term plans on the assumption that Britain and the United States offered a threat to Soviet security.[32] Glazebrook was dissatisfied with the paper's political analysis, and with the frequent imprecision of its military estimates.[33] Both would require revision; and then the cabinet would face an important decision.

'My impression is that the Americans are pressing for sweeping measures of defence and that our view must be in degree rather than in kind. The implementation of any decision would have serious consequences. I presume some at least of the steps taken would be obvious and therefore cause political repercussions abroad. There would be heavy expenditure and also the probability of suggested American installations on Canadian territory. The last, I think, should be watched particularly carefully.'

Hume Wrong, in his paper of 28 June, noted that while the task of the government's military advisers was to assess Soviet military capacities, it was External's responsibility to estimate whether war was a possibility.[34] (He was discreetly silent about the quality of the military assessment, as he had not been in his less formal comment of 11 June.) While it was improbable that the American government would deliberately provoke war with Russia, Wrong believed it still conceivable that, if the United States were sufficiently provoked, 'there might grow up a wide-spread popular sentiment that war with the Soviet Union was inevitable and should, therefore, be undertaken at a time of their own choosing, while they possessed the enormous advantage of the atomic bomb.' It was less likely that Russia would deliberately seek war with the United States. 'Although it is apparent, both from secret intelligence and from public information about the plans for Soviet reconstruction and development, that they intend to continue to concentrate effort on the building up of their military potential, nevertheless most well-informed persons agree that devastation, war weariness and the needs for raising standards of living make it highly unlikely that the Soviet Government will deliberately seek involvement in another great trial of arms within the next fifteen years.'

The short-term danger was that some local conflict might escalate out of control into a general war; and 'the blundering diplomacy and inability to compromise of the Soviet Government seem almost certain to lead to some local conflagrations.' This danger was likely to increase rather than diminish over time, once the United States lost its atomic monopoly. The Soviet Union was 'essentially self-regarding and nationalistic' and desired 'a troubled and uneasy world.' Its leaders seemed to favour 'a constant war of nerves' which would perpetuate the mood of insecurity. Although the prospect would not change, Wrong asserted that Soviet policy was essentially defensive, and that any comparison with Nazi Germany was misleading. He shared the cool judgment of Dana Wilgress and Frank Roberts from Moscow, rather than the fervour and self-interest of the Pentagon.

The Canadian chiefs of staff, in contrast (while admitting that they had no independent intelligence on which to judge the American assessment of Russian offensive capabilities), offered their support for the joint assessment and recommended its approval to the Canadian cabinet on 15 July 1946.[35]

Faced with the dilemmas posed by this evidence of apparent American pressure on Canada, and the division between Canadian civil and military advisers on the issue, Prime Minister King welcomed the chance to seek advice from Field Marshal Bernard Montgomery, the chief of the Imperial General Staff, during his extended visit to Canada at the beginning of September 1946.[36] Montgomery was both reassuring and unsettling in his views, which were unmistakably European in their perspective on the world crisis. General Foulkes recorded that: 'He took a very grave view of the Russian attitude towards world peace, and he felt that no matter how much we desired world peace there was no doubt we should be prepared for another war with [sic] a period of between ten and fifteen years,' probably to be fought with advanced chemical, bacteriological, and atomic weapons.[37] Montgomery insisted that 'there was no possibility of Russia attempting to invade the North American Continent at any time during the next fifteen years, but that she might attempt air raids either direct or from a base, or bases, established in the Arctic Islands.'[38] A major Russian attack, when it came, would occur against Britain, Western Europe, and the oil states of the Middle East. The primary defensive effort, accordingly, would have to be directed at countering that Russian threat. American and Canadian air forces, in particular, would be needed in Europe, alongside those of Great Britain; Montgomery hoped that the two North American governments would not limit their defence planning to their own continent. Mackenzie King wondered why the United States and the Soviet Union could not agree, as Canada and the United States had after the war of 1812, to avoid competitive rearmament. Montgomery told him that 'Neither country would trust the other, and no one knows what goes on behind the iron curtain.'[39]

When King questioned Montgomery about the proposed joint defence plan, the response was complicated and perhaps tactless.[40]

The Field Marshal reiterated his view that an adequate Air Defence Scheme, well up in the Arctic, was essential so as to prevent the odd raid interfering with the preparations of Canada and America to come to Great Britain's aid. The Field Marshal pointed out that invasion of Canada was not feasible for many years to come. The Prime Minister then interjected that he would like to know whether, in the Field Marshal's view, it was feasible for this country to be invaded by air forces, and that in the next ten or fifteen years air forces may have so progressed that invasion of this country by air was a feasible proposal. The Field Marshal replied that in his opinion the question of invasion by air was not on; that invasion could only be feasible when an adequate supply and maintenance plan could be worked out. This was not feasible in the Canadian North, especially if we refrain from building large air fields which could be used by the enemy in that area. In other words, he considered that the inaccessability [sic] of our Canadian North is our best defence. He did, however, consider that raids were possible and in order to carry out these raids, either by guided missiles or by aircraft, that the enemy may attempt to established [sic] bases in the Canadian Arctic and we therefore must be in a position to reject anyone attempting to establish a base … The question of … an Air Defence Scheme was discussed, and it was emphasized by the Field Marshal that he considered Canada's sovereignty should be maintained. The Field Marshal appeared to have a rather loose appreciation of the Canadian financial position, and, as the Prime Minister pointed out, all development in the Canadian North was frightfully expensive, and he also explained the difficulty of securing large appropriations from Parliament for this purpose without disclosing the reason these appropriations were necessary. The Field Marshal made the remark that he thought Canada was a very rich country and not groaning under a burden of taxation like the Englishmen.[41]

The general nature of the Canadian-American defence discussions had been revealed to the public in the spring, when James Reston of the *New York Times* (abetted by his friend the Canadian ambassador in Washington, Lester Pearson) reported their occurrence.[42] The Canadian editorial response to this news had been positive. Inevitably Montgomery's visit focused attention, once again, on questions of joint defence, and this time the Department of External Affairs was reminded by Radio Moscow that the Russians were watching. Reuters reported on 4 September that a Soviet commentator had pointed to the military significance of Montgomery's travels.

Moscow Radio said that many correspondents felt that Montgomery's Canadian visit should be interpreted in the light of the strategic problem of Canada's arctic frontier, and Canada's preparation for a future war.

Canadian papers, said the Soviet broadcaster, have commented that it is obvious from Montgomery's speeches that Canada is taking 'serious measures' in areas lying opposite her 'northern neighbour.' He added that it will be difficult to convince this 'neighbour' that these measures are innocent. Hence ... it must surprise no one if that neighbour takes counter measures.[44]

While the joint military appreciation awaited consideration by the Canadian cabinet, the American members of the Permanent Joint Board on Defence pressed their case for technical agreements on the sharing of military bases, northern military training exercises, the standardization of equipment, and special agreements on northern weather stations and an advanced American bomber base at Goose Bay, Labrador.[45] On 20 September 1946, the board heard an extensive summary of the State Department's view of the Soviet Union, based very closely on the Kennan 'long telegram.'[46] This account, in echoing Kennan, discounted the likelihood of an early war and held the long-term intentions of the Soviet Union to be 'even more difficult to assess.' R.M. Macdonnell, in his minute on the American briefing, reported that 'the evidence is far from conclusive and the State Department are not certain that the lines of Soviet policy have been firmly fixed in the direction of armed conquest. They have some hope that the Soviet Government can be convinced that a war would be unnecessary and disastrous, and that a somewhat uneasy peace would therefore continue for a long time.' Whether or not it was consciously intended, the occasion revealed to the Canadians a gap between the State Department's and the War Department's estimates of the Russian challenge. 'It is worth noting that the State Department assessment of Soviet intentions, while cheerless enough, is less grim and depressing than that of the War Department. The United States Army doctrine appears to be that a Soviet ("oriental") bid for world domination is only a matter of time, with the inscrutabilities of the oriental mind making it more than usually difficult for the western mind to predict when this time would occur.'

Despite the differing assessments, however, the State Department spokesman made clear that there was a single American policy towards the Soviet Union. American military strength abroad would be maintained, and the United States 'will adopt a combination of firmness and fairness in its dealings with the Soviet Union.' All Soviet proposals would be considered on their own merits, but there would be no gratuitous concessions which might indicate weakness; concessions would only be traded for equally valuable counter-concessions. The permanent commitment to firmness meant that North American defence had to be carefully prepared as one element in America's posture.

This assertion of American determination reflected the Truman administration's embarrassment over the appeal for peaceful accommodation with the Soviet Union made the week before by the secretary of commerce, Henry Wallace, in a major speech at Madison Square Gardens. After a few days of uncertain blundering, President Truman repudiated the speech and received Wallace's resignation from the cabinet. Lester Pearson, in his dispatch from Washington about the affair on 24 September, concluded that the incident had 'greatly lessened' the faith of the outside world in the ability of the United States to follow a consistent foreign policy. Wallace had 'gravely weakened' the administration, given President Truman's domestic and foreign opponents useful evidence for attack, and forced the president, paradoxically, into a position of greater intransigence towards the Soviet Union.[47]

Meanwhile Canadian officials were feeling increasingly uneasy in the face of mounting American pressure to endorse the military view of the Soviet challenge and to undertake the joint measures recommended by the Permanent Joint Board. The joint appreciation and the revised war plan awaited formal consideration by the Canadian cabinet; and in early October Hume Wrong reflected on the delicate problem of giving publicity to the Canadian-American military arrangements once they had been concluded.[48] While the Truman administration purged itself of internal critics in order to maintain a public stance of unwavering firmness toward the Soviet Union, Wrong canvassed the advantages of mounting the defences more quietly. The PJBD's proposals for military co-operation, if published, 'would be treated as the announcement of a defensive alliance against the USSR.'

That, indeed, is what it is in essence, although not in form. Since it was drafted, the beam of Soviet propaganda has been turned on defences in the far North and undoubtedly publication of the recommendation would provide a further occasion for attacks on us and the United States. The decision must be essentially a political one and I am not clear what we should do. On the one hand, Soviet propaganda does not need much in the way of fuel and the addition of a little more may not make much difference. On the other hand, publication would make it more difficult to carry out even modest and essential work in the far North without giving rise to alarmist reports.

The Cabinet Defence Committee had delayed recommending approval of the joint appreciation and basic security plan to the cabinet over the summer, but it had nevertheless authorized continued Canadian-American defence planning on the basis of these documents. Planning proceeded at an intense pace through a series of bilateral military staff committees: by the middle of October the major committee had held seventy-three meetings, and was ready for early cabinet approval of a wide range of specific defence programs.[49] The most substantial of these involved a four-year development plan for air interceptors and warning, estimated to involve 105,000 personnel and 2,478 aircraft, at a total capital cost to the two countries of $407,372,950. In Washington both State and War departments were anxious to maintain the pressure for decision on the Canadian government. On 1 October the acting secretary of state, Dean Acheson, suggested to President Truman that the time had come for a firm nudge at the political level.[50] While the Canadians were 'tacitly permitting' the development of close military collaboration, they had not formally given their approval. 'Our military authorities,' wrote Acheson, 'are naturally insistent on closing the gap between Alaska and Greenland and on pushing the defense of our industrial centers north of our own border. For this we are dependent on the cooperation of the Canadian Government.' Acheson noted that a shift to still closer military association with the United States, and away from Britain, 'is a matter of great moment in Canada and one which involves a considerable political risk for the present Government. Some Canadians fear that we would encroach on their sovereignty and some fear that Canada might ultimately have to withdraw from the British Commonwealth.' 'I am sure,' he concluded, 'that it would help a great deal if you felt inclined to express to the (Canadian) Ambassador your interest in the effective carrying out of joint defense plans.' (Subsequent evidence suggests that he did so.)

In mid-October 1946 the three senior members of the Department of External Affairs engaged in a round of musical chairs which sent Norman Robertson to London as high commissioner, Lester Pearson to Ottawa as under-secretary, and Hume Wrong to Washington as ambassador.[51] (This followed the separation of External Affairs from the prime minister, and the appointment of Louis St Laurent as minister, in September.) Without missing a beat, Wrong and Pearson exchanged places at this crucial occasion for Canadian-American relations. In Ottawa on 23 October, Pearson met the American ambassador, Ray Atherton, who conveyed to him an invitation for Prime Minister King to visit President Truman in Washington the following week to discuss northern defence.[52] Pearson was convinced, he told St Laurent, that the Americans placed the need for a quick and satisfactory settlement of the issue very high.

The flood of specific American proposals for military co-operation on Canadian territory during 1946 had by this time somewhat displaced the joint appreciation of the Soviet threat as a preoccupation of the Department of External Affairs, although the joint appreciation hovered in the background as the rationalization for the detailed proposals. When Hume Wrong wrote to Prime Minister King from Washington on 26 October in preparation for his meeting with Harry Truman, Wrong concentrated his comments on the difficulties for Canada raised by the specific American requests – and added that 'There is still ... a lot to be learned in Washington about our position and our problems.'[53] Wrong was worried that Canadian sovereignty would be threatened by American air defences on Canadian territory; that Canadian financial resources would be strained; and (following Montgomery's argument) that the capacity to respond to Soviet aggression where it was more likely would be diminished by the concentration of military resources in the Canadian north. He recommended that the general line to be taken with President Truman should be to temporize, while assuring him of Canada's 'hearty agreement' with the principle of close military co-operation. In the end Wrong reiterated his dissatisfaction with the joint appreciation as the foundation for the kind of military integration the Americans were suggesting:

You might finally express the hope that we shall be taken fully into the confidence of the U.S. authorities not only on their plans for continental defence, but also on their appreciation of the dangers of war and their estimates of the international and strategic situation. They have been more forthcoming in the last year or so, and this might be recognized. They still, however, have some way to go before we can ourselves assess the bases on which they are doing their own planning and seeking our active co-operation with them.

Wrong did not suggest (what in retrospect appears evident) that Canada had in fact received as much hard intelligence about Soviet intentions as the Americans possessed – that is, remarkably little. Nor did he consider that repeated appeals for more confidential information on which to judge American policy might make an independent Canadian assessment of the Soviet Union more politically difficult – not less.[54]

Mackenzie King met Harry Truman at the White House on 28 October 1946 to discuss North American defence. As Hume Wrong reported, 'the discussion was in general terms and no specific proposals were put forward.'[55] The leaders agreed in principle on close co-operation in defence and information-sharing, and King expressed his wish to inform the United Kingdom of any arrangements between the United States and Canada. Truman mentioned the American desire to develop a forward bomber base at Goose Bay, Labrador, and agreed with King that further talks should proceed on the diplomatic or ministerial level. King gained Truman's agreement that 'the greatest care and fullest consultation' would have to occur before any publicity was given to mutual defence arrangements. Finally, President Truman offered King his views on the likelihood of Soviet aggression.

These were very closely in accord with those expressed by Mr. Wilgress. Their general tenor was that the Soviet Government would be in no position to participate in a great war for a considerable period, and that the aggressiveness of Soviet foreign policy might well be caused in part by the desire of the masters of Russia to maintain a feeling of strain and insecurity at home so as to diminish discontent with the rigours of the existing regime.[56]

The conversation was reassuring: it seemed that King's and Truman's experience of the Russians during the year had calmed the exaggerated anxieties of 1945. Nevertheless, the American commitment to diplomatic firmness had a military corollary in North America. The US administration had decided that northern air defences would have to be developed for the long term, whether or not there was a significant threat of Soviet aggression against the continent. Wrong reported that the way was open for further discussion, but that initiative had been left in the hands of the Americans. What had been accomplished was to check, for the moment, the momentum of the military planners of the two countries, and to raise the discussion to the level of strategic principle among the politicians and diplomats.

Two days later, in Washington and Ottawa, the Canadian government was presented with a long written statement, described as an 'oral message,' from President Truman to Prime Minister King.[57] It put directly and emphatically, in the language of the State Department, what Truman had said less precisely during their interview. The conclusions differed dramatically from those King had brought back from Washington. There should be quick concurrence in the joint appreciation of the Soviet threat, and rapid implementation of a North American defence scheme, because the military advisers of the two governments considered that within five years 'another major power will be capable of jeopardizing North American security.' The document assured Canada of the American desire to respect 'the traditional relations of the two countries' and to share defence costs equitably. Permission for the maintenance of US air force units at Goose Bay was again requested; and the paper suggested that all these things could be accomplished without a treaty and within the framework of co-operation under the PJBD that had been customary since 1940.

As the cabinet prepared to discuss the American requests, Lester Pearson offered the prime minister his personal views on 12 November.[58] Pearson focused his attention on the world political situation, as the proper background for examining questions of Canadian defence. He quickly dismissed the ability of the United Nations to guarantee international security, and turned to the relations of the United States and the USSR.

If the relations between these two powers deteriorate to the point of conflict, we in Canada cannot escape from becoming involved at once. If we think that such a result is probable, or even possible, we would be negligent if we did not plan our defence policies with that end in view. The U.S.A. is certainly not going to provoke such a conflict and will not consciously shape its policies in such a way that they might be interpreted as aggressive and provocative, though it will make many mistakes and may even on occasion adopt bellicose and unreasonable attitudes. But what about Russia? Is it possible for the western democratic world to work out, if not a friendly, at least a tolerable relationship with a state, organized on a police basis, governed by ruthless despots, inhabited by millions of fighting men to whom life is hard and cheap, and with a dynamic communist ideology[?]

His response to this rhetorical question was decisive. 'My own view, for what it may be worth, is that without some fundamental change in the Soviet state system and in the policies and views of its leaders, the U.S.S.R. is ultimately bound to come into open conflict with western democracy ... The Russian leaders themselves insist on this. We should not make the mistake we made with Hitler, of refusing to take seriously the words those leaders utter for home consumption.' This judgment seemed to challenge the King-Truman consensus that Russian tough talk could be faced with equanimity. For Pearson, Soviet domestic and foreign policy could not be disentangled; Russia's ruthless despots were bound to carry their policy of conquest abroad. 'All this does not mean war today or tomorrow,' he added. 'I cannot believe that Russia – even crediting her with the most evil intentions – would be ready to strike within five years or ten years. But the way the world is now going, there can only be one ultimate result – war.'

The lesson of current history was that Canadians should 'limit our thoughts of peace to a short period of time.'

In the strategy of a future war, there could be no isolation for Canada or the United Kingdom – although 'the centre and pivot' of the 'freedom loving world' would be the United States. Careful planning by Canada now might limit unreasonable claims on Canada in the future. 'But the inescapable facts of the world situation dictate close co-operation with both these countries in working out combined plans based on sound principles. This may, for us, result in obligations which, economically, will be difficult to carry.' Pearson drew the somewhat veiled conclusions that national strength should be effectively organized for the coming dangers; that this would require 'combination and co-operation' above all with the United States; and that Canadian defence plans should fit this combined effort rather than reflecting 'merely traditional and possibly outworn concepts.' He seemed to be recommending acceptance of the American strategic assessment and joint defence plan; he was certainly gingering the prime minister's thoughts with a renewed dose of fear.

Accompanying his memorandum, Pearson sent King two statements on the Soviet Union: one a recent leading article from the *Economist*, the other a paper, 'Russia from the Political Angle,' given by an unidentified British diplomat to a conference of UK military attachés in London.[59] He urged that King should read these, and implied that they supported his view that eventually there would be war. Curiously, they did not. The *Economist* argued, on the contrary, against taking 'the melodramatic view' of Russian expansionism. A consistent Western policy of diplomatic firmness, it believed, would make possible a long period of practical (though not friendly) collaboration. 'The chief buttress of peace at the moment is the much abused balance of power, which is strongly against Russia, and will remain so, unless Western carelessness allows the atomic bomb to get on to the wrong side. The reasonable attitude for the liberal-minded Westerner to adopt towards Russia is one of dislike and even of distrust, but neither of fear nor of hostility.'

The Foreign Office paper was a painstaking account of the historical background of Russian tyranny, insecurity, underdevelopment, and expansionism, similar to earlier dispatches from the British Embassy in Moscow. While it gave a pessimistic account of Soviet aims in Europe, the Middle East, and Asia, and foresaw worsening rather than improving relations as Russian power increased, the paper concluded: 'It does not seem likely that we are confronted with the threat of a major war in the near future. Russia, so far as we can judge, is neither prepared for nor in the mood for war, and Stalin is a sober realist. But the general outlook is one of friction, disputes, recrimination and unrest.' In his paper for the prime minister, Lester Pearson preferred instead to blur the line between a calculating Soviet Union determined to make gains by relentless annoyance, subversion, and diplomatic pressure, and a Soviet Union dedicated ultimately to war.

The cabinet and Cabinet Defence Committee now, in mid-November, entered three days of intensive meetings primarily devoted to the accumulated questions of the Soviet challenge, North American defence, and Canadian-American relations, in which differing interpretations of Soviet policy played a crucial role.[60] At the Defence Committee meeting on 13 November, Mackenzie King asked the chiefs of staff for their comments on the general strategic situation before discussion of President Truman's requests in his 'oral message.' The chief of the air staff, Air Marshal Leckie, reviewed the history of the joint appreciation and basic security plan, and noted that the most important detailed plan to follow from these general directives had been the air defence scheme. He was dissatisfied both with the defence plan (particularly its cost) and the strategic judgment from which it derived.

The intelligence upon which the draft appreciation was founded had been drawn largely from United States sources. The military view in Washington was that, in any future war, an aggressor would attempt to neutralize the war potential of this continent before embarking on a programme of expansion elsewhere. He did not altogether share this view, and felt that any attacks which might develop would be of a diversionary nature which would not warrant the establishment of an elaborate defence scheme employing our resources in a static role. With this in mind, and, in view of the immense financial outlays involved, it might be more appropriate to adopt measures of more modest proportions.[61]

The army chief of staff agreed that defences aimed at 'complete protection against sporadic raids' were unjustified, and that more realistic planning would allow for an offensive capacity as well as static defences. But he added that the British military appreciation of the risks of war 'did not differ materially' from the Canadian-American military appreciation. The Defence Committee decided that the chiefs of staff should repeat their reports to the cabinet the next day. At the same meeting, the committee agreed to recommend approval of the PJBD's 35th recommendation on principles of military co-operation to the cabinet, while deferring discussion of publicity for the agreement.

When the full cabinet met the next morning, the military staff had apparently closed ranks. Service intelligence officers, using maps and charts, explained the joint military appreciation of Soviet aims, capabilities, and potential objectives in North America; the chief of the general staff, Lieutenant-General Foulkes, reported that the chiefs of staff had concurred in the appreciation and defence plan as a basis for detailed planning, and that planning had proceeded with the support of the Cabinet Defence Committee and the prime minister; and Air Marshal Leckie reported that both the Canadian and UK General Staffs disagreed with the view of US staff that the main Soviet attack, in the event of war, would be delivered against the United States.[62] Later in the day, in the absence of the chiefs of staff and their advisers, Mackenzie King told the cabinet that there was no doubt that Canadian and American defences were inseparable; that further diplomatic discussion on the basis for joint planning should proceed; but that – in the words of the cabinet *Conclusions* – 'It was questionable, however, how far the government should accept, in any event at this stage, the strategic concept upon which the conclusions of the joint draft appreciation had been based.' A decision on this question was deferred, but 'after considerable discussion' the cabinet accepted the Defence Committee's recommendation that the Permanent Joint Board's 35th recommendation should be approved.[63]

Messages were now flying in profusion to and from the East Block, and a line of delicate compromise with the United States seemed to be emerging. On 13 November in New York (where the UN General Assembly was in session), Ernest Bevin gave Louis St Laurent an *aide-mémoire* from Britain about US bases in Canada.[64] Although he recognized that Canadian proximity to the United States made defence co-operation essential, Bevin urged caution. While it was important 'that both Canada and ourselves should co-operate with the United States ... and that we should not appear to rebuff their present advances,' there was also a 'grave danger of provoking Soviet reactions which would tend to divide the world into two armed camps.' '[W]e should beware of military measures which, because of their unfavourable reaction on political sentiment, make themselves the more essential. This is a vicious circle which leads inevitably to war. Consequently, military measures, however great their technical advantages, should be subordinate to political considerations.' Above all the British proposed delay: 'We suggest that the matter is one that should not be hurried. Although four or five years is little enough time in which to set up a defensive system in the Arctic regions and in which to train personnel, it does leave sufficient time for the matter to be given the close study which it deserves.'

From Washington, Hume Wrong also appealed for a lead at the political rather than the military level.[65] His purpose seemed to be not necessarily to alter the judgments of the joint appreciation or the defence plan, but rather to transcend them in a common political assessment which could more easily be accepted by the cabinet. He wrote personally to Lester Pearson:

The more I think of it, the more I am convinced that a joint appreciation and forecast of the global strategical situation, developed by our two great prospective Allies in another war, would be of great value in reaching intelligent decisions on our own domestic policies, provided that it is well done and carries conviction. If these talks fulfill their purpose and the results are accepted in London and Washington, it seems to me that we shall have to accept the conclusions as a matter of practical necessity. Unless we run the risks involved in junior partnership in the formulation of the strategical concepts, I am fairly certain that there would be greater difficulty in securing consent in Ottawa on the political level, since the advisers of the Government would not be able to explain fully the processes whereby the conclusions were reached.

At the decisive cabinet meeting on 15 November 1946, a consensus emerged that the joint appreciation should be superseded by immediate negotiations with the United States at the diplomatic level.[66] Brooke Claxton set the tone with his reminder that, on the basis of the joint appreciation, there was a 'fundamental difference of view' between the American and Canadian military staffs: 'the Americans say that they are to be the object of the main attack, and we say that at the outset we would be the object of a diversionary attack.'[67] In consequence the Canadian military favoured a modest defence plan in comparison with the American scheme put forward by the joint planners.

It seems to me that in these circumstances, and against this background, our approval of the appreciation and endorsement of the joint planning that is now going on could not but mislead our American partners into the belief that we were going along with them in their concept.

It seems to me that each day that we allow them to continue along the present course will commit us further to acceptance of that course.

It seems to me that as this proceeds we will find that in their view at least we will have acquiesced in the action they have been taking, so that all that remains will be to settle the details and allocate the cost.

The prime minister read to the cabinet the British *aide-mémoire* of 13 November, and said that it would be improper for Canada to give its support to the military appreciation or its consequences until there had been political agreement on the Soviet threat. Other ministers expressed their approval, and eventually the cabinet concluded:

1 that while general endorsement could be given to the principle of joint defence planning with the United States, the government could not concur in the draft joint appreciation submitted through the Canadian and U.S. Joint Chiefs of Staff, pending the outcome of forthcoming discussions between the two governments on the diplomatic level; as a result of these discussions it was hoped that a general appreciation, taking account of all relevant factors, would be agreed between the two governments;
2 that no decision could be taken respecting the U.S. government's proposal to station additional forces at Goose Bay, Labrador, pending the forthcoming discussions with the United States, and pending discussion of this subject with the U.K. government and Newfoundland;
3 that joint defence planning should not proceed beyond the present stage, pending the forthcoming discussions and pending agreement between the two governments as to the lines upon which further planning should proceed and joint measures be undertaken;
4 that the Chiefs of Staff be directed to prepare forthwith a joint defence programme for the immediate future – including a joint appreciation and joint plan, due weight being given therein to:
   (a) the course of joint planning with the United States; and
   (b) other relevant factors from the Canadian point of view (e.g. local defence, Commonwealth relationships, possible United Nations obligation).[68]

On the Canadian side, preparations were undertaken at once for diplomatic discussions with the United States. In a preliminary meeting between Canadian and American officials on 21 November, led by Lester Pearson for Canada and the American ambassador, Ray Atherton, for the United States, an agenda based on the Canadian concerns was accepted.[69] The talks would begin with consideration of a political estimate of Russian intentions (as opposed to an estimate of military capabilities), which

Canada was particularly invited to provide; an analysis of possible Soviet reactions to North American defence measures; and a discussion of global strategy. Detailed consideration of North American defence planning would then follow. On 30 November R.M. Macdonnell produced the key Canadian paper on the objectives of Soviet foreign policy, which was subsequently made available to the American participants as well.[70]

Macdonnell's paper began by repeating the frequently asserted judgment of the Department of External Affairs that it was 'most unlikely,' 'highly improbable,' that the Soviet Union would enter a major war in the coming fifteen years, while accepting that Russian economic power and war potential would steadily grow. But three qualifications were added to this estimate of short-run dangers: the possibility of Russian acquisition of atomic bombs or 'some new weapon of mass destruction'; the unpredictable consequences of a succession crisis following the death of Stalin; and the remote chance of a local war that might grow into a general conflict. Since these qualifications were either undeveloped or dismissed, the judgment of the short-term danger remained optimistic.

However, the paper took a gloomier view 'that there are powerful forces at work which may in the end precipitate the struggle between the Soviet Union and the Western World.' The Marxist vision of the 'ultimate struggle between communism and capitalism' was a fact in Russian policy, although 'It may be assumed, however, that Soviet foreign policy will be dictated less by ideological considerations than by a realistic estimate of Soviet interests as they are understood in the Kremlin.' The Soviet dictators would engage in 'unceasing propaganda to instill into the population fear and suspicion of the intentions of the Western democracies,' which would itself be a danger to world peace. 'Apart from the desire to further world revolution,' the paper continued (without examining the evidence for this supposition, which Dana Wilgress had firmly discounted), 'the Soviet Government may be led in the direction of war by two other motives. One is the desire for expansion – perhaps for eventual world domination – and the other is fear of a threat to Soviet security by the Western powers.'

It was 'perfectly obvious' that the Soviet Union was an expanding power: the lists of Soviet conquests, zones of exclusive influence, and pressure points 'represent formidable acquisitions of power and influence; and there are no signs that the Soviet Government is willing to set bounds to its appetite for further expansion.' But this absence of finite goals had to be carefully interpreted:

There is, perhaps, however, a valid distinction between admitting Russia's expansionist tendencies and attributing to her schemes for world domination, although the distinction may be rather one of method than of eventual objective. It seems unlikely that the Soviet Government is contemplating grandiose schemes for world domination of the kind which fascinated the restless dictators of the thirties. The Soviet rulers have always despised what they term 'bourgeois adventurism.' The gambling spirit that is willing to take great risks in the hope of immense returns seems to have little appeal for the Soviet Government. On the record of their past policies, it is rather difficult to imagine the rulers of the Soviet Union unleashing at a stroke a world struggle. It seems more probable that the Soviet Government will pursue a course of deliberate and cautious consolidation of positions already acquired together with a process of probing for weak spots in the adversary's positions. Such a policy might operate on the political, economic or military planes.

The Soviets sought to divide the Western powers and to encourage 'discord and instability.' Such aims were incompatible with conventional friendship and co-operation, but they did not imply a desire for world war.

Macdonnell examined the matter of Soviet reactions to Western policy judiciously. In the first place, the Russian leaders respected American industrial power, recognized the attractions of democratic ideas to other peoples, and were worried that socialism in Britain might undermine the appeal of the Communist alternative on the European continent. So long as they believed that the Western democracies were strong, united, and firm in their foreign policies, the Soviets would act with caution. But if the Western economies faltered, or if Western firmness collapsed, the Russians might be tempted into a more aggressive policy. 'They will certainly seize upon any evidence of appeasement as an encouraging sign of weakness.' At the other extreme, the West had to avoid any impression that it had aggressive goals, since the Soviets 'might feel impelled to provide in haste for their security by further annexations of territory or infiltration into countries in strategic positions.'

The paper recommended a policy of prudent anticipation which reflected the existing attitudes of the United States and United Kingdom governments to the Soviet Union.

Thus while the threat of immediate aggression seems slight, there is little prospect of sincere cooperation with the Soviet Union. A period of deteriorating relations between the Soviet Union and the Western world is to be anticipated. It is all too probable that this situation may end in war. The best likelihood of averting such a catastrophe would be for the Soviet Government to be convinced of the strength and unity of the western democracies and at the same time persuaded that they have nothing to fear from them. It is possible that they might then postpone indefinitely the accomplishment of their ultimate aims and the world might settle into a period of uneasy peace.

If this analysis is correct, we cannot afford to risk being unprepared in the event of war. The danger that Soviet policies may end in aggression cannot safely be ignored and it becomes essential in self-protection to consider the defensive measures entailed by the possibility of Soviet aggression.

On 16 and 17 December 1946, senior Canadian and American diplomatic and military representatives met in Ottawa, once again under the joint chairmanship of Lester Pearson and Ray Atherton, in what was described as an informal (but minuted) meeting.[71] The most significant addition to the American delegation was George Kennan, who was then on secondment from the State Department to the National War College in Washington. (In a letter to Dean Acheson in October, he had foreseen 'occasions where it might be possible for someone who, like myself, is not too far from the Department of State and at the same time not too near to it, to accomplish something valuable in the support of our present policies.'[72] This was such an occasion.) As the diplomatic catalyst of the policy of firmness, and the American diplomat most respected by the Canadian Department for his judgment of the Soviet Union, Kennan was an inspired choice for the American delegation.

The finesse with which the meeting reached its conclusions on the Soviet challenge, indeed, suggests the possibility that there was some skilful prearrangement of the outcome – perhaps at the hands of Lester Pearson and Hume Wrong, who both saw the need for an amicable agreement which would be tolerable to the Canadian cabinet and the prime minister. The document presented for discussion was a Canadian one, and it was clear in advance that this Canadian appreciation coincided very closely with George Kennan's position. Not surprisingly, Kennan responded flatteringly to the paper on behalf of the US delegation that he was in general agreement with the Canadian conclusions. He emphasized the need to balance firmness with moderation, and applied the lesson to North American policy. 'Defensive weapons in the Arctic were a logical security development and the U.S.S.R. would expect precautions of this nature to be taken. These should, however, be carried out in such a way as to minimize the possibility of their being exploited as a threat to peace. They should be treated as co-operative arrangements of a continuing nature and not as indicating a new policy.' Although Arnold Heeney warned that the Canadian government believed there would be 'some element of provocation in the overt planning of joint defence measures in the Arctic,' he recognized that this disadvantage 'had to be balanced against the deterrent element in the policy of firmness.' The meeting agreed that 'there was no substantial difference between the viewpoint of the u.s. and Canadian representatives as to the objectives of the Soviet Union and as to the effect upon the Soviet foreign policy of undertaking joint Canadian-u.s. defence measures.'[73] 'The Canadians ...,' writes Joseph Jockel, 'discovered that the views of the Soviet threat expressed in the Appreciation exaggerated the US perception.'[74]

On the relationship of North American defence to global strategy, the Americans took the lead and succeeded equally in reassuring the Canadians. Lester Pearson reported to the prime minister that American planning was based above all upon the ability to take the strategic offensive outside North America in case of war, and that continental defence was seen simply as an essential complement to this war-making capacity abroad.[75] The United States did 'not favour the enormous diversion of resources that would be needed to provide one hundred percent protection for North America'; by extension the Canadians apparently need not fear pressure for a defence effort that would be beyond Canadian means.

On the second day of the talks, the American military delegates offered what Pearson described as 'very important information' about US strategic planning.

We had been talking on the previous day about 'stop lines' beyond which the United States could not allow the U.S.S.R. to advance. On the next day, General Lincoln made it clear that the stand taken by the United States delegation at diplomatic conferences in the last six months gave a very clear indication of where that 'stop line' was; that it moved through the centre of Germany to Trieste, and from there through Greece to the Dardanelles. The United States, however, made a very sensible distinction between a geographical and an ethical stop line; in other words, it was not merely a question of an advance of the U.S.S.R. beyond a certain line so much as whether this advance was made with the genuine consent to [sic] the people concerned or aggressively and against their wishes. A concrete example would be Trieste. If the people of that city of their own free will decided to attach themselves to the Yugoslav Federation there could not be any objection on anybody's part. It would be quite another matter, however, if that change took place by aggressive action against the will of the people.

Once a general understanding on the Soviet Union and global strategy had been achieved at the meeting, it was possible for both parties to define away the problem before which Canada had balked. The military representatives pointed out that the basic security plan was 'a purely military plan' which committed neither government to specific action. Arnold Heeney added that the original joint appreciation was not something to be accepted or rejected by the Canadian cabinet. What remained for cabinet consideration, therefore, were the particular joint defence projects, on which decisions would be taken as the projects were presented one by one. There would be no single, comprehensive document to bind the two countries in a common defence policy.[76]

The Americans indicated their intention to make specific proposals related to the air defence plan, mapping, weather forecasting, and joint testing; the principles of cost-sharing were discussed amicably but inconclusively; the delegates agreed, at Canadian insistence, that some general publicity would have to be given to the acceptance of the PJBD's 35th recommendation, emphasizing it as 'a natural continuation of wartime co-operation'; the Americans accepted Canada's desire to inform the United Kingdom of the general nature of joint planning; and the Canadians agreed to seek the concurrence of the UK and Newfoundland governments in placing a United States heavy bomber group at Goose Bay, Labrador.[77]

It appeared that this outcome was entirely satisfactory for all participants, civil and military, Canadian and American. Official attitudes to the Soviet Union now seemed to coincide (or speculative differences, at least, seem to have been repressed); measures of common defence could proceed; and these measures would not be unduly provocative or an excessive strain on the Canadian treasury. In Lester Pearson's view, the Americans had behaved impeccably. They made their case reasonably and moderately, allowed the Canadians to reach their own conclusions, and made no attempt 'to present demands or to insist on certain things being done.'[78] As a result, they gained the essential Canadian agreement they had sought to proceed step by step with measures of common defence in Canadian territory – although at a slower pace than the US members of the Military Co-operation Committee had originally desired. That pace suited the Truman administration as well as it did the Canadian government. Over the next two months the budgetary and logistical implications were worked out for the short-term, and on 12 February 1947 the prime minister told the House of Commons that military co-operation between the two countries, through the Permanent Joint Board on Defence, would continue on the limited basis of staff interchanges, common testing and exercises, the encouragement of standardization, mutual use of bases, and the maintenance of sovereignty.[79] No new treaty or contractual obligations were involved, and Mackenzie King emphasized that the policy stemmed directly from the Ogdensburg agreement. In his peroration King was studiously unprovocative, seeking to discharge any suspicion – Russian or Canadian – that anything unusual was going on.

In conclusion, I should like to comment briefly on problems of northern defence. The subject has naturally engaged the attention of many people both here and abroad and some quite unfounded suggestions have been put forward. There is a persistent rumour, for example, that the United States Government has asked for bases in the Canadian North. This is a rumour which I should like to deny emphatically. There has been talk of Maginot lines, of large-scale defence projects, all of which is unwarranted and much of it fantastic. What we are trying to do is to view the situation soberly, realistically, and undramatically.

It is apparent to anyone who has reflected even casually on the technological advances of recent years that new geographic factors have been brought into play. The polar regions assume new importance as the shortest routes between North American and the principal centres of population of the world. In consequence, we must think and learn more about these regions. When we think of the defence of Canada, we must, in addition to looking East and West as in the past, take the North into consideration as well. Our defence forces must, of course, have experience of conditions in these regions, but it is clear that most of the things that should be done are required apart altogether from considerations of defence. We must know more about such fundamental facts as topography and weather. We must improve facilities for flying. We must develop better means of communication. The general economic development of the North will be greatly aided by tests and projects carried out by both civilian and defence services. As the Government views it, our primary objective should be to expand our knowledge of the North and of the conditions necessary for life and work there with the object of developing its resources.

Thus Mackenzie King drew a gigantic veil of euphemisms over the beginnings of a northern defence policy undertaken on American initiative and in response, initially, to American perceptions of the Soviet challenge.

He might have encouraged Canadian self-understanding if he had been more straightforward – but that was never one of his main objectives. But was this preparation for war? In rhetoric, certainly not; and in fact, despite the anxious and interminable military and political discussions of the previous months, the defence preparations which resulted in the north were minimal. The Canadian government would move slowly, but in tandem with the American – which seemed to be all, for the moment, that the policy of 'firmness and fairness' towards the Russians required. In 1947 the two administrations reached agreement on the Goose Bay establishment and a system of northern weather stations, while the new minister of national defence, Brooke Claxton, undertook a rigorous campaign of budgetary cost-cutting.[80] The message the Soviet Union received from these activities could not have been alarming.

Pax Americana

While the American military rationalized their ambitions with assertions about Russian capabilities, President Truman sought his own advice from the White House staff on the nature of the Soviet challenge. On 24 September 1946 the special counsel to the president, Clark Clifford, presented the president with an eighty-page report on 'American Relations with the Soviet Union,' the first comprehensive briefing on Soviet-American relations to be received by the new president.[1] The paper, prepared on the basis of documents and advice from the State, War, and Navy departments as well as the White House, relentlessly catalogued the Soviet Union's alleged violations of wartime and post-war agreements as they were interpreted by the American administration, concentrating at length upon the Yalta Declaration on Liberated Europe of February 1945.[2] George Kennan's account of the historical and ideological elements in Soviet expansionism was compressed and coupled with the War Department's assessment of the 'growing ability of the U.S.S.R. to wage an offensive war against the United States' – an ability which was declared to be 'the ultimate goal of Soviet military policy.'[3] While the report conceded that this ability had not yet been achieved, it brought the threat home with the assertion that large-scale espionage networks operated in the United States under diplomatic cover, and that the American Communist party provided 'thousands of invaluable sources of information in various industrial establishments as well as in the departments of the Government' – a reflection that echoed the recent conclusions of the Canadian Royal Commission on espionage about Canadian Communists.[4] ('In this regard,' said the Clifford report, 'it must be remembered that every American Communist is potentially an espionage agent of the Soviet Government, requiring only the direct instruction of a Soviet superior to make the potentiality a reality.'[5] This remarkable generalization was not justified on the basis of the specific evidence presented in the *Gouzenko Report,* and there was no indication that it arose from any other reliable source of evidence.) Soviet policy was presented as implacably threatening and evil, without any element of moderation. In the guise of understanding the Soviet Union the paper offered, on close reading, no understanding at all.

American policy was presented equally simply. While the Soviet Union's 'aggressive militaristic imperialism' was the source of conflict, the United States sought only co-operation, mutual security, and prosperity for all; it was driven to a defensive response by Soviet belligerence.[6] A political vacuum had permitted Russia the 'easy success' of expansion into 'the Balkans, Eastern Europe, the Near East, Manchuria and Korea because no other nation was both willing and able to prevent it,' but henceforth the United States would have to halt further Russian 'aggression' for the sake of stability. No distinction was drawn between the circumstances permitting Russian military advances during the Second World War and those of peacetime: by the end of the paper the assumption was that the Soviets acted in 1946 as aggressors at war. The appropriate American response was seen in military rather than diplomatic terms. The line between the two spheres of influence would have to be drawn where it then existed, and would have to be maintained by a permanent display of American military superiority.

The main deterrent to Soviet attack on the United States, or to attack on areas of the world which are vital to our security, will be the military power of this country. It must be made apparent to the Soviet Government that our strength will be sufficient to repel any attack and sufficient to defeat the U.S.S.R. decisively if a war should start. The prospect of defeat is the only sure means of deterring the Soviet Union.

The Soviet Union's vulnerability is limited due to the vast area over which its key industries and natural resources are widely dispersed, but it is vulnerable to atomic weapons, biological warfare, and long-range air power. Therefore, in order to maintain our strength at a level which will be effective in restraining the Soviet Union, the United States must be prepared to wage atomic and biological warfare. A highly mechanized army, which can be moved either by sea or by air, capable of seizing and holding strategic areas, must be supported by powerful naval and air forces. A war with the U.S.S.R. would be 'total' in a more horrible sense than any previous war and there must be constant research for both offensive and defensive weapons.

182 Diplomacy of Fear

Whether it would actually be in this country's interest to employ atomic and biological weapons against the Soviet Union in the event of hostilities is a question which would require careful consideration in the light of the circumstances prevailing at the time. The decision would probably be influenced by a number of factors, such as the Soviet Union's capacity to employ similar weapons, which can not now be estimated. But the important point is that the United States must be prepared to wage atomic and biological warfare if necessary. The mere fact of preparedness may be the only powerful deterrent to Soviet aggressive action and in this sense the only sure guaranty of peace.

The United States, with a military potential composed primarily of highly effective technical weapons, should entertain no proposal for disarmament or limitation of armament as long as the possibility of Soviet aggression exists.[7]

This emphasis upon the military basis of American power and the aggressive purposes of the USSR reflected the strong views of the secretary of the navy, James Forrestal.

From its insistence on military readiness, the report elaborated the case for the 'effective co-ordination' of the policies of the United States and its allies towards Russia and her satellite states. American policy would have to be 'consistent and forceful' and 'global in scope,' because 'any uncertainty or discrepancy will be seized immediately by the Soviets and exploited at our cost.'[8] American policy in all areas bordering on the Soviet sphere would henceforth have to be assessed in the light of Soviet objectives; economic aid and 'political support' should be extended generously to countries outside the Soviet sphere in order to stem further Russian advances; the American people should be informed and instructed about 'the record of Soviet evasion, misrepresentation, aggression and militarism'; and Communist penetration into the military services, government, and industry in the United States 'should be exposed and eliminated whenever the national security is endangered.'[9] The report concluded paradoxically (in a muddled simplification of Kennan's conclusion in the Long Telegram) that the only hope for an understanding with the Soviet Union lay in such a general display of American resolution. 'Even though Soviet leaders profess to believe that the conflict between Capitalism and Communism is irreconcilable and must eventually be resolved by the triumph of the latter, it is our hope that they will change their minds and work out with us a fair and equitable settlement when they realize that we are too strong to be beaten and too determined to be frightened.'[10]

Truman considered the document 'much too explosive' for distribution to his cabinet; its circulation was apparently restricted to the president, Clark Clifford, and Admiral Leahy (although the president's journalist friend Arthur Krock of the *New York Times* published a full copy in his *Memoirs* in 1968).[11] While the paper lacked detailed proposals for policy, it conveyed a mood of fierce determination. The document echoed and concentrated the dominant messages now being transmitted to the White House from within the administration. Those messages were strident and alarmist, with little of the realistic complexity of the diplomatic dispatches from Moscow familiar to the foreign offices in London, Washington, and Ottawa.[12] The principal recommendations for strategic atomic armament, the unification of defence planning, the purging of Communists from the government service, the assessment of foreign policy from a global anti-Soviet perspective, the direction of American propaganda against the Soviet Union, and the extension of massive American economic aid to countries outside the Soviet bloc soon became the foundations of policy for the Truman administration.

The message of events in late 1946 and early 1947 was, by contrast, more confusing. Russian forces had withdrawn from Iran earlier in the year under diplomatic pressure; the draft peace treaties with Italy and the former German satellite states were on their way to signature; the situation in China was confused but an accommodation between the Nationalists and Communists still seemed conceivable to General George C. Marshall, the US ambassador; managed Polish elections were approaching in January 1947; no progress was evident in the Four Power efforts to work out a common policy on the revival of Germany and as a result its permanent division between the two power blocs was rapidly becoming the assumption of American and Soviet policy; the Soviet government was engaged in a crude propaganda campaign at home and abroad against the purported evils and warlike intentions of the capitalist powers; the Greek Communists were involved in guerrilla activity against government forces with logistical support from Yugoslavia and Bulgaria; and the economy of Western Europe was approaching bankruptcy and possible collapse, while the strong Communist parties of France and Italy appeared the likely beneficiaries of economic disaster. Viewed with dispassion, the actions of the Soviet Union and its agents (where they could be understood from the evidence) frequently did not match its aggressive rhetoric. But the White House was impatient with the rhetoric, and was increasingly inclined to make sense of the world by imposing on it a harsh and monolithic interpretation of Soviet aims. That would at least reduce the confusions of the post-war world and permit the United States government to act with a sense of purpose as it had done in wartime.

The administration's own need for clarity of purpose was matched by its anxiety to carry Congress and the public, once and for all, in an outward-looking foreign policy; and that seemed to require some dramatic gesture. The opportunity came in February 1947, soon after General George C. Marshall replaced James Byrnes as secretary of state. The story of the next few months of transformation in American foreign policy is familiar, and the account as related in the Canadian archives coincides with the published record.[13]

The United Kingdom government, strained by economic crisis at home and expensive obligations abroad, informed the governments of the dominions on 21 February 1947 that it had come to a momentous decision.[14] After 31 March Britain's economic and military aid to Greece (amounting to forty million pounds in the first three months of 1947 alone), and its lesser aid to Turkey, would cease. The British ambassador in Washington, Lord Inverchapel, had been instructed the same day to convey this warning to the secretary of state, with the urgent request that the necessary aid to sustain the two governments should henceforth come from the United States. Without such aid, the United Kingdom foresaw imminent economic and political collapse in Greece, with strategic consequences which it said had been previously considered by the two partners.

Towards the end of the last year, 1946, Mr. Byrnes made it clear to Foreign Secretary that United States Government considered it a matter of utmost importance on strategic and political grounds that Greece and Turkey should not be allowed to fall under Soviet influence, and proposed that United States Government should give active help in sustaining economic and military position in those two countries, in particular on economic side. The United States Government has subsequently reminded us on many occasions of keen interest which they take in future of Greece.[15]

'We are bound to make General Marshall realize quite clearly,' the dispatch to Ottawa concluded, 'that if a joint policy of effective and practical support for Greece is to be maintained, United States Government must bear, as from 1st April 1947, financial burden of which major part has hitherto been borne by United Kingdom Government ... Matter is one of extreme urgency.'[16]

This sense was shared in the State Department, where hectic activity began at once to prepare a positive American response to the British ultimatum. The administration's own, direct advice on the European crisis was as bleak as the account of the British, and Hume Wrong told Ottawa on 3 March that 'During the last week or so there have been indicators of possible new developments in the foreign policy of the United States which may become of the first importance.'[17] Wrong reported that a crucial meeting had occurred on 27 February among President Truman, General Marshall, assistant secretary of state Acheson, and Congressional leaders. 'Unusual secrecy surrounded the discussion. It is now known, however, that as a result of it a not unfavourable, but inevitably tentative, reply has been dispatched to the British Ambassador on March 1st.'[18] According to Joseph Jones, secretary of state Marshall made a 'summary and cryptic presentation' of the strategic case for American aid which failed to convince the Congressional delegation. Dean Acheson intervened to speak as a 'fervent advocate' of the American mission to defend democracy and liberty throughout the world against Soviet aggression, to which Senator Vandenberg replied gravely that the request to Congress for aid to Greece and Turkey should be accompanied by a presidential message 'in which the grim facts of the larger situation should be laid publicly on the line as they had been at their meeting there that day.' The administration's policy was thus framed in those terms. 'It was Vandenberg's 'condition' that made it possible, even necessary, to launch the global policy that broke through the remaining barriers of American isolationism,' Jones judged. Acheson told the same story to Hume Wrong, indicating his own decisive role in linking American aid to 'the openly anti-Communist aspects which were incorporated in the President's speech to Congress.'[19]

There was a sudden realization in Washington, shared by 'both the informed and the ignorant,' Wrong reported, that British power was collapsing everywhere.

The effect of these developments is to increase consciousness that the United States must exert itself all around the world, and a common approach is to discuss what responsibilities hitherto assumed by the British should now be taken over by the United States. A programme to 'aid Britain' would have little popular appeal, although Mr. Lippman [sic] among others conceives the issue in those terms. The basic approach might be the strengthening of anti-Communist forces by large-scale action to restore economic stability in the democratic countries.[20]

Wrong elaborated on this justification for an enhanced American role in the world, which was gaining ground rapidly after the meeting of 27 February.

In private discussion during the last few days Senator Vandenberg, Mr. Walter Lippmann, Mr. Eugene Meyer, and a number of other prominent people have all been critical of a piecemeal approach to the current situation. They share the view that a broad and imaginative initiative is required, while not committing themselves to any particular plan. Many of them are conscious that public resistance to reversion to isolationism is often emotional rather than the result of intellectual conviction, and is inspired mainly by fear of Russia. Perhaps fortunately, fear of Russia is particularly strong among those who otherwise are most inclined towards isolationism. There is a feeling abroad among those who wish to see the United States execute her full responsibilities as the strongest Power in the world that the time is arriving when opinion can best be solidified through bold action on a comprehensive scale. This is, of course, extremely vague. Those taking this line are partly influenced by fears of the domestic political results of a series of separate controversies over aid to Greece, aid to Turkey, wider United States commitments in Germany and Western Europe, and so on.

The result of the 'shift of atmosphere' in Washington was 'a possibility – and no more than a possibility – that the United States may take more vigorous action to restore the economies of friendly European countries than seemed feasible a few weeks ago.' When Americans pointed out to him that only the United States and Canada were able to offer such assistance, Wrong was careful to distinguish Canadian from American policy: 'I have not failed to point out the limitations on Canadian action and the inhibitions resulting from the exclusion of Canada from participation in the central decisions on the European settlement.' Nevertheless, he wrote: 'There can be no doubt that it is in our interest that the United States should adopt a more forward policy.'[21]

In a separate letter to L.B. Pearson written the same day, Wrong reported the views of Senator Vandenberg expressed at dinner on 28 February, the day after the president's meeting with Congressional leaders.[22] 'Vandenberg looked towards a foreign policy "from top to bottom". He said that the American people would rise to such a foreign policy as a "trout to a fly" ... Vandenberg's thinking in essence seemed to be clear. The U.S.A. is unwilling to step into Britain's boots, muddied by imperialism, but it is ready to pursue a vigorous 100% American foreign policy, which would combat on a world scale the spread of Communism.' Two days later Wrong wrote to reaffirm that this concentration on the Communist challenge had been the key element in the understanding reached between the president and members of Congress: 'At the President's meeting on February 27th with Congressional leaders it was agreed that Congress could be persuaded to provide the funds if the reasons were presented with complete frankness. This would involve a good deal of emphasis on the necessity of preventing the advance of Soviet influence in the Eastern Mediterranean.'[23]

Wrong said that the administration had little confidence in the Greek government, would prefer to see it replaced by a centre or left-of-centre cabinet, and would insist on placing American advisers 'in key positions to guard against any abuses.' The White House's analysis of Soviet motives in the area, as described by Wrong, involved an early version of the domino theory: 'They regard Soviet interest in Greece as being inspired mainly by their desire to outflank Turkey with the purpose of securing the installation in Turkey of "a friendly Government" – in other words a satellite Government. Turkey is thus the key point, the control of which by Russia would clear the way to the south, and Greece politically is only part of the outer defences of Turkey.'[24]

By now the State Department had discussed whether Canada had a role to play in Greece, and had made informal approaches to the Canadian ambassador.

It seems there has been some discussion in the Department of State on the question of whether they should seek Canadlan participation in the programme of aid to Greece, both by the provision of a share of the funds and by furnishing some experts to direct the disbursement in Greece. I have held out no hope that we should be ready to participate, and have argued on the theme of the very difficult position of a junior partner in a scheme of this sort which would be inspired not by humanitarian aims, but by large considerations of foreign policy and power politics.[25]

President Truman's address to Congress on 12 March 1947 calling for emergency aid to Greece and Turkey, Hume Wrong reported the next day, was generally viewed as 'a re-statement of foreign policy of the highest importance, comparable to the Monroe Doctrine and the inauguration of the Lend-Lease program in 1941.'[26] The passages chosen for quotation in the press, he said, were those broad assertions 'that the United States must resist the imposition of totalitarian regimes.' Supporters and critics alike were anxious about where the president's policy might lead.

How far, people are asking, will the supply of dollars to eastern Mediterranean countries serve to resist Soviet influence, without the supply of armed forces to back them up. The chaotic nature of Greek politics is another source of concern. If the United States helps Greece financially and by the provision of advisers, can the Greeks do the rest, especially after the withdrawal of the remaining British forces? If the United States is to help free peoples to resist Communist infiltration, is there any stopping place short of the overthrow of the Soviet regime in Russia? How do the principles expressed in the message apply to the situation in China? The one-world conception is laid aside, but, in place of reverting to the traditional alternative of aiming at an American world in the western hemisphere, the President's policy divides the world between the Soviet sphere and the rest.[27]

Wrong expressed cautious reservations about the prudence of the president's emphasis on the Soviet challenge as the basis for the American initiative.

Although the President did not mention the Soviet Union in his speech, he nevertheless lived up to his private commitment to the Congressional leaders that he would state frankly the reasons for his proposals. Indeed, the necessity of appealing to as wide a public as possible led him to use, for domestic political purposes, language which he would probably have modified in other circumstances, especially when he simplified the issues to resistance to Communist infiltration and described Soviet methods and aims in words not long ago reserved for use against the Nazis.[28]

This judgment probably reflected reservations existing also within the American administration; but State Department surveys of opinion showed that popular support for the president's program was indeed based on approval of the determination to resist Soviet expansion.[29]

Wrong offered further analysis in a dispatch five days later.[30] The prospects for 'fairly early' congressional approval of the president's requests remained good, since 'the critics have not discovered a common line of attack.' 'They are a curious mixture of Communists and fellow travellers, wishful thinkers about Soviet policy such as Henry Wallace, hopeful supporters of the United Nations such as Mrs. Roosevelt and Mr. La Guardia who are worried that the proposals will "harm the strength of the United Nations", old line isolationists and twisters of the lion's tail, idealists with pacifist leanings and ardent champions of budgetary economy.'[31] The administration accepted that there would be 'a public inquisition' in congressional committees to probe the program and its implications; congressional discussion was bound to focus on the growing realization that aid to Greece and Turkey was only the first step in a wider scheme of American support for recovery in Western Europe. The acting secretary of state, Dean Acheson, would speak for the policy in committee in the absence of the secretary of state at the Council of Foreign Ministers in Moscow; and Acheson would speak frankly, 'even when frank replies will cause further complications with Russia and other countries.' ('Speaking frankly' had become the code phrase in the debate for naming the Soviet Union as the omnipresent source of tension.)

This exercise in public education, in Wrong's view, marked a notable substitution of realism for illusion in American diplomacy.

The way in which the issues are being faced by the Administration involves giving up much of the public pretense which has surrounded the conduct of relations with the U.S.S.R. and support of the United Nations. The United States Government will speak more bluntly and briefly than hitherto. They are likely deliberately to make use of United Nations meetings as a forum for putting the Russians on the spot by the methods of psychological warfare. They will be more unready to continue to take part in protracted and unproductive discussions such as those in the Atomic Energy Commission. The effect would be to employ the United Nations as a means for building up an anti-Soviet bloc; senior members of the State Department have said as much to me in private conversation.[32]

Wrong's dispatches on the emergence of the Truman Doctrine were the object of unusual interest in the Prime Minister's Office. On 25 March James Gibson wrote to the Canadian ambassador: 'These telegrams have been specially brought to the Prime Minister's attention and I know that Mr. King has found them particularly helpful in giving a judicious appreciation of the more recent developments in United States policy abroad.'[33]

In April, the Canadian Embassy's briefings to Ottawa on the implications of the president's statement were supplemented by a copy of a seven-page commentary prepared for London by John Balfour of the British Embassy.[34] The paper confirmed the background sketch already provided by Hume Wrong, and noted the care with which the administration had now begun to hedge the universal pledges made by the president in March.

As regards the decision of the Administration to lift the statement out of the limited framework of an appeal for aid for Greece and Turkey, it should be borne in mind that the President's task in approaching Congress was greatly complicated by the fact that he is a minority President and that, when the need for action arose, the two Houses of the legislature were fully launched on a programme of domestic economies from which they were naturally most loath to turn aside. In these circumstances, the best, if not the only, hope for Mr. Truman to secure Congressional approval for his proposals lay in arousing the missionary fervour of liberals as well as the Russo-phobia of most conservatives by presenting the immediate requirements of Greece and Turkey within the larger setting of totalitarian threats to the American way of life. The time factor in the case of aid to Greece also made it necessary for the administration to dramatise the situation to Congress and the public to a greater extent than it might otherwise have deemed wise.[35]

The purpose of the president, in Balfour's words, was 'to prevent the imposition of Communist regimes in countries into which they have not yet crept.' But the administration insisted that it possessed no 'blue print for United States foreign policy at all times and towards all countries.' 'Indeed in his testimony Acheson made it very clear that, although the United States would doubtless "react" if any other country became exposed to like threats which now confront Greece and Turkey, it should not be assumed that such a reaction would be similar in character.'[36] This was especially true, Acheson had told Congress, in the case of the Chiang Kai-shek government of China.

Balfour concluded that the Truman Doctrine was designed to meet a specific, not a general case, and that it reflected the strategic wisdom of the new secretary of state, who 'as an experienced soldier, has always been a great believer in the concentration of resources at the time and at the place where they can be most effectively employed.' The policy was not due wholly either to a new realization of the Soviet menace, or to the judgment that Greece and Turkey were of more strategic importance to the United States than other countries already within the Soviet sphere. It was prompted largely by the belief that it could succeed, and that, as Senator Vandenberg had said on 18 April, 'if at this strategic point we surrender to Communist aggression, we have set in motion a chain reaction that may make it impossible for us ever again peacefully to meet the Russian menace.'[37]

Circumstances would accordingly determine whether the Truman Doctrine would be given general application. If it succeeded in Greece and

Turkey, the United States would be encouraged 'to repeat the experiment of intervention whenever other analogous instances occur. In that event the statement might well be pushed to its logical conclusion and become as essential a feature of American policy as the Monroe Doctrine.' If it failed, it might fall into disuse. In any event, 'The costs involved in each instance, and the need to persuade Congress whenever it may be decided that action is required, should ... operate against any wholesale application of this so-called doctrine.'[38] The course of action was 'still in an embryo state and hardly to be dignified by the name of a policy.' It was, as Senator Vandenberg had described it, only 'a plan; ... a part of a pattern.'

The doctrine certainly did not imply a fixed policy of American encouragement to political oppositions in Communist countries. And while the United States would be 'somewhat more resolute and consistent' in aiding non-Communist countries to achieve stability and resist Communist domination, the White House had so far given 'no firm clue as to how the United States would react either to an apparent legal Communist victory in another country or to one achieved by a *coup d'état*.'[39] Balfour argued that the American policy was designed not 'to impose its own way of life on the rest of the world' (as a Foreign Office paper had suggested), but 'rather to create a balance of power in the world' which might lead to the reduction of conflict (just as the Clifford report had proposed). 'It is the hope of the Administration that this new move will serve to convince the Kremlin that intransigence does not pay and that the prospects of an adjustment of interests between the East and the West will thus be promoted.'[40]

The creation of balance could be expressed in other words as the rejection of isolationism and appeasement; Balfour concluded that the essential issue was to lay the ghost of the thirties.

The most encouraging conclusion that we can draw from the fact that the President's lead in regard to Greece and Turkey has already been endorsed by a majority of the American people and seems assured of overwhelming support in Congress is that the United States does not intend to reproduce in regard to the Kremlin the spectacle of indifference to embryonic aggression which it offered to the pre-war Nazi-Fascist dictators when their thirst for world power was gathering momentum. Lastly, it looks on present showing as though America, unlike the permanent members of the League of Nations Council after World War I, does not intend to fall into the error which proved fatal to the Geneva experiment of evading her responsibilities as a world power on the pretext that ... the initiative in meeting international emergencies must properly rest with the community of nations as a whole.[41]

The Greek and Turkish aid bill passed both House and Senate by mid-May.[42] Once its passage was assured, Hume Wrong wrote, the administration sought to turn public attention from the containment of Russia to the 'more important' issue of 'the urgent need for economic recovery in western Europe.'[43] This new emphasis was reflected in a speech of Dean Acheson to the Delta Council in Cleveland, Mississippi, on 8 May, which Wrong described as 'a clear and coherent account of the reasons whereby the United States should, in its own interest, take further steps to encourage reconstruction abroad.'[44] The press had given prominence to Acheson's insistence on the need to reconstruct 'those two great workshops of Europe and Asia – Germany and Japan – upon which the ultimate recovery of the two continents so largely depends.' Acheson also urged that the United States should 'take as large a volume of imports as possible from abroad'; undertake further emergency financing of foreign purchasing in the United States in 1948 and 1949; concentrate its emergency aid 'where it will be most effective in restoring stability, promoting democracy, furthering international trade, and strengthening the United Nations'; and control domestic allocation and transport to permit such a foreign aid program.

Wrong said that the president had not yet committed himself publicly to the policies suggested by the under-secretary of state, although there seemed little doubt that he had approved Acheson's text before delivery. The press, with the exception of the *Daily Worker*, had given the speech prominent display and favourable comment. The reaction of Congress to such proposals, however, was still uncertain and could not be reliably estimated from the easy majorities of the Greek and Turkish aid bill, because 'It is impossible to determine how large a proportion of those voting for the Greco-Turkish program supported it because of its directly anti-Soviet character.'[45]

The imminence of further American initiatives in European aid was emphasized in another Canadian dispatch from Washington on 26 May 1947.[46] Public and press discussion of the international dollar shortage and the economic plight of Europe was intense; but Wrong remained sceptical that the president or a conservative Congress possessed the 'greatness and imagination' which Franklin Roosevelt would have brought to the crisis of post-war reconstruction.

The first great opportunity was missed when the lend-lease system was abruptly terminated after the surrender of Japan, and the second during the negotiation of the British loan.

The passage of time and the change in the party complexion of Congress have made it more difficult for the President, no matter how willing he may be, to display successfully statesmanship of the bold and high order required. It is still, however, not too late. Domestically, the partly-learned lesson that the prosperity of the United States depends on its export trade, and that this depends on the customer's ability to pay, must be repeated many times before it can overcome isolationist traditions and national vested interests. That process of education is going on; a recent Gallup poll showed a very considerable majority favouring a low rather than a high tariff. In this as in other matters, Republican leaders in Congress seem to be lagging behind the country. As so often happens, especially in great issues of foreign policy, it is probably necessary that the world should at least reach the brink of catastrophe before the machinery of the Constitution of the United States can be made to operate to apply remedial measures.[47]

In spite of the preparations for a fresh American initiative which Wrong had noted, the secretary of state's Harvard University speech of 5 June 1947 still came as a surprise to the Canadian ambassador. 'It is strange,' Hume Wrong wrote in a short message to Ottawa the next day, 'that in all the important conversations which we have been having with members of the Department of State during the past week and as late as yesterday lunch time with Mr. Hickerson when the speech was actually being delivered, ... no reference whatsoever was made to the fact that the Secretary of State was going to make this statement.'[48] Wrong's ignorance was probably a simple reflection of the casual preparation for the speech itself. Marshall had decided eight days before that he should soon speak on the European situation, and 'a day or two later' (according to Joseph Jones) had chosen the Harvard commencement as the occasion. But he was still rewriting the speech as he flew to Boston on 4 June.[49]

The secretary of state's address set out, briefly and bleakly, 'the dislocation of the entire fabric of European economy,' 'the visible destruction of cities, factories, mines, and railroads,' and the less visible collapse of trading institutions and currencies.[50] By now, the basic division of labour and system of exchange between city and countryside were near breakdown, as both sought in vain for fuel, machinery, and credit. Rehabilitation, Marshall said, 'quite evidently will require a much longer time and greater effort than had been foreseen.' The bulk of aid necessary to break the vicious circle of economic decline would have to come from America. Marshall called for a great and restrained act of enlightened self-interest from both the United States and Europe. 'It is logical,' he said, 'that the United States should do whatever it is able to do to assist in the return of normal economic health in the world, without which there can be no political stability and no assured peace.' But the countries of Europe would have to produce a plan for recovery before such aid would be provided. 'It would be neither fitting nor efficacious for this Government to undertake to draw up unilaterally a program designed to place Europe on its feet economically. This is the business of the Europeans. The initiative, I think, must come from Europe.'[51]

Marshall insisted that American aid 'is directed not against any country or doctrine but against hunger, poverty, desperation and chaos.' Any government that wished to co-operate in a recovery program could do so. The limitations were discreetly phrased: the purpose of American policy would be 'the revival of a working economy in the world so as to permit the emergence of political and social conditions in which free institutions can exist'; and any governments, parties, or groups seeking 'to perpetuate human misery in order to profit therefrom politically or otherwise will encounter the opposition of the United States.' If those conditions ruled out Russian participation, as they probably would, they did so without the dramatic provocation to the Soviet Union offered by President Truman for domestic political reasons in the Truman Doctrine speech three months earlier. The invitation to join in planning seemed open equally to the countries of Eastern and Western Europe.

The initial reactions of Canadian diplomats to Marshall's address were sceptical. On 26 June Hume Wrong endorsed a *New York Times* report from London which said that 'Britain's leaders know perfectly well that our State Department has no programme, no plan and not even a very clear idea of how the United States can help and how much Congress will stand for.'[52] Wrong added that James Reston's depiction of the debate on Greek-Turkish aid as having been conducted in 'an atmosphere of intense vagueness' applied even more to the 'Marshall Plan,' which was still so indefinite that it allowed only speculation, not debate. (Both Wrong and Pearson referred to the scheme in quotation marks at this time, apparently to reinforce the ironic point that it was not in fact a plan.) 'A great work of education' would be required before Congress would vote the necessary resources; and in Europe the position of the Russians created an obvious dilemma. 'If Russia and her satellites stay aloof, no general European plan can be developed and the Communist parties in Western Europe will adopt wrecking tactics. On the other hand, if Russia participates and is ready honestly to pay the price of a profound change in her current policies, it will be difficult to persuade this Russophobe Congress to take any action which could be regarded as increasing Russian strength.'[53]

Arrangements were made for preliminary European discussions on Marshall's proposal (including the Soviet Union) immediately following the Harvard speech, to take place at the end of June. The State Department expected that the UK foreign secretary, Ernest Bevin, would play the key role in extracting satisfactory terms of collaboration from the Russians, or provoking their withdrawal.[54]

Wrong repeated a private remark of Dean Acheson that 'probably the fairest judgment to reach is that action *will* be taken on a large scale because it *must* be taken to maintain economic prosperity in the United States.' But Congress would have to be convinced that massive foreign aid was cheaper than a depression, and that persuasion would take months. 'I fear, however, that it will take actual disaster to come, to make the political wheels go round in Washington.'[55] L.B. Pearson underlined this pessimistic judgment in a covering memorandum to Prime Minister King on 28 June, while noting that the adoption of the Marshall Plan would incidentally ease Canada's dollar problem by putting fresh purchasing power in European hands.[56]

The dilemma over potential Russian participation in the program for European recovery disappeared quickly in July, when the Soviet foreign minister rejected any comprehensive European planning for reconstruction as interference in domestic affairs, and made clear that neither the Soviet Union nor its East European clients would participate.[57] Planning among the countries of Western Europe proceeded over the summer, and in the early autumn a European proposal was received by President Truman. The American administration acted vigorously over the next six months to convince Congress and the public of the urgency of the crisis, and in April 1948 the president signed the European Recovery Act, which eventually resulted in the provision of thirteen billion dollars in aid to Western Europe over four years.[58] Hume Wrong had predicted the outcome accurately in a dispatch to Ottawa on 18 July 1947 that moved beyond his doubts of the previous month:

In the Department of State there is satisfaction over the political results of

Marshall's suggestions coupled with concern at the domestic difficulties of carrying them through. One senior official has said to me that for the first time since the end of the war they have gained the initiative against Russia and put the Soviet Government on the defensive. I believe that those concerned, from the Secretary of State down, were fully satisfied in advance that Russia would refuse to co-operate, and they are therefore pleased that the Soviet position has been made clear so quickly and so nakedly.

They are fully aware that failure on the American side to carry through would be a disaster of the first magnitude, and I am sure that the Secretary of State more than anyone else is determined to do his utmost, by a steady programme of public education, by constant pressure on the Congressional leaders and by encouraging the Western European countries to do their part. I believe that he will succeed because public opinion will come to recognize the terrific cost of failure.[59]

The Truman Doctrine signalled Washington's decision in principle to enter world-wide competition with the Soviet Union, and to accept the certainty of this contest as the basis for American foreign policy. Britain's precipitate withdrawal from the front rank, and America's epoch-making acceptance of its role in the great game, shook the pattern of relationships among their friends as well. At the end of March 1947 Lester Pearson noted in a letter to Dana Wilgress that this rearrangement required Canada to reconsider some basic elements of her foreign policy, and invited Wilgress to examine Soviet relations with the Western world from this fresh perspective. Wilgress did so in a dispatch from Geneva on 25 April 1947.[60]

He urged first of all that the Western powers should desist from their efforts to use Eastern Europe 'as the testing ground for the clash between Western and Soviet policies.' To challenge the Soviet Union in the countries on its borders where it had already imposed its influence was doubly wrong, because it was futile and because it aroused Russian suspicion 'that we wished to gain a foothold in the very security belt which they had been able to establish as a result of the war.' Western support for 'the Yalta formula on free and unfettered elections' in Poland and Romania suggested that Britain and the United States favoured governments there which would be unfriendly to Soviet Russia. In fact the West was powerless to achieve that result; but if it were achieved, it 'would be, in Soviet eyes, tantamount to depriving them of any sphere of influence in Eastern Europe and would confine Soviet influence to the borders of the Soviet Union.' Instead of supporting politicians hostile to the Soviet

Union, Britain and America should adopt an attitude of 'mild tolerance' toward the Communist-dominated governments of Eastern Europe, neither blindly opposing them nor becoming their dupes. Modest economic aid should be offered, measured carefully so that it would counter potential Soviet criticism of the West for refusing assistance, maintain some economic links, but not undermine Soviet domination.[61]

British and American policy toward the Soviet Union should follow a similar pattern of realism: 'Here too we should endeavour to follow a course which is neither that of excessive flattery nor that of excessive ostracism.' Economic co-operation should be encouraged, but 'on a strictly commercial basis, free from the taint of political considerations.'

Wilgress saw the possibility of a long period of relative stability between the two great powers and their clearly delineated spheres of influence, each respecting and tolerating the other, neither interfering in the other's realm. Western firmness, relative indifference, and non-interference should be accompanied by diplomatic good manners: 'Our detestation of totalitarianism and all that it stands for should not lead us into treating the Russians differently to the manner with which we would treat any other country with which we were not on particularly friendly terms.'

Throughout this dispatch Wilgress used the collective 'we' to refer to Britain and the United States, rarely distinguishing any separate role or attitude for Canada: writing, indeed, as though he were either an American or a British diplomat. In one paragraph, however, he wrote as a Canadian and made his understanding of this general subordination explicit.

Undoubtedly the 'Truman doctrine' will bring us into still greater dependence upon the United States and to this extent away from the United Kingdom. It is really the coming into being of that 'Atlantic Community' envisaged by Walter Lippman [sic] in his book on 'United States War Aims'. The Atlantic Community envisaged by Lippman was one dominated by the United States but in the same benevolent fashion as the world susceptible to sea power used to be dominated by Great Britain. In other words the Pax Britannica of the nineteenth century is to be replaced in the later twentieth century by a Pax Americana. On account of our proximity to the United States this gives rise to all sorts of problems for us and it makes it necessary for us to subscribe to the main lines of the United States policy. Hence, in our relations with the Soviet Union, we have no alternative than to accept and follow the 'Truman doctrine.'[62]

The overriding implication for Canada of America's acceptance of its competitive global role, as Wilgress saw it, was simply resignation. Canada was part of the American sphere, and could not (or should not) challenge that fate. This momentous assumption, which would henceforth, if accepted, prescribe the narrow limits of Canadian foreign policy, deserved elaboration and critical analysis.

Wilgress's April dispatch contributed essential background for External's definitive effort to understand the nature of the post-war struggle for power. This effort took initial shape in a study paper prepared by Escott Reid in February 1947 titled 'Political Appreciation of the Possibility of the Soviet Union Precipitating War against the United States,'[63] which followed out of the previous year's paper by R.M. Macdonnell designed to counter the US estimate of Soviet military capabilities.[64] Reid argued once again, in summary, that the Soviet Union had no intention of provoking a general war, but that it was an expansionist power which would not only consolidate its defence perimeter but constantly prod for weak points along that perimeter. Six months elapsed between this draft and a much altered version dated 30 August 1947 which was prepared for wide distribution and comment within the department.[65] These were the months of the Truman Doctrine and the Marshall Plan, and Reid's title changed significantly to 'The United States and the Soviet Union: A Study of the Possibility of War and Some of the Implications for Canadian Policy.' What Reid had previously described as a problem solely of Russian behaviour had now become a matter of mutual behaviour between the two great powers. Reid noted in a preface that the paper was 'nothing more than a rough first draft of the kind of memorandum which I think it would be useful if we were to prepare in the Department in order to help us clear our minds on this fundamental question.'

In an opening section on 'The Source of Conflict,' Reid carefully (and perhaps too self-consciously) attempted to balance the expansionist ambitions of the two states against one another. Although the table of charges weighed heavily against the Soviet Union in Reid's reckoning, he emphasized the equality of responsibility for conflict by juxtaposing virtually identical paragraphs directed first against one power, then against the other, and summed up as follows:

The desire on the part of both the Soviet Union and the United States to expand their defence areas brings them into conflict in all the borderlands between their present defence areas from Korea to Finland. It is idle to suppose that this source of conflict could for long be removed by an agreement between the two powers on the boundaries of their respective defence areas. Such an agreement might stabilize the situation for a few years, but by its very nature a desire on the part of a great power to expand its defence area is an illimitable process. The appetite for security grows with eating.[66]

In part two, 'The Conditions under Which Conflict Might Lead to War,' Reid dismissed the likelihood of deliberate resort to war with the other by either contestant, with the caveat that either power, if it saw the balance tipping steadily against it, might precipitate a preventive war. Because the Soviets were patient realists, however, Reid believed that 'the danger of war diminishes if the forces on the United States side of the balance are much greater than the forces on the Soviet side, provided that the Soviet leaders are not driven by too relentless an increase of United States power to risk a desperate gamble.' Here the objective observer shifted by degree into the role of advocate for an armed and superior Western alliance (an alliance which, he asserted, existed already in fact 'though not on paper').

Reid's argument was more paradoxical than it appeared. There was no realistic chance, he believed, that Russia would either provoke or blunder into a war with the United States in the next decade; the Soviets were too careful and calculating for that. On the contrary, 'A war, if it comes, is more likely to arise out of panic in the United States, should there occur, as is possible, a steady increase over the next ten years of Soviet power in relation to that of the United States.' The maintenance of 'an overwhelming balance of force' in the West, to be used to deter further extensions of Soviet power, would reduce the risk of war primarily by reassuring the American public of its security.

Reid took substantial chunks of his paper from Wilgress's 25 April dispatch, and from George Kennan's 'x' article, 'The Sources of Soviet Conduct' (which had appeared in the July issue of *Foreign Affairs*), emphasizing with them that a policy of 'containment' should be maintained without bluster or provocation toward the USSR. Neither should the Soviets, according to Reid, be elbowed out of the United Nations. But he did advocate the creation of a new regional military alliance among 'the Western nations,' 'which would become immediately effective if the Soviet Union should commit aggression.' (He had made the plea openly at the Couchiching Conference earlier in August.)

'Most of the implications of all this for Canadian policy,' Reid held, 'are obvious and need not be developed'; but some did deserve attention. As Wilgress had said, Canada was being thrust into greater dependence on the

United States as Lippmann's 'Atlantic Community' came into existence. In the extreme event of war, 'we shall have no freedom of action in any matter which the United States considers essential.' But short of war, because it was so close in spirit to the United States, Canada could 'exert an influence at Washington out of all proportion to the relative importance of our strength in war compared with that of the United States. The game is difficult; the issues will be delicate; but with skill we can play it successfully.' Reid, like Wilgress, took for granted that there was no other option for Canada; and in default of alternatives, he took final, sentimental refuge with George Kennan in the romantic notion that in the long run the grim competition between the United States and Russia might be transcended because 'the Soviet system may mellow or collapse.'

Reid admitted in his preface that the reflections on Canadian policy were 'particularly weak.' His 'scissors and paste job,' as he called it, did not make a consistent whole. The judgment that the Soviets did not intend general war was familiar in the department, befitting not only the evidence but the Canadians' moderating temperament, and belying the more alarmist claims being made in public against the Soviet regime. The judgment that both great powers were expansionist, and prone to conflict with one another, was more unusual. But neither insight led Reid to any unorthodox conclusions about what Canada might do in this world of conflict: rather, he argued for a formal alliance to contain Soviet expansion under American leadership, just as he might have done if he had believed that the Soviet Union intended war against a wholly innocent United States. Given the unexamined assumption that Canada could not deviate from the general line of American policy towards Soviet Russia, any genuine effort to comprehend the behaviour of the two powers from an independent perspective was an academic exercise that it might be frustrating or dangerous to pursue too far. There was no basis for debate on an independent Canadian foreign policy in the Department of External Affairs.

Maurice Pope, the mordant head of the Canadian military mission in Berlin, was the first to respond to Mike Pearson's request for comments on Reid's paper at the end of September 1947.[67] Pope noticed the paper's lack of conviction, its sometimes wishful tone, and its sentimental peroration. He urged 'the amiable Escott' and his colleagues to see the world realistically: to recognize the 'unalterable antagonism' of the Soviet and Western systems, the product of nature, geography, and national character; to understand that the two systems, by keeping to themselves, might nevertheless fashion 'a welcome detente'; and to appreciate how little room for manoeuvre Canada possessed. 'I cannot avoid the thought,' he wrote, 'that Czechoslovakia's foreign policy position vis-à-vis Russia is really no different from Canada's position vis-à-vis the United States.' 'Rather than to say it would still be open to us to oppose the United States in certain issues in United States–Soviet relations, I think it would be truer to say that it would still be open to us to endeavour to restrain the United States. If I know anything of that country, it is that when they, rightly or wrongly, feel that their security is threatened or that their interests may suffer, they brook no opposition.' To Reid's suggestion that Canada, through consistency and diplomatic skill, 'might exert a very considerable influence upon United States policy,' Pope recalled an American naval friend who 'quietly observed to me that whereas it was inexcusable in one's course through life to try to kid others, it was far worse ever to kid one's self.'

R.A.D. Ford, the Canadian chargé d'affaires in Moscow, commented bleakly on Reid's paper in October that Kennan's notion that the Soviet system might eventually mellow or collapse was 'the weak point of his argument.'[68] Rather, the Western nations were confronted with 'a resourceful and dynamic group with vast ambitions, a philosophy attractive to millions, and with allies and sympathizers everywhere in the world ... it is a moot point if the Americans and ourselves are capable of withstanding successfully the impact of Soviet obstruction and propaganda over a long period of time, particularly if we are caught up in another depression.' A policy of containment was necessary, and would probably avert war in the short run; but it would not discourage Russia's continuing war of nerves outside its own sphere. Ford, like Pope, accepted the legitimacy of regarding Soviet-American rivalry as a mutual affair to which both powers contributed, and suggested the added explanation that 'there is also a deep-seated, almost mystical feeling in each nation of the rightness and justness of its own cause, the superiority of its system over all others, and the inevitability of (a) American democracy, or (b) Soviet Communism eventually spreading all over the globe. In Russia this is accompanied by a centuries-old imperialist history and a Messianic tradition.' To Reid's confident assertion about the prospects for Canadian influence in Washington, Ford proposed a notable addition:

But so long as we have relatively few people who are acquainted with Russia in an expert way, it will be difficult to exert influence on the State Department in the sphere of Soviet relations. We should at once, therefore, start training Canadian diplomats in the Russian language, history, psychology, Marxism, and so on. As soon as feasible we should increase the staff of the Embassy at Moscow to provide better facilities for training, and for more complete reporting, particularly in economic questions.

The most substantial responses to Escott Reid's paper were those of the Canadian ambassadors in Paris and Washington, Charles Ritchie and Hume Wrong. Almost half of Ritchie's twenty-one page commentary involved reflections on the complexities of American and Soviet states of mind.[69] Reid's conclusion that the most likely source of war in the coming decade would be American panic at the growth of Soviet power suggested a number of questions to Ritchie. One set concerned the attitudes of American leaders.

How far, if at all, does there exist in politically or militarily influential circles in Washington a group who are thinking seriously in terms of a preventative war? Is there a powerful and responsible body of opinion which is convinced that war is inevitable and that preparations for it should be put in hand lest the United States find itself in a relatively weaker position later on? If a body of opinion with such a clearly defined objective does not yet exist in the United States, are there signs that it may be in process of formation?

Another set of questions concerned the likelihood of 'a violent nerve-storm in American public opinion' arising not only from panic but from resentment, anger, and despair at Soviet 'treacheries and brutalities.' Yet more concerned the potentially demoralizing effects of an American economic depression. But Ritchie reflected that it would be especially difficult for the United States to prepare for a pre-emptive war.

Discussion of the likelihood of a preventative war waged by the United States is apt to seem unreal to those who know the United States and the profoundly peace-loving character of the American people. Nor is it easy to imagine the planning of a war under the United States constitution and in the full glare of publicity which plays upon all the processes of American Government. Indeed the vast and secret preparations, the sudden unleashing of surprise attack seem totally incompatible with American realities as we have learned to know them in the past ... It is highly improbable that in the United States the process would take the form of a conscious and deliberate preparation for waging an offensive war. But this does not exclude the possibility that the United States Government might come to the decision that as war was inevitable there was nothing to be gained and much to be lost from postponing it and might base its policy on this decision. Such a development would indeed only be possible if the decisive mass of public opinion was moving in the same direction. It would result from the interplay of Government policy and aroused national feeling. But the sole condition on which this whole developing process could come about would be the conviction of the American government, and people that they were acting in self-defense. This essential psychological condition could be provided by the continuing aggressive behaviour of the Soviet Union. War could be precipitated by some particularly gross manifestation of Soviet aggressiveness which would be regarded in the United States as the 'sticking point' beyond which it was impossible to tolerate Soviet pressure. At this stage, if United States offensive-defensive preparations were far enough advanced, the United States might launch the first blow in the belief that if they did not do so the Soviet Union would have the advantage of a surprise offensive.

On the Soviet side, Ritchie judged that the Kremlin might well accept its own propaganda about the aggressive intentions of the United States, and could conceivably launch a war in the desperate belief that its relative strength was declining. But it would probably do everything possible, 'short of abandoning power or giving up the militant leadership of world communism,' to avoid war as the weaker antagonist. Ritchie worried, however, that the Soviets might respond to the American policy of containment by unintended provocation, through sheer diplomatic ineptitude.

... the Soviet Union may play a cautious waiting-game and thus avoid war in the near future at any rate. On the other hand, no one who has followed the course of Soviet diplomacy since the end of the war can feel reassured about the quality of Soviet statesmanship. The Soviet Government have again and again behaved as though they were the victims of compulsive fears and suspicions rather than cooly [sic] rational judges of their own interests. They have again and again created the very dangers which they sought to avoid. In 1945 they had a unique opportunity to establish stable relations with the Western powers and thus to ensure for themselves a long period of security. This opportunity they are in the process of throwing away. They are also in danger of creating against themselves an overwhelmingly powerful alliance of Western nations many of whom will have been forced into such an alliance by the intransigence of Soviet diplomacy.

Similarly, within the countries of Western Europe they are forcing the moderate political parties, and particularly the Socialist parties, into the anti-Communist camp and are thus in danger of creating Right-wing dictatorships in the countries concerned. The Soviet rulers trapped in the narrow confines of their Marxist-Leninist analysis seem obsessed with the inevitability of war with the capitalist world and unable to make the statesman-like effort of adaptation which might have secured cooperation with the West on terms highly advantageous to themselves. With this record of blunders behind them, who can confidently prophecy that the Soviet Government will not by some crude piece of 'scratch and grab' give the signal to the United States that the moment has come beyond which it would be dangerous to hold their hand.

Ritchie emphasized the importance of restoring the economic strength of Europe according to the principles of the Marshall Plan, with the minimum of direct American intervention in the process. He concurred in Dana Wilgress's view that Central and Southeastern Europe were effectively within the Soviet sphere of influence, and could not be rescued from Soviet domination short of war.

The concentration of world power in Washington and Moscow was a dangerous and unnatural result of the Second World War. 'The sooner it is ended, the better are the prospects for world peace. The restoration of the states of Western Europe and the peaceful settlement of the disturbances that wrack the Chinese, Indian and Arab worlds would make for a balanced international community and are therefore in the interest of Canada as of every other peace-seeking nation.' Canada could work toward that objective by emphasizing as much as possible its independent position, by aiding the restoration of stability and strength in the nations shattered by war (especially in the United Kingdom), by maintaining and broadening her association with the middle and small powers of the Commonwealth, and by active participation in the United Nations and its agencies. 'These are indeed,' Ritchie noted, 'the broad policies which the Canadian Government has pursued since the end of the war to attain the objective of international peace and stability.'

Escott Reid's conclusion, drawn from George Kennan's *Foreign Affairs* article, that the steady application of Western counter-force against Russian pressures might lead to Soviet mellowing or collapse, seemed curious to Charles Ritchie.

Frustration has not usually lead [*sic*] either in an individual or a nation to mellowness, nor does it seem likely that the frustration of Soviet aims will lead to the collapse of the system. Such a collapse could only come about as the result of war or internal revolution and probably only as the result of internal revolution after defeat in war. The feeling of 'encirclement' perhaps accompanied by the fear of revolution which would grow up on the Soviet Government as they found themselves confronted in their expansion with 'unalterable force' might be more likely to produce an explosion of aggression than the nerveless collapse of the regime or its modification into milder forms ...

These arguments do not invalidate the necessity for the Western powers to command overwhelming force in relation to the Soviet Union. They illustrate how much self-restraint and moderation will be needed to employ this force wisely.

Ritchie foresaw no romantic dawn ahead, but only a long and dangerous twilight lived 'on the narrow edge of risk,' in which both sides would have to demonstrate unusual strength and restraint to avoid an unwanted war.

In December 1947, stimulated by Ritchie's comments, Hume Wrong replied to the Reid memorandum from Washington.[70] Wrong endorsed Ritchie's criticisms whole-heartedly, dismissing the possibility of an American-led preventive war, underlining Ritchie's view that Soviet policy was brutal and blundering rather than realistic, and rejecting Reid's optimistic hopes for Canadian influence in Washington or a mellowing international conflict. With his comments he enclosed a separate paper, 'Influences Shaping the Policy of the United States towards the Soviet Union,' which seemed to be directly prompted by Ritchie's appeal for a critical analysis of the sources and nature of American foreign policy.[71]

Wrong held that the broad outlines of US policy, as drawn by Marshall and Kennan – reviving the world economy and 'containing the Soviet Union patiently and firmly' – were beyond criticism and deserved Canadian support. He cautioned, however, that 'there are flaws in its structure which could become fissures.' There were elements in the United States that sought to dominate other nations, and advocates of 'dangerously noisy and provocative methods' towards the Soviet Union. Such tendencies might antagonize potential allies and drive the Soviets to war. Wrong quoted the warning of Justice Jackson of the Supreme Court against the use of 'careless, threatening or boastful words by Americans in places of responsibility.'

In the Canadian ambassador's view there were both institutional and historic reasons for the excesses of American foreign policy. The congressional system meant that the administration constantly had to appease congressional prejudices in order to gain its appropriations. 'In this general connection it is crystal clear ... that no single reason or combination of reasons can approach the basic motive of rabid anti-Communism as the driving motive for expending huge funds for a European recovery programme.' Before an economizing Congress, the administration was thus constantly tempted to play the anti-Communist line to the point of caricature. And the prejudices of Congress had public origins as well.

The Congressional factor ... is, however, multiplied and complicated by a complex of forces inside the United States which threaten to promote bluster and confusion in the short run. In the more distant future, the pressure of economic forces could lead to the abandonment of an adequate policy. The component parts of the mixture of more immediate concern may perhaps be listed as inexperience in international affairs, unbalanced and blinding hatred and fear of Communism, an inability to comprehend the state of the European mind, and lastly, plain ignorance of some elementary historical facts.

Inexperience and self-rightousness meant that Americans expected affection and respect in return for their country's generosity, and felt abused when American motives were challenged. 'The blinding unbalanced fear and hatred of Russia and Communism prevalent in this country' had sources which Wrong could not adequately explain; but he did not doubt their strength. They had 'vicious' and 'pernicious' expressions that threatened the domestic balance. Widespread ignorance of history meant that Americans failed to appreciate either that Russian expansionism pre-dated the Soviet regime, or that some American policies towards its small neighbours paralleled Soviet policies in Eastern Europe.

This complex of American traits meant that the United States tended to over-dramatize the world situation as though it involved nothing more subtle than the conflict between American light and Soviet darkness: 'The central factor of rabid anti-Communism produces a feeling that if every vestige of Communism were to disappear overnight, no real problems would remain.' In the extreme, such fantasy inspired the thought of preventive war, without consideration of its political aftermath.

Like others in External (and Walter Lippmann), Wrong insisted that the United States should discard any mischievous efforts to undermine Russian influence in Eastern Europe. 'It is illogical to suppose,' he wrote, 'that a victorious Russia, whether Czarist or Communist would not have spilled over the confining borders imposed by the Treaty of Brest-Litovsk. But, more to the point, it is difficult to see what means the western powers have at their disposal for eliminating Soviet domination from the belt of her satellites in eastern Europe. To act effectively in this region under the present conditions would mean to act aggressively; to act ineffectively and noisily would be to act provocatively.'

While he deplored the excesses of American anti-Communist rhetoric, Wrong concluded by accepting a paradox.

It is apparent ... that the consciousness of the people of the United States of their responsibilities in the world depends too greatly for comfort on their dislike and fear of the Soviet Union and the Communist ideology. This dislike and fear results in distortions and exaggerations which increase the difficulty of achieving a negotiated settlement between the U.S. and the U.S.S.R.. It also provides the Soviet propaganda mill with a steady supply of useable material. It has to be remembered, nevertheless, that if there had not been developed such powerful and widespread popular emotions, there would have been strong tendencies to move backwards from the wartime position of full involvement in international affairs all over the world, towards the pre-war aloofness which it took Pearl Harbor to terminate decisively. The contest between the U.S. and the U.S.S.R. is providing the necessary popular foundation for a vigorous foreign policy, and it has put those leaders who still possess strong isolationist leanings, such as Senator Taft and Speaker Martin, in the position of opening themselves to charges of lack of patriotism if they attack the general trend; they are therefore reduced to the role of critics of its details.

The extravagances appearing in the press and in speeches in Congress are, of course, embarrassing to those responsible for the actual conduct of U.S. policy; but we must bear with them, for without them the rest of the world would be worse off ... they are part of the price to be paid for the Marshall Plan.

None of the other commentaries on Reid's paper suggested that the international conflict was less serious than Reid had depicted it – although Dana Wilgress responded that, while North Americans tended to be obsessed with the possibility of war, Europeans took the long view and neither thought nor talked of it.[72] He recalled that British policy from 1878 to 1905 was aimed at checking Russian expansion, but that 'never once during this period was there a really serious threat of war between the two countries.' The policy of firmness now adopted by the United States was the proper one, deserving Canada's full and long-term support, without fear or panic over the dangers of war.

R.M. Macdonnell and D.M. Johnson commented that the effort in the paper to balance Russian and American responsibility for world tensions was misplaced.[73] Both accepted that the blame rested primarily with the Soviet Union, and that the Canadian interest lay in supporting the American position. From his experience of the previous year's negotiations over North American defence, however, Macdonnell could see one practical opportunity for asserting Canadian influence. If the United States desired defensive preparations in Canada in peacetime, its interest would dictate that these should be achieved by negotiation rather than fiat. Canada would thus have 'a certain bargaining power,' on condition that it was prepared to accept 'a respectable share of the responsibility and expense, a share that may be high in terms of Canada's manpower and national income.'

Macdonnell (who was writing from Prague) believed with other realist critics of the Reid paper that the conclusion was 'unduly optimistic,' the product of pious hope. He preferred an attitude of grim and sustained determination.

One of the great problems facing leaders of public opinion in the West in the coming years will be to convince the public of the need to maintain overwhelming strength, and there will be a natural temptation to hope for the best and to pin wistful faith on the mellowing or collapse of the Soviet system. It is always unrealistic and often dangerous to base policies on wishful thinking, and it must be recognized that the period of uneasy peace which requires adequate and expensive strength on the part of the West may extend for much longer than ... ten or fifteen years.

Three French-speaking members of the department, Laurent Beaudry, Marcel Cadieux, and Pierre Dupuy, differed profoundly with Escott Reid's attempt to offer a balanced perspective on Soviet and American expansionism.[74] For Beaudry the USSR was 'a massive tyranny' with whom no reconciliation was possible; the conflict was essentially one between materialism and Christianity. The West would have to remain 'calm, patient, vigilant and strong,' but in the end triumph was bound to come for the 'Christian World' because 'Christian thought is the greatest strengthening idea, and no other idea can prevail against it.' For Beaudry the outcome was equally a matter of faith, which he conceded 'may appear to be oblivious of certain realities. This may be true to some extent, particularly if we think too much in terms of material forces, but if we accept the fundamental fact that the world is mainly governed by ideas, that subversive ideas cannot prevail against constructive ideas in the highest sense of the world, we may conclude there is hope for peace and perhaps a long peace, despite the turmoil of subversive ideas which exists in large sections of the world.'

For Marcel Cadieux, 'the U.S.S.R. is waging war against us in all but a military sense'; for Pierre Dupuy, 'war is well past the stage of possibility and in fact is now being waged.' For both, the appropriate response of the Western powers was a militant and forward policy in all spheres, domestic and foreign. At home, Soviet subversion and propaganda should be matched by unusual measures of internal security and counter-propaganda. Cadieux suggested 'some sort of political and psychological defence committee with appropriate means of action'; Dupuy proposed 'a permanent press-government committee' or at least close liaison 'to adopt a consistent and effective propaganda line in the newspapers.' Special measures against domestic agents of the USSR would be necessary, in Dupuy's view, and these would have to be 'far more intensified than was necessary against the Germans and Japanese.' ('I assume that police bodies such as the R.C.M.P. and the F.B.I. are fully alert in this respect.') Public-spirited citizens should 'be encouraged to assume the duty of reporting on activities which appear to be designed to abet the Soviet cause.' Dupuy cautioned that, somehow, civil liberties would have to be safeguarded in this campaign, but the warning appeared flimsy in contrast to the vigilance he felt was required. These commentaries seemed to fit the pattern of 'rabid anti-Communism' that Hume Wrong worried about in the American debate. They were matched by Prime Minister King's private vision, conveyed to his diary on 2 April 1947: 'Each day emphasizes anew the appalling alignment that is shaping up between Capitalist and Communistic countries. The insidious nature of the Communist movement is its worst feature. It is the dragon in action. Destructive of all that is constructive. Undermining standards of morality, beauty and truth; religion and all else that makes for enduring peace, happiness and prosperity.'[75]

Arnold C. Smith, who had recently been appointed associate director at Canada's new National Defence College in Kingston, responded to the Reid paper on 10 December 1947 by letter, enclosing a memorandum he had prepared for the staff of the college titled 'The Russians and the Rest of Us.'[76] Smith believed that Reid's paper, once revised on the basis of the comments being solicited, 'should prove most valuable in clarifying our minds on the fundamental question of relations with the USSR, and in helping us toward a consensus which, while inevitably not final or dogmatic, should make for increased consistency and effectiveness in day-to-day policies.' For his part, Smith wished to see the paper significantly hardened in its attitudes to the Soviet Union. Reid's emphasis on 'bi-polarity,' the effort to explain the nature of international tension as a product of 'the interplay of u.s. and Soviet expansion,' was both incorrect and dangerous. The possibility of war, Smith thought, arose 'almost exclusively from the existence and expansionist policies of the present regime in the ussr.' In the absence of American power, the danger posed by Soviet power would be 'greater, not less.' The depiction of a bipolar world was dangerous because 'it tends to encourage a feeling of neutrality ("a pox on both your houses"), which is already dangerously widespread in such regions as Latin America, Scandinavia, and to some extent in Western Europe as a whole. This "neutral" psychology tends to favor the totalitarians by throwing on to one strong power (the u.s.) almost the whole weight of resistance to a common menace.'

Smith dismissed the optimistic judgment (most often expressed in the Canadian dispatches by Dana Wilgress) that the Soviet Union's basic motives were defensive. To the extent that the Russian leaders believed war to be inevitable – and Smith said that they did, out of ideological conviction – the distinction between offence and defence became meaningless: 'the two words represent merely different facets of the same thing.' 'For practical purposes,' he suggested, 'I am inclined to think that the determining motive of Soviet policy, external and internal, can best be described as a nihilist pursuit of power for its own sake.' The best hope of reducing the danger of war, therefore, was 'to organize an overwhelming and effective preponderance of strength in the non-Soviet three-quarters of the world.'

The most promising means of achieving this goal, in Smith's judgment, would be to transform the United Nations, minus the Soviet Union, into a comprehensive world association directed not only to mutual defence but also to 'the economic, cultural, and social welfare of the non-Soviet peoples.' He preferred this vision of a world-wide anti-Soviet alliance to Reid's suggestion for a regional treaty of mutual assistance within the terms of the un charter among the nations of Western Europe and North America. Smith admitted, however, that Reid's more modest scheme might be 'the best we can do in the immediate future,' and conceded that 'I am in general agreement with most of Mr. Reid's practical conclusions regarding desirable lines for western policy during the next few years.'

Smith's general analysis, while harsher and more radical than Reid's, was in fact absorbed without discomfort into the departmental consensus. Reid circulated Smith's paper to a dozen colleagues, pointing out that 'the difference between Arnold Smith and myself is not as profound as might appear on the surface since I would propose to organize our three-quarters of the world by means of a treaty of mutual defence ... [which] would actually go much further than a normal treaty of this kind and would provide machinery for carrying out the kind of things which Arnold Smith would do through UN machinery.'[77] Reid noted that he would take Smith's memorandum into account in revising his paper.[78]

Only one brief commentary, by R.A. Mackay, seemed to hint at the outlines of a Canadian strategy for independence between the great powers.[79] Mackay accepted Reid's general argument, but suggested that Canada should pursue, as far as possible, a 'buffer state policy.' He admitted that Canada's presence within the defence and ideological orbit of the United States meant that 'an out-and-out buffer state policy is impossible'; but Canada could assert its power by manning its own northern bases, insisting on 'the fullest information of the activities of the United States forces in Canadian territory,' and thus, in consequence, giving weight to its claim to the 'sector principle' of arctic sovereignty not yet recognized by the United States. As a counterweight to American and Russian power, Mackay urged that Canada should turn its attention to closer association with Britain, Western Europe, and the Commonwealth in a nascent third bloc. Although his thoughts paralleled those of Ritchie, Macdonnell, and Ford, they were not developed and apparently received no more than cursory attention.

Following this collective exercise in the fall of 1947, Escott Reid's efforts to revise his document came to nothing; the paper, whose ultimate disposition had always been uncertain, was overtaken by events. A final version was never distributed, but the process seemed to serve the purpose within the Department of External Affairs of clarifying Canada's drift within the hardening lines of the Soviet-American conflict into the territory of the Pax Americana. What was evident in Reid's paper and all the commentaries was a resigned acceptance of hostile American and Soviet blocs, based upon a psychological and ideological judgment of the Soviet Union, and an almost complete failure to examine particular acts as elements in the worsening conflict. Without such close analysis, the consideration of alternatives had become impossible. By the early spring of 1948, Escott Reid was more and more preoccupied with the preparation of drafts for a North Atlantic treaty, all attempts to explain the post-war world behind him.[80]

In the autumn of 1947 Mackenzie King was overtaken by renewed panic over the prospect of war with the Soviet Union. This mood was the product neither of the Department of External Affairs' sober briefings nor of his own unassisted reflections. In November the prime minister travelled to Britain with the Canadian high commissioner in London, Norman Robertson, to represent Canada at the royal wedding of Princess Elizabeth; and in the course of his three weeks in London, King participated in a series of meetings with members of the British cabinet, Commonwealth prime ministers and high commissioners, and political acquaintances whose views of the international situation he accepted on faith. A concurrent meeting of the Council of Foreign Ministers in London gave a sense of immediacy to these discussions. On 24 November, the day before the opening of the Council of Foreign Ministers, King and Robertson attended a special briefing for Commonwealth politicians and diplomats at 10 Downing Street.[81] Norman Robertson recorded Ernest Bevin's survey of the state of East-West relations with dispassion. Bevin told the meeting that he expected no agreement with the Soviet Union over Germany, increased Communist party efforts at disruption in Western Europe, and rapid elimination of non-Communists from the governments of Eastern and Central Europe. The source of this 'very marked acceleration of the Communist offensive, both on the diplomatic level and in the domestic policies of every country in which the Communist Party had a footing,' was probably fear that the Marshall Plan would make possible European recovery. Bevin believed, according to Robertson, that 'The Russians were pushing so hard and so vigorously that they could easily overstep themselves and lose their balance. He did not think they wanted war, but they might suddenly find themselves in a position from which they could not retreat.'[82] Robertson wrote that Field Marshal Smuts intervened at this point to counsel a firm and united British-American response to Soviet pressure:

He thought that if they took a firm line, and showed that they were determined to stand together and meant business, there would be no war. He did not think the Russians were prepared for it, or wanted it, and that their aggressiveness was an indication of their sense of western weakness. If they found themselves resolutely blocked, it would be within character of their historic policies for them to draw back, as at Brest-Litovsk, to take stock of the new situation and to alter their strategy in accordance with its requirements.

Bevin agreed, 'but he was very much afraid that their strategy and tactics might land them in a position in which they would find that they had forced a war on the world.'

According to Robertson, King said 'that he did not think that the Foreign Secretary over-estimated the political dangers of the situation which he had described. The United States' feeling towards the Soviet Union had hardened greatly during the past year. They might well be exasperated by the Russian tactics into calling a final bluff in the way that the Foreign Secretary feared.' But he recalled that in discussion a year earlier, the consensus of military and diplomatic opinion was that the Russians would not be in a position 'to invite a war with confidence about its outcome' for ten years. Bevin responded with two points. First, while the strategic appreciation was still valid, it had to be qualified by 'some evidence which indicated that Soviet military readiness might be further advanced than had previously been thought likely.' Second, the present danger was political and diplomatic, and thus harder to measure. He repeated that he 'did not believe that the Russians wished war, but he did fear that by their actions they might force a showdown, even though they were not really prepared for it in a military or industrial sense.'[83]

Following the formal meeting, King was told by the first lord of the admiralty, A.V. Alexander (in the presence of Clement Attlee), that British intelligence reports suggested the need to revise the previous estimate of Russian military capability. Soviet jet aircraft and submarines were more advanced than formerly believed, and there were also 'quite well-substantiated reports that the Russians had reassembled a German army of 200,000 to 300,000 men.'[84] Beyond this, and 'to be most feared,' King told his diary, were the unknown prospects of Russian atomic and bacteriological weapons.[85] 'At any rate,' wrote King, 'there were very strong evidences that she was preparing for war and that, soon. What she was waiting for was the unrest in other nations in Europe and the hope of depression in the States.' Attlee and Alexander told him that 'the British people would fight rather than suffer the encroachment of Russian power over the whole of Europe which would mean their own extinction in a short time.'[86] This was scare talk, unsubstantiated and unrelated to any concrete evidence of Soviet intentions for Western Europe; but it reflected accurately the mood of pessimism and anxiety among European leaders.

King and Robertson left this meeting in profound depression.

We each agreed it was the most serious situation that we could possibly have imagined and indeed was altogether beyond anything I had hitherto thought possible. In a word, it came down to this: that within three weeks, there may be another world war. This world war will grow out of the unwillingness of the Russians to make any peace settlement with respect to Germany at this time, and their determination to go on fomenting unrest in all countries ... I felt that instead of going on to a dinner at night with High Commissioners and others, we should all be on our knees praying for guidance.[87]

In the absence of a heavenly communication, King's guidance came at lunch the next day from Winston Churchill. The ex–prime minister's combination of emphatic conviction and extravagant surmise overwhelmed King. When he asked how the United States could possibly meet a Soviet challenge in Europe, King was astonished by Churchill's reply. 'He turned to me sharply, his eyes bulging out of his head, and said: they would, of course, begin the attack in Russia itself. You must know they have had plans all laid for this, for over a year.'[88] Churchill asserted that the time had come for an American ultimatum to Stalin.

What the Russians should be told at the present conference, if they are unwilling to co-operate, is that the nations that have fought the last war for freedom, have had enough of this war of nerves and intimidation ... We will give you what you want and is reasonable in the matter of boundaries. We will give you ports in the North. We will meet you in regard to conditions generally. What we will not allow you to do is to destroy Western Europe; to extend your regime further there. If you do not agree to that here and now, within so many days, we will attack Moscow and your other cities and destroy them with atomic bombs from the air. We will not allow tyranny to be continued.[89]

King was transfixed. He wrote that Churchill's 'whole face and eyes were like those of a man whose whole being was filled with the belief which he had ... I confess that while he was talking, I myself had a sort of vision of a welter of the world. It might just be the effect of his own words but they were strong and powerful and deeply felt.' Churchill recalled his predictions of the Second World War, and King accepted his view that if a stand were not made now, 'within five years or a much shorter time, there would be another world war in which we shall all be finished.'[90]

For the Canadian prime minister, what he heard from Churchill was more than private reflection. He concluded that Churchill was speaking officially on behalf of the British government, filling out the background to what had been conveyed at Downing Street the previous day. King judged as well that when Churchill spoke of American stockpiles of atomic bombs and plans to bomb Moscow, he was repeating privileged information about American intentions rather than asserting his own preferences.[91]

On his return to Ottawa in early December, King told the cabinet 'perhaps more than I should' about the European crisis.

I could see what I said had a very sobering effect among all the Members. They were not surprised about conditions in France, but they seemed stunned at the thought of a possible conflict coming on immediately between Russia and the other nations. It is just too terrible to contemplate, but it does look to me increasingly as if the men at the head of affairs in Russia have got into their minds that they can conquer the world. What they may have in the way of secret weapons and missiles and poisons, no one knows.[92]

On 4 December and again on the 6th King exchanged views at length with the governor general, Lord Alexander. Churchill's view of events had become King's touchstone.

I said to him my understanding was that Marshall and Bevin, perhaps together, would finally say to Molotov that they wanted to know at once whether there was to be an end of this frustration and stirring up of Communism in Europe at the instance of Russia. Unless there were, the two countries would have to say at once that the moment had come when they could not allow matters to proceed further and to give Molotov to understand that Moscow would be destroyed within a certain number of hours if there were further delay.[93]

Alexander did not challenge King's statement, although he must have known it was nonsense; instead King wrote that Alexander shared the belief that this stand was necessary, and that the Soviets would 'climb down' in response to it.

The prime minister left Government House on 6 December confident that his own judgment in world affairs 'has not had to take second place to that of anyone else. I am most anxious to make the most of every moment and be prepared to speak fearlessly on the present day issues.'[94] The same day, however, Norman Robertson wrote to Mike Pearson to suggest that he had found no evidence, after further enquiries in London, to indicate the likelihood of a serious crisis, or any British and American preparations to meet it.[95] The threat to bomb Moscow (or as King said he had spoken of it to Alexander, 'the thought of blasting gangsters out of Moscow') was apparently Churchillian hyperbole which reflected, in crude form, the American strategic doctrine of 'atomic blitz' incorporated in an evolving American war plan, developed in 1946 and 1947, and calling for an attack on Russia using 'about fifty atomic bombs' – although in fact 'even the working figure of fifty was wishful thinking.'[96]

When the Council of Foreign Ministers meeting in London adjourned on 15 December without progress on the German and Austrian treaties, King wrote: 'We have now reached the point that Bevin feared might lead to war.'[97] The United Kingdom, France, and the United States were determined to reconstruct Western Europe through the Marshall Plan; the Soviets sought its conquest; and at the moment when Russia decided to prevent Western access to Berlin, 'war will be inevitable.' In the event, when the Berlin crisis developed in 1948, the objectives of the antagonists were conceived more narrowly, and pursued by means more restrained, than Mackenzie King had anticipated. But during this winter the Canadian prime minister lived in fear of war.

In London King had expressed solidarity with Bevin and Churchill over the joint determination of Britain and the United States to resist further Russian encroachment in Europe. The commitment rested safely under the umbrella of Anglo-American unity, and in the short run it cost Canada nothing beyond King's fear because she was not a party to the negotiations over Germany and Austria. But in mid-December the Canadian cabinet was confronted with a commitment of a different kind, undertaken by the Canadian delegation to the United Nations, to participate in the UN Temporary Commission on Korea, whose unlikely task was to arrange and supervise elections in both the American and Russian occupation zones of that country.[98] The Russians promised obstruction; the Americans hoped to make use of the commission to legitimize the creation of a government of South Korea; the Canadians had been persuaded to join by Washington; and neither King nor his cabinet had received prior warning of the nomination. Given Mackenzie King's bleak view of the coming Soviet-American conflict, the prospect of direct Canadian participation in an exercise displeasing to the Soviet Union was predictably distasteful to him. As in the Gouzenko case, King's instinct for Canada was to retreat into isolation and inaction, to avoid giving offence to the Russians. When the issue came before cabinet, King refused to sign the order-in-council appointing a Canadian representative to the commission, and lectured the two ministers responsible (J.L. Ilsley and Louis St Laurent) on the uselessness of the United Nations, Canadian ignorance of distant lands, and the indignity of American pressure on Canada to serve. At subsequent cabinet meetings King threatened to resign and stump the country against his former colleagues, warning of the dangers of involvement in a Soviet-American war. A decision was deferred while Mike Pearson acted as intermediary to Washington: or more precisely, as the State Department's adviser on how to deal with Canada's eccentric prime minister.[99] Finally a letter from President Truman to the prime minister, drafted with Pearson's advice, flattered King and emphasized the need for Canadian statesmanship.[100] Louis St Laurent met King's challenge with the threat of his own resignation, and King agreed to a paper compromise which permitted Canada to serve on the Commission on the understanding that it would only operate within the range of Russian-American consensus.[101] (In fact the commission failed to do so, and performed the service desired by the United States of supervising elections in South Korea alone. Canada continued to participate in spite of her previously recorded interpretation of the commission's mission.)[102]

The Korean affair was virtually King's last, and unsuccessful, attempt to impose his isolationist will on the conduct of Canadian foreign relations. He blamed the Department of External Affairs, and especially the under-secretary, L.B. Pearson, for excessive ambition and independence. But he seemed to recognize that the drift of opinion in cabinet and country was with them rather than with him – or at least, he lacked the energy to make the test. He protested further in cabinet against too much Canadian involvement in United Nations mediation efforts in Kashmir and Palestine, always with the 'appalling possibility' of direct Soviet-American confrontation in mind.[103] Following lunch at Laurier House in February 1948 with Norman Robertson, he reflected to the diary that he would prefer to see Robertson return from London to replace Pearson as under-secretary. 'I really think Robertson's judgment is sounder than Pearson's on these international affairs, and that he would be better at the head of the Department here. Is less fond of speaking or of travelling or of participating in the United Nations, etc. Less likely to get the Government into trouble.'[104] But the drift into American internationalism was not Pearson's alone. King saw it all around him, in speeches by St Laurent and Claxton as well, and resigned himself increasingly to his own retirement. [105] If he could not persuade the cabinet to resist Canadian activism, he could at least avoid personal responsibility for leading the country to disaster. According to his moral calculus, that would put him right with God, if not necessarily with the historians.

By the summer of 1947 the nature of the Soviet problem, which had been the source of perplexity and endless analysis in Western chancelleries since the spring of 1945, was understood enough to offer the basis for a consistent policy. (That is, since the United States now had a consistent policy, it had become possible to understand the nature of the Soviet problem.) As a British dispatch from Moscow put it in October 1947, 'nothing the Western world can do at present will remove from the Soviet mind in the foreseeable future the fatalistic conviction that a collision between East and West is inevitable and the consequent determination to push through the preparations deemed necessary to face the clash successfully when it arrives.'[106] The paper emphasized the theme familiar to the diplomats that 'the clash is not, however, necessarily imminent, and in the meantime the Soviet Union is prepared to rub along with the rest of the world, provided always that this entails no weakening of her position for the ultimate struggle.' The futility of attempting to co-operate with or appease the Soviet Union on all matters of high policy was now taken for granted in Whitehall and Washington; and in place of co-operation, a policy of consolidating the Western sphere of influence was emerging. This involved, above all, the irreversible commitment of the United States to a forward policy as a great power, already signified in the Truman Doctrine and the Marshall Plan. Although the diplomatic assessment was that the Soviets did not want war, there were inevitable military implications in an American determination to accept and consolidate a Western sphere against Soviet expansion. These implications had at least two potentially dangerous senses: one propagandist, the other concrete. The British dispatch of 10 October illuminated the first danger: 'although Soviet policy is conceived as strategically defensive, its execution involves the same military preparedness, the same striving after self-sufficiency, the same propaganda campaigns and the same tactics of stalling, intervention and attempts at disruption as would a policy planned for aggression. It therefore carries with it the same dangers and enforces upon us preparedness and vigilance.'[107] Given the difficulty of distinguishing between defensive and offensive measures, there would be a continuing temptation, in the democracies, to exaggerate or misinterpret Russian aims in justification of the budgets and policies required for 'preparedness and vigilance.'

The second potential military danger was implicit in the very conception of a stable Western sphere of interest. A sphere of interest has boundaries; a stable sphere has stable boundaries. If it is to be defended, lines of defence must be drawn – and advertised. In July 1947 an internal State Department memorandum defined the issue: 'Are we,' it asked, 'prepared to use armed force against the Soviet Union on any given conditions, and if so, what are the given conditions upon which we could not for our own safety allow Russian action to proceed unchecked? ... Unless we are prepared to call a halt somewhere – whenever that point or line is reached – we should certainly avoid strong courses whose only outcomes could be tough talk, and (because of weak action following) demoralization in the countries which we may ultimately need as allies.'[108] The memorandum added both that the Western line was already being drawn 'by default in the absence of a reasoned conscious position' in a series of particular responses to Soviet actions; and that the Soviet Union probably failed to understand American determination as it applied in many regions of the world. Russian choices, in that case, 'may turn out to lead to a basic miscalculation which could precipitate war.'

Both George Marshall and Ernest Bevin, on behalf of their governments, had come to the view in the fall of 1947 that the line against Soviet expansion must be drawn at the boundaries of the existing Soviet sphere in Europe. (In Asia the strategic picture was not yet so clear.) The Soviets increasingly seemed to take note of Anglo-American firmness (even if there were still uncertainties on the margins), and after June hastened their own crude acts of consolidation in their realm. For both sides, the decisions of the other on European policy appeared menacing; for both the rationalizations were defensive. The Soviets had the added advantage of powerful Communist parties and trade unions in France and Italy, which threatened Western unity from within and added to a sense of desperate vulnerability. The November Council of Foreign Ministers was the last occasion for compromise on the future of Germany, but it was evident before the meeting began that there would be no compromise. The conference's collapse, when it came, was the final disenchanting signal that the two power blocs would live in conflict, more or less active. For many in the West, that conflict could only be understood or justified in the simplest moralistic and alarmist terms, as a potential military conflict between the forces of good and evil. It is not so difficult to appreciate how Mackenzie King, pietistic, cautious, neurotic, and ignorant of international politics, could draw the most frightening conclusions from his briefings when he arrived in London in November 1947; he was encouraged to do so. The fear of war was in the air. In a dispatch to Washington from Moscow on 15 November, General Walter Bedell Smith, the American ambassador, had written of 'the terrible and developing fear of imminent war which is overpowering Europe.'[109] King could sniff it.

By this time, officials in the State Department who were sympathetic to the idea of a North Atlantic treaty of mutual guarantee were actively consulting with their British and Canadian counterparts about the best timing for such a project. They believed it was still premature to broach the subject publicly, however, before Congress had authorized Marshall Plan aid to Europe; and they favoured an initiative, when it did come, 'from some source other than themselves.'[110] The need to counter Western Europe's developing psychology of fear was a powerful element in these calculations.

Once the Council of Foreign Ministers had collapsed, Britain moved quickly to dispel that fear and acknowledge the new era. On 14 January 1948 Prime Minister Attlee cabled Mackenzie King: 'we feel that the time has come on the one hand to give a moral lead to the friendly countries of Western Europe and, on the other hand, to take a more active line against Communism.'[111]

Soviet Government have formed a solid block behind a line from the Baltic along the Oder, through Trieste to the Black Sea. Countries behind that line are dominated by Communists and there is no prospect in immediate future of our re-establishing normal relations with them. In Germany, France, Trieste, Italy and Greece, Soviet policy is exerting a constantly increasing pressure. Soviet policy is based on expectation of economic chaos in Western Europe and will be checked if Marshall Plan succeeds, but economic program alone will not suffice. Indeed if we are to stem further encroachment of Soviet tide we should organise ethical and spiritual forces of Western Europe backed by the power and resources of the Commonwealth and of the Americas, thus creating a solid foundation for the defence of Western civilization in the widest sense. The countries of Western Europe already sense Communist peril and are seeking some assurance of salvation. They are likely to welcome a lead from Britain. We believe, therefore, that we should seek to form a Western democratic system comprising at any rate France, the Low Countries, and Scandinavia, Portugal, Italy and Greece. When circumstances permit it could be extended to Spain and Germany.

Attlee left open whether a formal alliance was necessary, but foresaw an alliance in fact: 'Essence of the system would be an understanding backed by resources and resolution of participants bound together by common ideals.' The Russians would regard it as hostile. 'We realise that Soviet Government would react fiercely to what they would describe as an offensive alliance directed against Soviet Union. Nevertheless we are convinced that, if we are to preserve peace and our own safety, we must mobilize moral and material force which will create confidence and energy in our friends and inspire respect and caution in others. Alternative would be to acquiesce in continued Russian infiltration and undermining of one Western country after another.'

Attlee noted that Ernest Bevin would 'probably ventilate the idea of a Western system' in the House of Commons later in the month, 'and we should thereafter pursue it as occasion demands with the Governments concerned.' Bevin's statement came on 22 January 1948. He reviewed briefly 'a policy on the part of the Soviet Union to use every means in their power to get Communist control in Eastern Europe, and, as it now appears, in the West as well.'[112] In response to these 'facts as they are,' he defined Britain's task as 'not to make spectacular declarations nor to use threats or intimidation, but to proceed swiftly and resolutely with the steps we consider necessary to meet the situation which now confronts the world.'[113] British policy was to seek the unity of Europe, without its domination by any single power: 'I am sure this House and the world will realise that if a policy is pursued by any one Power to try to dominate Europe by whatever means, direct or indirect – one has to be frank – one is driven to the conclusion that it will inevitably lead again to another world war.'[114] Rather than seeking great power co-operation in European recovery, however, the Soviet Union had decided to create its own exclusive bloc in Eastern Europe, and to 'wreck or intimidate Western Europe by political upsets, economic chaos and even revolutionary methods.'[115] Just as Molotov had threatened at the European recovery meetings in June 1947, economic disruptions had occurred on his schedule in the autumn, and the Cominform had been created in September. But the planning for European recovery had proceeded none the less, and the scheme was now before the American Congress. In the face of Soviet vituperation and disruption, however, something more was now necessary: 'the free nations of Western Europe must now draw closely together.'[116] Bevin revealed that he had initiated talks with France and the Low Countries leading to a political alliance, and that a broader association, to include Italy, was also desirable. His words repeated those of Attlee in his private message to Mackenzie King of the previous week: 'If we are to preserve peace and our own safety at the same time we can only do so by the mobilisation of such a moral and material force as will create confidence and energy in the West and inspire respect elsewhere.'[117] While the immediate task was to reinvigorate Western Europe, Bevin looked beyond it to 'the power and resources of all the countries on the continent of America' to bring that about.[118] A Western bloc was in the making to balance the Eastern bloc.

Czechoslovakia was the last nation in Eastern Europe to maintain a semblance of multiparty democracy, although the Communist party had exercised steadily increasing domination since 1945. Western diplomats universally recognized that the country fell within the Soviet sphere, and would suffer the same political fate as Poland, Hungary, and the rest at a time of Moscow's choosing. In July 1947, for example, Hume Wrong wrote to Mike Pearson from Washington to report on a conversation with Llewellyn Thompson, the chief of the East European Division of the State Department.[119] Thompson interpreted two recent Soviet articles to mean (in Wrong's words) 'that popular front governments such as now exist in Poland, Czechoslovakia and Rumania were transitional and must be expected in time to give way to a solid bloc – i.e., a one party system. He was sure that the articles were intended as directives to the Communist Parties in the satellite states, and their appearance had been followed by overt moves against other parties in Hungary and in Rumania ... He felt fairly sure that the Politburo had reached firm decisions on their objectives without setting any time limits. It would obviously take a good deal longer to bring about the desired results in Czechoslovakia than it would in some of the other satellites.' Pearson expressed his agreement with Thompson's judgments in a letter to John Holmes in London on 9 September 1947: 'the Soviet Union has no intention of allowing any opposition groups in the Eastern European states to steer their nations away from complete dependence upon and subservience to the Soviet Union.'[120] He repeated this conviction in a letter to Dana Wilgress the same day.[121]

This calm recognition of Soviet geopolitical logic, however, did not anticipate the profound emotional reaction to the reorganization of the government in Prague, under Communist domination, following the resignation of its conservative members on 24 February 1948. The West's sentimental attachment to Czechoslovak democracy, coupled with its current forebodings about Russian intentions, meant that the Czech events were greeted with horror and panic, as an example not of ruthless consolidation within the Soviet sphere, but of rank Soviet aggression.[122] For two weeks the shock reverberated on the diplomatic wires and in the press. While the United States, Britain, and France expressed their immediate condemnation of the coup, and the negotiations for a Western European Union accelerated, the Canadian prime minister responded with instinctive passivity. When Louis St Laurent showed him a draft statement on 3 March intended for use in the House of Commons, King recoiled.

I confess I was perfectly horrified if not terrified at the thought of anything of the kind read in the House of Commons at this time. It was a long story of what the press had contained of how the Government had changed. To me, it was a real interference with the domestic affairs of Czechoslovakia in an unpardonable way ... It was almost equivalent to an open declaration against Russia on the part of Canada. I confess that I get increasingly alarmed at the lack of judgment on the part of External Affairs in these matters and am beginning to mistrust St Laurent's judgment in them.[123]

St Laurent made no statement of substance on Czechoslovakia in the House that day, but delivered his harsh condemnation of 'a frightening case history of communist totalitarianism in action' in his general survey of world affairs on 29 April 1948.[124] There were no shadings to match the real complexity of the crisis in St Laurent's account.

The mysterious death of Jan Masaryk in a fall from a window of the Czech Foreign Ministry on 10 March coincided with an urgent message from Clement Attlee to Mackenzie King delivered personally the next day by the British high commissioner, Alexander Clutterbuck.[125] He told King that the Czech events 'had alarmed the [UK] ministers greatly as to what might take place in other countries, for example, Italy, etc.' Attlee wrote that 'events are moving ever quicker than we at first apprehended and there are grave indications from many sources that the next Russian move will be to make demands on Norway ... Norwegian Government have consulted United States and ourselves as to the help that they could expect if attacked.'[126] Attlee said that the Norwegians had been advised to resist Soviet demands, but 'We cannot be sure ... that encouragement of this kind will alone induce Norwegian Government to hold out.' Their defection, however, 'would not only involve the collapse of the whole Scandinavian system but would also prejudice our chances of calling a halt to expansion of Soviet influence over Western Europe and would in fact mean the appearance of Russia on the Atlantic.' The British conclusion was that 'only a bold move can avert the danger and the pace already set by Russia tells us that there is no time to lose.' What was necessary was 'a regional Atlantic pact of mutual assistance' to be joined by 'all the countries threatened by a Russian move on the Atlantic ... the United States and the United Kingdom, Canada, Eire, Iceland, Norway, Denmark, France, Portugal and Spain when it again has a democratic regime.'

Failure to act now may mean a repetition of our experience with Hitler and we should again have to witness the slow deterioration of our position until we were forced to resort to war in much less favourable circumstances.

In this grave situation I think it right to put our ideas at once before you and the United States Secretary of State. I am convinced that we should study without delay the establishment of such an Atlantic security system so that we inspire necessary confidence to consolidate the west against Soviet infiltration and at the same time inspire Soviet Government with sufficient respect for the west to remove temptation from them and so ensure a long period of peace. Our idea would be that if the Canadian and United States Governments agree, officials of the three Governments should meet in Washington and very secretly explore the proposal for an Atlantic system.

King mentioned the message only to St Laurent, Claxton, and Pearson, who met with him in the Prime Minister's Office that afternoon. They 'agreed that collective security was essential to preservation of safety and preservation of Canada. That no time should be lost in seeking to bring this about.'[127] They did not, apparently, question the nature of the supposed challenge to Norway, or the appropriateness of the historical analogy to the 1930s.[128] A reply – drafted by Pearson – was agreed upon and dispatched that evening. In it King made Canada's commitment to join in a treaty of mutual assistance under Anglo-American sponsorship.

I am deeply impressed with the gravity of these developments. Certainly everything possible should be done, and that speedily, to avoid a possible repetition of the disastrous experiences of pre-war years when peaceful states allowed themselves to become victims of aggression, one by one. Collective measures seem to me to be essential to establish some sense of security and to preserve the peace. Such collective measures will, of course, require the active leadership of the United Kingdom and of the United States. To permit of the earliest possible consideration by the Canadian Government of the proposal for an Atlantic system, I shall arrange to send one of our officials to Washington just as soon as he is required, to join officials of the United Kingdom and the United States Governments in the exploratory talks suggested.[129]

King called in the three opposition party leaders, John Bracken, M.J. Coldwell, and Solon Low, to warn them of the gravity of the international crisis, but without informing them of the joint action now contemplated.[130] On 15 March he gave cabinet the same sombre warnings, again without revealing his hand.[131] On 17 March, 'one of the most anxious days of my life' and also 'a memorable day in the world's history,' the conclusion of the Brussels Treaty and President Truman's broadcast committing the United States to the integrity of Western Europe allowed Mackenzie King to bring Canada's policy out of the closet.[132] The Liberal caucus listened to Truman's broadcast together, and King then summoned the cabinet upstairs, where he informed them of Attlee's message and his reply. The cabinet concurred without dissent in the decision to engage in security talks, and later in the day King informed the House that 'Canada was in line with the United Kingdom and the United States in the matter of security pacts.'[133]

In the coming days the prime minister would continue to wring his hands at the deplorable audacity of the Soviet Union, and to lament privately over the likelihood of war. He would remind Mike Pearson to keep Canada in the background of the security talks, and to ensure that the United States and Britain were firmly and safely in the lead. Nevertheless, his government had made its commitment to the Western alliance, and there could be no doubt it would carry parliament and the country in that commitment. 'The rest,' as Louis St Laurent told the cabinet, 'was a matter of implementation.'[134]

The Politics of Fear

Political misunderstanding and conflict between the United States and the Soviet Union in the early post-war period were inevitable. The seeds of conflict lay primarily in Europe, the shattered battlefield and focus of diplomatic attention of both great powers, and secondarily in the Northern Tier of Greece, Turkey, and Iran, an area of traditional but declining British influence and Russian aspiration. In victory, the Soviet Union assumed that it would exercise predominant influence in Europe for its own security. In the areas of Russian military occupation the Western powers reluctantly conceded that influence because they could not resist it. Initially, however, Joseph Stalin did not limit his ambitions to the line of Soviet military occupation; nor did he seem to take for granted that Russian influence meant a chain of exclusively Communist regimes along the western borders. Rather, he hoped to secure general European compliance with Soviet interests by less direct means, and with the overriding acquiescence of the United Kingdom and the United States. This Soviet version of the Grand Design emerged from the desperate Russian sense of insecurity, the heightened expectation of post-war co-operation unexpectedly aroused by the wartime alliance, and the chaos of Europe in 1945.

The Soviet view of Europe was not shared by the United States, which foresaw instead a restored system of independent states, democratic and capitalist, living within an open, world-wide trading and security system that would avoid another depression and another war. As Western governments observed the brutal means by which the Soviet Union set out to ensure pliability in the countries under Soviet occupation, they abandoned any wishful belief in benevolent co-operation with the Soviets elsewhere. By the spring of 1947 American policy involved a clear determination to prevent the extension of Soviet influence in Europe beyond its zone of military occupation. As the easy hopes of wartime dissolved, the Soviets on their side hardened their determination to assert absolute authority in their East European sphere; and from September 1947 they launched, as well, a campaign of challenge in Western Europe to upset the Marshall Plan. This was a political and economic campaign of disruption aimed at frustrating recovery; it contained no perceptible element of an aggressive military threat. Thus the Cold War, in its initial stages, was the product of two incompatible visions of post-war Europe, and was essentially diplomatic and political, not military, in nature. But other elements gave the conflict darker and more ominous shadings.

While the Soviet Union sought to ensure its security from invasion in the West, and to discourage (in ways that proved self-defeating) the creation of an anti-Soviet concert or alliance, the United States sought post-war security in other senses. The liberal and utopian objective of American policy was to remake the world in the American image, not by conquest but by example and persuasion – and by the free exercise of American economic power. The realist objective of American policy was to prevent renewed aggression in the Nazi pattern, both by re-creating an international collective security agency, and by ensuring that predominant military power rested in American hands. Exclusive possession of the atomic bomb appeared to give the United States that ultimate predominance in the early post-war years, despite the vast demobilization of US forces.

The United States assumed its predominance, while the Soviet Union sought equality as a great power; and both justified their new roles in the universalist claims of ideology. Both visions and interests were in conflict, and in the West, under American leadership, the initially puzzling nature of Soviet policy soon appeared alarming. The generation that had lived through a devastating world war was accustomed to alarm as the basis for policy, and perhaps unused to the less dramatic ways of peacetime diplomacy. By 1948 its political leaders had chosen to live by fear and alarm.

Mackenzie King's decision of 11 March 1948 to take Canada into a peacetime alliance of the North Atlantic nations fitted this pattern, and had the hallmarks, as well, of his traditional approach to foreign policy: it was not only impelled by fear, but was adopted in secrecy and sanctified by the endorsement of the United Kingdom and the United States. It was evident that some kind of commitment to mutual defence among the countries of the region, including Canada, was emerging as a complement to the economic alliance of the Marshall Plan. The decision had been germinating for months in the Department of External Affairs, coincidental with developments in the Foreign Office and the State Department. But it was taken only when Clement Attlee made a direct appeal to King in the anxious aftermath of the Czech crisis, in an atmosphere of panic and without study of the immediate pretext. By 1948 Canada enjoyed the public reputation of independence, but for the prime minister (and perhaps for his advisers as well) the ties of psychological dependence remained. For King the world beyond the borders was a realm of wayward forces and malevolent demons, best kept at bay by closing the doors on them. When the doors could not be closed, he still relied on the comforting protection of the two Anglo-American neighbours. King knew that Canada would fall under American protection in the Soviet-American conflict, whether this was tacit or explicit. But his instinct still was to avoid commitments, especially if they could be considered unfriendly by the Soviet Union. In addition, as power had shifted from London to Washington, King had grown more suspicious of American purposes and less suspicious of British; the old Canadian nationalist was now more willing to accept British than American advice. While he might have balked at an American invitation to join talks on an alliance, he acceded at once to the British proposal. His advisers were undoubtedly sensitive to the distinction.

For Louis St Laurent, Lester Pearson, and the senior officials of the Department of External Affairs, the Soviet challenge in the spring of 1948 was equally real, while the opportunities for Canada created by a new Western alliance soared beyond the prime minister's restricted vision. If American leadership was necessary and inevitable, the limitations imposed on Canada's actions by membership in the alliance were best played down, and the potential gains emphasized. At best, the Soviets would be deterred; confidence and prosperity in Western Europe would return, with great economic benefit to Canada; Canada would have an established place in the councils of the alliance, and the means to restrain American excess quietly from within; and Canadian diplomatic talents could be exercised beyond the alliance as well, in the spaces between the spheres of influence of the two great powers. Fear of the Soviet Union overrode and suppressed Canadian anxieties about the potential misuse of American power. In the spring of 1948 the governments of Britain, the United States, and Canada all made use of the atmosphere of fear to consolidate their own particular interests in an anti-Soviet system. For Canada, as R.D. Cuff and J.L. Granatstein say, 'Pearson and Reid decided to seize their advantage at the imperial center, capitalize on an inflamed public opinion, and negotiate an alliance that would best serve Canada's long-term interests as they defined them.'[1] Norman Robertson put the case most euphorically in April 1948 when he wrote: 'A situation in which our special relationship with the United Kingdom can be identified with our special relationships with other countries in western Europe and in which the United States will be providing a firm basis, both economically and probably militarily, for the link across the North Atlantic' would be 'a providential solution for so many of our problems.'[2]

If Norman Robertson's benediction put the benefits of the alliance complacently high, it is not clear – except on the margins of policy – how Canada's alternative choices might have differed from the collective choices of the other Western powers. The overriding desire to commit the United States to a forward role in world politics was shared by all their governments, who were willing to defer to and conspire with American leadership in order to ensure it. In that atmosphere – a product of the catastrophic failure of the interwar system – it is unlikely that Canada could have stood aside from and discouraged American activism. Great Britain, faltering in status and financially dependent on the United States, was the leading advocate of the new Western alliance; but she retained as well the assumptions of a great power and struggled to maintain an independent strategic role by secretly undertaking (at crippling expense) the development of her own atomic arsenal. The West European nations gratefully accepted American aid and entered the alliance, but also commenced their own efforts of historic co-operation aimed at the recovery of independent influence in world politics (while France under de Gaulle later added its atomic weapons to the balance). For both Britain and Western Europe, the post-war link with the United States was primary; the effort to recover world status depended first upon American support and protection. Canada shared Western Europe's desire for American leadership, without Europe's ambitions. She was too far in spirit from the experience of the great powers, new or old, to think in the same way about seeking great power status for herself.

Canadian diplomats sensed, and sought increasingly to make use of, the country's limited range of diplomatic manoeuvre in the United Nations and the Commonwealth, where Canada could exploit her ambiguous position as both a newly independent nation and an intimate of Britain and America. Beyond this, in the analysis of Canadian options prepared in the Department of External Affairs in 1947, there seemed to be only two substantial proposals for maximizing Canadian freedom of action within the constraints of the East-West confrontation. One was the suggestion of R.M. Macdonnell and R.A. Mackay that the major effort of air reconnaisance, warning, and interception in the Canadian north should be undertaken by Canada alone. This would have given Canada real bargaining power in Washington; but it seemed to be far from Canadian political reality in the age of Mackenzie King, and was never seriously considered by the cabinet. Failure to confront the issue in the 1940s has dogged Canadian defence and foreign policy ever since. The other was the suggestion of R.A.D. Ford that Canada should begin a crash program of training experts in Russian language, politics, and economics, to give External Affairs an enhanced capacity to judge Soviet politics and intentions on its own, and thus to influence Washington. Both the United States and the United Kingdom undertook such programs; Canada did not. It could be argued that this failure was simply the complement of Canada's larger incapacity to imagine itself in the front rank of international diplomacy, and that an enhanced ability to understand Soviet policy would have served no purpose (except to create frustration) in the absence of any independent desire to use that knowledge. The Canadian government failed equally to recognize the need for any special effort to train experts in American politics and foreign policy. These joint lapses in the provision of knowledge about the post-war world were perhaps more blameworthy than the larger failure of imagination about the use of Canadian power, because they were well within the capacity of Canada, both financial and intellectual, and could have been accomplished without domestic controversy. Enhanced expertise about the United States and the Soviet Union would have sharpened Canadian perspectives and created fresh opportunities for Canadian initiatives on the margin in the worst years of the Cold War after 1948. Yet even the Department of External Affairs failed to promote such programs; R.A.D. Ford's suggestion struck no chords.

By the time of the Czech crisis, the international mood was scarcely conducive to reason and moderation. In the West, deep and exaggerated mistrust had replaced the Panglossian faith in the Soviet Union stimulated by the wartime alliance and its accompanying propaganda. In the Department of External Affairs, detailed reporting from Moscow and Washington, and the open interchanges of information and opinion among Canadian, American, and British diplomats in the two foreign capitals, meant that those who applied themselves to the dispatches and reports could gain a complex sense of the sources and range of conflict and Anglo-American reactions to it. Until the autumn of 1947 the utility of departmental debate on the meaning of Soviet acts and the appropriate Western responses was still recognized. In External Affairs the dominant view of the Soviets (with some individual variations of mood and emphasis) paralleled the views in the State Department and the Foreign Office. Canada's contribution to this shared understanding was the result of copious reporting from the Canadian Embassy in Moscow, and reflection on the part of other Canadian officers in Ottawa, Washington, London, Paris, Prague, and other posts abroad. The Canadians had no special sources of intelligence beyond this, and very few officers with extended knowledge of Russia. As American policy became clear, the picture they drew more and more accommodated itself to that policy. The perception was increasingly pessimistic but usually not alarmist: the Soviets were seen as crude adventurers, determined to assert power within the sphere secured for them by the Red Army, to probe for weaknesses in Western Europe and elsewhere along the perimeters of that sphere, to enhance their economic and military power as rapidly as possible, but not to provoke direct military conflict with the United States or its leading partners. The danger of war was seen to lie in mutual misperception or desperate error rather than in aggressive intention on either side (although surprisingly often the diplomats worried over the prospect of an American pre-emptive attack on the Soviet Union).

Up to this point, the analysis might have coincided with traditional notions of power politics and pointed to traditional measures of balance and reassurance. But it went further to suggest that the Soviet Union was also moved by a faith calling eventually for world conquest. The prescription of containment (which the Canadian diplomats accepted) was therefore designed not just to meet specific and limited Soviet pressures, but also to break Russia's universal drive for conquest. There was a comforting implication in the doctrine as well that successful containment would somehow result in the collapse of Soviet power at home. (Although many of the diplomatic commentators rejected this belief as wishful thinking, it was a recurring and essential element in both official and popular analyses of the Cold War.) Thus, even when the explanations of Soviet behaviour were expressed in restrained language, they tended to imply a titanic struggle between profoundly differing rivals for ultimate goals. The most influential source of this general position, from February 1946 on, was George Kennan of the State Department, whose words were quoted and reflected in the papers of the Department of External Affairs and the Foreign Office. By the spring of 1948 the orthodoxy of containment was accepted in Ottawa as in Washington and London as the foundation of Western policy. There may still have been controversy in the State Department about its meaning and application (Kennan himself opposed both the Truman Doctrine and the North Atlantic Treaty); but in the East Block debate had effectively ended.

In the three foreign ministries, the uncertain balance between a relatively sophisticated and cool-headed perception of the Soviet Union on the one hand, and an alarmist perception on the other hand, tipped decisively in favour of the alarmist position by the late autumn of 1947. In Britain, the Attlee government entered the post-war period in a mood of optimism, although it tended to see the world in traditional terms as a realm of perpetual struggle requiring continual bargaining for advantage and balancing of forces to prevent domination by any single power. Britain had lost its pre-eminent balancing role, which it had previously exercised against the expansionism of Germany and Russia. It recognized the Soviet Union after 1945 as the major potential source of instability, and the United States as the balancing force which required its support. For the British political audience (except for a minority on the Labour left) this undramatic analysis was probably a sufficient basis for policy. Ernest Bevin hesitated to commit the government to an active anti-Soviet policy until after the failure of the Council of Foreign Ministers in December 1947; but as the Attlee government observed and shared in the collapse of European morale in 1946 and 1947, and saw its recovery more and more as dependent on an explicit American guarantee, it became less discriminating in the kind of appeal it made for American and Canadian support.

The first and most spectacular British attempt to influence American opinion and policy directly in the post-war period was a vigilante effort rather than an official one: Winston Churchill's Iron Curtain speech at Fulton, Missouri, in March 1946. Churchill took extraordinary care in the preparation of this address to inform and consult both President Truman and Prime Minister King (but not Prime Minister Attlee). Both Truman and King approved of it, presumably both as an accurate description of Soviet objectives and as a rationalization for emerging Western policy. Attlee was less enthusiastic, as were the American press and public, still under the spell of wartime propaganda and goodwill. But the sustaining echoes of Churchill's rhetoric did more than anything else in the next two years to shape public language and attitudes towards the Soviet Union as the spell evaporated and popular anxiety increased.

The disjunction of views about the Soviet Union between the realists and the alarmists in the United States was first revealed in the confusing alterations of approach during the period of James F. Byrnes's incumbency as secretary of state. Once the administration had determined on a forward policy in the spring of 1947, it was prepared to justify that policy in the universalist language of an anti-Communist crusade as the price of congressional and popular approval, or increasingly out of conviction – and without prudent consideration of Soviet reactions to such rhetoric. (The crude domestic consequences, the loyalty investigations and persecutions, were also unforeseen.) This popular justification for an activist foreign policy found its sources in some of George Kennan's ambiguities, in Churchill's rallying cries, and in the projections of American military planners. Kennan's formula for containment was imprecise about the balance of diplomatic, economic, and military elements. That lack of precision, and his sentimental conclusion about eventual Soviet collapse, played to those who emphasized the absolute and military nature of the conflict. Churchill's appeal for an alliance to guarantee Western superiority (not balance) did the same. These elements, combined with the military assessment of Russian capabilities and ambitions, were reflected in the Clifford report to President Truman of September 1946, which permitted no room for compromise with the Soviets, and set the pattern for American policy towards Russia in the following three decades. Behind that policy rested the confidence, sublime and innocently arrogant, of nuclear superiority. The bomb was not only exclusively in American hands; it was there to be used both as persuasive deterrent and, if necessary, as a weapon of war. By the summer of 1950 the contest, seen from the American side, was primarily a military competition for superiority, driven both by ideological sloganeering and by technological innovation in atomic weapons and their means of delivery. Over the following thirty-five years the source of danger in that contest has become, increasingly, the weapons themselves.

The Canadian record reveals that, whatever the subtlety of the message about the Soviet-American conflict which was conveyed by the Department of External Affairs to Prime Minister King, in the end what he and his government absorbed was an undiscriminating mood of anxiety. The foreign politician who best understood and knew how to exploit King's foibles was Winston Churchill who – even out of office – exercised a crucial influence on the Canadian prime minister at three key points in the period of post-war confusion. In October 1945, February-March 1946, and November 1947, Churchill used his formidable skills to flatter and frighten

King into participation in a renewed Anglo-American alliance. On the first and third occasions Churchill may have been acting in concert with Clement Attlee and Ernest Bevin to move King in the direction they also thought desirable. In October 1945 Churchill complemented Attlee in urging on King calm but resolute public steps against the Soviet spy ring; in February 1946, through William Stephenson, he probably forced King to act. In November 1947 Churchill's performance was even more melodramatic, when he encouraged King to believe there were American plans to blitz Moscow with atomic bombs following an ultimatum demanding Soviet good behaviour. Although King claimed to think that such intimidation was desirable, the prospect nevertheless terrified him, and prepared him for Prime Minister Attlee's formal request to join in discussion of a peacetime alliance of deterrence three months later. By that time his closest colleagues and advisers on foreign policy, Louis St Laurent and Lester Pearson – whether out of conviction or opportunism – were also ready to make use of fear as the goad to action.

From the Canadian perspective, the revelation of Soviet espionage in 1946 was a substantial and perhaps dominant element in the transformation of early post-war attitudes about the wartime ally. For the Americans, who were engaged in a much larger range of dealings with the Soviets, the Canadian spy case was a less important part of the emerging pattern. For the British, it was accepted more easily still as one more example of a perpetual feature of international politics – in which they also engaged. None of the Western countries understood until later the unusual centrality of espionage in the conduct of Soviet foreign policy, and none managed to make effective use of the hints and evidence provided by the Gouzenko case to strengthen their own counter-intelligence capacity. Soviet spies continued to penetrate Anglo-American diplomacy and military research for the next decade and longer.

Aside from its public impact in the West when the case was finally revealed in February 1946, the most significant effect of the Gouzenko affair as a factor in the Cold War was probably its unintended influence on official Soviet behaviour before the public revelations. The naive assumption may be that defections and the exposure of spy rings should moderate the behaviour of the offending nation, at least for a time. But great powers are more hard-bitten than that, and in 1945 this was certainly not the result. On the contrary, the affair must, at least marginally, have reinforced the Soviet Union's tendency to adventurism: for what it revealed to Joseph Stalin was the Canadian government's lack of certainty and self-confidence, shared or tolerated by the United States and the United Kingdom. Mackenzie King's attempt to suppress the evidence was bound to perpetuate the wartime Soviet image of Western moral weakness at the very moment when the diplomats were urging their governments to reject soft responses because they fed rather than satisfied Soviet ambitions. The uncertain Canadian reaction not only indicated that Canada was irresolute, but also gave the Soviet government time to repatriate the officials responsible, to mend and reactivate their spy networks, and to calculate their formal response with care. The limited Soviet admission of guilt in February 1946 was the hypocritical counterpart to a dazzling private display of diplomatic contempt towards the King administration – which King meekly accepted. With his elaborate capacity for self-deception he may have been unaware of his own humiliation, or of how his feckless display may have contributed to more general Soviet intransigence.

Soviet diplomatic intransigence, however, was not necessarily military aggressiveness outside its established sphere, or the expression of any coherent plan for world domination. The evidence in Finland, Iran, Turkey, Greece, Germany, and Norway in these years indicates that it was not. The circumstances of the 1940s, however, allowed Russian pressure to be interpreted that way, while the domestic politics of bringing the United States permanently onto the world stage encouraged that interpretation. So, from an initial state of confused and flaccid incomprehension of the Soviet Union, the West had moved by 1948 to a state of resolute incomprehension controlled by fear and exaggeration.

The American nuclear monopoly, coupled with American firmness of intent, might have been an effective deterrent to Soviet aggression in Europe if that had been necessary in 1948. When the Soviets tested that intent in Berlin later in the year, they found it firm in the absence of a formal Western alliance; and as a result the Soviets demonstrated anew their willingness to temper conflict with the United States when that seemed prudent. But by this time the democracies of Western Europe were not primarily seeking to halt Soviet aggression; instead they were seeking to banish their fears of appeasement, war, and occupation, the recurring nightmares of the Nazi period, by calling American power explicitly into the balance in advance. (Implicitly it was already there.) This was a magical act of exorcism for the Europeans, and as a cure for demoralization the summons and the American commitment worked. For American administrations, it was an unprecedented demonstration of the legitimacy of American hegemony. But, in the long run, the creation of the alliance had a high political price as well: for the common Western commitment to united defence, strategic superiority, and rearmament, defended in the language of demagogy, provoked the very response in kind from the Soviet Union that the Canadian realists like Charles Ritchie and Robert Ford (among others) predicted. The confusion of purpose inherent in the conception of the alliance made sober assessment of the international situation even more difficult for both governments and publics in the years that followed, for the Soviet Union was not repeating the Nazi pattern of aggression. The criminal excesses of Stalin's domestic tyranny, Soviet brutality in Eastern Europe, and the regime's heated rhetoric, however, were too easily equated in the West with the Nazi model, and rejected in panic. Ironically, the Western alliance was intended to banish fear in Europe, but it was justified in North America by calling forth fear. That was a historic miscalculation. For fear was malignant: henceforth it paralysed thought, sustained ignorance, and bred intolerance. The world still lives with its consequences.

Notes

CAB	Cabinet Papers (United Kingdom)
CP	Cabinet Paper (United Kingdom)
DCER	*Documents on Canadian External Relations*
DEA	Department of External Affairs
DO	Dominions Office
FRUS	*Foreign Relations of the United States*
MKR	*The Mackenzie King Record*
OUSSEA	Office of the Under-Secretary of State for External Affairs
PCO	Privy Council Office
PJBD	Permanent Joint Board on Defence
PRO	Public Record Office (United Kingdom)
SSDA	Secretary of State for Dominion Affairs (United Kingdom)
SSEA	Secretary of State for External Affairs

Introduction

1 See, for example, Alan Bullock's wise summation in the first chapter of his *Ernest Bevin: Foreign Secretary, 1945–1951*, 6–12.
2 Among the leading revisionist works were: David Horowitz, *The Free World Colossus*; Walter LaFeber, *America, Russia, and the Cold War*; Gabriel Kolko, *The Politics of War: Allied Diplomacy and the World Crisis of 1943–1945*; Gar Alperovitz, *Atomic Diplomacy: Hiroshima and Potsdam*; Gar Alperovitz, *Cold War Essays*; Barton J. Bernstein, 'American Foreign Policy and the Origins of the Cold War,' in Barton J. Bernstein, ed., *Politics and Policies of the Truman Administration;* Lloyd C. Gardner, *Architects of Illusion: Men and Ideas in American Foreign Policy, 1941–1949*; Gabriel and Joyce Kolko, *The Limits of Power: The World and United States Foreign Policy, 1945–1954*.
3 See, for example, J. Samuel Walker, 'Historians and Cold War Origins: The New Consensus,' in Gerald K. Haines and Samuel Walker, eds, *American Foreign*

Relations: A Historiographical Review; and John Lewis Gaddis, 'The Emerging
Post-Revisionist Synthesis on the Origins of the Cold War.' One example of the
rejection of a post-revisionist consensus is Warren F. Kimball's response to the
Gaddis paper, in which he suggests that 'postrevisionism is, at best, just what
Gaddis fears we will call it, orthodoxy plus archives' (in *Diplomatic History*, VII,
3 [1983], 198–200).

4 Gaddis makes this point in his paper 'The Emerging Post-Revisionist Synthesis'
(176–7) in relation to Scandinavia and the Near East, when he discusses Geir
Lundestad's *America, Scandinavia, and the Cold War, 1945–1949* and Bruce R.
Kuniholm's *The Origins of the Cold War in the Near East: Great Power Conflict
and Diplomacy in Iran, Turkey, and Greece*. It is illustrated further in Terry H.
Anderson's *The United States, Great Britain and the Cold War 1944–1947*; in
Ritchie Ovendale's *The English-Speaking Alliance: Britain, the United States, the
Dominions and the Cold War, 1945–51*; in Fraser J. Harbutt's *The Iron Curtain:
Churchill, America, and the Origins of the Cold War*; and in Alan Bullock's defini-
tive work on Ernest Bevin – although Bullock's commitment to his subject pre-
dates the period of post-revisionism.

5 Don Page and Don Munton, in their 1977 article, 'Canadian Images of the Cold War,
1946–47,' claim that there is a coherent body of Canadian revisionist history, but
mention only two books (one of them a polemic) and two short magazine pieces in
justification of their assertion. They then erect a straw man version of the Canadian revisionist position in order to knock it down on the basis of a study of one major
document (and its departmental commentaries) produced in the Department of
External Affairs in 1947. But this paper was not, by itself, the basis for Canada's
decisive actions in the Cold War. (See below, chapter 6.) The sources cited by
Page and Munton are John Warnock, *Partner to Behemoth: The Military Policy of a
Satellite Canada*; R.D. Cuff and J.L. Granatstein, *Canadian-American Relations
in Wartime: From the Great War to the Cold War*; J.L. Granatstein and R.D. Cuff,
'Looking back at the Cold War: 1945–1954,' and Granatstein and Cuff, 'Looking
Back Once More – A Rejoinder.' Cuff and Granatstein's later *American Dollars –
Canadian Prosperity: Canadian-American Economic Relations, 1945–1950* is a
penetrating study, from a revisionist perspective, of Canada's economic relations
with her great power neighbour.

6 See, for example, L.B. Pearson, *Mike: The Memoirs of the Right Honourable Lester
B. Pearson*, vol. 1: *1897–1948* and vol. 2: *1948–1957*; Escott Reid, *Time of
Fear and Hope: The Making of the North Atlantic Treaty 1947–1949*; Escott Reid,
On Duty: A Canadian at the Making of the United Nations, 1945–1946; John W.
Holmes, *The Shaping of Peace: Canada and the Search for World Order 1943–
1957*, vols 1 and 2; and George Ignatieff, *The Making of a Peacemonger*. Two
memoirists and diarists who are more inclined to iconoclasm are Lt.-Gen. Maurice
A. Pope, *Soldiers and Politicians*, and Charles Ritchie, *The Siren Years: A
Canadian Diplomat Abroad, 1937–1945* and *Diplomatic Passport: More Undiplomatic Diaries, 1946–1962*. Among scholarly works, in addition to the two Cuff
and Granatstein books previously cited, see especially James G. Eayrs, *In Defence of*

Canada, vols 1–5; Denis Stairs, *The Diplomacy of Constraint: Canada, The Korean War, and the United States*; J.L. Granatstein, *A Man of Influence: Norman A. Robertson and Canadian Statecraft 1929–68*; and J.L. Granatstein, *The Ottawa Men: The Civil Service Mandarins, 1935–1957*. One recent example of a more critical (indeed, revisionist) study is James Littleton's *Target Nation: Canada and the Western Intelligence Network*; two others, dealing with broader questions about the nature of the Cold War and the arms race, are Robert Malcolmson's *Nuclear Fallacies: How We Have Been Misguided since Hiroshima* and Reg Whitaker's 'What Is the Cold War about and Why Is It Still with Us?'

7 In his memoirs (*Mike*, 2: 24) Mike Pearson (the historian manqué) takes a brief, sharp swipe at the revisionists, whose arguments he finds 'singularly unimpressive': 'The pendulum of historical judgment on events and conditions, on their nature and causes, customarily swings from one conclusion to the extreme opposite. The first judgment is often determined as much by immediate emotion as by evidence, or is based on official explanations perhaps motivated by immediate circumstances. Subsequently, the inevitable swing to revision takes place, leading to an entirely different conclusion by ignoring factors and feelings dominant at the time, which were often valid reasons for what took place and are certainly essential to an understanding of the period. This is true of what we now know as the Cold War.'

Chapter 1: Between America and Russia, 1941–1943

1 Anthony Eden, *The Reckoning*, 460
2 Ibid, 316–20
3 C.P. Stacey, *Canada and the Age of Conflict*, vol. 2: *1921–1948*, 324–45. Stacey comments (p. 337): 'Enough has been said to make it quite clear that the Canadian government had no effective share in the higher direction of the war. In the beginning it sought no share; and when in the later stages it made some attempt at achieving influence, the attempt was limited, half-hearted, and largely ineffective.'
4 From June 1940 to February 1944, there were at least eight major External Affairs documents dealing with Canada's general concerns over the imbalance of American and Canadian power, and the potentially unfortunate results for Canada of American attitudes and behaviour.
5 Office of the Under-Secretary of State for External Affairs (OUSSEA) files, vol. 781, 17 June 1940
6 C.P. Stacey, *Age of Conflict*, 2: 309–10; J.L. Granatstein, *Canada's War: The Politics of the Mackenzie King Government, 1939–1945*, 119–22; *Documents on Canadian External Relations* (DCER), 8: 65–97
7 Keenleyside seemed here to be referring, probably with excessive alarm, to a memorandum written by the Canadian journalist Bruce Hutchison following an interview in Washington with A.A. Berle, an assistant secretary of state, and forwarded to the prime minister just before the date of the Keenleyside paper. Berle told Hutchison grandly that he had been working on 'the re-organization of the economy of all North and South America.' According to Hutchison, 'His whole assumption was that Canada's economy would be merged with that of the U.S., but he did not foresee political union.' (Memorandum, 12 June 1940, Black Binders, vol. 19,

King Papers; see also Cuff and Granatstein, *Canadian-American Relations in Wartime*, 98–100, and Granatstein, *Canada's War*, 126.)

8 In particular, the paper mentioned three 'lines along which Washington is likely to require Canadian co-operation': construction of the Alaska Highway, Atlantic and Pacific coastal defences, and standardization of war materials.

9 See Stacey, *Age of Conflict*, 2: 310–15; Granatstein, *Canada's War*, 124–32; DCER, 8: 139–41.

10 Cuff and Granatstein, *Canadian-American Relations in Wartime*, 103

11 See, for example, DCER, 8: 80–147.

12 'Memorandum to the Prime Minister,' 22.12.41, in DCER, 9: 1125–31. Lester Pearson claims authorship of this document in his memoirs, noting that Robertson made it a departmental paper for the prime minister 'after modifying some of my stronger expressions of concern' (*Mike*, 1: 212). See also Cuff and Granatstein, *Canadian-American Relations in Wartime*, 104–6; Granatstein, *Canada's War*, 149–51.

13 See, for example, Pearson, *Mike*, 1: 202–20.

14 DCER, 9: 1131–6

15 Reid Papers, vol. 6, file 10; also in Pearson Papers, vol. 11. According to Reid's file notes, the paper was sent to sixteen senior members of the department. Six of them replied with comments in writing.

16 The memorandum quoted Prime Minister King, from the files, as having declared in September 1941: 'There is no reason why we should put ourselves in the position where if it suits British interests, we can be held responsible for having determined or unduly influenced British policy towards Japan.'

17 Reid Papers, vol. 6, file 10

18 'Memorandum from Assistant Under-Secretary of State for External Affairs to Under-Secretary of State for External Affairs, April 14, 1942,' DCER, 9: 1136–8

19 J.W. Pickersgill, *The Mackenzie King Record* (MKR), 1: 318

20 'Memorandum for the Minister: Certain Developments in Canada–United States Relations,' 18 March 1943, DCER, 9: 1138–42; also in Pearson Papers, vol. 11

21 Pearson cited as recent examples of American disregard the strict application of the selective service laws against Canadian residents in the United States; a demand for exclusive jurisdiction over American armed forces in Canada; Canada's failure to gain adequate representation in the various combined boards; conflict over Canadian status in the United Nations Relief and Rehabilitation Administration; a 'mix-up' over a proposed refugee conference in Ottawa; and unilateral American action over the control of exports to South America.

22 In his memoirs (*Mike*, 1: 199), Pearson comments more benevolently on Canadian-American relations in this period: 'If occasionally Washington acted as though Canada were another state of the union, we tried to be tolerant, realizing that our American friends, unlike the British, had not been educated to respect our national sovereign status – and our sensitivity. They too would learn this, under our firm but friendly teaching, or so we hoped.' The comment seems to be based on

Pearson's 1943 memorandum; but its tone of gentle self-deprecation blunts the force of the original.

23 'Some Problems in the Relations between Canada and the United States,' 16 April 1943, Reid Papers, vol. 6, file 10. The paper was initially circulated for comments to H.L. Keenleyside, H.H. Wrong, L.B. Pearson, A.D.P. Heeney, and J.W. Pickersgill. Reid's copy contains the marginal comments of Keenleyside.

24 The italicized words are a handwritten substitute over the typewritten original, which reads with slightly less equivocation: 'If another world war occurs, it is probable that the principal protagonists will be ...' The amendment was apparently that of H.L. Keenleyside.

25 Reid was confusing what was possible with what was preferable. With the benefit of hindsight it is clear that Reid's internationalist reasoning was fuzzy and overly formalist. Canada subsequently entered the United Nations, and was a member of the Security Council (charged with responsibility under the charter for dealing with threats to international peace and security) in June 1950 when North Korea invaded South Korea. The council, with Canada's support, authorized military assistance to South Korea, but only *after* President Truman had taken a unilateral American decision to enter the war. The allies of the United States, despite the existence of the UN framework, had in effect surrendered the power of decision over peace and war to Washington. Later, when the Canadian effort to influence American dominance had been substantially diverted from the United Nations to the North Atlantic Treaty Organization, it seems equally true that the institutional framework, while providing a continuing forum for exerting multilateral influence upon the United States, had left the fundamental power to decide on peace or war against the USSR in the hands of Washington. But 'effective military cooperation' between Canada and the United States has existed in this period despite this reality: which suggests that such co-operation is dependent, not on 'an effective world order of which both Canada and the United States are loyal members,' but rather on Canada's realistic recognition of the country's subordination to the power of the United States.

26 'Canada's position on the main air routes between North America and Northern and Central Europe and Northern Asia: some general political and security considerations,' 2 August 1943, 3rd draft, Reid Papers, vol. 6, file 10

27 Alexander P. de Seversky's *Victory through Air Power*, which touted the revolutionary possibilities of air warfare, was a North American best-seller, widely excerpted in the press. The *Ottawa Evening Citizen* published thirteen instalments in August 1942.

28 'Memorandum for the Under Secretary: United States Policy toward Canada,' 29 February 1944, OUSSEA files, vol. 823; see also Granatstein, *Canada's War*, 323–4.

29 See Stacey, *Age of Conflict*, 2: 194–269.

30 Ibid, 239–42; King Diary, 24 March 1939

31 Stacey, *Age of Conflict*, 2: 242; King Diary, 25 April 1939

32 Stacey, *Age of Conflict*, 2: 253

33 *DCER*, 8: 1093–4

34 Eden, *Reckoning,* 268–9; W.S. Churchill, *The Second World War*, vol. III: *The Grand Alliance,* 298–9

35 Quoted in Churchill, *Grand Alliance,* 299

36 Stacey, *Age of Conflict,* 2: 319; DCER, 8: 1099; King Diary, 22 June 1941. For the text of Churchill's speech, see Churchill, *Grand Alliance,* 300–1.

37 DCER, 8: 1099–1102; 'Canadian Comment on Recent Developments in Canadian-Russian Relations,' 30 July 1941, DCER, 8: 1106–9; Stacey, *Age of Conflict,* 2: 319–20. 'In due course,' Stacey adds, 'a good deal of aid would go to the USSR from Canada.'

38 Vojtech Mastny, in his book *Russia's Road to the Cold War* (pp. 39–40), argues that after the crude and cynical record of Soviet foreign policy following the signing of the Nazi-Soviet Pact, and its frigid reception by Britain, her allies, and the United States, the Western allies' sudden embrace of the Soviet Union after 22 June 1941 must have come as an unexpected windfall to Moscow.

39 See Pearson, *Mike,* 1: 198; Escott Reid, 'Note for Mr. Robertson. Release of Communists from Detention in Canada,' 24 June 1941, Reid Papers, vol. 6, file 10; Louis St Laurent, 'Memorandum for the Prime Minister's Secretary,' 6 January 1943, King Papers, vol. 246, C165441–3; HSF, 'Memorandum for Mr. Turnbull,' 15/7/43, King Papers, vol. 246, C165446–8. Reid's paper contained the surprising proposal that the Canadian authorities might make use of 'the branch of the Comintern in Canada' to disseminate propaganda among Ukrainian Canadians in order to undermine 'Nazi claims that Germany is freeing the Ukrainians.' Apparently nothing came of this suggestion.

40 'Canadian Comment on Recent Developments in Canadian-Russian Relationships,' 30 July 1941, DCER, 8: 1107

41 See Arnold C. Smith, 'Memorandum D, "Our Own Cards: Some Reflections on the Materials for a 'Strong Policy,' "' 12 April 1945, enclosed with L. Mayrand to SSEA, No. 193, 16 April 1945, DEA files, 2-AE(S).

42 'Canadian Comment,' 1108

43 Ibid, 1109

44 Ibid

45 H.H. Wrong to SSEA, 8 August 1941, DEA files, 4901-40C; see also George C. Herring, Jr., *Aid to Russia, 1941–1946: Strategy, Diplomacy, and the Origins of the Cold War,* 2–24.

46 Eden, *Reckoning,* 270–5; Churchill, *Grand Alliance,* 311–12

47 See, for example, DCER, 8: 1110–17; G.P. Glazebrook, 'Memorandum for the Prime Minister,' 14/4/42, PCO files, vol. 43.

48 Churchill, *Grand Alliance,* 352

49 Mastny, *Russia's Road,* 41

50 Quoted in Eden, *Reckoning,* 296

51 Ibid, 270–1

52 Ibid, 271–5

53 Ibid, 277–81

54 Ibid, 273

55 Ibid, 289
56 Ibid
57 Eden, *Reckoning*, 297. A reference to this point in the Stalin-Eden conversation is made by Vincent Massey, the Canadian high commissioner in London, in his dispatch of 22 April 1942, which suggests that Eden's comment was in response to a question, and may have been more equivocal than Eden recounts: 'Stalin asked Eden in Moscow whether the Dominions would be signatories to these treaties and Maisky raised the question again recently in London without, however, pressing the point' (*DCER* 9: 1856). See also Graham Ross, ed., *The Foreign Office and the Kremlin: British Documents on Anglo-Soviet Relations 1941–45*, 82–7.
58 Eden, *Reckoning*, 318
59 Ibid, 319–20
60 The negotiations are recounted in detail in Eden, *Reckoning*, 320–30.
61 See Eden memorandum, 10 April 1942, W.P. (42) 156, CAB 66/23; Mastny, *Russia's Road*, 44–5.
62 'Memorandum for the Prime Minister,' 14/4/42, PCO files, vol. 43
63 High Commissioner in Great Britain to SSEA, Telegram 1104, 22 April 1942, *DCER*, 9: 1856. The cable refers to the 'proposed Anglo-Russian treaties' in the plural, since at this stage, in accordance with the original Russian initiative, separate political-al and military treaties were still under negotiation.
64 Extract from Minutes of Cabinet War Committee, 29 April 1942, *DCER*, 9: 1857.
65 SSEA to High Commissioner in Great Britain, Telegram 868, 1 May 1942, *DCER*, 9: 1857.
66 'British-Soviet Negotiations Looking Forward to the Conclusion of a Treaty of a Political Character with Particular Reference to Soviet Suggestions that Certain Territories Taken Over by the Soviet Union during the Period September 1, 1939–June 22, 1941, Be Recognized as Soviet Territory,' 4 February 1942, *FRUS, 1942*, III: 505–12; *Memoirs of Cordell Hull*, II: 1172; Mastny, *Russia's Road*, 45–6
67 Eden, *Reckoning*, 326–9
68 Ibid, 329. The text of the treaty appears in *DCER*, 9: 1859–60.
69 'Memorandum by Special Wartime Assistant to Under-Secretary of State for External Affairs,' 2 June 1942, *DCER*, 9: 1858–62.
70 'Memorandum from Under-Secretary of State for External Affairs to Prime Minister,' June 1942, *DCER*, 9: 1858.
71 'Extract from Minutes of Cabinet War Committee,' 11 June 1942, *DCER*, 9: 1863; *House of Commons Debates*, 11 June 1942: 3252–3.
72 John Lewis Gaddis, *The United States and the Origins of the Cold War, 1941–1947*, 16–17; Mark A. Stoler, *The Politics of the Second Front*, 36–51
73 Eden, *Reckoning*, 330; see also Herbert Feis, *Churchill-Roosevelt-Stalin*, 57–70; Stoler, *Second Front*, 44–51.
74 Eden, *Reckoning*, 330. The disagreement over a second front is noted in a Depart-ment of External Affairs paper by Escott Reid of 18 September 1942, in Reid Papers, vol. 6, file 10.
75 On the government's sensitivity to the church's anti-Communism, see the comments

of the minister of justice, Louis St Laurent, writing in early 1943: 'Memorandum for the Prime Minister's Secretary,' 6 January 1943, King Papers, 246: C165441–3.

76 See Aloysius Balawyder, 'Canada in the Uneasy War Alliance,' in Balawyder, ed., *Canadian-Soviet Relations, 1939–1980*, 5.

77 He was preceded by the counsellor and first secretary in September (Balawyder, *Canadian-Soviet Relations*, 6).

78 Balawyder, 'Canada in the Uneasy War Alliance,' 5; L.D. Wilgress, Memoirs, 123–4. Wilgress had an itinerant upbringing in Vancouver, Hong Kong, and Japan as son of a Canadian Pacific Steamships agent, and attended McGill University from 1910 to 1914. On the recommendation of Stephen Leacock he entered the Trade Commissioner Service, and in 1915, aged 23, he received the unlikely appointment of Canadian trade commissioner in Omsk, Siberia, a post he reached in 1916. His token – apparently futile – duties were eventually interrupted by the Civil War in March 1918, when he moved by uncertain steps to Vladivostok as a member of the short-lived Canadian Economic Commission to Siberia. When the Allied intervention collapsed in the summer of 1919 the commission dispersed. Wilgress returned to Ottawa with his Russian bride, and continued his peripatetic career with postings in Bucharest, Milan, London, and Hamburg. In 1931 he returned to Ottawa, rising to deputy minister by October 1940. During his interwar career he participated in Canada's major trade negotiations and visited the USSR with Canadian trade delegations in 1921 and 1936.

79 L.D. Wilgress to SSEA, 8, 9 March and 19 April 1943; King Papers, 353: 306852–53, 306879; Kieran Simpson, ed., *Canadian Who's Who* (Toronto: University of Toronto Press 1984), 1105.

80 Wilgress, *Memoirs*, 129

81 Wilgress to N.A. Robertson, 23 April 1943, King Papers, 353: 306890–1. According to the typist's initials, the letter was actually written by R.M. Macdonnell.

82 Wilgress to SSEA, No. 17, 26 April 1943, King Papers, 353: 306893–9

83 Wilgress to N.A. Robertson, 6 May 1943, King Papers, 353: 306923–5

84 See also William H. Standley and Arthur A. Ageton, *Admiral Ambassador to Russia*.

85 Wilgress to SSEA, No. 17, 26 April 1943

86 Wilgress to N.A. Robertson, 6 May 1943. Vojtech Mastny comments that Fierlinger 'was always more inclined to defend to the Soviet viewpoint to his own government than vice-versa,' and 'was much more Moscow's ambassador' than Czechoslovakia's (*Russia's Road*, 103, 228).

87 Wilgress to SSEA, No. 17, 26 April 1943

88 'What One Clerk Said to Another,' 5

89 Sir A. Clark Kerr to Mr Eden, 25 November 1942 (received 5 January 1943), No. 340, King Papers, 344: C237631–2

90 L.D. Wilgress to SSEA, No. 26, 6 May 1943, DEA files, 2-AE(S)

91 Wilgress to SSEA, No. 75, 24 May 1943, King Papers, 353: 306956

92 Wilgress to SSEA, No. 41, 24 May 1943, King Papers, 353: 306958–9

93 'Memorandum from the Under-Secretary of State for External Affairs to the Prime

Minister,' 25 May 1943, *DCER*, 9: 1865. Later, in recoil from the shock of the Gouzenko revelations of Soviet espionage in Canada, it became the view in External Affairs (as in the State Department) that the dissolution had not, in fact, occurred. Gouzenko testified that the Comintern's central files on foreign Communists and sympathizers continued to be kept, and used by the Russian intelligence services, during this period. When Milovan Djilas visited Moscow in March 1944 with the Yugoslav Military Mission, however, he found that 'the Comintern had really been dissolved' and that its former director, Georgi Dimitrov, had thus lost his influential position: 'his only job now was to gather information about Communist parties and to give advice to the Soviet Government and Party' (*Conversations with Stalin*, 33). The slender basis for the change of opinion about the Comintern suggests both the paucity of information that was available to Western diplomats about the Soviet Union in the early post-war period, and the ease with which stereotyped convictions could take hold in this absence of information.

94 Wilgress to SSEA, No. 82, 6 July 1943, DEA files, 2-AE(S)
95 L.D. Wilgress to SSEA, 23, 24, and 31 August 1943, Nos 107, 108, 112, DEA files, 2-AE(S). The quotations are from the letter of 31 August.
96 W.L.M. King to L.D. Wilgress, 24 June 1943, King Papers, 353: 306984

Chapter 2: The Enigma

1 See Mastny, *Russia's Road*, 77–8, 83–4; Wilgress to SSEA, 24 August 1943, No. 108; 26 August 1943, No. 171; 23 September 1943, No. 137, King Papers, 353: 307039–41, 307042, 307078–80.
2 The 'Grand Design' was first publicly sketched by Forrest Davis in an article on 'Roosevelt's World Blueprint' based upon conversations with Roosevelt and published in the *Saturday Evening Post* of 10 April 1943. It was evident, as Dana Wilgress reported in October 1943 in a dispatch examining recent issues of the Soviet magazine *War and the Working Class* (which he called 'an excellent barometer of the official Soviet attitude towards international questions'), that the Soviet foreign ministry showed interest in this article. (See Daniel S. Yergin, *Shattered Peace*, 43–4; 'Oral History Interview with Elbridge Durbrow,' Harry S. Truman Library, pp. 15–17; Wilgress to SSEA, 13 October 1943, No. 164, King Papers, 353: 307097–8.)
3 Gaddis, *Origins*, 33
4 On 22 June 1943, for example (the second anniversary of the German invasion of Russia), Davies was the principal speaker at a Canadian-Soviet Friendship Rally in Toronto, where he was introduced by Prime Minister W.L. Mackenzie King (W.L.M. King to L.D. Wilgress, 24 June 1943, King Papers, 353: 306984).
5 *Life*, 29 March 1943, quoted in Gaddis, *Origins*, 38
6 Gaddis, *Origins*, 42–6; Gardner, *Architects of Illusion*, 307
7 The variety and flexibility of Russian diplomatic dealings with these nations in wartime is illustrated, inter alia, in Mastny, *Russia's Road*, 111–82.
8 See Mastny, *Russia's Road*, 133–44; SSEA to Wilgress, 22 June 1943, No. 69;

Wilgress to SSEA, 18, 21, 28 December 1943, Nos 231, 304, 233, 235, and 239, King Papers, 353: 306891, 307231–7, 307240–1, 307259–61.

9 See Mastny, *Russia's Road*, especially 167–82; Gaddis, *Origins*, 139–49; Wilgress to SSEA, 27 April 1943, No. 19, King Papers, 353: 306902–7.

10 Wilgress to SSEA, 21, 26, 27 April and 12 May 1943, Nos 41, 44, 46, 19, 27, King Papers, 353: 306886, 306892, 306908–9, 306902–7, 306931–5

11 'There is great danger,' reported Dana Wilgress to Ottawa, 'of relations between Soviet Union and other United Nations being prejudiced if situation not handled carefully.' (Canadian Minister to USSR to SSEA, No. 44, 26 April 1943, King Papers, 353:306892. See also SSEA to Canadian Minister to USSR, 3 May 1943, No. 32, King Papers, 353: 306918; Wilgress to SSEA, 13 January 1944, No. 20, King Papers, 376: 327864–6; Mastny, *Russia's Road*, 77–8; Gaddis, *Origins*, 135; Standley and Ageton, *Admiral Ambassador*, 401–11.)

12 SSEA to Canadian Minister to USSR, No. 34, 4 May 1943, King Papers, 353: 306919

13 SSEA to Canadian Minister to USSR, No, 37, 5 May 1943, King Papers, 353: 306920

14 Canadian Minister to USSR to SSEA, No. 68, 16 May 1943, King Papers, 353: 306944.

15 Wilgress, *Memoirs*, 128

16 Canadian Minister to USSR to SSEA, No. 166, 23 August 1943, King Papers, 353: 307037.

17 Quoted in Gaddis, *Origins*, 64

18 Quoted in Mastny, *Russia's Road*, 108; Bernstein, *Truman Administration*, 19

19 Mastny, *Russia's Road*, 108

20 Ibid, 110

21 'The Moscow Conference, October 19–30, 1943,' in US Senate Committee on Foreign Relations, *A Decade of American Foreign Policy, Basic Documents, 1941–49* (Washington: US Government Printing Office 1950), 9–11

22 Speech of 18 November 1943, quoted in Mastny, *Russia's Road*, 120–1

23 Wilgress to SSEA, 16, 24, 25, 27 October 1943, Nos 225, 239, 240, and 245, King Papers, 353: 307107, 307118–19, 307120, 307128; Mastny, *Russia's Road*, 112–22; W.S. Churchill, *Closing the Ring*, 224–39; Eden, *Reckoning*, 410–18

24 See Churchill, *Closing the Ring*, 239; Mastny, *Russia's Road*, 121–2.

25 Wilgress to SSEA, No. 239, 24 October 1943, King Papers, 353: 307118–19. Wilgress sent this dispatch before Eden withdrew his draft declaration proscribing spheres of influence on 26 October. See also Wilgress to SSEA, 27 October and 3, 9, 11, 13 November 1943, Nos 245, 254, 189, 264, and 193, King Papers, 353: 307128, 307146–7, 307156–7, 307160–2, 307165–71.

26 Wilgress to SSEA, No. 50, 16 February 1944, King Papers, 376: 327946–9.

27 The American record of the conference is in *FRUS: Tehran, 1943*. For recent assessments, see Gaddis, *Origins*, 136–9, and Mastny, *Russia's Road*, 122–33.

28 Gaddis, *Origins*, 139

29 Ibid, 150–1

30 Memorandum by Bohlen, 15 December 1943, in *FRUS: Tehran*, 846, quoted in Mastny, *Russia's Road*, 132

31 L.D. Wilgress to SSEA, No. 45, 10 February 1944, DEA files, 2-D(s). This dispatch followed another long one, of 11 January 1944, on Soviet nationalities policy.

32 Mastny notes that in his major speech to the Supreme Soviet of 1 February 1944 which was the occasion for Wilgress's dispatch on Soviet constitutional changes, Molotov 'extolled the relationship with Czechoslovakia as a model for other countries' (*Russia's Road*, 143).

33 Wilgress to SSEA, No. 45, 10 February 1944

34 'Soviet Constitutional Changes,' 19 February 1944, DEA files, 2-D(s). Malania had been recruited to the department as a temporary assistant in April 1943, along with H.G. Skilling and Professor F.H. Soward. He was a recent graduate in history and political science from the University of Toronto. (See N.A.R., 'Memo for P.M.,' 25 February 1943, King Papers, 250: C167458; 'Minute of a Meeting of the Treasury Board,' 5 May 1943, P.C. 23/3711 [obtained under the Access to Information Act].)

35 Wilgress to N.A. Robertson, 9 March 1944, DEA files, 7-H(s)

36 Wilgress to SSEA, No. 74, 9 March 1944, DEA files, 7-H(s)

37 Ibid

38 N.A. Robertson, 'Memorandum for the Prime Minister,' 21 June 1944, enclosing 'Recent Indications of Soviet Policy,' King Papers, 344: C237841–4; and L.M., 'Memorandum for Mr. Robertson et al,' enclosing 'Conversation between Mr. Charles E. Bohlen ... and members of the Department of External Affairs, Ottawa, November 3, 1944,' DEA files, 7-H(s)

39 'Recent Indications of Soviet Policy'

40 L.D. Wilgress to SSEA, No. 111, 7 April 1944, OUSSEA files, vol. 823

41 For accounts of these events in the summer of 1944 see Mastny, *Russia's Road*, 183–6, 194–5; George F. Kennan, *Memoirs, 1925–1950*, 210–11; Churchill, *Triumph and Tragedy*, 116–29; Wilgress to SSEA, 10, 16, 22, 23, 24 August and 28 September 1944, Nos 243, 262, 271, 262, 275, 264, and 330, King Papers, 376: 328200–2, 328210–15, 328217–24, 328285–8. See also the detailed account of the military and diplomatic struggle over Warsaw in John Erickson, *The Road to Berlin: Continuing the History of Stalin's War with Germany*, 266–90.

42 George F. Kennan, 'Russia – Seven Years Later,' in his *Memoirs*, 528

43 Kennan, *Memoirs*, 230

44 Ibid, 530–1

45 See W.S. Churchill, *Triumph and Tragedy*, 194–206; Martin Gilbert, *Road to Victory: Winston S. Churchill 1941–1945*, 989–1005; W. Averell Harriman and Elie Abel, *Special Envoy to Churchill and Stalin, 1941–1946*, 356–8; FRUS: *Malta and Yalta 1945*, 103–8; Mastny, *Russia's Road*, 207–12; Feis, *Churchill-Roosevelt-Stalin*, 451; Gaddis, *Origins*, 91; Ross, ed., *Foreign Office*, 175–83.

46 Churchill wrote apologetically to his war cabinet: 'The system of percentages is not intended to prescribe the numbers sitting on commissions for the different Balkan countries, but rather to express the interest and sentiment with which the British and Soviet Governments approach the problems of these countries, and so that they might reveal their minds to each other in some way that could be comprehended. It is

not intended to be more than a guide, and of course in no way commits the United States, nor does it attempt to set up a rigid system of spheres of interest. It may however help the United States to see how their two principal Allies feel about these regions when the picture is presented as a whole.' (Churchill, 12 October 1944, quoted in his *Triumph and Tragedy*, 199.)

47 See Wilgress to SSEA, 11, 12, 19, 23, 24 October 1944, Nos 316, 318, 328, 364, and 370, King Papers, 376: 328308, 328310–11, 328324–5, 328330–3, 328342–5. Mackenzie King recorded a conversation with Churchill in May 1946 in which Churchill told King of his agreement with Stalin to 'let Stalin look after Roumania, etc. while he would be busy getting peace restored in Greece. This involved killing large numbers of Communists in Greece' (King Papers, Diaries, 22 May 1946).

48 Wilgress to SSEA, No. 402, 9 November 1944, King Papers, 376: 328371–9

49 See the exchanges recorded in Churchill, *Triumph and Tragedy*, 274–9; Feis, *Churchill-Roosevelt-Stalin*, 453–60, 518–29; FRUS: *Malta and Yalta 1945*, 202–37.

50 Churchill, *Triumph and Tragedy*, 278–9

51 Ibid, 279

52 Mastny, *Russia's Road*, 240

53 'Joint Statement by the President, Prime Minister Churchill, and Marshal Stalin on Crimea Conference – Yalta. February 11, 1945,' in *The Public Papers and Addresses of Franklin D. Roosevelt*, vol. 13, 1944–5: 531–48; FRUS: *Malta and Yalta, 1945*, 968–75; Churchill, *Triumph and Tragedy*, 286–323; Feis, *Churchill-Roosevelt-Stalin*, 489–558; Anderson, *United States, Great Britain*, 28–32. One of the most judicious summaries of the conference is in Mastny, *Russia's Road*, 239–53.

54 Mastny, *Russia's Road*, 253

Chapter 3: Disenchantment

1 On the breakdown of trust in 1945, see Gaddis, *Origins*, 171–3; Mastny, *Russia's Road*, 253–66; Churchill, *Triumph and Tragedy*, 343–69; Kennan, *Memoirs*, 236; Anderson, *United States, Great Britain*, 39–51.

2 Mastny, *Russia's Road*, 261

3 Djilas, *Conversations*, 114

4 Churchill to Stalin, 1 April 1945, quoted in Churchill, *Triumph and Tragedy*, 357

5 Quoted in Churchill, *Triumph and Tragedy*, 581

6 Churchill, *Triumph and Tragedy*, 359–69; Mastny, *Russia's Road*, 258–60

7 Churchill, *Triumph and Tragedy*, 360–1

8 Quoted in Churchill, *Triumph and Tragedy*, 364

9 Quoted in Churchill, *Triumph and Tragedy*, 365

10 Ibid, 368

11 Roosevelt to Stalin, 12 April 1945, quoted in Churchill, *Triumph and Tragedy*, 369. The entire incident is reviewed, on the basis of privileged access through the

British Embassy in Moscow to the Roosevelt-Churchill-Stalin correspondence, in Leon Mayrand to N.A. Robertson, 18 April 1945, DEA files, 2-AE(s). Mackenzie King was briefed by Robertson and Wrong on 19 April in San Francisco, reporting to his diary that Stalin had been 'quite rough in some of his telegrams & apparently things are smoothing out a little now. The whole matter is too secret to record' (King Diary, 19 April 1945).

12 Leon Mayrand to SSEA, No. 193, 16 April 1945, DEA files, 7-H(s)

13 Smith also drafted this covering dispatch (letter from Arnold C. Smith, 6 October 1985).

14 Arnold C. Smith, 'Memorandum "A": Soviet Attitude to Relief and Economic Reorganization Problems in Europe,' 12 April 1945, DEA files, 7-H(s)

15 Arnold C. Smith, 'Memorandum "C": Certain Aspects of Soviet Diplomatic Techniques,' 15 April 1945

16 Arnold C. Smith, 'Memo "D": "Our Own Cards," Some Reflections on the Materials for a "Strong Policy,"' 12 April 1945, DEA files, 7-H(s)

17 Kennan, *Memoirs*, 224–5

18 See below, pp. 122 – 4. Smith has noted subsequently that in Moscow he was on close terms with Averell Harriman, George Kennan, and Llewellyn Thompson at the American Embassy, and Sir Archibald Clark Kerr, Jock Balfour, Tom Brimelow, and Frank Roberts at the British Embassy. Terry Anderson's comment about the shared views of Averell Harriman and Clark Kerr at this time applies also to those of Arnold Smith and his colleagues in the Canadian Embassy: 'The more contact British and American representatives had with the Soviets, the sooner they arrived at the same conclusions about Russian behavior, cooperated with each other during negotiations, and advocated similar if not joint policies against the Kremlin' (Anderson, *United States, Great Britain*, 39; letter from Arnold Smith, 6 October 1985).

19 See Gaddis, *Origins*, 230–6; Anderson, *United States, Great Britain*, 53–72.

20 See Gaddis, *Origins*, 200–5; Harry S. Truman, *Year of Decisions: Memoirs*, I: 79–82; FRUS: 1945, V: 252–8; Walter Millis, ed., *The Forrestal Diaries*, 48–51; J.L. Richardson, 'Cold-War Revisionism: A Critique,' 579–612, esp. 583.

21 Gaddis, *Origins*, 205–6

22 Gaddis, *Origins*, 230–6; FRUS: Potsdam, I: 64–5; Truman, *Year of Decisions*, 257–63; Churchill, *Triumph and Tragedy*, 492–6; Mastny, *Russia's Road*, 284–8; Anderson, *United States, Great Britain*, 66–72

23 Gaddis, *Origins*, 230–6; Sir A. Clark Kerr to Mr Eden, No. 468, 17 July 1945, King Papers, 344: C237905; Richardson, 'Cold-War Revisionism,' 583–4; Bullock, *Bevin*, 17–18

24 Churchill, *Triumph and Tragedy*, 478–84; Mastny, *Russia's Road*, 291

25 See, inter alia, Mastny, *Russia's Road*, 284; Gilbert, *Road to Victory*, 1024; Nikolai Tolstoy, *Stalin's Secret War*, 296–330; Nikolai Tolstoy, *The Minister and the Massacres*, passim; Harold Macmillan, *Tides of Fortune*, 16–18.

26 The British minister in Washington, Jock Balfour, devoted a long dispatch to this subject in August 1945. A copy of it was conveyed through the Canadian Embassy

to Norman Robertson (T.A. Stone to Norman Robertson, 21 August 1945, DEA files, 4380–40c).

27 Stacey, *Age of Conflict*, 2: 382

28 J.L. Granatstein, *A Man of Influence*, 151; Pope, *Soldiers and Politicians*, 269

29 Granatstein, *A Man of Influence*, 150–6; Stacey, *Age of Conflict*, 2: 381–2

30 Reid, *On Duty*, 56

31 Ibid, 57

32 Ibid, 59. It is curious that, in the seven pages of his memoirs devoted to San Francisco, Lester Pearson (who, as Canadian ambassador in Washington, was one of the leading members of the Canadian delegation) makes no mention of the conflict with the Soviet Union, other than to say that 'It soon became clear that the Big Three had agreed at Yalta to stand firm on their draft. Any changes, not acceptable by all three, would be opposed. This set the scene, of course, for our major arguments at San Francisco.' There is no sign here that Soviet attitudes generated any differences of view in the Canadian delegation or the Department of External Affairs. (Pearson, *Mike*, 1: 272–8, esp. 272.)

33 Reid, *On Duty*, 30

34 Ibid, 50–1

35 Granatstein, *A Man of Influence*, 154–5

36 J.E.R., 'Memorandum for Mr. Robertson,' 4.5.45, enclosing 'Recent Trends in Soviet Foreign Policy,' 4 May 1945, DEA files, 2-AE(s)

37 Arnold Smith recalled in 1985: 'Naturally I disagreed with [Malania's] views, but I felt that he was well meaning and that if he had had the opportunity of seeing Stalin's policies close up, as I had, he would probably come to share my assessments' (letter from Arnold C. Smith, 6 October 1985).

38 Leon Mayrand to SSEA, No. 242, 18 May 1945, DEA files, 7-H(s)

39 Agreement on interim occupation lines in Venezia-Giulia was reached by the British, Americans, and Yugoslavs on 9 June 1945, although Anglo-American troops remained in the Allied zones until October 1954, when Italy and Yugoslavia accepted the existing division of territory (with small adjustments). (Macmillan, *Tides of Fortune*, 18–21.)

40 T.A. Stone to G. de T. Glazebrook, 18 June 1945, DEA files, 2-AE(s)

41 J.E. Read, 'Memorandum for the Prime Minister Re: Despatch No. 193 of April 16th from Moscow,' King Papers, 344: C237899–903

42 See, for example, L.M., 'Re: Despatch No. 272 of June 19 from Moscow,' 31 July 1945; L.M., 'Memorandum to: Mr. Ritchie, Legal Adviser,' 3 August 1945, DEA files, 7-CA-8(s); L.M., 'Re: Despatches Nos. 194 of April 19, 222 of May 2, and 242 of May 18,' 17 August 1945, DEA files, 2-AE(s).

43 Sir A. Clark Kerr to Mr. Eden, No. 468, 17 July 1945, King Papers, 344: C237904–7; J. Balfour to Ernest Bevin, No. 1038, 9 August 1945, DEA files, 4380–40C.

44 C.P. Stacey, *Arms, Men and Governments*, 514–28

45 King Diary, 6 August 1945

46 H.H. Wrong, 'Memorandum to the Prime Minister,' 18 August 1945, King Papers, file 2284, C157717–19

47 Mayrand to SSEA, No. 307, 3 August 1945, DEA files, 2-AE(S)

48 *MKR*, III: 7–8

49 Ibid., 8–9

50 Ibid, 9

51 Ibid, 10; Granatstein, *A Man of Influence*, 172; David Stafford, *Camp X: Canada's School for Secret Agents, 1941–45*, 258–9

52 *MKR*, III: 11

53 Ibid, 11–12

54 Ibid, 12–15; Granatstein, *A Man of Influence*, 173; Chapman Pincher, *Too Secret Too Long*, 104–5. The senior M16 representative was Peter Dwyer, who was then on secondment to British Security Co-ordination in New York (Pincher, *Too Secret*, 104; Stafford, *Camp X*, 260–5). See also Malcolm MacDonald, *People and Places*, 182–4.

55 *MKR*, III: 14

56 MacDonald, *People and Places*, 184

57 *MKR*, III: 14

58 Ibid, 17–18, 33; MacDonald, *People and Places*, 196–8

59 Pincher, *Too Secret*, 105–8; Granatstein, *A Man of Influence*, 173; *Globe and Mail*, Toronto, 27 March 1981

60 Chapman Pincher's *Too Secret Too Long* is a comprehensive attempt to demonstrate, on circumstantial grounds, that Hollis was 'Elli.' Prime Minister Thatcher told the House of Commons in March 1981 that renewed security investigations arising from the claims in Pincher's previous book, *Their Trade Is Treachery*, left the case against Hollis unproven. Pincher's 1984 survey of the evidence (which depends upon confidential intelligence sources as well as published materials and thus cannot be fully substantiated) challenges the official denial. (For Gouzenko's claims about 'Elli,' see Pincher's *Too Secret Too Long*, 81–2, 104–11.) In August 1986, in Australian court proceedings aimed at halting publication of a memoir by Peter Wright (a former MI5 officer involved in the investigation of Hollis), lawyers for the United Kingdom government admitted the truth of Wright's assertions, including the claim that Hollis was a Soviet agent. Almost immediately, in London, the government's law officers issued a statement that 'Except for the limited procedural purposes of this case, the Government does not admit the truth of any of the allegations in Mr. Wright's book relating to the activities or personnel of the security services' (*Globe and Mail*, Toronto, 26 August 1986). The case for suppression of publication was pursued in the Australian courts later in 1986 and 1987; the book was published in the United States and Canada in 1987 under the title *Spycatcher*. Wright's evidence that Hollis was a Soviet deep penetration agent, as he presents it in *Spycatcher*, remains inconclusive.

61 *MKR*, III: 28. Those present at this meeting were King, Robertson, Wrong, Sir William Stephenson, Charles Rivett-Carnac of the RCMP, and Malcolm MacDonald and Stephen Holmes of the UK High Commission (Granatstein, *A Man of Influence*, 175).

62 *MKR*, III, 20

63 Ibid, 30
64 Ibid, 34
65 Ibid, 38–9
66 L.B. Pearson to H.H. Wrong, 1 October 1945, Pearson Papers, vol. 6; *MKR*, III: 39
67 *MKR*, III: 40–1
68 Ibid, 41. The diary reference to this incident reads: 'I told the President of my mission to England at the instance of Theodore Roosevelt in regard to Japan; of my having seized passports in Vancouver; of Edward Grey's passing on to Komura, information, etc.' King's role in the Japanese-American dispute over immigration of 1908 is recounted in detail in R.M. Dawson's *William Lyon Mackenzie King: A Political Biography 1874–1923*, 151–66. King (then the Canadian deputy minister of labour) was invited by President Roosevelt to act as his secret emissary to the British foreign secretary, Sir Edward Grey, to express American determination to halt Japanese immigration. Roosevelt expected that Britain, as Japan's ally, would convey this determination to the Japanese, and Grey assured King that he would do so. For King the parallels between the two situations must have been remarkable: in both he could see the risk of war between the great powers; in both his role was to 'confront' an 'oriental' power with the outrage and determination of the Western nations in order to gain its promise of good behaviour. It is apparent that King exaggerated both the dangers and the benefits (or potential benefits) of his personal intervention in the two crises. Dawson concludes about King's role in 1908 that Japanese-American relations were already improving before his mission, and that his efforts 'doubtless played a small part in accelerating this trend' (Dawson, *King*, 165). By the end of the year the immigration issue was settled to American satisfaction.
69 *MKR*, III: 41
70 Ibid, 41–2
71 Ibid, 43–4
72 William Stevenson, *Intrepid's Last Case*, 115
73 *MKR*, III: 42
74 In Acheson's briefing paper for the president on the prime minister's visit, the subject of Canadian adoption of American military training, organization, and equipment is the exclusive preoccupation of the covering memorandum. During the King-Truman interview, however, no matter aside from the Gouzenko affair was discussed. (Dean Acheson, 'Memorandum for the President: Visit of Prime Minister of Canada,' 28 September 1945, Truman Papers, President's Secretary's File; Pearson to Wrong, 1 October 1945, Pearson Papers, vol. 6.)
75 *MKR*, III: 47; *Report* of the Royal Commission Appointed under Order in Council P.C. 411 of 5 February 1946 (Ottawa, 27 June 1946), 7–8, 649–50. (Henceforth referred to as Royal Commission on Espionage, *Report*.)
76 Pincher, *Too Secret*, 108–9; *House of Commons Debates*, 18 March 1946: 51
77 The saga is recounted from King's perspective in chapter three of *MKR*, III: 46–102.
78 Ibid, 58–9

79 Ibid, 52–4. See also Ross, *Foreign Office*, 251–63.
80 *MKR*, III: 55
81 Ibid, 69
82 Ibid, 71, 74
83 Ibid, 71, 74
84 Ibid, 75
85 Ibid, 80. King wrote that Robertson had consulted with 'two representatives of the British Secret Service … MI5 people …' Since Hollis had already been assigned to the role of liaison in the case, his presence seems likely.
86 Ibid, 83. According to Bullock (*Bevin*, 187), Prime Minister Attlee favoured delay, while Ernest Bevin favoured immediate action to interrogate and prosecute suspects.
87 Stevenson, *Intrepid's Last Case*, 136–40
88 *MKR*, III: 91–2
89 Ibid, 49; Millis, *Forrestal Diaries*, 95–6
90 *MKR*, III: 86. This image too had an early history: the Spanish socialist prime minister Largo Caballero spoke in 1937 of the 'reptilian intrigues' of the Communist party in the first months of the Spanish Civil War (Raymond Carr, *Modern Spain, 1875–1980* [Oxford: Oxford University Press 1980], 143).
91 *MKR*, III: 86. William Stevenson suggests that Churchill had already been privately briefed on the Corby case by William Stephenson (*Intrepid's Last Case*, 140). Stephenson confirmed this claim by telegram to the author, 31 August 1985. Churchill's preference for public exposure of the case coincided with Stephenson's; if Churchill was informed by Stephenson, it would not have been the first time that Churchill, out of power, had made use of his own private intelligence network on matters of high policy.
92 *MKR*, III: 87
93 Ibid, 88. The detail of King's thoughts and activities over the next two months is lost, however, since the King Diaries for the period 10 November to 31 December 1945 were missing from his papers when these were collected after his death. (See *MKR*, III: 96; Granatstein, *A Man of Influence*, 168.)
94 'Joint Declaration by the President of the United States, the Prime Minister of the United Kingdom, and the Prime Minister of Canada, November 15, 1945,' *A Decade of American Foreign Policy*, 1076–8. See also Kenneth Harris, *Attlee*, 281–3.
95 *MKR*, III: 98
96 'Draft agreement on procedure for dealing with the "Corby" case,' undated, King Papers, 272: C187018–25. The King Diary may refer to this document when it mentions 'a draft to be sent to Wrong' that Norman Robertson was preparing in London on 22 October 1945. When Robertson persuaded King on 23 October that no immediate action should be taken, the message to Ottawa would have lost its urgency, which may partly explain why it remains in draft form – although it would not explain why the draft was not formally confirmed in Washington (if that, indeed, was the case). The document includes a two-page agreement, an annex

on the British aspect of the case, a draft public statement by Prime Minister King, and Gouzenko's three-page formal statement made on 10 October 1945.

97 *MKR*, III: 136. See also Granatstein, *A Man of Influence*, 176–7.

98 Dean Acheson, 'Memorandum for the President, Subject: Corby Case,' 22 December 1945, Truman Papers, President's Secretary File

Chapter 4: The Curtain Descends

1 Wilgress to SSEA, No. 368, 25 September 1945, DEA files, 2-AE(s)

2 At the London meeting of the Conference of Foreign Ministers, then in session, the Soviet Union had made the proposal (which appeared outrageous to the British and Americans) that it should assume trusteeship over Tripolitania. (It subsequently withdrew the proposal.)

3 'Present Trends of Soviet Foreign Policy,' 28 September 1945, King Papers, 344: C237913–21

4 Royal Commission on Espionage, *Report*, 502; letter from John W. Holmes, 11 April 1985; letter from Escott Reid, 15 April 1985. See also June Callwood, *Emma*, for an account of Emma Woikin's life and her role in the GRU spy ring. Malania's notice of separation from the department is dated 11 July 1946, to take effect 12 August 1946. (Information obtained under the Access to Information Act.)

5 Wilgress to SSEA, No. 400, 9 October 1945, DEA files, 7-CZ(s). Excerpts from this dispatch, along with Foreign Office comments upon it, appear in Ross, ed., *Foreign Office*, 259–63.

6 Wilgress continued his efforts of analysis throughout the autumn. Three long dispatches, in particular, described the emergence of a new, privileged class in the Soviet Union, and argued to the conclusion that this class pursued a defensive foreign policy 'designed in the first place to hold the gains they have so far acquired and in the second place to improve their bargaining position for the struggle that is to come' against powers which appeared to be on the diplomatic offensive against Russia. These dispatches were drawn specifically to the prime minister's attention by Hume Wrong in December 1945. (H.H.W., 'Memorandum for the Prime Minister,' 18 December 1945; Wilgress to SSEA, No. 378, 29 September 1945; No. 413, 15 October 1945; No. 437, 29 October 1945, King Papers, 344: C237724–50.)

7 L.B. Pearson to Acting SSEA, No. 2407, 10 October 1945, King Papers, 397: 349876–8

8 Mr Roberts to Mr Bevin, No. 799, 16 November 1945, King Papers, 344: C237719–23

9 Wilgress to SSEA, No. 462, 14 November 1945, King Papers, 389: 359440–2

10 The confused state of discussion in the American administration and in Congress over the control of atomic energy, which formed the background to the Anglo-American-Canadian statement of 15 November, demonstrated more clearly still that American policy was not 'tough,' but in disarray. See, for example, Gaddis, *Origins*, 245–73.

11 Gaddis, *Origins*, 276; Bullock, *Bevin*, 198–200

12 Gaddis, *Origins*, 276–7
13 Ibid, 279–80
14 Secretary of State for Foreign Affairs to Lord Halifax, No. 12252, 7 December 1945, Dominions Office 35/1515
15 Dominions Office to Canada (High Commission), No. 2171, 7 December 1945, Dominions Office 35/1515
16 Canada (High Commission) to Dominions Office, No. 2496, 7 December 1945, Dominions Office 35/1515
17 Halifax to Foreign Office, No. 8185, 7 December 1945, Dominions Office 35/1515
18 Wilgress to Norman Robertson, 12 December 1945, King Papers, 389: 359471–2
19 Wilgress's account of Bevin's desire for the definition of three great spheres of interest or 'Monroes' coincides with Bevin's views as expressed in his memorandum to the UK Cabinet of 8 November 1945, 'The Foreign Situation.' (See Bullock, *Bevin*, 193–5.)
20 On the Moscow conference, see Byrnes, *Speaking Frankly*, 110–22; Bullock, *Bevin*, 206–13; Gaddis, *Origins*, 280–3; FRUS: 1945, II: 560–826; Patricia Dawson Ward, *The Threat of Peace*, 50–77.
21 Wilgress to N.A. Robertson, 15 January 1946, DEA files, 2-AE(s)
22 Gaddis, *Origins*, 283–90; Ward, *Threat of Peace*, 72–7
23 Truman, *Year of Decisions*, 552
24 Gaddis, *Origins*, 285–96; Ward, *Threat of Peace*, 78
25 In December 1945, following agreement on the post-war US loan to Britain, the American ambassador to Russia, Averell Harriman, told his staff: 'England is so weak she must follow our leadership ... She will do anything that we insist upon and she won't go out on a limb alone' (Harriman and Abel, *Special Envoy*, 531).
26 Gaddis, *Origins*, 299–301
27 Millis, *Forrestal Diaries*, 134–5
28 Gardner, *Architects of Illusion*, 315–16
29 The Chargé in the Soviet Union (Kennan) to the Secretary of State, 22 February 1946, FRUS: 1946, VI: 696–709
30 Millis, *Forrestal Diaries*, 135–40; Kennan, *Memoirs*, 294–5; Gaddis, *Origins*, 303–4; Anderson, *United States, Great Britain*, 105–6
31 Kennan, *Memoirs*, 294–5
32 Ibid, 294
33 L.B. Pearson to N.A. Robertson, 12 February 1946; L.B. Pearson to W.L. Mackenzie King, 12 February 1946, DEA files, 51-B(s)
34 Pearson to King, 12 February 1946, DEA files, 51-B(s)
35 MKR, III: 180–1
36 Ibid, 181
37 Ibid
38 Ibid 182
39 Pearson to King, 4 March 1946, Pearson Papers, file: King, W.L.M., 1942–1950. Admiral Leahy reported to his diary that he found no fault with the draft speech, read at Churchill's bedside, with Churchill smoking a cigar and 'scattering ashes

together with pages of manuscript about the bed' (Leahy Papers, Diary, 3 March 1946).

40 Gaddis, *Origins*, 306–10; Anderson, *United States, Great Britain*, 110–16; Gabriel and Joyce Kolko, *Limits of Power*, 44–5

41 The text of the speech appears in the *New York Times*, 6 March 1946.

42 *MKR*, III: 185

43 King to Attlee, No. 53, 5 March 1946, DEA files, 51-B(s)

44 *MKR*, III: 184–5. King was gilding history. Ogdensburg was, as he had recorded at the time, the inspiration of President Roosevelt, sprung upon King without notice but accepted gratefully.

45 L.B. Pearson to SSEA, No. 511, 11 March 1946, enclosing Press Analysis Section, C.I.S., Canadian Embassy, Washington, D.C., 'Churchill's Westminster College Address,' Special Report No. 30, 11 March 1946, King Papers, 411: 371383–93

46 Ibid

47 Ibid, 371392. See also Ronald Steel, *Walter Lippmann and the American Century*, 428–30.

· 48 Canadian High Commission to SSEA, No. 660, 8 March 1946, DEA files, 51-B(s); Harris, *Attlee*, 298, 301–3; Bullock, *Bevin*, 224–7

49 L.B. Pearson to N.A. Robertson, 11 March 1946, Pearson Papers, vol. 3, file: Robertson, N.A., 1942–1946

50 *MKR*, III: 133. Leahy's pretext for the visit to Ottawa was an invitation to attend a dinner given by the US ambassador for the retiring governor general, the Earl of Athlone. Leahy's unrevealing diary notes that 'This journey was made to meet an urgent request by the Ambassador and with the President's approval.' The diary entry for 1 February 1946 offers an unwitting metaphor for the secrecy of Leahy's discussion with King: 'During yesterday and last night a continuous fall of snow covered the ground to a depth of nearly three feet, making as beautiful a winter picture as I have ever seen.' Admiral Leahy explicitly mentions the spy affair in his diary for the first time on 16 February 1946 following the Canadian detentions, when he records: 'This is the case related to me by Prime Minister Mackenzie King in which a number of Canadian and Englishmen gave secret information to the Soviet spy system. One might hope that this action by Canada might eliminate some of the alleged Soviet agents employed by our Department of State.' (Leahy Papers, Diary, 30 January, 1 February, 16 February 1946.)

51 *MKR*, III, 134

52 On the reported death of Zabotin, see MacDonald, *People and Places*, 186–7; Sir P. Clutterbuck to Lord Addison, No. 346, 22 August 1946, DO 35, 1207, X/L 05183.

53 *MKR*, III: 133–5

54 Ibid, 135

55 The claim is made in William Stevenson's *Intrepid's Last Case* (155–60) and repeated by William Stephenson in a telegram to the author, 31 August 1985. In John Sawatsky's oral history *Gouzenko: The Untold Story* (p. 75), Stephenson says that 'King refused to take the necessary action for fear of offending Stalin. The Soviet

penetration in the U.S.A. was so widespread and their agents were preparing to escape. After consultation with [J. Edgar] Hoover and President Roosevelt's so-called brain-trust coordinator, Ernest Cuneo, we agreed that the story should be released by way of Drew Pearson, Sunday night broadcast, *Nationwide* [*sic*].' In an earlier book, Sawatsky suggests that 'The Americans grew impatient with Canada's procrastination and leaked the story' to Pearson. Gregg Herken also implies that the leak to Pearson (and another to the columnist Frank McNaughton) was from a source in the American administration (probably the FBI). He suggests that its purpose was, through a spy scare, 'to ensure passage of domestic legislation that would provide for significant military representation in the atomic energy commission and preclude the sharing of information on atomic energy with other nations, including even America's partners in creating the bomb, Great Britain and Canada.' This interpretation of events contradicts that of Stephenson, unless the leak came simultaneously from more than one source, for more than one motive. But whatever the source, its consequence in the United States was, as Herken suggests, to influence Congress against the maintenance of post-war co-operation in atomic development. (See John Sawatsky, *Men in the Shadows*, 81; Gregg Herken, *The Winning Weapon: The Atomic Bomb in the Cold War 1945–1950*, 116, 129–32, 146.)

56 William Stephenson, telegram to author, 31 August 1985. David Stafford's account of Stephenson's involvement in the Gouzenko affair is consistent with this suggestion (*Camp X*, 267–9).
57 *Cabinet Conclusions*, 5 February 1946
58 *MKR*, III: 134
59 Ibid, 135–6
60 Ibid, 136. In spite of the publicity and the likelihood of Russian knowledge of the matter, the cabinet was told that 'the subject was one of the highest secrecy and it was essential that no reference of any kind be made thereto' (*Cabinet Conclusions*, 5 February 1946).
61 *MKR*, III: 136
62 Ibid, 139; *Cabinet Conclusions*, 14 February 1946
63 *MKR*, III: 139
64 Ibid, 140
65 Ibid, 140
66 'Press Release of Department of External Affairs,' No. 17, 15 February 1946, *DCER*, 12: 2040
67 *MKR*, III: 143
68 Ibid, 142–3
69 Ibid, 143
70 Ibid, 144, 147
71 Ibid, 146
72 Ibid, 147
73 Ibid, 150
74 Chargé d'Affaires in Soviet Union to SSEA, Telegram 25, 21 February 1946, *DCER*, 12: 2041–2

75 *House of Commons Debates*, 18 March 1946: 53
76 MKR, III: 151, 154–8; Granatstein, *A Man of Influence*, 177–9; Dale C. Thomson, *Louis St. Laurent: Canadian*, 182–6
77 MKR, III: 156–7
78 Ibid, 158
79 'Memorandum from Government of Canada to Embassy of Soviet Union,' 12 July 1946, DCER, 12: 2058–9
80 Chargé d'Affaires of Soviet Union to Prime Minister, No. 21, 15 July 1946, DCER, 12: 2059–60
81 See the *Report*, Royal Commission on Espionage, passim; MKR, III: 284; J.A.G., 'Espionage: RCE etc. / Chronology and Commentary,' 31 January 1947, King Papers, 390: C274025–31.
82 MKR, III: 284
83 Clutterbuck to Addison, No. 346, 22 August 1946, DO 35, 1207 X/L 05183
84 Sir M. Peterson to Foreign Office, No. 2585, 4 August 1946, DO 35, 1207, X/L 05183
85 Escott Reid, 'An Approach to Some of the Basic Problems of Foreign Policy,' 9–11 February 1946, Reid Papers
86 The Ottawa correspondent of the *Winnipeg Free Press*, Grant Dexter, noted privately in March 1946, after a long discussion with Reid, that whereas 'in 1941 or 1942, he was a tremendous Russian man,' now 'He is cured on Russia, beyond all danger of relapse. Indeed I never heard more envenomed comment on Uncle Joe and Co. than from Escott.' Reid approved the government's methods in the spy affair, Dexter reported, on the ground that 'we are now up against an idealogical [*sic*] conflict without parallel since Elizabethan times ... Just as Elizabeth had to resort to the star chamber so we must look to the Rockcliffe [*sic*] police barracks. To stand by our system of habeas corpus and so forth just doesn't make sense. It is equivalent to turning our inner government workings over to Moscow.' (Grant Dexter, Memo, 17 March 1946, Grant Dexter Papers, Queen's University Archives.)
87 Reid made this contrast clear in a draft speech he prepared for the prime minister on 23 March 1946 (after Churchill's Fulton speech) and based closely on his memorandum of 9–11 February. In it he wrote that 'it would be folly to believe that in the long run in the world as it exists today war can be averted by one side building up a so-called preponderance of armed force over the other. This belief would be true only under three conditions: that the force which one side is able and willing to use is so much greater than the force which the other side is able and willing to use that the weaker side will not provoke war; that the stronger side exercise its power with calm restraint so as not to provoke the other side to war; that the weaker side has no chance of redressing the balance.' This was a telling criticism of the weakness of Churchill's position; but it did not mean that Reid's alternative was more practical. The draft speech appears not to have been used by Mackenzie King. (Escott Reid, 'Prepared for P.M.'s speech,' 23 March 1946, Reid Papers.)
88 H.H. Wrong, 'Impressions of the First General Assembly of the United Nations,' 27 February 1946, Reid Papers

89 Reid made clear his disagreement with the approach of Wrong's paper in a memorandum of 25 February, offering a number of suggestions for change which would
invest the document with some of Reid's utopian optimism about an international
parliament. Wrong rejected most of the suggestions. (Escott Reid, 'Memorandum
for Mr. Wrong,' 25 February 1946, Reid Papers.)

90 Mr Roberts to Mr Bevin, No. 189, 17 March 1946; No. 190, 18 March 1946, DEA
files, 2-AE(s). See also Ray Merrick, 'The Russia Committee of the British Foreign
Office and the Cold War, 1946–47,' 453–68, esp. 453–4. Soon afterwards, in
April 1946, the Foreign Office created the Russia Committee, an interdepartmen-
tal body charged with reviewing all aspects of Soviet policy and activities, and
recommending policy to the foreign secretary. This committee took a particularly
hard line in its interpretation of Russian purposes from the beginning (Merrick,
455–66).

91 Wilgress to SSEA, No. 110, 21 March 1946, DEA files, 2-AE(s)

92 The Soviet Union had failed to withdraw its troops from northern Iran on the date
agreed with Britain and the United States, 2 March 1946. The issue was taken at
once by Iran to the Security Council, where Britain and the United States were
unyielding in their demands for Soviet withdrawal. In the face of this pressure,
the Soviet Union renewed its pledge to withdraw and did so on 1 April 1946.
Wilgress had prophesied that an Anglo-American diplomatic victory in the affair
would offer 'a definite check' to Soviet expansion and restore 'Anglo-Saxon hegemony over the world outside of the Soviet sphere.'

93 Wilgress to N.A. Robertson, 15 April 1946, King Papers, 345: C238178–9

94 King, however, kept the prospect (and Wilgress's judgment) in the back of his mind.
When he met Igor Gouzenko for the first time on 16 July 1946, he asked Gouzenko
what he thought of the idea, and whether it 'would be looked upon as an effort at
appeasement.' Gouzenko's reply, as reported by King, was that 'the Russians
always advertise any distinguished visitor as an evidence of the great respect the rest
of the world had for Russia.' (MKR, III: 282–3.)

95 Wilgress to SSEA, No. 185, 24 April 1946, King Papers, 418: 380062–71

96 N.A. Robertson, 'Memorandum for the Prime Minister,' 7 May 1946, King Papers,
344: C237771–2; Escott Reid to Prime Minister et al, 10 May 1946, DEA files, 2-AE(s)

97 21 May 1946, DEA files, 52-C(s)

Chapter 5: Preparing for War?

1 Gaddis, *Origins*, 323; Canadian Ambassador to the United States to SSEA, 6 May
1946, King Papers, 412: 371654–62

2 Gaddis, *Origins*, 323–4; MKR, III: 287–327; Bullock, *Bevin*, 259–74, 279–86;
FRUS: 1946, vols II, III, IV, passim

3 See MKR, III, 287–327; Stacey, *Age of Conflict*, 2: 387–9; Pope, *Soldiers and
Politicians*, 281, 311–20. Brooke Claxton made a detailed final report on the
conference to King at the end of October (Claxton to SSEA, Delca No. 72, 31 October
1946, King Papers, 401: 362187–215).

4 *MKR*, III: 327
5 Gaddis, *Origins*, 328–31
6 Quoted in Gaddis, *Origins*, 329
7 Gaddis, *Origins*, 328–31; Byrnes, *Speaking Frankly*, 187–92
8 Eayrs, *Peacemaking and Deterrence*, 142–6; H.H. Wrong to Wilgress, No. 97, 13 May 1944, DEA files, 7-AB(s). For further discussion of post-war defence arrangements with the United States, see Holmes, *Shaping of Peace*, 2: 76–88, and Eayrs, *Peacemaking and Deterrence*, 319–72.
9 Under-Secretary of State for External Affairs to Wilgress, 5 August 1944, DEA files, 7-AB(s)
10 Quoted in N.A.R., 'Memorandum for the Prime Minister,' 10 April 1944, DEA files, 52-C(s)
11 J.A.G., 'For the Under-Secretary,' 12 April 1944, DEA files, 52-C(s)
12 'Minutes of the Working Committee on Post-Hostilities Problems,' 19 May 1944, DEA files, 7-AD(s)
13 'Report to the Advisory Committee from the Working Committee on Post-Hostilities Problems,' 16 June 1944, DEA files, 7-AB(s)
14 Maurice Pope to Colonel J.H. Jenkins, 27 June 1944, DEA files, 7-AB(s)
15 E.R., 'Canada's postwar defence relationship with the United States,' 11 April 1944 (revised 29 June 1944), DEA files, 52-C(s); E.R., 'Comments on P.H.P. Memorandum of June 16, 1944 ...,' 29 June 1944, DEA files, 7-AB(s)
16 'Memorandum to the Cabinet War Committee from the Advisory Committee on Post-Hostilities Problems,' 6 July 1944, DEA files, 7-AB(s). The original is amended in handwriting 'as approved by the War Committee, July 19, 1944,' and a corrected and retyped copy appears in the same file.
17 Canadian Joint Staff to Chiefs of Staff, JS 101, 5 August 1944, DEA files, 7-AB(s)
18 N.A.R., 'Postwar defence relationships with the United States,' 28 February 1945, DEA files, 52-C(s). See also H.W., 'Memorandum for Mr. Robertson,' 3 November 1944, DEA files, 52-C(s).
19 See, for example, J.E. Read, 'Memorandum for the Prime Minister: Permanent Joint Board on Defence,' 18 June 1945; J.A.G. to the Prime Minister, 29 September 1945, King Papers, 318: C220111–13, C220136–44.
20 'Permanent Joint Board on Defence, Note on General Henry's statements ...,' 3 September 1945, King Papers, 318: C220140–44, esp. C220142–3
21 R.M. Macdonnell, 'Memorandum for Cabinet: Postwar Defence Collaboration with the United States,' 12 December 1945, DEA files, 52-C(s)
22 Ibid
23 'Memorandum from Secretary to the Cabinet to Under-Secretary of State for External Affairs: Re: Joint Planning with the United States,' 1 February 1946, DCER, 12: 1605–7.
24 See DCER, 12: 1598–1725; Eayrs, *Peacemaking and Deterrence*, 319–56.
25 See, in particular, 'Memorandum by Secretary, Canadian Section, PJBD,' 18 January 1946, DCER, 12: 1600–4; Ambassador in United States to SSEA, 29 January 1946,

DCER, 12: 1604–5; 'Memorandum from Secretary to the Cabinet to Under-Secretary of State for External Affairs,' 1 February 1946, *DCER*, 12: 1605–7.

26 'Memorandum from Associate Under-Secretary of State for External Affairs to Prime Minister,' 2 May 1946, *DCER*, 12: 1610–12; 'Memorandum by Joint Canadian–United States Military Co-operation Committee,' 23 May 1946, *DCER*, 12: 1615–23; Joseph T. Jockel, 'The Canada–United States Military Co-operation Committee and Continental Air Defence, 1946'

27 G.P. de T. Glazebrook, 'Memorandum for Mr. Macdonnell,' 2 February 1946, DEA files, 52-C(s). The assessment seems to have been revised later in February or March 1946, and bears a handwritten date, 'April 2, 1946.'

28 'Memorandum by Joint Canadian–United States Military Co-operation Committee,' 23 May 1946, *DCER*, 12: 1615–23; Jockel, 'The Canada–United States Military Co-operation Committee,' 360–2

29 'Memorandum from Secretary to the Cabinet to Prime Minister Re: Defence of North America; Canada-U.S. Joint planning,' 12 June 1946, *DCER*, 12: 1627–9. Hume Wrong wrote that the original had 'not been changed substantially' (Wrong to N.A. Robertson, 12 June 1946, DEA files, 52-C[s]). Joseph Jockel suggests that the American members of the joint committee had received 'considerable latitude' from the joint chiefs of staff to draw defence plans 'guided by their own strategic insights and institutional interests,' and in the absence of any general American strategic plan. The Appreciation, he concludes, did not reflect the considered view of the joint chiefs on the nature of the Soviet threat. He dates formal JCS approval of the Appreciation, according to JCS records, at 22 June 1946; even then, he suggests, the joint chiefs of staff were indicating their general approval of the effort to 'sign Canada on' rather than giving serious expression to a political judgment of Soviet intentions and capabilities. (Jockel, 359–67.)

30 H.W., 'Note,' 11 June 1946, DEA files, 52-C(s)

31 'Memorandum from Secretary to the Cabinet to Prime Minister,' 12 June 1946, *DCER*, 12: 1627–9.

32 C.S.A.R., 'Memorandum on the Appreciation of the Requirements of Canadian–United States Security,' 14 June 1946, DEA files, 52-C(s)

33 G.G., 'Memorandum for Mr. Wrong,' 15 June 1946, DEA files, 52-C(s)

34 'Memorandum by Associate Under-Secretary of State for External Affairs: The Possibility of War with the Soviet Union (in connection with the Joint Appreciation of the Requirements for Canadian-U.S. Security and Joint Basic Security Plan),' 28 June 1946, *DCER*, 12: 1632–5. In October 1946, when Wrong went to Washington as ambassador and Lester Pearson returned to Ottawa as under-secretary, Wrong told Pearson, in the course of passing on to him copies of the joint appreciation and basic security plan (which he had not previously seen), that this memo of 28 June had been given to no one except Arnold Heeney. Now Pearson might want to use it 'if you have to produce something in a hurry.' Instead Pearson produced his own markedly different document, as indicated below. (H.H.W., 'Memorandum for Mr. Pearson,' 10 October 1946, DEA files, 52-C[s]).

35 'Memorandum from Chiefs of Staff Committee to Cabinet Defence Committee,' 15 July 1946, *DCER*, 12: 1638–40

36 D.C.A., 'Notes re conversation at Laurier House ... between the Prime Minister, Field Marshal Montgomery, Lieutenant General Foulkes, and the Minister of National Defence,' 9 September 1946; Charles Foulkes, 'Notes on Conference, Prime Minister–Field Marshal Montgomery,' 10 September 1946, King Papers, 389: C274007–13

37 Foulkes, 'Notes on Conference ...'

38 D.C.A., 'Notes re conversation ...'

39 Foulkes, 'Notes on Conference ...'

40 Although King reported to his diary that Montgomery was 'exceedingly pleasant' (*MKR*, III: 343).

41 Foulkes, 'Notes on Conference ...'

42 L.B. Pearson to H.H. Wrong, 28 May 1946, DEA files, 52-C(S)

43 Canadian Ambassador in Washington to SSEA, Ex-1453, 4 June 1946, DEA files, 52-C(S)

44 Cable, 4PN27, 4 September 1946, King Papers, 389: C274016

45 See, for example, 'Memorandum from Senior United States Army Member, PJBD, to PJBD,' 9 September 1946, *DCER*, 12: 1642–5.

46 R.M.M., 'United States Foreign Policy towards the Soviet Union,' 21 September 1946, King Papers, 344: C237543–5

47 L.B. Pearson to SSEA, No. 1873, 24 September 1946, DEA files, 4901–40C.

48 'Memorandum from Associate Under-Secretary of State for External Affairs to Under-Secretary of State for External Affairs,' 8 October 1946, *DCER*, 12: 1649.

49 'Chiefs of Staff Committee: Joint Planning Committee: Progress Report No. 7,' 29 October 1946, DEA files, 52-C(S)

50 Dean Acheson, 'Memorandum for the President, Subject: Joint Defense Measures with Canada,' 1 October 1946, Truman Papers, President's Secretary's File. Jockel suggests that in fact Acheson probably knew little of the detail of the Military Co-operation Committee's proposals ('Canada–United States Military Co-operation Committee,' 366–7, 375–6).

51 The shift is recounted in the King diaries. See *MKR*, III: 333–7.

52 'Memorandum from Under-Secretary of State for External Affairs to Secretary of State for External Affairs,' 23 October 1946, *DCER*, 12: 1653.

53 'Memorandum from Ambassador in United States to Prime Minister,' 26 October 1946, *DCER*, 12: 1654–8.

54 The call for closer sharing and evaluation of intelligence reports was also being made at the official military level, where the practical dangers of losing the capacity for independent judgment were even more obvious. The Canadian chiefs of staff received a request from their joint planning committee on 29 October 1946 which called for the interpretation and presentation of intelligence reports (both military and diplomatic) to combined Canadian-US committees or boards by combined intelligence teams, even though 'It is appreciated that the majority of this information will emanate from United States sources.' As in the case of the original joint appreciation

263 Notes to pages 165–70

of 23 May, one result would be to make Canadian officials responsible for American intelligence assessments, before any political consideration had been given to these reports by the Canadian authorities. This was the very difficulty the Canadians were trying to overcome in their elaborate and circuitous treatment of the joint appreciation. (See 'Memorandum from Joint Planning Committee to Chiefs of Staff Committee,' 29 October 1946, DCER, 12: 1660–1.)

55 Ambassador in United States to SSEA, 29 October 1946, Telegram WA-3862, DCER, 12: 1661–2

56 Ibid. Wrong's account was based on a conversation with King immediately after his visit to the White House. It may be that what Truman said was affected to some degree in King's account by what King wanted to hear. In an interview with Grant Dexter ten days before seeing Truman, King had expressed the same opinion that 'the prevailing view – which he shares – is that internal strains have much to do' with Russian intransigence in foreign policy, and that there was no serious danger of war. 'It would not happen in our time but what might occur 30 years hence, was another matter.' King's diary account of the conversation says that he exchanged views with Truman, and told him that Wilgress's assessment of Soviet internal problems coincided with Truman's. There was certainly no serious disagreement on the question. (Grant Dexter, 'Memorandum, Talk with Mr. King – Thursday afternoon, October 17, 1946,' Grant Dexter Papers; MKR, III: 361–3.)

57 'Memorandum from Under-Secretary of State for External Affairs to Prime Minister,' 30 October 1946, DCER, 12: 1662–6

58 'Memorandum from Under-Secretary of State for External Affairs to Prime Minister,' 12 November 1946, DCER, 12: 1670–2

59 'Reason and Russia,' from the *Economist*, 2 November 1946, appears in the King Papers with the original memorandum to the prime minister. The British document does not, but a copy can be found in the Canada House files, enclosed with a letter from Pearson to Robertson of 28 November 1946. (King Papers, 389: C273479–851; Canada House files, vol. 2077, file AR 5/7.)

60 The minutes and conclusions of these meetings are reproduced in DCER, 12: 1673–95.

61 'Minutes of a Meeting of the Cabinet Defence Committee,' 13 November 1946, DCER, 12: 1673–9, esp. 1674–5

62 A.D.P. Heeney, 'Extract from Cabinet Conclusions,' 14 November 1946, DCER, 12: 1679–83. Leckie's statement to the cabinet is not reported in the *Conclusions*, but is referred to in a statement to the cabinet the next day by Brooke Claxton, reprinted in DCER, 12: 1684–6.

63 In its polite dance, the cabinet did not actually approve the 35th recommendation at this meeting, but 'agreed that a recommendation along the lines of the draft submitted would be favourably considered by the government and that the Board be informed to that effect.' Final approval was given by the cabinet on 16 January 1947.

64 'Aide-mémoire by Government of Great Britain: United States Bases in Canada,' DCER, 12: 1678–9

65 Wrong to Pearson, 14 November 1946, DCER, 12: 1683–4
66 *Cabinet Conclusions,* 15 November 1946, DCER, 12: 1686–95
67 Brooke Claxton, 'Statement by Minister of National Health and Welfare to Cabinet,' 15 November 1946, DCER, 12: 1684–6. Claxton's statement was especially important because, at the same meeting, the cabinet approved the appointment of a single minister of defence for the three services; and on 12 December Claxton was appointed to that post.
68 *Cabinet Conclusions,* 15 November 1946
69 'Record of Conclusions, Informal Canada–United States Meeting, November 21,' 26 November 1946, DCER, 12: 1699–1702. See also 'Memorandum on the Agenda for Canada–United States Defence Talks,' 21 November 1946, DCER, 12: 1697–9.
70 'Working Papers for Use in Discussions with the United States,' 6 December 1946, DCER, 12: 1702–7
71 'Minutes of a Meeting between Representatives of Canada and the United States,' 21 December 1946, DCER, 12: 1712–20.
72 George F. Kennan to Dean Acheson, 8 October 1946, Dean Acheson Papers
73 See 'Minutes ...,' 21 December 1946.
74 Jockel, 'Canada–United States Military Co-operation Committee,' 373
75 'Memorandum from Under-Secretary of State for External Affairs to Prime Minister: Defence Discussions with the United States,' 23 December 1946, DCER, 12: 1721–5
76 See 'Minutes ...,' 21 December 1946: 1717.
77 Ibid, 1717–20
78 'Memorandum ...,' 23 December 1946, DCER, 12: 1721–5
79 'Statement to be made in the House of Commons by the Prime Minister on Defence Cooperation with the United States,' 12 February 1947, DEA files, 52-C(s)
80 Stacey, *Age of Conflict,* 2: 396, 410

Chapter 6: Pax Americana

1 'American Relations with the Soviet Union,' 24 September 1946, Elsey Papers. The genesis of the paper from a request by the president is explained by its primary author, George Elsey, in his oral history interview for the Truman Library. See also Gaddis, *Origins,* 321–3; Arthur Krock, *Memoirs: Sixty Years on the Firing Line,* 223; Harbutt, *Iron Curtain,* 276–7.
2 'American Relations with the Soviet Union,' 38–42
3 Ibid, 59, 62
4 Royal Commission on Espionage, *Report,* 44–9
5 'American Relations with the Soviet Union,' 65–9
6 Ibid, 71
7 Ibid, 73–4
8 Ibid, 78
9 Ibid, 75–9

10 Ibid, 79
11 See the oral history interview with George M. Elsey, Truman Library, February 1974, pp. 265–7; Krock, *Memoirs*, 421–82.
12 For example, in August 1946, in an atmosphere of anxiety prompted by Soviet diplomatic pressure on Turkey and the shooting down of two US military transports by Yugoslavia, the director of the Central Intelligence Group, General Hoyt Vandenberg, sent a memo to President Truman expressing 'both alarm and puzzlement' over secret reports that Russian rockets had been fired over Norway and Sweden. Vandenberg accepted the orthodox view of British intelligence (apparently the source of the reports) that the events were Soviet acts of intimidation; they were actually sightings of meteors. Trevor Barnes concludes that 'the incident illustrates the panic atmosphere which made such an erroneous interpretation possible and the dependence of the C.I.A. on British intelligence at this time.' (Trevor Barnes, 'The Secret Cold War: The C.I.A. and American Foreign Policy in Europe, 1946–1956. Part I,' 399–415, esp. 402–3.)
13 See especially Joseph M. Jones, *The Fifteen Weeks*, passim; Harris, *Attlee*, 303–6; Bullock, *Bevin*, 368–71.
14 SSDA to SSEA, 21 February 1947, Circular D.54, King Papers, 430: 391405–8
15 Ibid
16 Ibid
17 Canadian Ambassador to US to SSEA, 3 March 1947, WA-702, King Papers, 433: 395559–64. In a personal letter to Mike Pearson on 5 July 1947 Hume Wrong offered more detailed background to these events gained in conversation with Dean Acheson at his Maryland farm following his retirement from the State Department at the beginning of July. Acheson told Wrong that the State Department knew that a crisis was approaching in Greece that would require 'drastic American action' and was prepared in spirit for it: 'The British approach late in February was the occasion and not the cause for their action.' (H.H. Wrong to L.B. Pearson, 5 July 1947, Pearson Papers, vol. 6.)
18 Canadian Ambassador to US to SSEA, 3 March 1947
19 Jones, *Fifteen Weeks*, 138–43; Wrong to Pearson, 5 July 1947
20 Canadian Ambassador to US to SSEA, 3 March 1947
21 Ibid
22 H.H. Wrong to L.B. Pearson, 3 March 1947, King Papers, 433: 395565–7
23 Canadian Ambassador to US to SSEA, 5 March 1947, WA-732, King Papers, 433: 395572–3
24 Ibid. This point too coincides with Joseph Jones's account of Acheson's polemic on 27 February (*Fifteen Weeks*, 139–41).
25 Ibid
26 Canadian Ambassador to US to SSEA, 13 March 1947, WA-821, King Papers, 433: 395574–7
27 Ibid
28 Ibid
29 Jones, *Fifteen Weeks*, 175–6

30 Canadian Ambassador to US to SSEA, 18 March 1947, WA-862, King Papers, 433: 395578–80
31 Ibid
32 Ibid
33 J.A. Gibson to Hume Wrong, 25 March 1947, King Papers 433: 395588
34 H.H. Wrong to L.B. Pearson, 28 April 1947, enclosing J. Balfour to H.M.G. Jebb, 19 April 1947, King Papers, 433: 395669–77
35 Ibid
36 Ibid
37 Quoted in ibid
38 Ibid
39 Ibid. Within a year the United States had thrown its weight (by both overt and covert means) behind the defeat of the Communist party in the Italian elections, but had responded passively to the Czechoslovak coup. The differing calculations seemed to be based, as Balfour had foreseen, on the realistic prospects for success and the existence of recognized spheres of influence.
40 Ibid
41 Ibid
42 Jones, *Fifteen Weeks*, 197–8
43 Canadian Ambassador to US to SSEA, 10 May 1947, WA-1469, King Papers, 433: 395696–701
44 Ibid. The full text of Acheson's speech is reprinted in the Appendix to Jones, *Fifteen Weeks*, 27–81.
45 Canadian Ambassador to US to SSEA, 10 May 1947, WA-1469
46 Canadian Ambassador to US to SSEA, 26 May 1947, DEA files, 4901–40C
47 Ibid
48 Canadian Ambassador to US to SSEA, 6 June 1947, WA-1743, King Papers, 433: 395771–2
49 Jones, *Fifteen Weeks*, 33. At the urging of under-secretary Acheson's office, however, Marshall had authorized the release of a final text to the press on the evening of 4 June. See also Bullock, *Bevin*, 404.
50 The speech appears in the Appendix to Jones, *Fifteen Weeks*, 281–4. Alan S. Milward argues against conventional accounts of the 1947 economic crisis (which owe much to Marshall's speech and the background papers which led to it) that the crisis was not the result of 'the deteriorating domestic economic situation of the western European economies. Even less was it attributable to an impending political, moral and spiritual collapse. It was, on the contrary, attributable to the remarkable speed and success of western Europe's economic recovery. It was caused by the widening gap in the first six months of 1947 between increasing imports and increasing exports in some European economies, particularly Britain, Italy and the Netherlands, and the failure of that gap to continue to narrow in others, notably France ... It was the success and vigour of the European recovery, not its incipient failure, which exacerbated [the] payments problem. Marshall Aid did not save Western Europe from economic collapse. In order to defend America's own strategic

interests it allowed some Western European governments to continue to pursue by means of an extensive array of trade and payments controls the extremely ambitious, expansionist domestic policies which had provoked the 1947 payments crisis and destroyed the Bretton Woods agreements almost at birth.' (Alan S. Milward, *The Reconstruction of Western Europe 1945–51*, 465–6; see also pp. 1–55.)

51 Jones, *Fifteen Weeks*, 283–4
52 Canadian Ambassador to US to SSEA, 26 June 1947, WA-2006, King Papers, 433: 395833–6, esp. 395836
53 Canadian Ambassador to US to SSEA, 25 June 1947, WA-1979, King Papers, 433: 395829–32
54 Ibid; Bullock, *Bevin*, 409–17
55 Canadian Ambassador to US to SSEA, 25 June 1947
56 L.B. Pearson, Memorandum for the Prime Minister, 28 June 1947, King Papers, 433: 395840–1. The Canadian government's persistent and successful compaign to ensure the eligibility of European purchases of Canadian goods and commodities under Marshall aid is recounted in detail in Cuff and Granatstein, *American Dollars – Canadian Prosperity*, 21–131.
57 Truman, *Years of Trial and Hope*, 116; SSDA to SSEA, Circular D.568, 2 July 1947, King Papers, 431: 392930–3; Bullock, *Bevin*, 417–22
58 Truman, *Trial and Hope*, 116–19
59 Canadian Ambassador to the US to SSEA, 18 July 1947, WA-2260, King Papers, 434: 395883–9
60 L.D. Wilgress to SSEA, 25 April 1947, No. G.1, King Papers, 433: 395253–6. Wilgress had become Canadian minister-designate in Switzerland in order to participate as chief Canadian delegate to the meeting of the preparatory committee for the International Trade Organization in Geneva (Wilgress, *Memoirs*, 150).
61 Ibid. Wilgress's comments on Western policy toward the satellite countries reinforced those of Robert Ford, the Canadian chargé d'affaires in Moscow, made following the Polish elections of January 1947 and circulated to Wilgress with L.B. Pearson's letter of 21 March 1947.
62 Wilgress to SSEA, 25 April 1947
63 18 February 1947, Reid Papers
64 See above, pp. 173–6. Hume Wrong wrote in December that he was uncertain about the purpose of Reid's paper, but 'I suppose that it is probably intended to be a political appreciation on the chances of war with the Soviet Union, intended to supplement a military appreciation approved by the Chiefs of Staff' (Hume Wrong to L.B. Pearson, 5 December 1947, DEA files, 52-F[s]).
65 'The United States and the Soviet Union,' 30 August 1947, DEA files, 52-F(s)). The paper was distributed in September 1947 to more than two dozen senior officers of the department and to the minister, Louis St Laurent. For other discussions of this paper and its commentaries, see Don Page and Don Munton, 'Canadian Images of the Cold War, 1946–47,' 582–604; Cuff and Granatstein, *American Dollars – Canadian Prosperity*, 201–18.
66 'The United States and the Soviet Union.' DEA files, 52–F(s). In the February draft,

this claim about the ever-expanding appetite had been directed only at the Soviet Union.

67 Maurice Pope to L.B. Pearson, 29 September 1947, DEA files, 52-F(s)

68 R.A.D. Ford to L.B. Pearson, 10 October 1947, DEA files, 52-F(s)

69 Charles Ritchie to N.A. Robertson, 13 December 1947, Canada House files, vol. 2078, file AR 5/17

70 Hume Wrong to L.B. Pearson, 5 December 1947, DEA files, 52-F(s)

71 4 December 1947, DEA files, 52-F(s). Wrong pointed out that the paper, with the exception of two paragraphs in conclusion of his own, was based on a draft written by Hume Wright of the embassy staff.

72 Dana Wilgress to L.B. Pearson, 6 November 1947, DEA files, 52-F(s)

73 R.M. Macdonnell to L.B. Pearson, 25 September 1947, DEA files, 2-AE(s); D.M. Johnson, 'Memorandum to Under-Secretary,' 4 December 1947, DEA files, 52-F(s)

74 Laurent Beaudry, 'The United States and the Soviet Union,' 15 December 1947; M. Cadieux, 'Memorandum for Mr. Teakles,' 17 October 1947; Pierre Dupuy to SSEA, 1 December 1947, all in DEA files, 52-F(s)

75 MKR, IV: 29

76 Arnold C. Smith to Under Secretary of State for External Affairs, 10 December 1947, DEA files, 52-F(s)

77 Escott Reid, 'Memorandum for Mr. Pearson,' 10 January 1948, DEA files, 52-F(s). Here, perhaps, in response to Smith's case for a universal organization to promote Western values and policies, was the origin of what eventually became article 2 of the NATO treaty. Reid and Smith were both, at heart, romantics who believed in the secular mission of the West, the ultimate challenge of the evil empire to the East, and the mellowing or collapse of Soviet power when confronted with the preponderant strength of the West.

78 Ibid.

79 R.A. Mackay, 'Comment on Mr. Reid's paper of September 13, 1947, Entitled "The United States and the Soviet Union,"' 2 November 1947, DEA files, 52-F(s)

80 See Reid, Time of Fear and Hope, 11; letter from Escott Reid, 15 April 1985.

81 King recorded his impressions of the meeting in his diary; Robertson produced an outline memo of notes, and a narrative memo the next day. As background, the Foreign Office distributed to participants twenty-two pages of summary notes on current international questions.

82 NAR, 'Memorandum,' 25.11.47, King Papers, 272: c187427–32, esp. c187428–9

83 Ibid, c187430–1

84 Ibid, c187432

85 MKR, IV: 111. King's hold on fact was, by his own admission, somewhat vague. In reporting Bevin's remarks about Berlin, he had confessed, 'I am not sure that I have this wholly correct'; and he added here, 'I am not sure that Alexander spoke of the bacteriological warfare. Someone else in authority did so in some conversation with me' (MKR, IV: 108, 111). Robertson did not report the remarks.

86 MKR, IV: 111

87 Ibid

88 Ibid, 112

89 Ibid

90 Ibid, 113

91 Ibid, 112–113. The lunch, which took place at the home of Sir John Anderson, was also attended by Harold Macmillan and Jan Christian Smuts; and King concluded that Churchill's words gained significance because of the presence of the others (ibid, 117).

92 Ibid, 119

93 Ibid, 120

94 Ibid

95 NAR to L.B. Pearson, 6 December 1947, DEA files, 270(s); J.L. Granatstein, *A Man of Influence*, 234

96 See Thomas Powers, 'How Nuclear War Could Start,' *New York Review of Books*, 17 January 1985, 33. The American atomic bomb stockpile in August 1947 was only thirteen; the plan had been devised by the military in ignorance of the number of bombs available for use in war (Gregg Herken, *Counsels of War*, 27; David Alan Rosenberg, 'The Origins of Overkill: Nuclear Weapons and American Strategy, 1945–1960,' in Steven E. Miller, ed., *Strategy and Nuclear Deterrence*, 113–81, esp. 121–4). In April 1948 the American ambassador in London, Lewis Douglas, reported to Washington that Churchill 'believes that now is the time, promptly, to tell the Soviet that if they do not retire from Berlin and abandon Eastern Germany, withdrawing to the Polish frontier, we will raze their cities.' This suggests that Churchill's talk of an ultimatum in November was something more than a passing effort to frighten Mackenzie King. Douglas's response was calmer than King's: he told Robert Lovett: 'You know better than I the practical infirmities in this suggestion.' Ernest Bevin too was firmly opposed to such provocation. (See Douglas to Lovett, 17 April 1948, *FRUS: 1948*, III: 90–1; Bullock, *Bevin*, 557.)

97 *MKR*, IV: 133

98 Korea–Canadian Membership UNCOK – 1947–1948, Pearson Papers; Pearson, *Mike*, 2: 135–45; *MKR*, IV: 133–53; Stairs, *Diplomacy of Constraint*, 5–17; Ignatieff, *Making of a Peacemonger*, 99–102

99 See especially L.B. Pearson's memo, 'Mission to Washington on the Korean Commission, January 1–6, 1948,' 10.1.48, in Korea–Canadian Membership UNCOK – 1947–1948, Pearson Papers, and Pearson, *Mike*, 2: 140–1.

100 The letter was conveyed by telegram in Canadian Consulate General, New York City, to SSEA, No. 26, 6 January 1948, in Korea–Canadian Membership UNCOK – 1947–1948, Pearson Papers.

101 SSEA to Canadian Ambassador to the United States, No. EX-61, 9 January 1948, in Korea–Canadian Membership UNCOK – 1947–1948, Pearson Papers

102 Stairs, *Diplomacy of Constraint*, 17–25

103 *MKR*, IV: 155–9

104 Ibid, 161

105 Ibid, 153–4, 157–8, 161–2.

106 'Soviet Post-War Policy,' Mr Roberts to Mr Bevin, No. 774, 10 October 1947, DEA files, 2-AE(s). The paper was received in the Department of External Affairs on 6 March 1948, in the wake of the Czech coup d'état.

107 Ibid

108 'Memorandum by the Adviser in the Office of Special Political Affairs (Notter) to the Director of the Office of Special Political Affairs (Rusk),' 14 July 1947, FRUS, 1947, IV: 577–9

109 The Ambassador in the Soviet Union (Smith) to the Secretary of State, 15 November 1947, FRUS, 1947, IV: 621

110 R.G. Riddell to L.B. Pearson, 5 December 1947, DEA files, 211-J(s); Reid, Time of Fear and Hope, 34–8

111 'Personal message to Mr. Mackenzie King from Mr. Attlee,' 14 January 1948, Reid Papers

112 United Kingdom House of Commons Debates, 22 January 1948, col. 384. See also Bullock, Bevin, 513–22.

113 UK House of Commons Debates, 22 January 1948, col. 386.

114 Ibid, col. 388

115 Ibid, col. 392

116 Ibid, col. 395

117 Ibid, col. 397

118 Ibid, col. 402

119 H.H. Wrong to L.B. Pearson, 26 July 1947, Canada House files, vol. 2077, file AR 5/7; see also Steel, Walter Lippmann, 452

120 L.B. Pearson to J.W. Holmes, 9 September 1947, Canada House files, vol. 2077, file AR 5/7

121 L.B. Pearson to D. Wilgress, 9 September 1947, DEA files, 2 AE(s). See also Trevor Barnes, 'The Secret Cold War: The C.I.A. and American Foreign Policy in Europe, 1946–1956. Part I,' 408. The detail of the Czech case illustrated the self-fulfilling nature of such predictions. Lloyd C. Gardner writes: 'In Prague during the summer of 1947, Czech leaders were trapped between American rhetoric and foreign bayonets. James Warburg personally witnessed their agony with a sense of foreboding about the future that grew day by day. Conversations with Jan Masaryk and the American Ambassador, Lawrence Steinhardt, convinced him that it was wrong to write off Czechoslovakia – and with it any last chance to avoid the Cold War. Returning home, Warburg pleaded with State Department officials to grant Prague credits for cotton purchases. But his private memos to the new Under Secretary of State, Robert Lovett, were politely disregarded. Either the Department had simply abandoned Czechoslovakia, or it was afraid of the effect such a credit would have on congressional attitudes toward the Marshall Plan, or both. "The gist of my reportage was that, if an Iron Curtain had been drawn around Czechoslovakia, it had been drawn by us – not by the Soviet Union."' The Kolkos quote Trygve Lie's comment: '[T]here are times when I wonder – in the light of hind sight – whether the West does not now and then suffer pangs of conscience when reviewing the fate of that country.'

(Gardner, *Architects of Illusion*, 228–9; Gabriel and Joyce Kolko, *Limits of Power*, 397.)

122 See, for example, 'Memorandum for the Minister of National Defence,' 8 March 1948; G.H. Southam, 'Memorandum: Western Union,' 2 April 1948, DEA files, 277(s); Trevor Barnes, 'The Secret Cold War,' 409; Bullock, *Bevin*, 530–1; Steel, *Lippmann*, 450–2; Gabriel and Joyce Kolko, *Limits of Power*, 384–98.

123 MKR, IV: 164

124 *House of Commons Debates*, 29 April 1948: 3440–1. It is not clear whether the 29 April statement, now part of a larger *tour d'horizon*, was the same one shown to the prime minister on 3 March. (See also Eayrs, *Growing Up Allied*, 29.)

125 MKR, IV: 165. On this day St Laurent made a short statement of sympathy for Masaryk's family and the Czech people, and followed it by endorsing the Anglo-French-US declaration on the coup of 26 February (*House of Commons Debates*, 10 March 1948: 2055).

126 Secretary of State for Commonwealth Relations to High Commissioner for the United Kingdom, Ottawa, No. 220, 10 March 1948, DEA files, 283(s). The message from the British ambassador in Oslo on which Attlee's statement was based was also relayed to External Affairs the same day (Secretary of State for Commonwealth Relations to High Commissioner for the United Kingdom, Ottawa, No. 217, 10 March 1948, DEA files, 283(s)). A further and possibly influential background document that appears to have been provided by the British high commissioner at the same time was a three-page paper, 'Situation in Europe,' which repeated the substance of one of Ernest Bevin's personal memoranda to the United Kingdom cabinet of 3 March 1948. (The title of Bevin's paper was 'The Threat to Western Civilisation.') The key paragraph in the version made available to the Canadian government said: 'Since the European Recovery Programme was devised, the Soviet Government have been conducting a war of nerves and appear to intend to expand their influence over the whole of Europe. In other words, despite every effort on our part in the past three years to get a real and friendly settlement in Europe on a four-power basis, not only are the Soviet Government not prepared to co-operate in any real sense with any non-Communist Government, but they appear to be actually preparing to extend their influence over the whole of continental Europe and subsequently over the Middle East and no doubt the rest of the Asian land-mass. Unless positive and vigorous steps are taken shortly by other States in a position to do so, it may well be that the Soviet Union will gain political and strategic advantages which will set the great Communist machine in action culminating either in the establishment of a world dictatorship or more probably in the collapse of organised society in great stretches of the globe. We cannot be sure where the next move will be made, but all our information goes to show that further moves are to be expected in the immediate future with the object of frustrating the European Recovery Programme by one means or another and developing a situation in which Communism will succeed in many countries through economic decay.' The two documents have the flavour of desperate opportunism prompted by panic. (See 'The Threat to Western Civilisation: Memorandum by the Secretary of State

for Foreign Affairs,' 3 March 1948, C.P. (48) 72, CAB 129/25; 'Situation in Europe,' Earnscliffe, Ottawa, 10 March 1948, Reid Papers, vol. 6, file 12. See also Bullock, *Bevin*, 526–31.)

127 *MKR*, IV: 166

128 The nature of the Norwegian challenge remains obscure; it was apparently not heard of again. For Escott Reid, Attlee's message instilled 'fear because the news from Norway indicated that the Soviet Union intended to expand its power more rapidly and recklessly than I had anticipated' (*Time of Fear and Hope*, 43). The immediate Norwegian concern was that the Soviet Union might request negotiations for a pact of friendship and alliance, as it had just proposed between Finland and the Soviet Union. Norway's information was speculative, but in the atmosphere of extreme Western anxiety following the Czech coup, rumours of a possible Soviet request for talks were easily equated with undue pressure, and even the threat of military action. In his memoirs, Lester Pearson transforms the Norwegian anxiety into 'increased Russian pressure on Norway' (*Mike*, 2: 42). Western leaders were willing to believe the worst of the Soviets, and to act on that belief for their own peace of mind. They lacked any direct intelligence reports which might have given them firmer information on Russian intentions.

129 Prime Minister for the Prime Minister, 11 March 1948 ('Handed by Pearson,to Clutterbuck, 7.30 p.m. March 11'), Reid Papers. Cuff and Granatstein, in their account of Canadian entry into the North Atlantic alliance, emphasize the calculation and missionary zeal of its advocates in the Department of External Affairs, especially Pearson and Reid, and their determination to persuade the prime minister of its desirability. (They tended in this period to argue an extremist view of the dangers of Soviet military aggression in Europe, even after alarmists in Europe and Washington had moderated their warnings in the late spring.) But King did not fully trust his foreign policy advisers, and made the fateful commitment not on their initiative but because the United Kingdom sought it at a propitious moment. The pattern of events, for Canada, seems less rational and less self-contained than Cuff and Granatstein imply. (See Cuff and Granatstein, *American Dollars – Canadian Prosperity*, 201–18.)

130 *MKR*, IV: 167

131 Ibid, 168

132 Ibid, 170–6

133 Ibid, 174; *Cabinet Conclusions*, 17 March 1948

134 *MKR*, IV, 172

Chapter 7: The Politics of Fear

1 Cuff and Granatstein, *American Dollars – Canadian Prosperity*, 216

2 Canadian High Commissioner to Secretary of State for External Affairs, 2 April 1948, DEA files, 264(s); also quoted in Reid, *Time of Fear and Hope*, 132, and Granatstein, *A Man of Influence*, 236

Sources

DOCUMENTS

Most of the unpublished documents referred to in the text originated in or were received by the Department of External Affairs. They are filed either in the Historical Division of the department or in the Public Archives of Canada under a variety of categories. Correspondence and memoranda on a single subject are sometimes found distributed among several collections, the richest of which is the King Papers. (The Papers include the King Diary, which is also available on microfiche from the University of Toronto Press.) The collections consulted are indicated below.

Government papers

Canada: *House of Commons Debates*
Canada: *Cabinet Conclusions* (Public Archives of Canada)
Canada: *The Report of the Royal Commission Appointed under Order in Council P.C. 411 of February 5, 1946*. Ottawa: Edmond Cloutier, Printer to the King's Most Excellent Majesty 1946
Canada House, London, files (Public Archives of Canada)
Department of External Affairs (DEA), files (Department of External Affairs)
Office of the Under Secretary of State for External Affairs (OUSSEA), files (Public Archives of Canada)
Privy Council Office (PCO), files (Public Archives of Canada)
United Kingdom: Cabinet Office (CAB), files (Public Record Office, London)
United Kingdom: Dominions Office (DO), files (Public Record Office, London)
United Kingdom: *House of Commons Debates (Hansard)*

Personal papers

Dean Acheson Papers (Truman Library, Independence, Missouri)
Grant Dexter Papers (Queen's University Archives)

Elbridge Durbrow, 'Oral History Interview,' 31 May 1973 (Truman Library)
George M. Elsey Papers (Truman Library)
George M. Elsey, 'Oral History Interview,' February 1964–July 1970 (Truman Library)
A.D.P. Heeney Papers (Public Archives of Canada)
W.L. Mackenzie King Papers (Public Archives of Canada)
Admiral William D. Leahy Papers (Library of Congress)
H. Freeman Matthews, 'Oral History Interview,' 7 June 1973 (Truman Library)
L.B. Pearson Papers (Public Archives of Canada)
Escott Reid Papers (Public Archives of Canada)
Harry S. Truman papers (Truman Library)
Hume Wrong Papers (Public Archives of Canada)

The major published collections of documents referred to are the incomplete *Documents on Canadian External Relations (DCER)* (Ottawa: Department of External Affairs) and the comprehensive and excellent *Foreign Relations of the United States (FRUS)* (Washington: Department of State Publications).

BOOKS

Acheson, Dean. *Present at the Creation*. New York: Norton 1967
Alperovitz, Gar. *Atomic Diplomacy: Hiroshima and Potsdam*. London: Secker & Warburg 1968
– *Cold War Essays*. Garden City, NY: Doubleday Anchor Books 1970
Ambrose, Stephen E. *Rise to Globalism: American Foreign Policy, 1938–1970*. Harmondsworth: Penguin 1971
Anderson, Terry H. *The United States, Great Britain and the Cold War 1944–1947*. Columbia and London: University of Missouri Press 1981
Andrew, Christopher. *Secret Service*. London: Heinemann 1985
Avakumovic, Ivan. *The Communist Party in Canada*. Toronto: McClelland and Stewart 1975
Balawyder, Aloysius, ed. *Canadian-Soviet Relations, 1939–1980*. Oakville, Ont.: Mosaic Press 1980
Barros, James. *No Sense of Evil: Espionage, the Case of Herbert Norman*. Toronto: Deneau 1986
Bernstein, Barton J., ed. *Politics and Policies of the Truman Administration*. Chicago: Quadrangle Books 1970
Birkenhead, Earl of. *Halifax*. London: Hamish Hamilton 1965
Blum, John M. *The Price of Vision: The Diary of Henry A. Wallace*. Boston: Houghton Mifflin 1973
Bohlen, Charles E. *The Transformation of American Foreign Policy*. New York: Norton 1969
– *Witness to History*. New York: Norton 1973
Bothwell, Robert; Drummond, Ian; and English, John. *Canada since 1945: Power, Politics, and Provincialism*. Toronto: University of Toronto Press 1981
Bothwell, Robert, and Granatstein, J.L. *The Gouzenko Transcripts*. Ottawa: Deneau 1982

Bowen, Roger W., ed. *E.H. Norman: His Life and Scholarship*. Toronto: University of Toronto Press 1984
– *Innocence Is Not Enough: The Life and Death of Herbert Norman*. Vancouver/Toronto: Douglas & McIntyre 1986
Bullock, Alan. *Ernest Bevin: Foreign Secretary, 1945–1951*. London: Heinemann 1983
Byrnes, James F. *Speaking Frankly*. New York: Harper & Brothers 1947
Callwood, June. *Emma*. Toronto: Stoddart 1984
Caute, David. *The Great Fear: The Anti-Communist Purge under Truman and Eisenhower*. New York: Simon and Schuster 1978
Cave-Brown, Anthony. *Bodyguard of Lies*. New York: Harper & Row 1975
Churchill, W.S. *The Second World War*, 6 vols: *The Gathering Storm*; *Their Finest Hour*; *The Grand Alliance*; *The Hinge of Fate*; *Closing the Ring*; *Triumph and Tragedy*. London: Cassell 1950–54
Cohen, Stephen F. *Rethinking the Soviet Experience: Politics and History since 1917*. London: Oxford University Press 1985
Colville, John. *The Fringes of Power*. London: Hodder and Stoughton 1985
Creighton, Donald. *The Forked Road*. Toronto: McClelland and Stewart 1976
Cuff, R.D., and Granatstein, J.L. *Canadian-American Relations in Wartime: From the Great War to the Cold War*. Toronto: Hakkert 1975
– *American Dollars – Canadian Prosperity: Canadian-American Economic Relations, 1945–1950*. Toronto: Samuel-Stevens 1978
Davies, Joseph E. *Mission to Moscow*. New York: Simon and Schuster 1941
Dawson, R.M. *William Lyon Mackenzie King: A Political Biography 1874–1923*. Toronto: University of Toronto Press 1958
De Santis, Hugh. *The Diplomacy of Silence: The American Foreign Service, The Soviet Union, and the Cold War, 1933–47*. Chicago: University of Chicago Press 1980
Djilas, Milovan. *Conversations with Stalin*. New York: Harcourt, Brace & World 1962
Donaldson, Robert H., and Nogee, Joseph L. *Soviet Foreign Policy since World War II*. Oxford: Oxford University Press 1981
Donovan, Robert J. *Conflict and Crisis: The Presidency of Harry S. Truman, 1945–1948*. New York: Norton 1977
Eayrs, James G. *In Defence of Canada*, 5 vols. Toronto: University of Toronto Press 1964–84
Eden, Anthony. *The Reckoning*. London: Cassell 1965
Erickson, John. *The Road to Berlin: Continuing the History of Stalin's War with Germany*. Boulder, Colo.: Westview Press 1983
Evans, Gary. *John Grierson and the National Film Board*. Toronto: University of Toronto Press 1984
Feis, Herbert. *Churchill-Roosevelt-Stalin*. Princeton: Princeton University Press 1957
Gaddis, John Lewis. *The United States and the Origins of the Cold War, 1941–1947*. New York: Columbia University Press 1972
– *Strategies of Containment*. New York: Oxford University Press: Quadrangle Books 1982
Gardner, Lloyd C. *Architects of Illusion: Men and Ideas in American Foreign Policy, 1941–1949*. Chicago: Quadrangle Books 1972

Gilbert, Martin. *Road to Victory: Winston S. Churchill 1941–1945*. London: Heinemann 1986

Gowing, Margaret. *Britain and Atomic Energy, 1939–1945*. London: Macmillan 1964

– *Independence and Deterrence: Britain and Atomic Energy, 1945–1952*, 2 vols. London: Macmillan 1974

Granatstein, J.L. *Canada's War: The Politics of the Mackenzie King Government, 1939–1945*. Toronto: Oxford University Press 1975

– *A Man of Influence: Norman A. Robertson and Canadian Statecraft 1929–68*. Ottawa: Deneau 1981

– *The Ottawa Men: The Civil Service Mandarins, 1935–1957*. Toronto: Oxford University Press 1982

Grosser, Alfred. *The Western Alliance: European-American Relations since 1945*. London: Macmillan 1980

Haines, Gerald K., and Walker, Samuel, eds. *American Foreign Relations: A Historiographical Review*. Westport, Conn.: Greenwood Press 1981

Halle, Louis J. *The Cold War as History*. New York: Harper Colophon Books 1971

Hammond, Thomas T., ed. *Witnesses to the Origins of the Cold War*. Seattle: University of Washington Press 1982

Harbutt, Fraser J., *The Iron Curtain: Churchill, America, and the Origins of the Cold War*. New York: Oxford University Press 1986

Harriman, W. Averell, and Abel, Elie. *Special Envoy to Churchill and Stalin, 1941–1946*. New York: Random House 1975

Harris, Kenneth. *Attlee*. London: Weidenfeld and Nicolson 1982

Herken, Gregg. *The Winning Weapon: The Atomic Bomb in the Cold War*. New York: Alfred A. Knopf 1980

– *Counsels of War*. New York: Alfred A. Knopf 1985

Herring, George C. Jr. *Aid to Russia, 1941–1946: Strategy, Diplomacy, and the Origins of the Cold War*. New York and London: Columbia University Press 1973

Holmes, John W. *The Shaping of Peace: Canada and the Search for World Order 1943–1957*, 2 vols. Toronto: University of Toronto Press 1979, 1982

Hoopes, Townsend. *The Devil and John Foster Dulles*. London: Andre Deutsch, 1974

Horowitz, David. *The Free World Colossus*. New York: Hill and Wang 1965

Hull, Cordell. *Memoirs of Cordell Hull*, 2 vols. New York: Macmillan 1948

Hyde, H. Montgomery. *Room 3603*. New York: Farrar, Strauss 1963

– *The Atom Bomb Spies*. London: Hamish Hamilton 1980

Ignatieff, George. *The Making of a Peacemonger: The Memoirs of George Ignatieff*. Toronto: University of Toronto Press 1985

Ireland, Timothy P. *Creating the Entangled Alliance: The Origins of the North Atlantic Treaty Organization*. London: Aldwych Press 1981

Jaffe, Philip J. *The Rise and Fall of American Communism*. New York: Horizon Books 1975

Jones, Joseph M. *The Fifteen Weeks*. New York: Harcourt, Brace & World 1955

Keenleyside, Hugh L. *On the Bridge of Time: Memoirs*, vol. 2. Toronto: McClelland and Stewart 1982

Kennan, George F. *Realities of American Foreign Policy*. London: Oxford University Press 1954
- *The Communist World and Ours*. London: Hamish Hamilton 1959
- *Memoirs, 1925–1950*. New York: Little, Brown & Co. 1967
- *The Nuclear Delusion: Soviet-American Relations in the Atomic Age*. New York: Pantheon Books 1982
Kimball, Warren F. *Churchill and Roosevelt: The Complete Correspondence*, 3 vols. Princeton: Princeton University Press 1984
Kolko, Gabriel. *The Politics of War: Allied Diplomacy and the World Crisis of 1943–1945*. London: Weidenfeld and Nicolson 1968
Kolko, Gabriel, and Kolko, Joyce. *The Limits of Power: The World and United States Foreign Policy, 1945–1954*. New York: Harper & Row 1972
Krock, Arthur. *Memoirs: Sixty Years on the Firing Line*. New York: Funk and Wagnalls 1968
Kuniholm, Bruce R. *The Origins of the Cold War in the Near East: Great Power Conflict and Diplomacy in Iran, Turkey, and Greece*. Princeton: Princeton University Press 1979
LaFeber, Walter. *America, Russia, and the Cold War, 1945–1980*. New York: Wiley 1980
Leahy, William D. *I Was There*. New York: Whittlesey House 1950
Levering, Ralph B. *American Opinion and the Russian Alliance 1939–1945*. Chapel Hill: University of North Carolina Press 1976
Lilienthal, David E. *The Journals of David E. Lilienthal*, vols 1 and 2: *1939–50*. New York: Harper & Row 1964
Lippmann, Walter. *The Cold War: A Study in U.S. Foreign Policy*. New York: Harper Torchbooks 1972
Littleton, James. *Target Nation: Canada and the Western Intelligence Network*. Toronto: Lester & Orpen Dennys / CBC Enterprises 1986
Lundestad, Geir. *America, Scandinavia, and the Cold War, 1945–1949*. New York: Columbia University Press 1980
MacDonald, Malcolm. *People and Places*. London: Collins 1969
Macmillan, Harold. *Tides of Fortune 1945–1955*. London: Macmillan 1969
Maddox, Robert James. *The New Left and the Origins of the Cold War*. Princeton: Princeton University Press 1973
Malcolmson, Robert. *Nuclear Fallacies: How We Have Been Misguided since Hiroshima*. Montreal and Kingston: McGill-Queen's University Press 1985
Mastny, Vojtech. *Russia's Road to the Cold War*. New York: Columbia University Press 1979
Miller, Steven E., ed. *Strategy and Nuclear Deterrence*. Princeton: Princeton University Press 1984
Millis, Walter, ed. *The Forrestal Diaries*. New York: Viking 1951
Milward, Alan S. *The Reconstruction of Western Europe 1945–1951*. London: Methuen 1984
Morgan, Kenneth O. *Labour in Power 1945–1951*. London: Oxford University Press 1984

Nye, Joseph S. Jr., ed. *The Making of America's Soviet Policy*. New Haven: Yale University Press 1984

Ovendale, Ritchie. *The English-Speaking Alliance: Britain, the United States, the Dominions and the Cold War, 1945–51*. London: Allen and Unwin 1985

Paterson, Thomas G. *Soviet-American Confrontation: Postwar Reconstruction and the Origins of the Cold War*. Baltimore: Johns Hopkins University Press 1973

– *The Origins of the Cold War*, 2nd ed. Lexington: D.C. Heath & Co. 1974

– *On Every Front: The Making of the Cold War*. New York: Norton 1979

Pearson, L.B. *Mike: The Memoirs of the Right Honourable Lester B. Pearson*, vol. 1: *1897–1948*; vol. 2: *1948–1957* (ed. John A. Munro and Alex I. Inglis). Toronto: University of Toronto Press 1972, 1973

Pickersgill, J.W. *The Mackenzie King Record*, vol. 1. Toronto: University of Toronto Press 1960

Pickersgill, J.W., and Forster, D.F. *The Mackenzie King Record*, vols 2–4. Toronto: University of Toronto Press 1968–70

Pincher, Chapman. *Too Secret Too Long*. London: Sidgwick and Jackson 1984

Pope, Lt.-Gen. Maurice A. *Soldiers and Politicians*. Toronto: University of Toronto Press 1962

Reid, Escott. *Time of Fear and Hope: The Making of the North Atlantic Treaty 1947–1949*. Toronto: McClelland and Stewart 1977

– *On Duty: A Canadian at the Making of the United Nations 1945–1946*. Toronto: McClelland and Stewart 1983

Ritchie, Charles. *The Siren Years: A Canadian Diplomat Abroad, 1937–1945*. Toronto: Macmillan 1974

– *Diplomatic Passport: More Undiplomatic Diaries, 1946–1962*. Toronto: Macmillan 1981

Roosevelt, Franklin Delano. *The Public Papers and Addresses of Franklin D. Roosevelt*. New York: Russell & Russell 1950

Ross, Graham, ed. *The Foreign Office and the Kremlin: British Documents on Anglo-Soviet Relations 1941–45*. Cambridge: Cambridge University Press 1984

Rothwell, Victor. *Britain and the Cold War*. London: Jonathan Cape, 1982

Sawatsky, John. *Men in the Shadows*. Toronto: Doubleday Canada 1980

– *Gouzenko: The Untold Story*. Toronto: Macmillan 1984

Schulzinger, Robert D. *American Diplomacy in the Twentieth Century*. New York: Oxford University Press 1984

Seversky, Alexander P. de. *Victory through Air Power*. New York: Simon and Schuster 1942

Sherwin, Martin J. *A World Destroyed: The Atomic Bomb and the Grand Alliance*. New York: Vintage Books 1977

Spencer, R.A. *Canada in World Affairs: 1946–49*. Toronto: Oxford University Press 1959

Stacey, C.P. *Arms, Men and Governments*. Ottawa: Information Canada 1970

– *Canada and the Age of Conflict*, vol. 2: *1921–1948*. Toronto: University of Toronto Press 1981

Stafford, David. *Camp x: Canada's School for Secret Agents 1941–45*. Toronto: Lester & Orpen Dennys 1986

Stairs, Denis. *The Diplomacy of Constraint: Canada, The Korean War, and the United States*. Toronto: University of Toronto Press 1974

Standley, William H., and Ageton, Arthur A. *Admiral Ambassador to Russia*. Chicago: Henry Regnery 1955

Steel, Ronald. *Walter Lippmann and the American Century*. Boston: Little, Brown and Co. 1980

Stevenson, William. *Intrepid's Last Case*. New York: Ballantine Books, 1983

Stimson, Henry L., and Bundy, McGeorge. *On Active Service in Peace and War*. New York: Harper 1948

Stoler, Mark A. *The Politics of the Second Front*. Westport, Conn.: Greenwood Press 1977

Taubman, William. *Stalin's American Policy: From Entente to Detente to Cold War*. New York: Norton 1982

Thomas, Hugh. *Armed Truce: The Beginnings of the Cold War 1945–46*. London: Hamish Hamilton 1986

Thomson, Dale C. *Louis St. Laurent: Canadian*. Toronto: Macmillan 1967

Tolstoy, Nicolai. *Stalin's Secret War*. London: Pan Books 1982

– *The Minister and the Massacres*. London: Hutchinson 1986

Truman, Harry S. *Year of Decisions: Memoirs*, vol. 1. Garden City: Doubleday 1955

– *Years of Trial and Hope: Memoirs*, vol. 2. Garden City: Doubleday 1956

Ulam, Adam B. *The Rivals: America and Russia since World War II*. New York: Penguin 1976

Vandenberg, A.H. *The Private Papers of Senator Vandenberg*. Boston: Houghton Mifflin 1952

Ward, Patricia Dawson. *The Threat of Peace*. Kent, Ohio: Kent State University Press 1979

Warnock, John. *Partner to Behemoth: The Military Policy of a Satellite Canada*. Toronto: New Press 1970

Weisbrod, Merrily. *The Strangest Dream*. Toronto: Lester & Orpen Dennys 1983

Werth, Alexander. *Russia at War, 1941–45*. New York: Dutton 1965

Wilgress, L.D. *Memoirs*. Toronto: Ryerson Press 1967

Williams, William Appleman. *American-Russian Relations, 1781–1947*. New York: Rinehart 1952

– *The Tragedy of American Diplomacy*. New York: Dell 1972

Willkie, Wendell. *One World*. Urbana: University of Illinois Press 1966

Woodward, Sir Ernest Llewellyn. *British Foreign Policy in the Second World War*. London: Her Majesty's Stationery Office 1962

Wright, Peter. *Spycatcher: The Candid Autobiography of a Senior Intelligence Officer*. Toronto: Stoddart 1987

Yergin, Daniel. *Shattered Peace: The Origins of the Cold War and the National Security State*. Boston: Houghton Mifflin 1978

ARTICLES

Barnes, Trevor. 'The Secret Cold War: The C.I.A. and American Foreign Policy in Europe, 1946–1956. Part I,' *The Historical Journal*, 24, 2 (1981), 399–415
Brzezinski, Zbigniew. 'Tragic Dilemmas of Soviet World Power,' *Encounter*, December 1983, 10–17
Charlton, Michael. 'The Eagle and the Small Birds: I. The Spectre of Yalta,' *Encounter*, June 1983, 7–28
Davis, Forrest. 'Roosevelt's World Blueprint,' *Saturday Evening Post*, CCXV (10 April 1943), 20
Gaddis, John Lewis. 'The Emerging Post-Revisionist Synthesis on the Origins of the Cold War,' *Diplomatic History*, VII, 3 (1983), 171–90
Granatstein, J.L. 'Getting on with the Americans: Changing Canadian Perceptions of the United States, 1939–1945,' *Canadian Review of American Studies*, V, 1 (Spring 1974), 3–17
Granatstein, J.L., and Cuff, R.D. 'Looking back at the Cold War: 1945–1954,' *The Canadian Forum*, LII, July-August 1972, 8–11
– 'Looking Back Once More – A Rejoinder,' *The Canadian Forum*, LII, December 1972, 19–20
Jockel, Joseph T. 'The Canada-United States Military Co-operation Committee and Continental Air Defence, 1946,' *Canadian Historical Review*, LXIV, 3 (1983), 352–77
Kennan, George F. ('Mr. X'). 'The Sources of Soviet Conduct,' *Foreign Affairs*, XXV (July 1947), 566–82
Keyserlingk, Robert H. 'Mackenzie King's Spiritualism and His View of Hitler in 1939,' *Journal of Canadian Studies*, 20, 4 (Winter 1985–86), 26–44
Lasch, Christopher. 'The Cold War, Revisited and Re-Visioned,' *New York Times Magazine*, 14 January 1968, 26
Mark, Edward. 'American Policy toward Eastern Europe and the Origins of the Cold War, 1941–1946: An Alternative Interpretation,' *Journal of American History*, LXVIII, 2 (1981), 313–36
Merrick, Ray. 'The Russia Committee of the British Foreign Office and the Cold War, 1946–47,' *Journal of Contemporary History*, 20 (1985), 453–68
Munro, John, and Inglis, Alex. 'The Atomic Conference of 1945 and the Pearson Memoirs,' *International Journal*, XXIX (Winter 1973–74), 90–109
Page, Donald M. 'Introduction,' *Documents on Canadian External Relations*, 12 (1946), xi–xxxv
Page, Don, and Munton, Don. 'Canadian Images of the Cold War 1946–47,' *International Journal*, XXXII, 3 (Summer 1977), 577–604
Paterson, Thomas G. 'Presidential Foreign Policy, Public Opinion, and Congress: The Truman Years,' *Diplomatic History*, III, 1 (1979), 1–18
Powers, Thomas. 'What Is It About?' *Atlantic Monthly*, June 1984, 35–55
– 'How Nuclear War Could Start,' *New York Review of Books*, 17 January 1985
Richardson, J.L. 'Cold-War Revisionism: A Critique,' *World Politics*, XXIV, 4 (1972), 579–612

Schlesinger, Arthur M., Jr. 'The Cold War Revisited,' *New York Review of Books*, 25 October 1979, 46–52

Seabury, Paul, 'Cold War Origins,' *Journal of Contemporary History*, III (January 1968), 169–82

Smith, Geoffrey. 'Harry, We hardly Know You: Revisionism, Politics and Diplomacy, 1945–54,' *American Political Science Review*, LXX, 2 (1976), 560–82

Taylor, A.J.P. 'What One Clerk Said to Another,' *London Review of Books*, 4, 3 (18 February–3 March 1982), 5

Wagner, J.R., and O'Neill, D.J. 'The Gouzenko Affair and the Civility Syndrome,' *American Review of Canadian Studies*, VIII (Spring 1978), 31–43

Whitaker, Reg. 'What Is the Cold War about and Why Is It Still with Us?' *Studies in Political Economy*, Spring 1986, 7–30

Wlibes, Lees, and Zeeman, Bert. 'The Pentagon Negotiations, March 1948: The Launching of the North Atlantic Treaty,' *International Affairs*, LXIX, 3 (1983), 351–63

Index